The United States and the Caribbean

Challenges of an Asymetrical Relationship

Anthony P. Maingot

Westview Press

BOULDER • SAN FRANCISCO

© Copyright text A. Maingot 1994

First published in 1994 by
THE MACMILLAN PRESS LTD.
London and Basingstoke

Published in 1994 in the United States by
WESTVIEW PRESS
5500 Central Avenue
Boulder, CO 80303

Maingot, Anthony P.
  The United States and the Caribbean / by Anthony P. Maingot.
    p.   cm.
  Includes bibliographical references.
  ISBN 0-8133-2242-1 (alk. paper). — ISBN 0-8133-2241-3 (pbk. : alk. paper)
    1. Caribbean Area—Relations—United States. 2. United States—Relations—Caribbean Area.   I. Title.
  F2178.U6M33   1994
  303.48′2729073—dc20   94-28673
                                                              CIP

Printed and bound in the United States of America

10   9   8   7   6   5   4   3   2   1

Contents

Preface

This author has taken to heart three strictures about writing on the Caribbean advanced by the late Gordon K. Lewis. First, that study has to have historical depth. Caribbean realities should be studied in terms of the process of becoming rather than purely as they presently appear to be. Secondly, that study has to be comparative for the simple reason that there is no 'cultural core' in the region, no single country, ethnic or linguistic group which can be studied as 'the Caribbean.'[1] One selects cases in terms of their longer term impacts on the region, and, in this case, on US-Caribbean relations.

To Lewis, both approaches are necessary if we are to reach what he called 'a reasonable sympathetic understanding' of the past, present and future of Caribbean peoples. I share with Lewis also his admonition that there should be nothing sentimental about this understanding. Lewis had a particular dislike for those who believed that they had to make a case for the Caribbean by 'going native' or becoming 'instant revolutionaries'. Precisely because he was himself of the socialist and anti-imperialist persuasion, this passionate Caribbeanist felt that the form most suited to an understanding of the Caribbean was the high essay. In that genre, clearly expressed ideas and opinions encourage – indeed, invite – review and critical analysis. The very nature of the field compels constant debates not only on facts but perhaps more critically on interpretations. Given the economic, political and social diversity of the region, there can be no claims to historical finality or sociological certainty. This explains Lewis' third methodological stricture: the study of the Caribbean has to be multidisciplinary. No one approach or body of theory can satisfactorily elucidate an area in which the Spanish, Dutch, French, British and American influences have blended with African and Asian cultural retentions to create extraordinarily complex, fluid and changing identities and identifications.

Certainly, all three approaches are necessary if we are to make any sense of the complex and changing relationships between the Caribbean and the US. It is difficult enough to trace the watersheds in US foreign policy towards the region; it is additionally difficult to describe and explain the varying responses of the region to the US.

This study attempts to do both things. But, in addition, it searches for the synergies which can result when a major power interacts respectfully and honourably with smaller states in a wide range of areas, both governmental and private. In other words, because of the large number of interactions, many cross cutting in nature, the total effect of those relationships taken together tends to be greater than the sum of the effects taken independently. Such synergies can be found, for example, in Caribbean migration to the US. While in some ways it represents a brain drain for the islands, that is not the whole story. For instance, it is evident that these small economies cannot employ all the highly-trained skilled labour they educate. Rather than curtailing that excellent education – which, aside from being politically unpopular, would deprive both the US and themselves of skilled workers – they continue to educate with the expectation that many will migrate. Those who migrate, in turn, remit monies home, come back as tourists, and serve as representatives for their islands in the metropolis. This process can grow to the point were the interrelations are so varied and beneficial to both societies that it becomes necessary to speak of 'binational' societies. The diaspora from the Dominican Republic has already been so designated,[2] the Jamaican and Haitian diasporas could probably also claim such a status.

One can also search for synergies in the political and international arenas. The issue of synergies is inferred in the central question posed by Robert Pastor in his excellent analysis of US-Latin American relations. Noting the difference between certain leaders such as Jamaica's Edward Seaga and Michael Manley and Panama's Omar Torrijos on the one hand and Nicaragua's Daniel Ortega and Panama's Manuel Noriega on the other, Pastor advises us that 'the issue for Latin America is why Noriega and Ortega brought out the worst in the US and Torrijos and the two Jamaicans brought the best.'[3]

In the post-Cold War era this is a question of vital importance. It is important for those nations which have maintained good relations with Washington but perhaps especially for those like Cuba which have not. The collapse of the socialist bloc, though arguably not necessarily of socialism, and the rise of new trading blocs with their emphasis on free enterprise and international competition, make good relations with the US indispensable for every country in the Caribbean.

Fortunately, such good relations are not as problematic as much of the literature which portrayed the US as the 'natural' enemy of the Caribbean would have us believe. That literature tended to be premised on a misreading of Caribbean society and, thus, of how it related to the US. It confused the Caribbean peoples' historical capacity and propensity to be morally indignant at injustice with a propensity for revolution. Applauding and celebrating every revolution and pseudo-revolution which came along, these authors overlooked the fact that the central thrust of Caribbean life has been the pursuit of progressive ends through moderate or conservative means.[4] Caribbean peoples have repeatedly 'surprised' observers with their attachment to liberal democratic institutions and respect for human rights.[5] Certainly the long memory of slavery and indentured bondage to the plantations partly explains this profound dislike of social or economic regimentation. Whatever shortcomings might derive from the testy individualism of Caribbean people, it also might explain why political pluralism is the preferred – and arguably, the most suited – form of governance.[6]

Fortunately, Caribbean intellectuals are reconsidering certain erstwhile radical premises. The lesson of Grenada's brief deviation from democracy was not lost on them, regardless of their ideological persuasions. Gordon Lewis himself was deeply moved by the tragic ending of that socialist experiment and agreed with one of the Caribbean's most respected socialist intellectuals, Clive Y. Thomas, who spoke for many in the Caribbean: 'after Grenada, no social project . . . will receive widespread support from the popular forces and their organizations if it does not clearly embrace political democracy as its norms of political conduct.'[7]

Even in those cases, such as Cuba, where there was an initial preference for centralized authoritarian politics and command economies, the tendency after 1990 has been towards both political and economic decentralization. There are few more urgent tasks in the Caribbean than to encourage those in Cuba who, since 1991, have been slowly but surely edging their system towards pluralism and democracy. The continued isolation of Cuba is counterproductive and out of step with the general relaxation of world tensions, the reduction of intransigence in state rhetoric and, fundamentally, to the need of a region-wide response to the new threats to state sovereignty and well-being which are far removed from the menaces identified during the Cold War.

Finally, the tendency to dismiss liberal democratic forms as merely 'formal' and thus presumably irrelevant in international relations, is fundamentally flawed. In a world in which the major powers – the US, the EC, Japan and multilateral agencies such as the IMF and the World Bank – all promote democratic values, possessing and practising them is a form of capital. Pierre Bourdieu calls such values which are widely shared 'symbolic capital.'[8] Like any other form of capital, it can be used in the ongoing bargaining these small states engage in with their powerful neighbour to the north. Retaining and enhancing that symbolic capital is crucial in the Caribbean's search for synergies in the very asymmetrical relationship they have with the US and to sustain the autonomy of their foreign policies. Because these two facts, autonomy and the use of symbolic capital, are central themes of this book, an example of their operation is now considered.

In 1992 the members of the English-speaking Caribbean established a CARICOM-Cuba Commission to explore opportunities for dialogue and practical co-operation. It seemed a logical step, given their equally autonomous establishment of diplomatic relations with Cuba in the 1970s and Cuba's search for reinsertion into the hemisphere. The news of this initiative elicited an 'outraged' response from the chairman of the sub-committee on Western Hemisphere Affairs of the US House of Representatives, Robert G. Torricelli and three of his Cuban-American colleagues on the sub-committee.[9] Even as they chastized and threatened the West Indians with dire consequences, the congressmen had to admit that they were aware that the West Indies represented 'the best in human rights in our hemisphere.' The West Indian response was not long in coming and, not surprisingly, they rejected the threats from the congressmen, underscoring their independence through a reassertion of the symbolic capital represented by their political practices:

> The decision of the Community was taken, very conscious of the deep-seated commitment of all CARICOM countries to the democratic process and to human rights . . . these matters speak for themselves and it has been noted that you yourself have acknowledged this. . . . The Caribbean Community has an extremely strong interest in the peaceful resolution of issues in the Region, including Cuba.[10]

One month after this exchange, four of the CARICOM prime ministers met with President Bill Clinton. The issue of relations with Cuba was not raised in public, that opportunity was taken to describe in the most effusive terms just how strong the democracies of these nations were.

The West Indians, along with virtually all others in the Caribbean, continue to strengthen their relationships with Cuba.

Notes

1 Cf. Anthony P. Maingot, *The Passionate Advocate: Gordon K. Lewis and the Caribbean Studies* (Centre for Caribbean Studies, University of Warwick, 1992).
2 Cf. Luis E. Guarnizo, 'The Emergence of a binational Society: Dominican Migrants at Home and Abroad', in Anthony P. Maingot (ed.) *Trends in US-Caribbean Relations* (*The Annals of the American Academy of Political and Social Science*, forthcoming May 1994).
3 Robert A. Pastor, *Whirlpool: US Foreign Policy Towards Latin America and the Caribbean* (Princeton, N.J.: Princeton University Press, 1992), p. 17.
4 Cf. Anthony P. Maingot, 'The Difficult Path to Socialism in the English-Speaking Caribbean', in Richard R. Fagen (ed.) *Capitalism and the State in US-Latin American Relations* (Stanford: Stanford University Press, 1979), pp. 254–301. See also Anthony P. Maingot, 'The Caribbean: The Structure of Modern-Conservative Societies', in Jan Knippers Black, *Latin America, Its Problems and Its Promise* (Boulder: Westview Press, 1984), pp. 362–78.

5 See, for instance, the imaginative essay by Jorge I. Dominguez, 'The Caribbean Question: Why Has Liberal Democracy (Surprisingly) Flourished?' in Jorge I. Dominguez, Robert A. Pastor, and R. Delisle Worrel (eds), *Democracy in the Caribbean* (Baltimore, MD.: The Johns Hopkins University Press, 1993), pp. 1–25.

6 Cf. Anthony Payne, 'Westminster Adapted: The Political Order of the Commonwealth Caribbean', in Dominguez, Pastor and Worrel, *op. cit.*, pp. 57–73.

7 Cited in Gordon K. Lewis, *Grenada, The Jewel Despoiled* (Baltimore, MD.: The Johns Hopkins University Press, l987), p. 197.

8 Cf. Pierre Bourdieu and Loic J.D. Wacquant, *An Invitation to Reflexive Sociology* (Chicago, Il.: The University of Chicago Press, 1992).

9 Letter from sub-committe, 26 July, l993.

10 Letter of response from CARICOM Secretariat, 19 August, 1993.

Introduction   The nature of complex interdependence

If one were to choose a single word to encapsulate Caribbean history, that word would have to be 'geopolitics', the relationship between geography and international relations. The most important part of Caribbean geography has been the sea, which has historically served less as the clichéd 'inner lake' than as a series of maritime highways linking the Caribbean to the rest of the world. These 'highways' explain why the Caribbean has never been isolated. In the fifteenth century the Caribbean became a centre of activity as direct sea mobility and contact changed the nature of movement in the world from an essentially land-centred basis to one in which trans-oceanic mobility was the key to empire and riches. As testaments to that sea's importance were the competitions over colonies and the attempts to manage that colonial competition through unilateral dictates. First came the Treaty of Tordesillas (1494) through which the Pope wished to separate that part of the new world which was 'rightfully' Spanish from that which was Portuguese. By Papal mandate other powers were to stay out. The Caribbean as we define it – the islands and the bordering mainland – fell into the portion that was assigned to Spain but, as would later be shown with another unilateral attempt at establishing a 'demarcation line' – The Monroe Doctrine – it was easier to proclaim a geopolitical doctrine than to enforce it.

What the history of archipelagic areas teaches us is that even the mightiest of naval powers cannot totally dominate each and every square mile of sea or island in the area. Even the presence of the greatest concentration of fortifications in the world would not secure total hegemony for any one power. This explains the presence of the British, Dutch, French and Danish alongside the Spaniards. It also explains the paradoxical nature of social change in the Caribbean. For instance, control of one small island off the coast of Haiti (Ile de la Tortue) was enough to provide an international band of pirates with a base from which to harass all merchant shipping and then, to penetrate the main island itself. Gradually that penetration turned into an occupation by more and more French corsairs. In 1697, at the Treaty of Ryswick, the eastern third of the island was turned over to France. In less than a century St Domingue became one of the richest pieces of real estate in the world, even as the larger Spanish part languished. The slaves of that island they called Haiti rose in an heroic liberation movement even as other lands (the US, Cuba, Brazil) were only then entering their most profitable phase of slave-based manufacturing.

Today, Haiti is among the poorest countries in the world, economically and politically out of step with the rest of the region. That island deserves, and gets, special attention in this study as we explore the balance between internal and external factors in social change.

Finally, and fatefully for the Caribbean, it was the US which ended the nineteenth century by taking Cuba, Puerto Rico and eventually – in 1917 – buying the Virgin Islands from the Danes. The $25 million the US paid the Danes was a considerable figure if we realize that the US had paid France $15 million for Louisiana (and its hinterland), had bought Florida from Spain for $10 million, and paid the Russians $7.2 million for Alaska. It was small, however, compared to the $300 million spent to build the Panama canal. American geopolitical interests in the Caribbean did not begin with the ownership of that canal but after 1914 the canal became the geopolitical centre of gravity in the region.

These were the actual territorial conquests or purchases. But geopolitics is not just a matter of creating colonies, it has also to do with the creation of spheres of influence. Certainly, gaining influence rather than occupying territory, was the American strategy in the Caribbean. This being the case, we need to define what we mean by a sphere of influence. A sphere of influence, says John P. Vlogantes, is an area into which is projected the power and influence of a country primarily for political, military-strategic, or economic purposes, but sometimes cultural purposes may be added.[1]

If explicit colonialism involves an outright exercise of power vested in a formal colonial authority, a sphere of influence involves any one of a range of possible uses of power: from informal persuasion to direct state coercion. There are some important consequences which flow from this. First and foremost is that the degree of Great Power control – and, thus, inversely, the degree of local independence – can vary greatly. As Vlogantes notes, a paramount power exercises a degree of influence consonant with the effects sought but modified by the resistance capability of the sphere state.[2] Just how consistently exclusive the American sphere of influence in the Caribbean has been, is a question for empirical research, not dogmatic assertion. Nowhere in this text will the reader find those facile assumptions that relate the description of being 'on the periphery' with being 'underdeveloped', 'dependent' and, consequently, 'lacking sovereignty' or self-determination.[3]

In his discussion of the various 'lenses' used to interpret events in Latin America and the Caribbean – the conservative, liberal and radical –

Robert Pastor notes that they all share one basic premise: that most developments in the region result from decisions made by the US.[4] Because of the disparity in size, power and wealth, 'it is logical that the US should simply work its will.' I agree with Pastor that this premise is flawed. The analysis of Costa Rica's turbulent search for democracy in the 1940s is precisely an effort to show how events with long-term region-wide consequences unfolded with little if any US involvement. Unfortunately, this example of successful self-determination was lost on US policymakers.

This author also agrees with Pastor's call for an 'interactive' lens: looking at the region in terms of actions which interact with each other and with the US. This perspective recognizes the vast asymmetry in power between the US and the rest but does not assume that this *ipso facto* means total control. 'Indeed', Pastor concludes, 'such power is reversible, with leaders or groups in the region trying to use the US to further their own political or economic ends.'[5] We show just such a relationship in our analysis of how Caribbean leaders 'played the Cuban card'. (See Chapter 6).

Additionally, even as we make the asymmetry in power between the US and the Caribbean a central point of our analysis, we believe that the degree of direct or indirect coercion or undue influence has also to be empirically established. This is so because spheres of influence can also result from a mutually acceptable relationship freely entered into by all parties. As we shall see, at least since World War II, Caribbean leaders – challenged as was the US by U-boats and fifth columns – have tended to share with Washington not only the definitions of the problems facing them but also the preferred solutions to them. Thus, it is not 'dependence' or lack of sovereignty which has often led Caribbean leaders to turn to the US leadership and initiative, but a coincidence or interdependence of interests.

This perspective is especially important if we keep in mind that there are other complex and non-coercive ways in which spheres of influence are established, as in transnational relations. The latter involves many of the processes described in this book such as the activities of the private sector, migration flows, private financial transfers and movements and even internationalized criminal activity. In the post-Cold War era such transnational relations have taken on primacy. As Henry Kissinger put it: ' . . . we are entering a new era. Old international patterns are crumbling; old slogans are uninstructive; old solutions are unravelling. The world has become interdependent in economics, in communications, in human aspirations.'[6]

The complexities of such an interdependent relationship should persuade us to ask a series of questions about US-Caribbean relations which are premised on the concept of a sphere of influence. Thus, we need to establish empirically four types of cases:

(1) Outright military intervention which had long-term and region-wide influences.
(2) Cases where we can prove that Caribbean actors have deferred to US policies despite their fundamental philosophical dissention from them and which have negative consequences for those actors.
(3) Cases where, despite initial reservations, Caribbean actors have made a rational calculation that US policies are desirable because accepting them results in a beneficial exchange of private or public goods.
(4) Cases where there have been legitimate philosophical and material convergences of goals.

No objective reading of US-Caribbean relations will leave much doubt that all four types of relationships have existed, sequentially or even simultaneously.

As we hope the chapters in this book will demonstrate, it is best to describe US-Caribbean relations as one of complex interdependence because it has involved at least three characteristics:[7]

(1) Societies in the region have historically been (and certainly are today) connected through multiple channels: governmental, private institutions and personal and familial. The non-governmental relations, called transnational relations in the literature, are often the most important.
(2) There has been no consistent hierarchy in the agenda of US-Caribbean relations. For instance, neither military nor economic issues can be assumed *a priori* to have consistently dominated the relationships between the US and one, or all, of the Caribbean nations. In a world in which the clear-cut distinctions between domestic and foreign policies are blurred, pertinent issues will often result from the interplay of sectoral interests. Throughout the analysis it will be clear that in the US, the departments of the Treasury, of Commerce and, increasingly, the Attorney-General's office, play international roles as significant as that of the State Department. In most Caribbean states, however, foreign affairs remains the exclusive domain of the head of government.[8] Prime Ministers, not Foreign Ministers, run foreign policy. Only they, it is believed, can fully co-ordinate policy on the complex, and interdependent, issues of today's world. And yet, they do not control many of the transnational relations of their societies.
(3) All this means that military force, while certainly an option of the major power, as we shall see, cedes in importance in direct relationship to the growth in complex interdependence.

If all this works to make complex interrelationships seem quite benign to the small state, that is not the intention here. Put simply, the absence of direct, coercive relationships does not mean the absence of influence, that outwardly quiet and possibly gradual exertion of power and persuasion.

The fact remains that even if the analysis reveals that the influence exercised did not stem from any undue degree of coercion or co-optation, there are still two delicate issues which flow from asymmetrical relationships. First, there is what C.J. Friedrich calls 'the rule of anticipated reaction.'[9] Leaders of small states are particularly prone to anticipate the reactions of the one who exercises the dominant influence in a region. As Friedrich noted, more often than not influence operates in these cases by changing the conduct of people without any outward appearance of change. One of the values which the leaders of small societies certainly internalize is a realistic sense of limits.

Beyond the anticipated reaction of leaders, there operates also in the Caribbean what sociologists term 'anticipatory socialization'. As we will note in the chapter on immigration, Caribbean people hardly wait until they arrive in the US to adopt 'American ways'. Migration and the international demonstration effect are operating to 'Americanize' the region.

Two points arise about these very real processes. First, there is little that economically open and politically democratic countries can do to stop these foreign influences. The argument that national cultures are too important to be abandoned to free market forces is an important one worth defending. It is necessary, however, to be realistic about the new roles of cable, satellite and video systems in making such cultural nationalism quite futile. Not even state-mandated censorship can work in as open an area as the Caribbean. In those cases where there have been attempts to prohibit the free movement of people and ideas (viz. Cuba and less intensely, Grenada), these attempts have failed. There is no isolation possible in a region such as the Caribbean. The second point is that even if US influences, both official and transnational, are the dominant ones, the traffic on those sea lanes which criss-cross the Caribbean hardly run in only one direction. America is itself yielding to the new cultural pressures of its new ethnic groups. Influences run in both directions, thus enriching the complexity of interdependence.

In such an interdependent world, many of the ongoing debates over the 'exact causes' of US geopolitical interests in the region have to be recast to accommodate the four possible relationships listed above. One can certainly understand those who believe that US imperial-like expansionism was purely a search for new markets which led to American interests in the Caribbean Basin.[10] One also finds plausible the argument which sees ideology as the driving force: fulfilling the 'White Man's Burden' in its peculiarly American Puritan form.[11]

The important task for US-Caribbean relations today is to discern how this past affected and continues to affect the perceptual predispositions which govern contemporary international relations. As Robert Jervis notes, whatever the theoretical disagreements among scholars of international politics, there is one area in which there is convergence among the students: it is the image, the perception, which leaders have of each other and of the nature of world politics, that is a fundamental determinant of what happens between states.[12] And it is crucial to understand that these perceptions are shaped before entering office. 'The convictions that leaders have formed before reaching high office', says Henry Kissinger, 'are the intellectual capital they will consume as long as they continue in office.'

Some of the most enduring attitudes and perceptions between peoples have to do with symbolic, not material grievances or satisfactions. Through the process of ethnic identifications, actions against particular countries are interpreted as offensive to the whole collectivity. This is especially the case when the major power justifies its international behaviour by advancing odious comparisons of race and culture. This, as we demonstrate in Chapter 1, is precisely what occurred in the Caribbean, feeding anti-Americanism throughout the whole hemisphere, as Professor Samuel Guy Inman of Columbia University discovered. Inman was part of the US State Department's post-World War II diplomatic offensive to reduce South American anti-Americanism.[13] In Chile, anticipating that the thrust of the questions would be on economic domination, he prepared to explain US economic policies thoroughly. This was not what the Chilean students wished to discuss. They asked rather: 'How do you explain the Baltimore Incident?' To Inman, Baltimore was an American city; to the Chileans it was the US Navy vessel which docked in Valparaiso where some of its sailors behaved as was their habit: fighting Chilean sailors in a night spot called the True Blue Saloon. In the riot which followed, one of the Americans was killed.

What followed was a test of wills between the US and Chile, both vowing to defend and redeem its national honour and dignity. The Chileans eventually backed-down, paying reparations and swallowing their pride. To Chilean students half a century later, this incident was more important than the claims of economic exploitation which Inman had come to explain, though not defend.

Again, in Argentina, knowing that Britain, not the US was the 'imperial power', Inman was surprised at the anti-Americanism of the Argentine students. He soon discovered that many Argentinean intellectuals had formed their opinion of American imperialism by studying US interventions in the Caribbean. Indeed, many had joined the Latin American Union, a continent-wide protest movement against US actions in the Dominican Republic, Haiti, Nicaragua and Cuba. This, not US investments, was what Inman found these scholars most eager to discuss.

It should come as no surprise, therefore, to anyone entering the museum of Cuban history in Havana when he or she is confronted with a picture of a drunken US sailor urinating on the statue of Cuba's most honoured hero, José Martí. The picture had originally been published in *Bohemia* in the early 1930s and has fuelled anti-American feelings since that date.

Thus, in international relations symbols are as important, if not more so, than cold statistics. Forging a sphere of influence is certainly not the same as an imperial conquest but the symbolic legacies can be strikingly similar. If the relationship is not based on mutual respect and consideration, no matter how materially beneficial that relationship might be, it will be regarded as colonial and offensive to national honour. For example, Williams Jennings Bryan's foreign policy might not have been 'classical colonialism', i.e. he did not advocate acquiring territory, but his assertion that 'the Filipinos cannot be citizens without endangering our civilization' was considered classical colonialism by the many who in other ways had been offended by American expressions of racial and cultural supremacy.

Having said this, it is wrong to draw blanket conclusions about US-'Caribbean' perceptions of each other. The reality is that Caribbean responses to American actions over the years have varied among Caribbean states according to the particular nature of their unique contacts with the Americans.

The dramatic expansion of US actions and interventions during the period 1803–1935 described in Chapter 2 generated very mixed feelings among the Caribbean peoples involved, i.e. those of the Spanish-speaking Caribbean. Mixed feelings because they invariably included a very strong admiration for what the Americans had accomplished at home with deep-seated resentment of their actions abroad. This ambiguity surely has been the basis of a consistent and often violent form of anti-Americanism in the region. Various Caribbean peoples have had to struggle with very mixed feelings towards the US. Panama was one such case. There, a complex love-hate relationship complicated their relations with the US, as a former US ambassador explains:

> Panamanian appreciation for the US role in their independence was profound. During three-quarters of a century after that momentous event, Panamanians knew that the Colossus of the North was the most reliable guarantor of their continued freedom. But, while one may take comfort from the protection a nearby friendly power affords, no one likes to be beholden. . . . As Balzac said: 'Gratitude is a charge upon the inheritance which the second generation is apt to repudiate.'[14]

Cuban anti-Americanism showed similar configurations. The influential Cuban historian, Emilio Roig de Leuchsenring, once wrote that the most sacred duty of any Cuban intellectual was to rescue Cuban honour by demolishing two historical fallacies: 1) that the US had always been 'generous' with Cuba, and 2) that because of that generosity Cubans ought to be 'grateful to the USA.'[15]

That purely material rewards are often not enough to satisfy the thirst for a stable identity is evident in the Puerto Rican case. While Puerto Ricans were ready to admit improvements in their material conditions, they were not convinced that they enjoyed complete citizenship, i.e. equality, with the Americans. As Gordon K. Lewis put it, citing Edmund Burke:

> This servitude, which makes men subject to a state without being citizens, may be more or less tolerable from many circumstances, but these circumstances, more or less favourable, do not alter the nature of the thing. The mildness by which absolute masters exercise their dominion, leaves them masters still.

The sentiment bred a virulent anti-American movement led by Pedro Albizu Campos; a movement which would give Americans many an anxious moment, both on the island and on the mainland. It continues to be a minority sentiment but not one to be easily dismissed.

Psychological ambiguity, therefore, has to be one of the most complex aspects of asymmetrical relationships, especially when they involve ethnic differences. How then can they be overridden in US-Caribbean relations? While there are no easy solutions to this issue, it is not something which has been ignored by Caribbean intellectuals.

It is an interesting fact that it was a Caribbean man, a Cuban specifically, who best described, explained and suggested remedies for the complex psychological results of such unequal relationships. José Martí understood Anglo-Saxon racism very well. 'They believe', he wrote, 'in the incomparable superiority of the Anglo-Saxon race over the Latin one. . . . They believe that the Hispanic American peoples are composed principally of Indians and blacks.'[16] He understood the consequences of this for his country's relations with the US. 'A people who disdain another', he wrote in 1892, 'is a dangerous friend.'[17] He lived in America for 15 years (1880–95) and admired much of the country; he also distrusted many American attitudes and motivations, especially what he perceived as racial haughtiness. 'Do you believe', he asked rhetorically, 'that a country, strong and very self-satisfied with its supremacy and which loathes the race they conquered . . . will treat as equals and recognize the sovereignty of a small society of heterogeneous population which includes a large number of those of the abhorred race.'[18]

Martí's views on the Americans were adopted selectively by all who wished to protest the ethnocentrism evident in America's international relations. For instance, the period's most celebrated Latin American attack on American culture, Rodó's *Ariel*, was a compendium of Martí's writings without attribution.

But those who used – and often misused – Martí to knock the Americans, tended to ignore or disregard a fundamental aspect of Martí's geopolitical thought: that leaders had to transcend such sentiments for the simple reason that friendly relations with the US were going to be indispensable to an independent Cuba. The first step in the process of dealing with the US was to study its system. 'It is necessary to study [the US]', he warned, 'so as not to stumble upon her.'[19] The next step – and in this he demonstrated a clear-headed understanding of asymmetrical relationships – had to be putting your own house in order. Just before leaving for Cuba (and his death) in 1895 he left the following advice to his compatriots:[20] (1) there is no other more sure and dignified way of obtaining the friendship of the North American people than to be seen to excel in their own capacities and virtues. 'We have to make up in merits what we lack in size.' (2) To adulate the strong and diminish yourself before him, he warned, is the sure way to merit 'the point of his foot as much as the flat of his hand.' (3) 'The indispensable friendship between Cuba and the US requires that Cubans constantly demonstrate their capacity to create, to organize, to join hands, to live under liberty and defend it, to learn and master better the language and habits of the North than they do ours. The virile and productive Cubans are the only ones who can contribute to the enduring and desirable friendship between Cuba and the US.'

Quite clearly Martí, whom Gonzalez and Schulman claim understood the US better than any other Latin American at the time, felt that even as he feared American expansionist ambitions, there were real grounds on which Cubans and Americans agreed. On more than one occasion he expressed this by saying, '*Amamos a la patria de Lincoln, tanto como tememos a la patria de Cutting.*' ('We love the land of Lincoln as much as we fear the land of Cutting'). The task for the smaller partner was to discover just where it shared a legitimate philosophical and material convergence of goals with the major power. For the many democracies in the Caribbean it means seeking out the 'Lincoln' in US policies.

It is a fundamental fact of Caribbean history that while most of the nations which entered independence in the 1960s implicitly understood Martí's realism, Martí's own homeland never did, neither before nor after the 1959 revolution. In that Cuban history lies a fundamental lesson worth retelling, given this book's emphasis on the wider threat which corruption represents to the region.

During the first four decades of Cuban independent life, a significant group of intellectuals understood Martí's message: if Cuba wanted to be respected it had to maintain high standards in its political and social life.

This the leaders of republican Cuba failed to do. That failure was encapsulated in the Martí-like lament of one of its important men, Manuel Marquez Sterling, that Cuba 'had not known how to confront external intervention with domestic virtue.'[21] This regret at the absence of domestic virtue became the dominant theme of the so-called 'generation of 1925'. They associated the social and political failures at home with their inability to put US-Cuban relations on a footing of mutual respect.

Throughout the first decades of the twentieth century, the island intellectuals gathered around such journals as *Cuba Contemporánea* and *Bohemia* which repeatedly called attention to the grievious failings of the Cuban political elite. There was perhaps no better account of a people condemned to stand by and watch as their country was being sacked and plundered by corrupt politicians than Charles E. Chapman's *History of the Cuban Republic* (1927). Chapman warned of terrible future consequences resulting from all these political betrayals of the Cuban people. He did not ignore the complex interrelationship between that island and the US:

> From the standpoint of her own interests, it may be no concern of the US that Cuba is in the grip of a corrupt political class, but it is conceivable that a continuance of present evils might arouse the Cubans to such a pitch of opposition to the politicians that they would confront both the home government and the US in an effort to gain real freedom for themselves.

This warning became the central theme of the campaign of Eduardo Chibás, to whose movement Fidel Castro originally belonged. Chibás' constant urging was for *verguenza contra dinero* (which can best be translated as countering money with decency or indignation). Fidel Castro was one of those who vowed to pursue Chibás' theme to the final consequences.

It was not just Cubans, however, who warned against the corroding effects of a corrupt system. In 1950, the International Bank of Reconstruction and Development also noted 'unconstructive attitudes' and 'a lack of confidence in Cuba among Cubans'. Central to the Bank's concern was what it considered to be an absolute absence of integrity in the public administration as well as personal political conduct. The Bank's conclusion proved prescient:

> If leaders have neglected to prepare Cuba [for more difficult times] they will be held to blame by the people. And, if that should happen, control may well pass into subversive but specious hands . . . .[22]

History records that the Cuban people did hold the existing political and social leaders responsible for a shameful lack of domestic virtue. That same history also records that the new revolutionary, political elite, out of what was perhaps an understandable excess of nationalistic zeal, disregarded the other side of Martí: geopolitical pragmatism. As Cuba seeks a 'reinsertion' into Latin America and the Caribbean, one can only hope that it will avoid both the corrosive corruption of the past as well as the counterproductive anti-Americanism of the revolution.

In many ways Cubans can take a lesson from many other Caribbean nations, including Puerto Rico who took to heart Martí's theme of 'the indispensable friendship' with the US, and who have known how to find the 'Lincoln' rather than the 'Cutting' in that superpower.

Dame Eugenia Charles, Prime Minister of Dominica and a model of both domestic virtue and geopolitical pragmatism, in February 1993 expressed the new realities of the Caribbean well:

> In a political sense the Caribbean in relation to the US has lost its strategic importance. But in a very real sense the Caribbean remains the frontier for domestic peace and stability in the US. Therefore we must be mindful that the socio-economic conditions that engendered and sustained political and social instability in the region are still with us.[23]

To Dame Charles the three fundamental areas of concern were: the protection and improvement of the human condition in the region, a continued privilege of migrating to the US and the threats posed by the narcotics trade.

In order to tackle this difficult agenda, the small nations of the Caribbean will have to muster their best talent, make the best use of their symbolic capital of democracy and respect for human rights and collectively, as a region, achieve a mutually respectful and beneficial working relationship with the US.

Notes

1 John P. Vlogantes, *Spheres of Influence: A Framework for Analysis* (Tucson, Arizona: Institute of Government Research, University of Arizona, 1970).

2 *Ibid.*, p. 8.

3 According to this 'dependency' approach, there is a direct relationship between the internationalization of the world market, and the dependence of non-industrialized societies. Notice, for instance, how Bruce Russett and Harvey Starr have distinct sections for ' "Interdependence" Among Industrialized Countries' and ' "Dependence" in the Less-Developed Countries', *World Politics: A Menu for Choice* (San Francisco, California: W. H. Freeman and Co., 1981), pp. 399–481.

4 Robert A. Pastor, *Whirlpool: US Foreign Policy Towards Latin America and the Caribbean* (Princeton, N.J.: Princeton University Press, 1992), p. 33.

5 *Ibid.*

6 Henry Kissinger, 'A New National Partnership', News Release, Department of State, Bureau of Public Affairs, 24 January, 1975, p. 1.

7   Much of the conceptualization for this section is drawn from Robert O. Keohane and Joseph S. Nye, *Power and Independence* (Boston: Little, Brown and Co., 1977), pp. 3–37.

8   Cf. Jacqueline Braveboy Wagner, *The Caribbean in World Affairs: The Foreign Policies of the English-Speaking States* (Boulder, Co: Westview Press, 1989).

9   Carl J. Friedrich, *Constitutional Government and Democracy* (Boston: Ginn and Co., 1946), p. 589.

10 Predominant in this school are Walter La Feber, *The New American Empire* (Ithaca, N.Y.: Cornell Univeristy Press, 1963), William Appelman Williams, *Roots of the Modern American Empire* (New York: Random House, 1969).

11 Cf. Ernest R. May, *Imperial Democracy* (New York: Harcourt, Brace and World, 1961).

12 Robert Jervis, *Perception and Misperception in International Politics* (Princeton, New Jersey: Princeton University Press, 1976).

13 See Inman's account in Carleton Beals, *et al.*, *What South Americans Think of US* (New York: Robert M. McBride & Co., 1945) pp. 348–51.

14 William J. Jorden, *Panama Odyssey* (Austin: University of Texas Press, 1984), p. 27.

15 Cited in Julio Le Riverend, 'La ciencia histórica en Cuba, 1920–1958', *Historia y Sociedad* (Mexico), No. 6 (verano, 1966), p. 11.

16 Cited in Manuel Pedro Gonzalez and Ivan Schulman (eds) *José Martí: Esquema Ideológico*, Vol. II (Mexico: Editorial Cultura, 1961), pp. 506–7.

17 José Martí, 'Carácter', *Patria*, 30 July, 1892 cited in Emilio Roig de Leuchsenring, *Martí Antimperialista* (Buenos Aires: Hemisferio, 1962), pp. 27–8.

18 *Ibid.*

19 Cited in González and Schulman, p. 513.

20 Cited in Roig de Leuchsenring, p. 36.

21 This section is drawn from Anthony P. Maingot, 'The Ideal and the Real in Cuban Political Culture', to appear in Lisandro Perez (ed.) *Cuba in Transition* (Miami, Florida: Cuban Research Institute, forthcoming).

22 International Bank for Reconstruction and Development, *Report on Cuba* (Baltimore, MD: The Johns Hopkins University Press, 1951), p. 9.

23 Dame Eugenia Charles, 'Frontier for Peace: US-Caribbean Relations', an address at Brown University, 10 February, 1993.

Part I

The US enters the Caribbean

CHAPTER 1 | Geopolitics and racial destiny: 1823–1903

Indicators that the New American State had already developed a strong perception of its geopolitical interests came early in its nationhood. In 1792 Thomas Jefferson, then the first Secretary of State, put American interests in perspective: the rights of navigation and deposit were 'natural rights', guaranteeing and securing justified purchasing – or taking – the lands and riverways occupied by Spain. This, to Jefferson, included the south-west, Florida and Cuba.[1] These and other geopolitical perceptions became law through the No-Transfer Resolution passed by the US Congress on 15 January, 1811. That resolution called attention to the 'peculiar' situation of Spain and her American provinces and warned that it could not 'without serious inquietude' see any of these territories pass into the hands of any foreign power. It also allowed, under certain contingencies, for the 'temporary occupation' of any territory in danger of passing into foreign hands. America had started the century with a unilateral statement of its geopolitical interests, a common enough practice at the time. What was not so common was that a nation as new and weak as the US was at the time, would be so ambitious and resolute about pursuing its interests, by force if necessary. There was little modesty in the geopolitical goals of the new Americans.

According to Samuel Flagg Bemis,[2] that policy had, at least since 1808, three goals: (1) the annexation of the adjacent Spanish borderlands, (2) the permanent opening to US trade of Spain's other colonies, and (3) the expulsion of European influence from the New World.

Not surprisingly, older and more potent nations were not going to stand by and accept American perceptions of how the collapsing Spanish empire should be dealt with. The British were the first to understand US intentions and the first to attempt diplomacy rather than gunboats to deal with them. In 1823 British Foreign Secretary George Canning suggested a joint British-US diplomatic initiative to keep other Europeans out of the New World. At first the sentiment of virtually all the American statesmen and politicians that President James Monroe consulted favoured Canning's plan.[3] It meant backing US interests with the British fleet. US Secretary of State John Quincy Adams, however, cleverly saw the catch in Canning's proposal, which was ostensibly to keep Europeans out but 'especially against the acquisition to the US themselves of any part of the Spanish-American possessions.'[4] Adams finally persuaded President Monroe that the US should not bind itself to any such collective commitments. Besides, there was the issue of national pride. 'It would be more candid, as well as more dignified, to avow our principles explicitly to Russia and France than to come in as a cockboat in the wake of the British man-of-war.'[5]

The British might have been correct in noting that there was a 'coincidence of principle' between themselves and their ex-colonials but to the latter this was limited to the goal of keeping other European powers out and securing the freedom of trade both Britain and the US were enjoying. Canning would later brag that he had 'called a New World into existence to redress the balance of the Old.' Whatever truth there was in such braggadocio about the Old World, the fact is that the New World had its own interests and ideas about the shape things would take.

President James Monroe's 1823 Annual Address to Congress unilaterally declared that 'the American continents, by the free and independent condition which they have assumed and maintain, are henceforth not to be considered as subjects for future colonization by any European Power.' Additionally, Monroe warned that any European intervention, in any part of this hemisphere, was to be regarded as 'the manifestation of an unfriendly disposition towards the US.' In return, in a clear recognition of the existence of spheres of influence, the Americans vowed not to interfere in European internal affairs.

One might well agree with Samuel Flagg Bemis that the Monroe Doctrine was the 'final printage in policy of the Era of Emancipation [from Monarchical Europe] . . . a perfect union of interest and ideal.'[6] It is an historical fact that the initial response of Latin American leaders was one of elation and joy.[7] Indeed, as Bemis notes, at least five Latin American countries proposed elevating the Doctrine to a general Pan-American defence pact. Not only was none of this ever agreed to, the Latins were soon disabused of any illusions about the new American doctrine.[8] Increasingly they tended to agree with Spanish thinker José Ortega y Gasset, who doubted that it was ever intended as a doctrine. It represented instead the earliest rumblings of incipient hegemony: 'a unilateral signal by the Americans that the Center of the Universe had been transferred from Europe to America.'[9]

In fact, the Doctrine violated two principles of international law already incorporated into the thought of the time: the prohibitions against intervention and against taking unoccupied territory. Europeans immediately recognized the unilateral nature of the American Doctrine, Latins were not far behind.[10] The US was to utilize the Doctrine as its perceptions of geopolitical interests changed, and as circumstances, leaders and collective climates of opinion changed. This explains the on-again, off-again application of the Doctrine. For instance, a bitter dispute with Argentina over fishing rights in waters the Argentines claimed were theirs, led to US inaction when the British annexed the Falkland-Malvinas islands in 1833. It was not invoked to stop France from engaging in Mexico-bashing in the 1838 'Pastry Cook' War; nor Britain taking the Bay Islands from Honduras, and Belize from Guatemala. There was silence on the Spanish recolonization of the Dominican Republic in 1861, a silence imposed by the political crisis at home. The Civil War was over, however, when in 1878 Sweden transferred the island of St Barthélemy to France without US objections.

The major explanation of such inaction lay in the fact that for a major part of the nineteenth century the US was preoccupied with *continental* expansion and security, not Caribbean geopolitics. As English historian W.F. Reddaway put it, with fertile adjacent territories 'crying out for settlement', a foreign policy had been 'superfluous'.[11]

Once that continental expansion, known as Manifest Destiny, was complete, American perceptions about its national security and interests turned to the Caribbean. It is in the Caribbean that it became clear, to quote Bemis, that the Monroe Doctrine was 'not a self-denial ordinance',[12] and that the right to intervene in the affairs of other states was an integral part of American action. This was especially the case *vis-à-vis* an island the Americans had always yearned for but which the Spaniards were determined to keep at any cost: Cuba.[13] Again, the Europeans anticipated American intentions and, as Canning had done in 1823, in 1852 the British and French proposed a 'hands off' agreement to the Americans. The then US Secretary of State, Edward Everett, disavowed any US coveting of Cuba. His response, however, not only put in doubt that disavowal, but it was one of the clearest statements of US geopolitical perceptions about Cuba, and thereore US trade routes about the Caribbean sea:

> The US . . . would . . . disable themselves from making an acquisition which might take place without any disturbance of existing foreign relations, and in the natural order of things. The island of Cuba lies at our doors. It commands the approach to the Gulf of Mexico, which washes the shores of five of our States. It bars the entrance of that great river which drains half the North American continent, and with its tributaries forms the largest system of internal water communication in the world. It keeps watch at the door-way of our intercourse with California by the Isthmus route. If an island like Cuba, belonging to the Spanish Crown, guarded the entrance of the Thames and the Seine, and the US should propose a convention like this to France and England, those powers would assuredly feel that the

disability assumed by ourselves was far less serious than that which we asked them to assume. . . . The history of the past – of the recent past – affords no assurance that twenty years hence France or England will even wish that Spain should retain Cuba. . . . Even now the President cannot doubt that both France and England would prefer any change in the condition of Cuba to that which is most to be apprehended, viz: an internal convulsion which should renew the horrors and the fate of San Domingo.[14]

The completion of continental expansion by the middle of the nineteenth century did not temper the urge to occupy new territory, it merely gave it two new dimensions: a 'scientific' justification and a racial one. Since they would both have extraordinary bearing on US-Caribbean relations they are worth exploring. We start with the new social science.

Among the most ardent intellectual exponents of expansion was the historian Frederick Jackson Turner. As early as 1891 his thesis was that stagnation would follow the end of expansion across unoccupied lands. America could adjust to that contraction and stagnation or find new frontiers. He advocated expansion:

For nearly three hundred years the dominant fact in American life has been expansion . . . That these energies of expansion will no longer operate would be a rash prediction; and the demands for a vigorous foreign policy, for an inter-ocean canal, for a revival of our power upon the seas, and for the extension of American influence to outlying islands and adjoining countries, are indications that the movement will continue.[15]

What Turner was intellectualizing was a theme which, as we have noted, was evident in US policy since early nationhood. In the early 1880s Secretary of State James G. Blaine reflected the then dominant theme of the search for foreign markets by warning that 'if the commercial empire which legitimately belongs to us [Latin America] is to be ours, we must not lie idle and witness its transfer to others.'[16] He would fail miserably, however, to coerce the Haitian government of Hyppolite (which he had helped put in power) into granting the bay, Mole St Nicolas, for a naval base. Equally unsuccessful was his attempt to persuade the Dominicans to part with Samaná Bay.[17]

Failure to secure foreign bases did not stop Americans from flexing their muscles. In 1891–92 the US forced Chile to pay reparations for the death on shore of a US sailor (the 'Baltimore' incident mentioned in the Preface). But if this action in Chile seemed close to bullying a weaker nation, the brash Americans showed themselves ready to take on some of the biggest boys.

In 1895 the US forced Great Britain to abandon any attempt at expanding its territorial claims *vis-à-vis* Venezuela in British Guiana. Britain agreed to arbitrate in 1895, a concession one scholar called a 'surrender',[18] while another says that in 1896 'the US replaced Britain as *caudillo* of the Western Hemisphere.'[19] The US certainly sounded like a *caudillo*. 'Today', boasted Secretary of State Olney with what became known as the Olney Extension of the Monroe Doctrine, 'the US is practically sovereign on this continent, and its fiat is law upon the subjects to which it confines its interposition.'[20] The US was now ready to take on the restless nations of the Caribbean.[21]

If early nineteenth century continental expansion had occurred because commercial and economic pressures turned American eyes to areas which, to repeat Reddaway's phrase, were 'crying out for settlement', what Frederick Merck calls the 'Caribbeanization' of Manifest Destiny[22] followed no such law of physics. This was, in fact, a quite explicit and conscious program of extending American influence and power into the international arena.[23] Already flushed with its ability to face down countries as weak as Chile or as powerful as Great Britain, the US did not perceive any problems in doing the same with the small insular or central American states. In fact, there was a growing sense that the US, as the major power, had a duty to police that area. As Walter La Feber notes: 'In essence he was interpreting the Monroe Doctrine as the catchall slogan which justified protecting what the US considered as its own interests.'[24] No one would articulate these sentiments more clearly than Theodore Roosevelt in 1904.

When, in this western hemisphere there were, as Roosevelt put it, cases of 'flagrant wrongdoing or impotence', the US would 'however reluctantly' adhere 'to the exercise of an international police power.'[25] Thus was announced the birth of the Roosevelt Corollary to the Monroe Doctrine.

It certainly appears to be the case that, as Dexter Perkins states, Roosevelt was 'by instinct a policeman'.[26] Biography, however, is an insufficient explanation for the dramatic change in US geopolitical codes. This Corollary represented a watershed for the US, and certainly for the Caribbean and other tropical areas.

What then, was behind this new geopolitical course? Howard K. Beale ranks the forces behind the new ideology of expansionism as follows:[27] (1) new-found American nationalism and pride; (2) a sense of American moral rectitude and rightfulness; (3) a sense of American racial superiority, which brings us to the second justification for American expansionism: the racial one. These stemmed from one central idea: the association made between ideas of racial superiority and ideas of imperial rights and obligations. As Beale notes of the thinking of the imperialists, expansionism by a 'masterful race' was not a matter of regret but of pride.[28]

It is of little comfort to the subjects of expansion that, as Beale intellectualizes, Roosevelt and his fellow American geopoliticians did not think about race in strictly biological terms. After all, they all spoke the language of the Social Darwinism which was popular at Harvard, Yale and other major universities at the time. The idea of the survival of the fittest invariably had a racial cast.[29] This is not to say that economics and trade, and the geopolitical codes designed to guarantee these, were secondary. It is merely to say that in the colonial situations which were now developing, symbols of self-worth perhaps meant more than the mysterious workings of trade balances and economic structures, both for the active conquerors and certainly for the conquered.

The language of Theodore Roosevelt and two of his most influential friends, Brooks Adams and Alfred T. Mahan, reveal the deep-seated racism which accompanied this new geopolitics. Roosevelt, as was the custom, divided the world into 'civilized' and 'barbarous' nations. Unfortunately, it was towards the barbarous that imperialism was directed. He opposed Chinese immigration to the US because 'his presence would be ruinous to the white race'.[30] He never referred to Latin Americans except contemptuously as 'Dagoes'. Such a sense of superiority had to come from more than just the possession of superior weapons. It was applied to the collectivity, not particular individuals. This explains why the threat of corrective, police action was directed at nations, not individual leaders. 'Sometime soon', Roosevelt wrote to his brother-in-law in 1905, 'I shall have to spank some little brigand of a South American republic.'[31]

In 1915 he justified his actions in Panama by explaining that the previous owners, Colombia, were 'an inferior people'. 'The analogy' of Colombians 'is with a group of Sicilian or Calabrian bandits. . . . You could no more make an agreement with the Colombian rulers than you could nail currant jelly to the wall.'[32] The point is not that Roosevelt had reasons to be exasperated with the Colombians. After fighting two major civil wars in less than a decade, the Colombian state was in disarray just as America was in its most self-confident activist and, possibly, racist phase. The long period of continental expansion had brought the Americans into contact with people for whom they not only had no respect but in fact held in open contempt. The catalyst to the racial ideology of the end of the century, according to Reginald Horsman, was the meeting of Americans and Mexicans in the south-west. To the Anglos, the Mexicans were 'a Mongrel race, adulterated by extensive intermarriage with an inferior Indian race.'[33] Thus, America enters its Caribbean phase with a full sense of racial destiny underpinning its equally well-developed geopolitical ambitions.

Even the economic determinist, Brooks Adams, could not refrain from packaging his economic arguments in racialism and ethnocentrism. Arguing that economic supremacy was shifting from Europe to the US, Adams argued that great forces and movements in history are not determined by argument but by forces which 'override the volition of man.'[34] To Adams these forces were economic and they required, as they had to Jefferson, acknowledgment of certain 'natural rights' such as safe passage of US goods to rich markets. One of the keys to understanding which forces would be successful in applying those natural rights, was to know which race was involved. Though Russians had the potential for economic predominance because of their land mass, their problem was that they were Asiatics, i.e. 'an archaic race' and thus 'ignorant, unimaginative, indolent, and improvident.'[35] Anglo-Saxons on the other hand, had little to fear in a trial of strength, 'for they have been the most successful of adventurers.' Additionally, the Anglo-Saxon race had preserved its ancient martial quality. Adams' Social Darwinism was blatant; he believed aggression on the part of nations seemed a less dangerous alternative than quiescence.[36] Without 'vitality', i.e. international competition, nations were condemned to what Adams called 'geographical eccentricity', and 'competition in its acutest form, is war.'[37]

How could Adams look upon the nations and peoples of the Caribbean except in racial terms, no matter what the economic reasoning. 'The Caribbean archipelago', he concluded, 'must, probably, either be absorbed by the economic system of the US or lapse into barbarism.'[38] To Adams, barbarism in the Caribbean had a name: Haiti.[39] It was this island which became the metaphor for 'mongrelization' (a very popular word at the time) and misrule. The racialist had an 'example' for those who would resist US paternalism.

The new foreign policy, being outward looking, needed a geopolitical framework. This it received magnificently from one of their own ideological persuasion, Alfred Thayer Mahan. It was Mahan more than anyone else who defined America's position *vis-à-vis* the world generally and the Caribbean specifically. His theories would dictate American perceptions and actions right through the twentieth century.

Mahan was no narrow naval strategist, he was a geopolitician with a very definite philosophy of history, of war and of man. He was, in the words of a biographer, 'more the larynx and cerebrum of American imperialism than its sword arm.'[40] Like Turner, he believed that nations either grew and expanded or they stagnated. Since the US had already completed its continental expansion, movement had to be elsewhere. This meant colonies, and on this he allowed no 'sentimentality', only 'realism'.

To Mahan, colonies did not have the function they had to Europeans, i.e. as sources of raw materials, markets and places to settle their bothersome or rebellious populations. To Mahan, colonies, especially islands, were to be strategic naval bases serving a navy which would guard the nation's foreign commerce. The Caribbean islands were perceived as little more than stepping stones towards the markets of Asia and Latin America. 'The first and most obvious light in which the sea presents itself from the political and social point of view', wrote Mahan, 'is that of a great highway; . . .'[41] On this score, Mahan made two central points about the Caribbean. First, its importance to the US was similar to that of the Mediterranean to Europe. 'A study of the strategic conditions of the Mediterranean', he wrote, 'which have received ample illustration, will be an excellent prelude to a similar study of the Caribbean, which has comparatively little history.' Secondly, and more importantly perhaps, he anticipated the building of a central American canal which would change the Caribbean 'from a terminus and place of local traffic, or at best a broken and imperfect line of travel, as it now is, into one of the great highways of the world.' This, he predicted, would radically change US geopolitical interests. But the US was not geographically situated nor did it have the proper Gulf ports to command the area. These 'defects', he noted, could be overcome by securing in the Caribbean 'stations fit for contingent, or secondary bases of operations . . .' 'Should this and the ancillary military preparations be accomplished', Mahan concluded, 'the preponderance of the US in this field follows, from her geographical position and her power, with mathematical certainty.'

The navy was the perfect instrument to achieve this. To back up his theory Mahan had an analogy from American expansion westward: the US Cavalry's campaigns against the American Indians of constant pursuit and attack. Using such a strategy – coaling stations and naval bases being the equivalent of the 'forts' – the US could control the strategic 'narrow straights', i.e. sea lanes. The surest way to maintain peace, he wrote in 1885, was to do as policemen do: 'occupy a position of menace'.[42] But this was not any ordinary policeman keeping law and order. He was also upholding proper civilization and pride of race. Like Roosevelt and the many members of the elite which guided US expansionism, Mahan's thoughts married race and geopolitics. He fervently believed in an 'English-speaking family', unified by 'race patriotism'.[43] In the dichotomized ethnic thinking of the time, Mahan believed the English to be 'a civilized race', while Latin Americans in general were the opposite.

Far from generating sentiments of friendship and hemispheric solidarity in Mahan, his participation in the increasing American naval diplomacy of 'showing the flag' throughout Latin America engendered disdain. As an important Mahan biographer explains, it left him with 'an abiding contempt for Latin Americans in general and for Latin American political, military, and diplomatic processes in particular.'[44]

Chileans were 'beggars' who had 'an absolute incapacity for governing themselves'. Argentines, he wrote, were strangers to any form of loyalty, civil or military, 'no man can depend on any man's truth; you cannot count upon any man's position tomorrow.'[45] Philippinos were 'in the childhood stage of race development.'[46]

Mahan's most cherished geopolitical scenario, making the Caribbean an area secure for American interests, was brought about by two extraordinarily bold moves: the Spanish-American war and the intervention in Panama. Both would return to haunt the US in the form of anti-Americanism. The first move was to declare war on Spain and enter Cuba, bringing that island's four-decade civil war to an end. Even though Spain was no longer a significant military power, the speedy success of American arms came as a surprise to all, including many Americans. After all, Spain had 200,000 trained fighting men in Cuba, while the whole US active army only stood at 26,000 poorly-trained men. Yet it was hardly a match. 'The success of our arms', wrote an American commander, 'far exceeded the expectations of the most sanguine. Prior to July 1st, no one would have regarded it possible for the purposes of the war to be accomplished in less than one or two years of hard fighting.'[47] In fact, the sea war, both in Santiago Bay, Cuba and Manila Bay, the Philippines, lasted only hours; the ground war was longer and more costly but hardly what the US military had expected.

Thus, the US opened the twentieth century with an intervention which confirmed its status as a world class military power. The Europeans, who sympathized with Spain,[48] dared not interfere in this new American sphere of influence. Indeed, Great Britain actively assisted the Americans by blocking possible Spanish naval moves. Latin Americans, with the exception of Ecuador which supported the Cuban rebels, stayed out of the fray.[49]

The reasons why the US finally decided to enter the Cuban War of Independence in April 1898 are various. Economic interests were important but certainly not the dominant reason. When war came, US investments were estimated at between $30 and $50 million. Other than in mining, US capital did not dominate any internal sector of the Cuban economy.[50] 'To say as a generalization that businessmen opposed war', concludes a historian partial to economic explanations, 'is as erroneous as saying that businessmen wanted war.'[51]

The reasons, rather, were much more profound and tied in with a longer trend, the outcome of which is best called the Caribbeanization of Manifest Destiny. The tropics, and the Caribbean specifically, both provided the opportunity and suited the new geopolitical codes emanating from a powerful group of politicians, academics, military and businessmen. The fact that these geopolitical codes married geopolitics to a sense of Anglo-Saxon racial destiny explains why so often good intentions were swamped by feelings of resentment on the part of Caribbean peoples. In other words, the symbolic dimensions of US actions often endured beyond the positive material gains engendered by that intervention. This fact, however, should not blind us to the complex reality of US motivations in intervening in the Caribbean. Because the Spanish American War set a precedent which would be followed with disappointing regularity in the Caribbean, it is worth understanding the reasons for the action given by President William McKinley himself in his message of 11 April, 1898 to Congress about entering the war.[52] The first reason was humanitarian: 'It is specially our duty for it is right at our door.' Secondly, McKinley cited a position in international law: the right to intervene to protect US citizens' life and property. The third was the serious injury to US commerce and trade which the destruction of the island was causing. The fourth reason McKinley felt was 'of the utmost importance': the war in Cuba kept the US government and society constantly preoccupied and focused on Cuba. In other words, Cuba's geographical proximity made ignoring the festering conflict there impossible. Geopolitics forced a decision to intervene and bring order and stability to a region 'so near us.'

If the US went to war to safeguard the law and order at its borders, a necessary condition for freedom to trade and act in distant shores, then the US should ensure that law and order remained after the war. This explains the Platt Amendment to the Cuban constitution: it gave the US the right to intervene in Cuba should the US perceive a threat to its interests, provided for the leasing of land for an American naval base (Guantanamo) and even prohibited Cubans from assuming a public debt larger than the ability of her ordinary revenues to liquidate. This amendment kept US-Cuban relations at boiling point until abrogated in 1934.

Criticisms of US actions were not long in coming and not limited to Cubans and Latin Americans. As Walter Millis put it in an articulate 1931 book, *The Martial Spirit*, the US had acquired a foreign policy almost as fatuous as the most elegant examples of monarchical Europe; it had seized a colonial empire in a manner entitling it to recognition by the very best diplomats.[53]

Perhaps the most critical legacy of Americans' actions during that period was the bitterness and resentment felt by Cubans. As Carlton Beals notes in describing the 'gross and unfair insults' to the Cuban patriots,[54] the Americans discovered early that the Cuban patriots they had come to save were – in the words of one general, S. B. M. Young – 'a lot of degenerates, absolutely devoid of humour or gratitude . . . no more capable of self-government than the savage of Africa.'[55] The reference to Africa was not accidental. Haiti and its black government represented Africa in the Caribbean and it would be official US policy during the military occupation of Cuba (1899–1902) to limit the participation of, as US Secretary of State Elihu Root put it in 1900, those members of the race which had brought ruin to Haiti.[56]

It is true that victory in the Spanish-American War, by adding Cuba,

Puerto Rico, the Philippines, and consolidating total control over Guam, Hawaii and the Mariana Islands, turned the US into a two-ocean international power. But the Spanish-American war was a prelude to the next and most significant US step in its expansion through the tropics: Panama.

In January, 1902 the British had already given tacit recognition to not only US rights to a canal but indeed to US predominance in the Caribbean.[57] More than that, the US was now clearly embarked on a role of global involvement which required an undisputed sphere of influence. Those geopoliticians who worried about controlling and defending the routes of that trade, made the defence of the Panama canal the cornerstone of their whole strategic plan. Protecting the Panama canal would now become the justification for a Pax-Americana in the Caribbean. Geopolitics had found its centre of gravity; strategic thinking and acute perceptions of national interests and especially national security would radiate from there. There was a clear cut sharpness and apparently irrefutable logic about the need to defend this international waterway. Mahan's most cherished scenario had been achieved. As David McCullough put it, to both Roosevelt and his geopolitical mentor Mahan, 'the canal was to be the first step to American supremacy of the sea,'[58] yet neither of them ever thought of themselves as imperialists. Expansion was different from imperialism; to Roosevelt it was 'growth, it was progress, it was the American grain.'[59]

In 1904 Secretary of War Taft put the nature of American interests quite clearly: 'My government does not covet one cent of Panama's money, or one acre of her land, but in the face of a probable outlay of $300,000,000, it is absolutely essential that a thorough and close understanding be maintained between the two governments.'[60]

Taft was correct on several counts, in particular that the canal did end up costing $300 million by the time the 10-mile wide, 41-mile long canal and its locks was finished. That was a considerable amount compared to the $3 million paid for Louisiana, $10 million for Florida and the $27 million that the US would pay the Danes in 1917 for the Virgin Islands. It was three times what the US had offered Spain for Cuba.

But the thorough and close understanding between Americans and Panamanians was more elusive than Taft thought. Two factors operated to make this so. First was the high-handed and unilateral fashion in which the US went about securing the rights to the canal. Panamanians had little or nothing to say about the purchase (for $40 million) by the US of the rights and assets of the French-run company of Ferdinand de Lesseps. De Lesseps had negotiated with the Colombians from whom the Panamanians took their independence in 1903. Secondly, there was from the start an issue over ultimate sovereignty of the canal zone. While the US got rights 'in perpetuity', they also agreed to pay $250,000 'rent' every year, even though they owned the land.

But, just as US imperialism was about the creation of a sphere of influence, not a landed empire, so also the attitudes prevalent in that sphere were no different from those of any colonial situation. From the moment in November, 1903 when the US gunboat *Nashville* prevented Colombian troops from reaching Panama City to put down the separatist rebellion, there has existed a love-hate ambivalence in US-Panamanian relations. As a former US Ambassador recalls, over the years Panamanian 'pride and irritation gradually overwhelmed any thankfulness.'[61] David McCullough was similarly struck by what he felt was the 'smouldering wrath' of aggrieved Panamanians who were initially only marginally concerned about this; there was, they thought, time enough to resolve such difficulties. Besides, there was the indifference born of racial haughtiness. 'To the average American', notes McCullough, 'Panama was a land of dark, ignorant, undersized people who very obviously dislike him.'[62]

Imperialism is more than the sum of conquered territory and commerce, it is also an attitude, a perception of how the world is, or should be ordered. In that sense it is crucial to understand that even as the Americans were not interested in territorial expansion but rather were reaching for influence and bases at strategic locations, they did enter the twentieth century with a well-developed imperial attitude. It was this attitude, loaded with feelings of racial and cultural superiority, which engendered the most enduring resentment and hostility.

But imperialism, from the social-psychological point of view, does not leave the colonized unaffected. The love-hate relationship tends to affect the colonized much more than the colonizer. This is part of the complex interrelationship. Note the tone of the following dispatch entitled 'The New Social Order in Havana' sent by Cuba-American War correspondent José de Olivares:

> The tourists complain that Cuba has not been Americanized, as they were led to believe. The great mass of the population talk the Spanish language, and this is an obstacle to visitors from the US who expected other conditions . . . It is the eating that frets the tourist most. The tourist from the States wants a heavy breakfast, and makes known with hearty American frankness his opinion of the degenerate Latin race for clinging to coffee and rolls[63].

Not surprisingly, de Olivares repeatedly makes the point that he prefers 'all things American including baseball (played in Cuba since at least 1875) without the least taint or colouring of Spanish.' The name of the smaller island should be '*Porto* Rico' since, he asserts, '*Puerto* Rico is un-American'. Not surprisingly the Puerto Rican is described with evident self-hatred as 'the most eloquent exponent of habitual somnambulism.'[64]

The complex interdependence between the US and the Caribbean would intensify as broadening US perceptions of its geopolitical interests led to wider involvements in the region.

Notes

1   Cf. Julius W. Pratt, *Expansionists of 1812* (Gloucester, Mass.: Peter Smith [1925], 1957), pp. 64–9.
2   Samuel Flagg Bemis, *The Latin American Policy of the US* (New York: Harcourt, Brace and Co., 1943), p. 27.
3   Cf. Graham F. Stuart, *Latin America and the US* (New York: Appleton, Century Crofts, 1955), pp. 53–5.
4   Cited in Bemis, pp. 61–2.
5   Cited in John A. Garraty and Peter Gay, (eds) *The Columbia University History of the World* (New York: Harper and Row Publishers, 1972), p. 798.
6   Bemis, *The Latin American Policy*, p. 49.
7   Stuart, *Latin America and the US*, pp. 56–7.
8   Bemis, p. 68.
9   Cited in Donald Marquand Dozer (ed.) *The Monroe Doctrine* (New York: Alfred A. Knopf, 1965), pp. 6–7.
10   Cf. W.S. Robertson, 'The Monroe Doctrine Abroad, 1823–1824', *The American Political Science Review*, Vol. VI (November 1912), p. 546.
11   Bemis, p. 73.
12   W.F. Reddaway, *The Monroe Doctrine* (Cambridge, 1888) quoted in La Feber, *The New Empire*, pp. 63–4.
17   'The aura of Manifest Destiny', says Bemis, was 'forever drifting over the island of Cuba.' (p. 94). The US offered Spain $100 million in 1848 but Spain responded that they would rather see it sunk in the ocean than transferred to another power.
14   Bemis, p. 96.
15   F.J. Turner, 'The Problem of the West', *Atlantic Monthly*, LXXVIII (September 1896), pp. 289–97 in LaFeber, 70.
16   Cited in LaFeber, p. 107.
17   Cf. Rayford W. Logan, *The Diplomatic Relations of the US with Haiti, 1776–1891* (Chapel Hill, NC, 1941), p. 408–25.
18   Arthur P. Whitaker, *The US and Latin America – The Northern Republics* (Cambridge, Mass.: 1948), p. 160.
19   Norman A. Bailey, *Latin America in World Politics* (New York: Walker and Co., 1967), p. 44.
20   Olney to Bayard, July 20, 1895, in La Feber, p. 262.
21   Walter La Feber, *The New Empire* (Ithaca, N.Y.: Cornell University Press, 1963), p. 242.
22   Frederick Merk, *Manifest Destiny and Mission in American History* (New York: Random House, Vintage Books, 1966), p. 210.
23   Cf. H. Wayne Morgan, *America's Road to Empire: The War with Spain and Overseas Expansion* (New York: Walker and Co., 1967), p. 44.
24   La Feber, p. 260.
25   Dexter Perkins, *A History of the Monroe Doctrine* (Boston: Little, Brown and Co., 1963), p. 240.
26   *Ibid.*

27 Howard K. Beale, *Theodore Roosevelt and the Rise of America to World Power* (New York: Collier Books, 1965), pp. 38–41.

28 *Ibid.*, p. 39.

29 Cf. Richard Hofstadter, *Social Darwinism and American Thought* (Boston: The Beacon Press, 1962), pp. 170–200.

30 Beale, p. 42.

31 *Ibid.*, p. 47.

32 *Ibid.*, p. 46.

33 Reginald Horsman, *Race and Manifest Destiny* (Cambridge: Harvard University Press, 1981), p. 210.

34 Brooks Adams, *America's Economic Supremacy* [1990] (Freeport, N.Y.: Books for Libraries Press, 1971), p. 81.

35 *Ibid.*, p. 179.

36 *Ibid.*, p. 82.

37 *Ibid.*, p. 72.

38 *Ibid.*, p. 130.

39 *Ibid.*, p. 108.

40 Robert Seager II, *Alfred Thayer Mahan. The Man and His Letters* (Annapolis, Md.: Naval Institute Press, 1977), p. xi.

41 All citations by Alfred T. Mahan from his, *The Influence of Sea Power Upon History, 1660–1783* (New York: Hill and Wang, 1957).

42 Seager, p. 147.

43 *Ibid.*, pp. 350–51.

44 *Ibid.*, p. 96.

45 *Ibid.*, p. 151.

46 *Ibid.*, p. 418.

47 Major General Joseph Wheeler, *Our Islands and Their People*, Vol. I (New York: N.D. Thompson, 1889), p. 3.

48 On European sympathy but no material support for Spain see L.D. Shippe, 'Germany and the Spanish American War', *American Historical Review*, VII (1927), pp. 25–44; L.M. Sears, 'French Opinion of the Spanish-American War', *Hispanic American Historical Review*, VII (1927), pp. 25–44.

49 Cf. Hugh Thomas, *Cuba* (New York: Harper and Row, 1971), p. 333.

50 Junes Robert Benjamin, *The US and Cuba: Hegemony and Dependent Development, 1880–1934* (Pittsburgh: University of Pittsburgh Press, 1977), p. 5.

51 LaFeber, p. 385.

52 The text of this message is printed verbatim in Russell H. Fitzgibbon, *Cuba and the US, 1900–1935* New York [1935] Russell and Russell, 1935, Appendix.

51 Walter Millis *The Martial Spirit* (1931).

54 Carlton Beals, *The Crime of Cuba* (Philadelphia: J.B. Lippincott Co., 1933), p. 155.

55 *Ibid.*, p. 159.

56 On US racial policies during this period see Louis A. Pérez, Jr., *Cuba Between Empires, 1878–1902* (Pittsburgh: University of Pittsburgh Press, 1983).

57 John A.W. Grenville, 'Great Britain and the Isthmian Canal, 1898–1901', *American Historical Review*, 61 (1955).

58 Cf. David McCullough, *The Path Between the Seas. The Creation of the Panama Canal, 1870–1914* (New York: Simon & Schuster, 1977), p. 250.

59 *Ibid.*, p. 255.

60 Cited in Ralph Emmett Avery, *The Greatest Engineering Feat in the World at Panama* New York: Leslie Judge Co., 1915), p. 263.

61 William J. Jorden, *Panama Odyssey* (Austin: University of Texas Press, 1984), pp. 27–8.

62 *Ibid.*, p. 556.
63 *Our Islands and Their People as Seen with Camera and Pencil*, introduced by Major-General Joseph Wheeler, with special descriptive matter by José de Olivares, edited by William S. Bryan, Two Quarts Volumes (St Louis: N.D. Thompson Publishing Co., 1899) Vol I., pp. 31–2.
64 *Ibid.*, p. 265.

CHAPTER 2 | Geopolitics and the perceived duties of the policeman: 1903–35

The US was rightly proud of that great feat of engineering, the Panama canal, and quite determined to protect and defend it. The final piece in Alfred T. Mahan's geopolitical vision of US interest in the Caribbean was now in place, and events would follow their natural course. After all, as noted earlier, it was Mahan who predicted that, given her geographical position and with the proper military preparation, US preponderance in the Caribbean would follow 'with mathematical certainty'.

The role of regional – if not international – policeman had found its most convincing rationale and *raison d'être* in what was now the US primary zone of defence. It is logical to ask, however, defence against whom? Britain had tacitly accepted the Caribbean as an American sphere of influence and America had in turn reconciled itself to living with British, French, Dutch and Danish colonies in the region. Be that as it may, defence presupposes a threat or at least a strong perception of one.

In the days before alliances and defence 'pacts' those assigned the task of preparing a nation's contingency plans of national defence had to assume no friends, only potential enemies or at best neutrals. Thus, US strategists such as A.T. Mahan perceived the Latin nations as disdainful neutrals, but all Europeans as jealous rivals or threatening adversaries. In the Caribbean, this could mean Britain. Before the US had compelled Britain to back down over the Venezuela-British Guiana border dispute in 1896, Americans such as Henry Cabot Lodge regarded the British presence in the Caribbean with deep suspicion. 'England', he warned somewhat unrealistically in 1895, 'has studded the West Indies with strong places which are a standing menace to our Atlantic seaboard.' Clearly, the American victory in the Spanish-American war, its securing of Puerto Rico, a major base in Cuba and its control over Panama and its canal project all made the US overwhelmingly predominant in the region. But predominance does not mean hegemony, invariably there were challengers. In the early twentieth century, Americans perceived that challenger to be Germany.

Gone were the days when the German Chancellor could say, as he did in 1871, that they would not think of penetrating the western hemisphere where 'we recognize . . . the predominant influence of the United States as found in the nature of things, and compatible with our interests.'[1] By 1897

Bismarck was describing the Monroe Doctrine as 'an extraordinary piece of insolence', and in 1898 he was predicting that with Spain out of the way in the Caribbean, England and France would drive the American 'pygmy navy' out of its waters. 'The Monroe Doctrine', he said, 'is a spectre that would vanish in plain daylight.'[2]

The Germans had eyes on the Danish Virgin Islands, Curaçao, the southern coast of Brazil, and the Galapagos Islands. It should come as no surprise that the Kaiser was an avid reader of A.T. Mahan's geopolitical doctrines and that he was determined not to abandon the sea lanes and commercial opportunities to the British. German capital and immigrants were deeply involved in both coffee and cocoa plantations and trade throughout the Caribbean Basin, and had made a bid to buy the Panama canal rights from the De Lesseps Company. In general, German capitalists behaved little differently from American or British, i.e. they expected their national navies to both protect, and where and when necessary, collect delinquent loans from Caribbean Basin countries. 'Dollar' diplomacy came in many denominations.[3] What perception did US military strategists have of their position in the region as this new competition began?

In 1901 the government assigned the General [Defence] Board the task of measuring 'the actual value of our power of and influence in the Caribbean Sea and upon the coasts of South America.' They reported back that if bases were kept in Cuba and new ones built in Puerto Rico, the 'principles of strategy and the defects in our geography' indicated that the navy could maintain 'mastery' of the Caribbean and 'predominance' on the Atlantic coast of South America 'as far as the mouth of the Orinoco.' Beyond that point control was 'doubtful' to 'improbable'.[4] In 1902 the US again virtually forced Germany, Britain and Italy to lift their blockade of Venezuela, proving the Board's estimates to be correct. Again, in 1903 the Board considered it 'sound strategy' to plan for the West Indies and not the Atlantic coast as a probable theatre of war. By then they had pinpointed the most likely enemy: the 'most important war problem to be studied is based on the supposition that Germany is the enemy'.[5]

It now appears that the Board had good intelligence. According to Grenville and Young, who researched the German archives, Germany had considered an attack as early as 1889, and in 1899 the Kaiser personally ordered a war plan against the US. The Caribbean, and Puerto Rico specifically, would be the first step towards not a conquest of the US, but in the Kaiser's words 'a firm base in the West Indies and a free hand in South America, which entails a breach of the "Monroe Doctrine".'[6] To what extent did these foreign investors and their governments pay heed to and find encouragement in President Theodore Roosevelt's message to Congress of 3 December, 1901 in which he sets some limits to his role as policeman? 'We do not', he declared 'guarantee any state against punishment if it misconducts itself, provided that punishment does not take the form of the acquisition of territory by any non-American power.'[7]

It was the language of a strict school teacher-cum-preacher-cum-policeman. All major powers at the time carried the patronizing belief of the white man's burden into their dealings with non-white people. In the US several men had such prominence in carrying out the mandate to improve America's position by bringing law and order to the Caribbean that their personalities seemed to characterize the whole period. Corporate lawyer Elihu Root was not only responsible for the Platt Amendment, he was the skilled negotiator and trouble-shooter whose attempts to put American policy on a legal track helped ameliorate the harshness of his boss's aggressiveness. That boss, T.R. Roosevelt, exemplified the Latin American characterization of a bully with a 'big stick'. Philadelphia corporate lawyer, Philander Knox, was so avid a defender of US banking and other financial interests he earned the name 'dollar diplomacy' for US actions in the Caribbean.

But it was President Woodrow Wilson who truly set the tone and style of US Caribbean policy up to the late 1920s. It was Wilson's actions as regional policeman that carried even further Roosevelt's 'Corollary' to the Monroe Doctrine, i.e. protective imperialism. According to Bemis, Wilson had a sincere zeal for 'saving the people from bad government, tyranny and economic exploitation. . . . All the Missionaries of Democracy desired that "benighted" peoples might be saved from themselves for themselves.'[8] But, as Cuban historian Ramiro Guerra y Sánchez noted in the 1930s, US haste at citing the national inferiority of Caribbean peoples appeared always to have been used to justify denying their rights.[9] It was not Wilson who started the policy of intervention; he did not even start the intervening of customs to collect debts and straighten the mess of many a Caribbean country's finances. Receiverships had already been set up in Nicaragua and the Dominican Republic. It was Wilson, however, who combined a moralizing approach with a heightened sense of strategic interests. Economic interests would hardly explain the numerous interventions in countries with minimal US investments. Wilson's actions in Mexico, Nicaragua, the Dominican Republic and Haiti illustrate the point.

There had been an American naval presence in Mexico since the days of President Taft (one battleship permanently at the oil port of Tampico, others patrolling off the main port of Veracruz). Secretary Knox once explained that the purpose of the battlewagons was to keep the Mexicans 'in a salutary equilibrium, between a dangerous and exaggerated apprehension and a proper degree of wholesome fear.'[10] The internal politics of nations seldom respond to such efforts at intimidation, however. Mexicans certainly did not.

In 1914, four years after the Mexicans had begun their revolutionary struggle, the nation was still being torn apart by civil war. The contenders were dictator General Victoriano Huerta and the so-called Constitutionalist forces led mainly (though not solely) by Venustiano Carranza. Revolutionary aspirations, personalities, regionalism, foreign involvement and traditional Mexican political attitudes all played a part in that struggle for power. Woodrow Wilson had just been elected President of the US and the Mexican situation was to involve him deeply in hemispheric affairs. It was vitally important to Wilson 'to teach the Latin American republics to elect good men.'[11] In Mexico the Constitutionalists were 'good men' and Huerta bad. The US 'acting on the behalf of the rest of the world', as Wilson put it, would not tolerate Huerta. When a financial loan which one historian has called a 'barefaced bribe'[12] in return for his resignation was refused by Huerta, Wilson turned to other strategies convinced, he stated, that 'The continuance of Huerta's rule is impossible without the consent of the US.'[13] With an American naval presence already in Mexico, armed intervention was only a question of when and how.

Wilson, later to become the greatest advocate of non-intervention and collective security, visualized the situation as directly involving the prestige and honour of the exalted office he occupied. On 9 April, 1914 an incident of little military importance provided him with the opportunity to carry out a complex scheme of intervention to oust Huerta. It was the political and symbolic significance of this incident which left enormous resentment in Mexico, just like the 'Baltimore' incident in Chile. They were, in fact, quite similar. In 1914, in the midst of one of the civil wars which had kept Mexico in a state of chaos since 1911, the crew members of the whaleboat USS *Dolphin* inadvertently entered an area of Veracruz designated off-limits by the Huerta government forces and were arrested by a local officer.[14] Their release and an apology to US Admiral Mayo came almost immediately from the local commander. The American response was that to salve this 'humiliating arrest' the Mexicans would have to do three things: court-martial the arresting officer, send a written apology to Admiral Mayo, and 'hoist the American flag on a prominent position on shore and salute it with twenty-one guns', a salute which would be duly returned by the US war ship. At first, Huerta was willing to accede to the first two demands but not to the third. The International Court, he stated, should adjudicate that one. Later, faced with the strains caused by the American blockade on his most important harbour, Huerta agreed to the third, provided the Americans would guarantee that the Mexican salute would be immediately returned by the American ships. Wilson refused to give any such promise and soon issued the order to take Veracruz. The Americans took Veracruz, staying for eight months or just long enough to bankrupt the Huerta government.

The same tactic was used in the American intervention in Nicaragua in 1909. Favouring the Conservative side in the civil war, US marines occupied the principal port of Bluefields and turned the custom house over to the Conservatives – who soon succeeded in the struggle for power. Interventions in Haiti and the Dominican Republic also centred around control of custom's revenues.

The Niagara Mediation Conference of May 1914 attempted to prevent all-out war between the US and Mexico. To the mediating countries, Argentina, Brazil and Chile (henceforth known as the 'ABC' powers) the Conference had been a success and had also established a precedent for inter-American mediation. No one in Mexico saw it that way. They believed, as does Howard Cline,[15] that Wilson wanted to have it both ways: to appear as a peacemaker, while also putting his political preference in power. He delayed the Conference hoping for a Constitutionalist sweep of Huerta, which occurred, and then he secured a dignified exit of US troops from Mexico.

The Constitutionalist side, while of course welcoming American arms and financial aid, condemned other forms of intervention. 'Carranza', says Cline, 'did not intend that Mexico should be treated in the highhanded way in which Wilson was treating Nicaragua and Haiti.'[16] He threatened to evict the Americans out of pure nationalism. In 1907 Theodore Roosevelt had negotiated a treaty with the Dominican Republic which gave the US the right to protect the receiver-general of customs in the performance of his duties. However, that treaty had not proved to be effective in keeping Dominican politics from repeatedly boiling over and irritating the US. President Taft and his Secretary of State Knox had tried repeatedly to cajole, co-opt and coerce Dominicans into stability. By the time Woodrow Wilson became president in 1913, the Dominican Republic was on the verge of anarchy. Partial US interventions were soon followed by a fully-fledged occupation by the US marine corps in 1916.

Samuel Flagg Bemis is one who believes that there was a material and moral benefit from stopping Dominicans from exercising their 'sovereign right to suicide'. He was content to conclude that 'after this timely tutelage, the Dominican Republic has been "running on its own" very successfully.'[17] Alas, it was the peace of the cemetery, a cemetery run with an iron hand by the man the US put in power, Rafael Leonidas Trujillo. As the new documentary research of Bernardo Vega has revealed, it was a network of officers of the US marine corps which not only trained Trujillo's new *gendarmerie* but, indeed, successfully lobbied for him with many a US administration.[18] They were so influential in the administrations of Hoover and especially F.D. Roosevelt, that they completely neutralized the anti-Trujillo sentiments of such important diplomats as Under-Secretary of State Summer Welles. Again, geopolitical and ideological perceptions, not economics, were at the core of this division. This, says Vega, created a two-track policy towards Trujillo, that of the State Department and that of the military. The latter invariably won, at least as we shall see, until the early 1960s when the friendship with Trujillo became an embarrassment. At that point the CIA took charge of US policy.

Just as US intervention in the Dominican Republic eventually brought Rafael Leonidas Trujillo to long-lasting power, so too its intervention in Nicaragua from 1927 to 1932 gave rise to the Anastacio Somoza dynasty.[19] They were part of a particularly nasty club of tyrants which helped keep the Caribbean Basin stable throughout the 1930s and 1940s. Geopolitical stability, not economics drove US policy, especially in the archipelagic Caribbean.[20] In Central America, as we shall see, economic interests might not have been predominant, but they certainly were important.

That the motives which impelled President Wilson to act as a moral policeman had little to do with economics is evident in the case of the intervention in Haiti. This did not mean, however, that American capital was not interested in profit. Some US investors, according to Ludwell Montague, had an exaggerated notion of Haitian resources. But even Montague agrees that it was fear of a foreign occupation which determined US actions.[21]

When the Americans intervened in that island in 1915 they had no major investments there. In fact there were only two significant foreign ownerships of land: an English investment in 10,000 acres and a German one in 7,100. The Americans would acquire these and others but by 1927 a report by six 'disinterested' Americans who opposed the US occupation, showed all major agricultural projects losing money. Only banks and utilities were profitable.

It was Woodrow Wilson, acting as regional policeman in the face of a breakdown of political order in Haiti, which led to the occupation. Haitian historians do not hesitate to describe the years before the American occupation as bordering on chaos. 'Anarchy', says a popular text, 'was permanent, generalized, and getting worse every day; the country was on the edge of a precipice . . . .'[22] They had had four presidents between May 1913 and July 1915. The last of these, Vilbrun Guillaume Sam, had all the political prisoners in the National Penitentiary massacred, then sought sanctuary in the French Embassy. An infuriated mob pulled him out of the legation and lynched him. The US marines landed that same day. Not surprisingly many Haitian intellectuals initially welcomed the marines.[23] That welcome was soon exhausted as American unilateralism, impatience and disdain for the Haitians revealed itself. 'The result of the arbitrary measures adopted', says Montague, 'was a system that had neither the virtues of a treaty regime based on true agreement nor those of a clean-cut military administration . . . but only the bad features of both.'[24] Reports of local American arrogance, and bullying even of the presidents they put in the palace, began to filter out to the American public. Even Republican presidential candidate Warren Harding took up the criticism in the 1920 campaign:

> I will not empower an Assistant Secretary of the Navy to draft a constitution for helpless neighbours in the West Indies and jam it down their throats at the point of bayonets borne by US marines . . . .'[25]

Also catching the attention of American civil-rights groups such as the NAACP were the racial attitudes of the occupation forces generally and one of its main commanders, Colonel Littleton W.T. Waller who could write the most insulting notes to the Haitian president himself.[26] Not surprisingly, historians would later discover just how deep the racial attitudes of men like Waller went. 'They are real niggers and no mistake', Waller wrote to a friend, 'What the people of Norfolk and Portsmouth would say if they saw me bowing and scraping to these coons, I do not know. All the same I do not wish to be outdone in formal politeness.'[27] Haitians, of course, saw through this 'politeness' and made the Americans' generalized lack of respect for them individually and collectively the basis of a strong nationalist movement, the 'Indigenous' movement. This movement became the incubator not just of a protest literature but, indeed, of black nationalists such as François Duvalier, who would tyrannize Haiti from 1957 to 1971.

Those who have studied the occupation from the Haitian perspective, agree that racial antagonism was probably the single most important reason why the Americans failed to achieve anything of enduring value, despite some significant contributions to improved health, roads and the infrastructure in general.[28] The racism which characterized the occupation administration turned Haitians of all classes and skin colour against them. As David Nicholls points out, 'Paradoxically, the Americans unintentionally succeeded . . . in writing all Haitians under the name "black".'[29]

This Haitian antagonism was hardly guarded, as was made evident to the members of an official US Commission in 1930. 'The commission was disappointed', it wrote, 'at the evidence it received of the lack of appreciation on the part of the educated and cultured Haitians of the services rendered them by the occupation . . .' They attributed this resentment to the 'brusque attempt to plant democracy there by drill and harrow' and 'its determination to set up a middle class.'[30] Both correct explanations, no doubt, but quite short of being the full story.

Even the war by the marines against the notorious mercenaries from northern Haiti, the *cacos*, turned Haitians against the Americans. These bandits were always available to any member of the Port-au-Prince elite who wished to overthrow an existing government, and were a major cause of the political instability which was a factor in the US decision to intervene. Certainly Haiti would be much better off without such elements. The problem is that the war against the *cacos*, especially against Charlemagne Peralte from Hinche in the Artibonite plains of central Haiti, turned into one of those irregular, guerrilla wars invariably accompanied by atrocities. 'For nineteen years', says Hans Schmidt, 'the marines fought people they defined as 'savages' and their tactics frequently degenerated into torture, systematic destruction of villages, and military tactics tantamount to genocide.'[31] In 1919 alone the marines killed 1,861 rebels and had killed 3,250 by the end of five years of occupation. The marines lost 14 men during that period, only one in actual combat.[32]

By far the greatest harm done to Haiti's political future, however, was the attempt to modernize the state materially but utilizing, and even reinforcing, some of the worst features of traditional exploitation of the peasantry. This was the case with the 1916 decision to reinstitute the *corvée*, a provision of the ancient rural code which forced peasants to contribute a few days a year free labour to keep the roads open. The Americans decided to build a modern road system with that method even though this meant moving peasants large distances from their homes and food plots. Evidence from a perspicacious US officer indicates the risks involved in the modernization-at-all-costs mentality:

> The results of this exploitation of labour were two: first, it created in the minds of the peasants a dislike for the American occupation and its two instruments – the marines and the gendarmerie – and, second, imbued the native enlisted man with an entirely false conception of his relations with the civil population. As the *corvée* became more and more unpopular, more and more difficulty caused the gendarme to resort to methods which were often brutal but quite consistent with their training under Haitian officials. I soon realized that one of the great causes of American unpopularity among the Haitians was the *corvée* . . . .'[33]

Despite Harding's ringing critique of the Wilsonian doctrine of moral policeman of the Caribbean, neither he nor his fellow Republicans who followed him in the White House removed the troops from Haiti. This would not occur until 1934.

While the Haitians' situation was kept before the eyes of Washington, largely through the efforts of the NAACP and especially of its Executive Secretary, James Weldon Johnson, the US was also involved in Nicaragua and the Dominican Republic. While major segments of both countries harboured a 'Yankeephobia' which would come into play later in the

century, the Nicaraguan case is especially relevant. The American perceptions about 'Third Party' subversion in the Caribbean were not born during
the Cold War, they were quite evident much earlier, in the Nicaraguan
case.[34] America's role as area policeman had survived the passing of
Woodrow Wilson.

After a decade and a half of marine presence in Nicaragua, American
supervised elections in 1916 brought a moderate Conservative President
with a Liberal Vice-President, Dr Juan B. Sacasa, into office. This government was almost immediately overthrown by the orthodox Conservative
General Emiliano Chamorro. The US pressured Chamorro out and accepted
the election by Congress of Adolfo Diaz who was more to their liking. The
Liberals did not accept this, maintaining that the Vice-President, Dr Sacasa,
was the legitimate successor to the office. Mexico recognized Sacasa,
which led President Diaz to notify President Coolidge that he could not
protect foreign nationals in Nicaragua; he blamed Mexican intervention.
Coolidge then informed Congress in 1927 that:

> The US cannot, therefore, fail to view with deep concern any
> serious threat to stability and constitutional government in Nica-
> ragua tending toward anarchy and jeopardizing American inter-
> ests, especially if a state of affairs is contributed or brought .
> about by outside influence or by any foreign power.[35]

The upshot of this was that US marines landed again, took the important
ports on both coasts, declared these and the vital Granada-Managua-Corinto
railroad passage 'neutral zones', and began pressing for their own political
formula.[36] But if we know who the good citizens in Nicaragua were, then
who or from where was the external threat which triggered geopolitical
concerns and therefore justified military intervention?

It was from Mexico, then governed by the independent-minded and
reform-oriented Plutarco Calles. He recognized Sacasa as President of
Nicaragua and welcomed him in exile to Mexico. Because of Calles' move
to expropriate American and European oil holdings and his open persecu-
tion of the Roman Catholic church and other socially oriented reforms, his
regime engendered wide hostility in American circles. With overtones of
the 'Red-Scare' of the early 1920s, the US government was apprehensive
about 'Bolshevik Aims and Policies in Mexico and Latin America', as a
paper released by Secretary of State Frank Kellogg was entitled. Nicaragua
was to be made a pawn in the diplomatic and geopolitical hostilities between Mexico and the US. Coolidge, one author writes, 'was playing a
game of power politics with Mexico. He chose to utilize the tremendous
strength of the US to drive President Calles into a corner.'[37] What this meant
for little Nicaragua is made plain by Neil Macaulay. 'The US', says Macaulay,
'could not allow a Sacasa victory which would augment the prestige of

Mexico in the area, especially since Mexico had just taken a sharp turn to the left. 'The US government feared that the Mexican revolutionary virus might infect Central America and lead to the formation of a block of revolutionary states directed by Mexico.'[38]

In the midst of the labyrinthine politics of Nicaragua, US geopolitical interests got caught up in the financial interests of US bankers and in the slippery self-interests of Nicaraguan and Mexican *caudillos*. In Nicaragua only one of those *caudillos*, the Liberal César Augusto Sandino, refused to accept either the American presence or their political formula. For five years he engaged the marines in a guerrilla war characterized by savagery on both sides. The story of Sandino has been told elsewhere[39] but here one should note the following: first, Sandino's anti-Americanisms as well as his ideology, which was an amalgam of anarchistic, Marxist and spiritualist influences, had been shaped while he was exiled in Mexico which was then under attack by the marines. 'It is in Tampico [Mexico]', writes Gregorio Selser, 'that every biographer must begin to search for the origins of Sandino's later struggle.'[40] Secondly, the history of the US-imposed 'order' throughout the area was already part of the popular culture's attitude towards the US. One of Sandino's Mexican lieutenants recalls why he adopted the red and black flag (communism and anarchism): these were the colours of his Mexican mentor, anarchist Ricardo Flores Magón, who, before he died in a US prison cell in Fort Leavenworth, Texas, would rail against 'the violators of Nicaragua, the ravishers of Haiti, the vandals who dismembered Colombia, the scourge of Puerto Rico, the butchers of Spain, and the stranglers of the rights of weak peoples.'[41]

What truth, then, in the charges of Secretary of State Frank Kellogg that Mexico under President Calles was under communist domination? The most recent research shows that while Calles' opposition to US policies in Central America, especially Nicaragua, and his support for anti-imperialist forces elicited positive responses from the Comintern and the American communist movement (Workers Party), they had little influence on his regime.[42] Calles was attempting to reconstruct Mexico on a national capitalist basis and communist support came in handy. And, in the final analysis, it was the Mexican communists and Comintern who felt duped by Calles. Following Comintern dictates, the Mexican Communist Party later accused Calles of having 'capitulated to Anglo-American imperialism'.[43] In fact, during the Party's 1925 Congress, Calles was described as 'the gendarme of the Yankee bankers and petroleum companies'.[44]

Driven by the momentum of Manifest Destiny, and racial destiny, cloaking their self-interest and geopolitical codes under the Monroe Doctrine and encouraged by the ease with which expansion had occurred, American policymakers were oblivious to key elements such as international law or nationalism. After all, the US claim to being the policeman had always been a unilateral doctrine without any standing in international law. As Charles E. Hughes, President Harding's Secretary of State, phrased it in 1923: 'As the policy embodied in the Monroe Doctrine is distinctly the policy of the United States, the Government of the United States reserves to itself its definition, interpretation, and applications.'[45] But nationalists have a way of responding in kind to perceived offences to national or ethnic honour, easily adopting the posture that the enemy of my enemy is my friend. These sentiments suited two international movements which had already reached the Caribbean: the communist international (Comintern) which followed Moscow's instructions, and the Alianza Popular Revolucionaria Americana (APRA), founded in 1924 in Mexico by Raúl Haya de la Torre, a Peruvian exile. While the former had the money (in the Caribbean it came from the American communists), the latter had a very strong appeal because of its racially-based notion of 'Indo America' vs. Anglo-America. APRA's five-point program started with a call to oppose 'Yankee imperialism', including a program for the internationalization of the Panama canal and for Latin American solidarity.[46] It soon had adepts around the Caribbean. In Nicaragua, Sandino was an early believer. He broke with APRA (and the Comintern), however, as soon as they were no longer useful to his cause. On the other hand, he never abandoned his opposition to what he called 'the blond beasts'. These and other epithets used to describe Americans indicated the racial bases of much of the anti-Americanism. The response to US racism was increased pride in what Sandino called the 'Spanish Indians of America', in the same way as US racism in Haiti gave rise to the first truly native or *autonomiste* movement asserting their African heritage.

The interventions in Haiti, the Dominican Republic and Nicaragua were under constant attack in the US. Commentator Walter Lippman put much of the American mood in perspective when he noted in 1928 that US interventions in the Caribbean had not only done no good, they had left these states with less sovereignty and worse governments.[47] If it had only been intellectuals like Lippmann and relatively powerless groups such as the NAACP, little attention would have been given to the protest, but other voices were being heard. An American coffee planter in Nicaragua complained that before the marine intervention, Americans were generally liked, now they are 'hated and despised' and even fearful for their lives.[48] Additionally, the intervention was incurring unusual costs in blood and capital. In one year, twenty-one marines had been killed and with the US economy already showing signs of faltering, there was little Congressional support for the action.

By the end of the 1920s the Wilsonian idea of extending the Roosevelt Corollary into a moral policeman role was under heavy attack by members of the Republican Herbert Hoover administration. The one who began redefining this role was Secretary of State Henry L. Stimson. His arguments had been set down in a document written by his Under-Secretary of State J. Reuben Clark, which stated specifically that the Monroe Doctrine was a unilateral policy decision which did not refer just to inter-American affairs. 'The Doctrine', said Clark, 'states a case of the US versus Europe, not of the US versus Latin America.'[49]

It was Democratic President Franklin Delano Roosevelt, however, who decided on a new initiative in the Americas. He called it the Good Neighbour Policy and spelt it out in his inaugural address of 4 March, 1933: 'I would dedicate this Nation to the policy of the good neighbour: the neighbour who resolutely respects himself and, because he does so, respects the rights of others.'

Roosevelt had two seasoned internationalists to carry out his ideas: Summer Welles and Cordell Hull. Welles in particular had ample Caribbean experience. He led the American mission to Honduras in 1924 which was in constant revolutionary upheaval. He helped draw up the Pact of Amapala (3 May, 1924) which committed other Central American countries to denying their borders to insurgents. His vision about US policy in the Caribbean was shaped by his stint as Commissioner of the United States in the occupied Dominican Republic, 1922–25, an occupation whose termination he oversaw. It was this experience which led him to write an important history of the Dominican Republic which contained a more generalized review of US-Caribbean relations. He described the US overall thrust as a policy of intimidation rather than cooperation which offended Latin American sensibilities and ignored their rights. He admits that T.R. Roosevelt 'took' the Panama canal, and that the Taft-Knox period of 'dollar diplomacy' was 'the most pernicious' period in US-Caribbean relations.[50] In general, Welles thought that American actions reflected 'a patronizing sentiment based on a supposed superiority' to the Latin Americans.

Welles' central criticism, however, had to do with what he called 'the extraordinary paradox' of Woodrow Wilson's Caribbean policy: on the one hand attempting to win Latin American friendship and confidence through relations based on 'terms of equality and honour', while at the same time repeatedly sending in the US marines to make them behave in terms of his conception of morality. Welles was very specific in locating the problem:

1   Neither Wilson nor any of his advisers had any knowledge of the 'psychology' of the Dominican people.
2   They never attempted to determine just what the limits of his influence could or should be. 'There was never a perspective', only *ad hoc* reactions to events. Each step taken led to further denials of the very moral principles enunciated. Through logical progression this led to the total denial of Dominican sovereignty.

The results have been disastrous: little gain materially and enormous losses in terms of goodwill. 'It had all left', he said, 'an enduring hostility' against Americans.

In 1933 President Roosevelt sent Welles to deal with a Cuban situation which was careening out of control. As Secretary of State Cordell Hull put it, the Gerardo Machado government 'was slipping its cinch after twelve years in the saddle, and revolution was plotting . . . .'[51]

This was Welles' chance to implement the new policy of Good Neighbours, bringing to it all his experience and skill in dealing with Latin Americans. His was a dual task: (1) to insure US interests (economic and geopolitical) but, (2) to do so without direct intervention. The history of Welles' travails and frustrations is instructive on several counts. First, good intentions are not enough. There is enough evidence of Summer Welles' good intentions; to give him the benefit of the doubt, therefore, means also giving others who have failed in US-Caribbean relations the benefit of the doubt. Seeking clarification and understanding, not recriminations, is the best approach. Secondly, policy decisions invariably were based on the information available at the time. Only hindsight is '20–20'. For instance, was communist influence – as Welles suggested and as Secretary of State Hull was inclined to believe – behind the problems in Cuba? It is a fact that the Cuban Communist Party controlled the largest trade unions which were generally well organized.'[52] On the other hand, there was no evidence that they controlled the nationalist, progressive movement. Welles operated with good intentions but without complete information from April to September, 1933.

His first move, the successful ousting of Machado – largely through his ability to win over the commander of the Cuban Army to US goals[53] – seemed an enormous accomplishment. But Welles had opened a Pandora's box which he could not handle without his government exerting the strongest form of intervention short of out-right military occupation – an intervention which became known as 'intervention by inertia'. What followed was a long struggle between the proud American Ambassador and various contending groups within the Cuban political system to control the destinies of the island.[54] One month after Welles' 'victory' in ousting Machado, two US destroyers were hastily summoned to make a show of force in Havana harbour. 'I feel confident', stated Welles, 'that the visit of these ships was essential for its moral effects alone'; shades of Mexico 1914. The Welles plan for Cuba, of support for the new regime of Cespedes, came to an abrupt end through one of the most singular events in the history of Latin American civil-military relations: a successful *coup d'état* by a non-commissioned officer corps. A self-taught and ambitious sergeant and ex-cane cutter named Fulgencio Batista emerged as the man with whom to contend.[55] Batista had joined one of the revolutionary student groups, the

ABC, and had in one fell swoop eliminated the complete officer corps of the Cuban army, deposed Céspedes and handed the government over to a revolutionary *junta*. This was totally unacceptable to Welles whom Batista had not consulted. To Welles the *junta* was nothing more nor less than 'a group of the most extreme radicals of the student organization and three university professors whose theories are frankly communistic.'[56] Professor Grau San Martín, who was made head of the government, was no communist but was an independent-minded and nationalistic leader who intended to 'Cubanize' the governing of the island. To some observers Cuba was at that point on the verge of a veritable social revolution.[57]

Secretary of State Hull and President Roosevelt were busy building the framework of their Good Neighbour Policy for the forthcoming Inter-American Conference at Montevideo in 1933. They were in no mood, therefore, for the military intervention Ambassador Welles felt was necessary. Intervention had to take a different form. Welles, convinced that 'no government here can survive for a protracted period without recognition by the US,' began to apply pressure on the Grau government. Along with a complete withdrawal of diplomatic recognition went a massive presence of the US navy.[58] Thirty warships, including at least two battleships, cruised in Cuban national waters for five solid months. With powerful enemies inside Cuba, with the Latin American nations waiting on the side and the European nations, which had long since come to recognize US dominance in the area, following the lead of the US, Grau's regime was isolated. Bryce Wood sums up the realities of the situation faced by the regime's confrontation with the US:

> The Cuban government must be changed if the Cuban sugar market in the US were to be expanded, if the Platt Amendment were to be repealed, and if Cuba were to emerge from economic distress so serious that it had brought many people to the verge of starvation.[59]

Grau resigned. His main source of support, the new Cuban army under Batista, had succumbed to American pressure and accepted the US candidate for the office, Colonel Mendieta. American recognition of the new regime came five days after its inauguration on 18 January, 1934. In the midst of the Good Neighbour Policy a sovereign nation had been forced to accept a foreign political formula and the other Latin American nations stood by meekly in silent witness.

The collective frustrations of US actions in 1933 became an integral part of Cuban political culture right up to the Revolution of 1959. In similar fashion, Sandino's revolution in Nicaragua had spawned – or at least helped sustain – many of the personalities, movements and ideas which would play roles in Central America and the Caribbean for decades to come. Among others there were Julio Antonio Mella, founder of the Cuban Communist Party, Farabundo Martí, founder of the El Salvador Communist Party; and the first 'Legiones del Caribe' composed of liberals, radicals and revolutionaries in general. But fundamentally, there was the growing resentment of the *Pax Americana* imposed by one US administration after the other. 'The same policy', writes Dana Munro, 'inspired the actions of successive American administrations towards the Caribbean during these decades.' The methods varied, 'more because of accumulating experience and increasing involvement than because of any differences in the ultimate goals'.[60]

Once a nation defines a region as a sphere of influence, its strategic goals are automatically set. The tactics may vary, but the geopolitics of spheres of influence operate by their own 'iron laws'. This is so until the costs force a redefinition of geopolitical interests. World War II brought about such a change but in the direction of reinforcing the security aspects of the area.

Notes

1   Dexter Perkins, p. 150.
2   See the discussion on German imperial designs in the Caribbean in Dexter Perkins, pp. 206–27.
3   Bemis, p. 115.
4   General Board Minutes, 14 April, 1901, cited in Grenville and Young, p. 303.
5   General Board Minutes, July 29, 1903 cited in Grenville and Young, p. 305.
6   See the discussion in Grenville and Young, pp. 304–7.
7   Bemis, p. 147.
8   Bemis, p. 185.
9   Ramiro Guerra y Sánchez, *La expansión territorial de los Estados Unidos* (La Habana: Editorial de Ciencias Sociales, 1975), p. 48.
10 Howard F. Cline, *The US and Mexico* (New York: Athenaeum, 1963) p. 155.
11 Quoted in Dexter Perkins, *A History of the Monroe Doctrine* (Boston: Little, Brown & Co., 1963) p. 258.
12 Cline, p. 155.
13 *Ibid.*, p. 149.
14 The most detailed study in print is Robert E. Quirk's appropriately titled *An Affair of Honour: Woodrow Wilson and the Occupation of Veracruz* (Lexington: University of Kentucky Press, 1962). Quirk, writing soon after the Bay of Pigs fiasco of 1962, correctly drew a parallel noting that 'we may profit from the realization that our failures today spring in part from the same attitude displayed in 1914' (p. vi), an optimism which, of course, I do not share.
15 Cline, p. 154.
16 *Ibid.*
17 Bemis, *The Latin American Policy*, p. 191.
18 Bernardo Vega, *Trujillo y Las Fuerzas Armadas Norteamericanas* (Santo Domingo: Fundación Cultural Dominicana, 1992).
19 For an interesting comparison of the creation of new armies in the Dominican Republic

and Nicaragua see Marvin Goldwert, The *Constabulary in the Dominican Republic and Nicaragua; Progeny and Legacy of US Intervention* (Gainesville, Fl.: University of Florida Press, 1962).

20   In 1939, then Assistant Secretary of State Adolph Berle, Jr. cited new evidence that even US banks in the Caribbean had became involved unwillingly and at the direct urging of the Department of State, 'lest European capital, affected with European politics, might find foothold on this side of the Atlantic.' Adolph Berle, Jr., *The Policy of the US in Latin America*, Department of State, Publication 1328 (2 May, 1939), p. 378.

21   Ludwell Lee Montague, *Haiti and the US, 1714–1938* (Durham: Duke University Press, 1940), pp. 210–11.

22   J.C. Dorsainvie, *Manuel D'Histoire D'Haiti* (Port-au-Prince, 1924), p. 289.

23   Montague, p. 212.

24   *Ibid.*, p. 215.

25   Cited in Arthur C. Millspaugh, *Haiti Under American Control, 1915–1930* (Boston: World Peace Foundation, 1931), p. 96n.

26   Cf. David Healy, *Gunboat Diplomacy in the Wilson Era. The US Navy in Haiti, 1915–1916* (Madison: The University of Wisconsin Press, 1976), p. 210.

27   *Ibid.*

28   Cf. J. Michael Dash, *Literature and Ideology in Haiti, 1915–1961* (Totowa, N.J.: Barnes and Noble Books, 1981).

29   David Nicholls, *From Dessalines to Duvalier* (London: Cambridge University Press, 1979), p. 142.

30   Report of the President's Commission for the Study and review of Conditions in the Republic of Haiti (26 March, 1930), reprinted in Arthur C. Millspaugh, *Haiti Under American Control*, pp. 242–9.

39   Hans Schmidt, *The US Occupation of Haiti, 1915–1934* (New Jersey: Rutgers University Press, 1971), p 7.

32   *Ibid.*, pp. 102–3.

33   Testimony of Lt. Col. A.S. Williams, *Inquiry into Occupation and Administration of Haiti and Santo Domingo*. Hearings. Select Committee on Haiti and Santo Domingo. US Senate, 67th Congress (Washington, D.C. 1922), p. 497.

34   Frederick Lewis Allen recounts how Americans emerged from World War I with an ingrained belief that anti-American spies and plots were everywhere. Especially suspect was anything which had to do with the rights of labour or setting limits on capital. (cf. *Only Yesterday* (New York: Bantam Books, 1959), p. 34.

35   Quoted in Bryce Wood, *The Making of the Good Neighbour Policy* (New York: Columbia University Press, 1967) p. 15.

36   The similarities to the situation in the Dominican Republic in 1965 are striking.

37   Lejeune Commins, *Quijote on a Burro, Sandino and the Marines, a Study in the Formulation of Foreign Policy* (Mexico, 1958), p. 22. Commins, like Quirk, draws a lesson from his cast study: that multilateral inter-American action is preferable to unilateral American intervention. Again, the moral was lost on policymakers.

38   Neill Macaulay, *The Sandino Affair* (Chicago, 1967) pp. 25–8. Writing at a time when American involvement in the Dominican Republic and Vietnam weighed heavily on the conscience of American intellectuals, Macaulay, like Quirk and Commins, attempts to draw a moral against this type of intervention.

39   Cf. Gregorio Selser, *Sandino, General de hombres libres* (Mexico: Diogenes, 1979).

40   *Ibid.*, p. 110.

41   Andrés García Salgado quoted in Donald C. Hodges, *Intellectual Foundations of the Nicaraguan Revolution* (Austin: University of Texas Press, 1986), p. 25.

42 Barry Carr, *Marxism and Communism in Twentieth Century Mexico* (Lincoln: University of Nebraska Press, 1992), pp. 40–2.

43 *Ibid.*, p. 8.

44 Cf. Robert Alexander, *Communism in Latin America* (New Brunswick: Rutgers University Press, 1957), p. 324.

45 Address delivered before the American Bar Association, August 20, 1923 cited in Henry Myron Blackmer, II *United States Policy and the Inter-American Peace System, 1889–1952* (Geneva: Institut Universitaire de Hautes Etudes Internationales, 1952), p. 13.

46 Cf. Harry Kantor, *Ideología y programa del movimiento Aprista* (Mexico: Ediciones Humanismo, 1955), pp. 25–6.

47 Walter W. Lippmann, 'Second Thoughts on Havana', *Foreign Affairs*, July, 1928, pp. 543–50.

48 Wood, p. 44.

49 Cited in Robert Klein, *The Idea of Equality in International Politics* (Geneva: Institut Universitaire de Hautes Etudes Internationales, 1966), p. 150.

50 Cf. Sumner Welles, *Naboth's Vineyard: The Dominican Republic, 1844–1924*, 2 vols. (Washington D.C.: Savile Books [reprint], 1966), pp. 349–83.

51 Cordell Hull, *The Memoirs of Cordell Hull* (New York, 1948), I, p. 309.

52 Cf. *Problems of the New Cuba. Report of the Commission on Cuba Affairs* (New York: Foreign Policy Association, 1935), pp. 182–200.

53 An interesting parallel to the Dominican case of 1961 – Trujillo's ousting in 1961 took place only after the US began actively to seek it. According to General Arturo Espaillat, the CIA played a key role in the dictator's final liquidation: *The Last Ceasar* (Chicago: Regnery, 1964), pp. 10–11.

54 Such was Welles' power that he could allegedly tell a group of mediators preceding the fall of Machado that they ought to speed up matters: 'I have here the fate of Cuba (pointing to his pockets). The President of the US can wait no longer.' Charles A. Thomson, 'The Cuban Revolution: The Fall of Machado', *Foreign Policy Reports*, XI (18 December, 1935).

55 There is no serious study of this enigmatic Caribbean *caudillo* yet. Some interesting insights are given in a favourable biography by Edmund A. Chester, *A Sargeant Named Batista* (New York, 1954).

56 Cited in Wood, p. 71. For an interesting but journalistic and chatty day-by-day account of events at this time see R. Hart Phillips, *Cuba Island of Paradox*, (New York, 1959) pp. 3–157.

57 Cf. Wyatt MacGaffey and Clifford R. Barnett, *Twentieth Century Cuba* (New York: Doubleday, 1965) pp. 145–66 *passim*.

58 Batista claims that Welles wanted US marines to establish several 'neutral zones' for the protection of American lives and property, but that he convinced him that widespread bloodshed would result. Fulgencio Batista, *The Growth and Decline of the Cuban Republic* (New York: Devin-Adair Co., 1964).

59 Wood, p. 95.

60 Dana G. Munroe, *Intervention and Dollar Diplomacy in the Caribbean 1900–1921* (New Jersey: Princeton University Press, 1964).

CHAPTER 3 | Reinforcing perceptions: U-boats and fifth columns in World War II

'Frankly', wrote Teddy Roosevelt in 1889, 'I don't know that I should be sorry to see a bit of a spar with Germany. The burning of New York and a few other sea coast cities would be a good object lesson in the need of an adequate system of coastal defences.'[1]

If this expressed the exasperation of the expansionists in the latter part of the nineteenth century, such attitudes would probably not have been prevalent in the first decades of the twentieth century. Quick victories over Spain had vindicated Mahan's geopolitical doctrines, perhaps beyond his own expectations. There were the bases in Cuba and Puerto Rico securing the entry into the protective zone of the Panama canal which would be opened to world maritime traffic in 1914. Multiple interventions in Nicaragua, Haiti, Dominican Republic and the purchase of the Virgin Islands in 1917 all tightened that security ring. In short, the American sense of territorial invulnerability was strong. Beyond those regional factors, there was also the assurance that should any European power decide to challenge the Monroe Doctrine, with its definition of spheres of influence, there was always the wide Atlantic Ocean and the British fleet to act as buffers. Not even the fact that German U-boats in World War I exacted a terrible toll of English and allied shipping seemed to have impressed itself on the US sense of territorial invulnerability. It should have.

In a single month, April 1917, U-boats sank 354 ships. A total of 2,430 ships were lost in 1917. From the outbreak of war to January 1917, the Allies lost 3.25 million tons of shipping to a German loss of only 54 submarines.[2] As fate and American luck would have it, Germany also failed to fully heed the lessons of U-boat warfare.

Traditional American isolationism also fed the sense that the US need not fear the happenings in Europe. Even as Nazi armies rolled into European country after country, Hitler consistently attempted to appease the Americans, as did, indeed, the Japanese. More than ever, the Monroe Doctrine's proclamation of a New World and an 'old' one appeared to have viability. In fact, even as late as 1939, Nazi Foreign Minister Ribbentrop – bolstered no doubt by the fact that the Munich Pact of 1938 recognized German territorial claims in Central Europe – kept up the theme that there were no divergences between Germany and the US: 'Germany, of all the countries in the world', he proclaimed, 'is the one which has most scrupulously respected the principles of the Monroe Doctrine . . .'.[3] Overlooked was the fact that similar German declarations had been made by the Kaiser, even as he was preparing to carve out a piece of the Caribbean for himself.

Certainly not all Americans were complacent, though. 'To me', Secretary of State Cordell Hull wrote later, 'the danger of the western hemisphere was real and imminent.'[4] Hull had ample experience in western hemisphere matters; he understood the resentment against the US which had built up over the years. Samuel Flagg Bemis was another who understood the military threat. He was, not surprisingly, an authority on submarine warfare and also had F.D. Roosevelt's ear.[5] Although Bemis had a very benign view of US imperialism – an 'imperialism against imperialism' he called it – he was concerned about anti-American sentiments in this hemisphere. He felt that the Axis powers were rapidly mobilizing German, Italian and even Japanese nationals in Latin America; activities he called 'cultural missions cloaking fifth-columns.'[6] All this led Bemis to question just how secure the hemisphere and its vital raw materials were for the US. Suddenly US imperial history did not seem so benign:

> How would those nations which had been the scene of US interventions respond when the Republic of the North met its time of trial? Would they welcome the discomfiture of the 'Colossus' whom they had regarded as an imperialist power? Or would they feel that their independence and liberty were bound up with that of their 'alien' neighbour and his Isthmian life line?[7]

This was precisely the thinking of those who had been arguing for a roll-back of the Roosevelt Corollary to the Monroe Doctrine. An end to unilateral interventions, a Good Neighbour Policy, was essential if the US was to secure Latin American backing for its chosen policy of neutrality in the face of the conflicts already agitating both Europe and the Far East. What the US needed was not a unilateral doctrine rejected legally and emotionally by all of Latin America, but rather a system of hemispheric collective security to keep outside forces at bay.[8] Since the Inter-American conference in Montevideo, Uruguay in 1933, Latin nations sought to consolidate the doctrines of sovereignty and non-intervention.

It all came to a head at the Inter-American Conference for the Maintenance of Peace in Buenos Aires, December 1936. The US message was that at a time of world political ferment and economic depression, US security depended upon the active and willing co-operation of all the republics in the hemisphere. This required treating them as equals. Secretary of State Cordell Hull made the desired rhetorical concession to the Plenary Session: 'We recognize the right of all nations to handle their affairs in the way they choose . . . even though their way may be different from our way, or even repugnant to our ideas.'[9] As long, of course, as this did not involve extra-hemispheric intervention.

By 1940, as war raged in Europe, the US was pushing even harder to secure Latin American support. After all, rumours were rampant that German submarines were refuelling from bases in Mexico, Central America, Haiti and the Dominican Republic.[10]

The Second Consultative Meeting of American Foreign Ministers in Havana, Cuba in July 1940 was called to ensure the continuing neutrality of this hemisphere but also most assuredly, its defence. It was the latter goal which led to the unanimous passing of a 'no transfer' principle which, in turn, was based on the principle of self-determination. Fearing that German conquests in Europe might mean that the European possessions in the Caribbean could be turned into 'strategic centres of aggression', the nations of the hemisphere decided that these territories should decide their own futures. They could even choose to be independent.

The US posture in these matters had clearly come in line with Latin American wishes and Cordell Hull worked assiduously to create a sense of hemispheric collective action. But US perceptions about its sphere of influence and its instinct for unilateral action had not disappeared. Even before the Havana meeting, the US Congress had legislated, as an Act of Congress, that the US would not allow any transfer of territory from one non-American power to another. As on past occasions, the Congressional mood appeared more decisive about the 'sacredness' of the Monroe Doctrine than that of the Executive.

Two trends finally shook America as a whole out of its smug sense of invulnerability. First there were the fears of Axis 'fifth column' activities, i.e. subversion. More importantly perhaps, was what Winston Churchill later confessed was 'the only thing that ever really frightened me during the War,' German submarines, the 'U-boat peril.'[11] To an America which was properly proud of its naval doctrines and performances, what came to be known as the 'Battle of the Caribbean' came close to being a major calamity. Dealing with perceived subversives was considerably easier.

The fifth columns

New words reflect new social realities. The term fifth column was popularized during the Spanish Civil War when four Nationalist (i.e. Francoist) columns attacking Madrid were supposed to be assisted by a 'Fifth' one inside the city. Not much later, a synonymous World War II usage became popular – 'to act like a Quisling' – after Norway's politician, Vidkun Quisling, who is said to have treacherously prepared the entry of German armies into his country. Both terms became part of American colloquial usage in the mid to late 1930s, not without reason.

To Berlin, *Unser Amerika*, i.e. the German community in America, was an important vehicle for propaganda and information. By 1935 a formal organization, the German-American Bund, was at the height of its activities. Despite the fact that in the US there had always existed a link between ethnicity and politics, these German activities soon became a matter of official concern. There was a Congressional investigation into the Bund's activities in 1935, and the FBI was kept busy keeping track of the *Abwehr*, the German espionage and sabotage agency.[12] As fear of a fifth column grew, the US government began to close German and German-American news agencies, travel concerns and other businesses, all of which were believed to be part of a vast network of spying and information gathering for Berlin.[13]

By 1940, there was the perception that Axis fifth columns had been brought under control in the US but not in Latin America where they were seen as a growing threat. Certainly there was a phenomenal growth in the number of books on the topic. As Hubert Herring, at the time a well-known historian of Latin America put it, tracking down fifth columns 'became the chief extracurricular activity of all good men and true in the summer of 1940 . . . .'[14] Ronald Newton notes that ' "fifth column" had become an international obsession' while Herring spoke of 'flitting journalists' who brought back 'horrid tales of Gestapo agents in every telephone booth.' But even the non-alarmist Herring concluded that 'after prudential discounts it was safe to say that Adolf Hitler had in Latin America a substantial body of sympathizers which may number from 100,000 to 500,000 . . .' And, even more ominous, in Herring's opinions were the Latin 'unwitting allies'[15] of the Axis: the Roman Catholic church, the military, the intellectuals and the upper classes. They were all portrayed as being pro-fascist.

To be sure there were quite a few Germans and Italians in Latin America. Argentina had between 200 – 300,000 Germans and 800,000 Italians; Brazil, perhaps a million Germans; Uruguay, 10,000; Chile, 50,000; Paraguay, 20,000, with fewer than 5,000 in each of the other South American countries. The Japanese were numerous, and unpopular, in Ecuador. The number of Germans in Central America was about 16,000, half in Guatemala and a substantial part of the rest in Costa Rica. More important than their numbers, however, was the fact that because of intermarriage with local upper classes and ownerships, especially in coffee, they wielded considerable influence in the economy and polity of Latin America. Even Newton, who down-plays the role of Nazi fifth columns and spying, admits that Nazi agents forced out of other Latin American countries congregated in Buenos Aires, and that it is hard to know just what economic influence they had since 'German firms began to disappear behind criollo cover.'[16]

Whether they and the many Spanish falangists were all the fifth columnists that the literature of the time claimed, or not, the fact is that they were so perceived in the US and in much of Latin America, and posed a special menace to the Panama canal.[17] Socialist and communist parties throughout the hemisphere joined the US and British agencies in agitating against Axis influence and activities.

One of the key sectors which it was thought the Germans came close to monopolizing throughout Latin America was air services. German built, owned and operated planes were said to crisscross the whole continent.[18] No wonder German intelligence reported that the Panama canal was not as invulnerable as the US believed. Their 'Project No. 14', a business front in Panama, was well placed to provide intelligence.[19] Yale University's Nicholas John Spykman, explained it this way: Germany believed (as US President Coolidge once did) that national sovereignty extended to German citizens and their property wherever they may be. This included not just those who were German born (*Reichdeutsche*) but also citizens of other countries who were of German descent (*Volksdeutsche*). They were all supposed to be willing and well-disciplined instruments of German foreign policy. 'The result is', concluded Spykman, 'that all nations with large German minorities are exposed to the danger of finding themselves some day with a small German state within their borders and a Nationalist Socialist state at that.'[20] The Latin American states were taking no chances. Fearing the activities of fifth columnists, all the Latin American republics adopted emergency measures in order to curtail potential fifth column activities, including preventing the acquisition of nationality by Axis subjects. 'It was not forgotten', stated a Mexican law in January, 1942, 'that the most dangerous fifth columnists for the defence of Holland, Belgium, and France were those Germans who went to these countries, saying they were being persecuted by the Nazi regime.'[21]

Despite the heightened fear of subversion and spying, the US was woefully relaxed about the impending storm. George Fielding Elliott lamented this smugness in his 1938 book, *If War Comes*. In 1939 he published *The Ramparts We Watch, A Study of the Problems of American National Defence* which had five printings. Elliott's message was simple: the US was totally unprepared for a war which everything indicated was on the horizon.[22] Saul Friedlander's review of German sources led him to agree with Elliott that in 1940 Berlin was well aware of the 'total unpreparedness of the American Armed Forces.'

In the wider Caribbean – the key to the defence of the canal and a region which the War Department had long designated as an 'area of main resistance'[23] – the situation was particularly acute, according to Elliott. He did not believe that the canal itself was susceptible to a direct attack, but he did worry that the US could lose control over *access* to it. A tightly defended canal was of little use if its approaches were vulnerable. Elliott noted that none of the European fortified ports in the area (Kingston, Jamaica; Fort de France, Martinique and Willemstad, Curaçao) had any significant defensive strength; they had garrisons of 600, 400, and 250 men respectively. Even Puerto Rico, long talked about as the lodestone of US-Caribbean defences, had one naval radio station and one regiment of local troops. Only by late 1939 did the US begin a rapid and expensive fortification of the island.[24]

While the multiple narrow straights which gave entrance to the Caribbean did provide the US with 'natural' geographical protection against an attack from enemy *surface* vessels, Elliott was prescient when he predicted that it was precisely in such narrow waters that submarines were going to have their maximum opportunity. He then outlined the strategic situation as it would indeed evolve three years later in what would be called 'the Battle of the Caribbean'.

> Through the Lesser Antilles . . . penetration of the Caribbean might be more easily achieved. There are half-a-score of channels available, and we could hardly plant a submarine division in each one and keep it there on station . . . to keep one patrol plane flying over the channel between Trinidad and Grenada, for example would require four patrol planes and six crews at the Eastern Outpost, allowing nothing for accident and bad weather.[25]

Aside from such logistical problems, there were sticky diplomatic issues affecting the defence of the Caribbean. Despite what appeared to be an Anglo-US bilateral co-operation, the British imperial disdain for the Americans had not dissipated. When President Roosevelt sent his friend and adviser on Caribbean affairs, Charles W. Taussig, on a fact-finding mission to the Caribbean in late 1940, Taussig received less than full co-operation from the British. In fact, the mission – and its leader – did come in for its full dose of patronizing criticisms. Contributing to the reaction of the British bureaucrats, notes Ken Post in a punctiliously researched study, was British 'arrogance towards Americans.'[26] They complained that conversations with Taussig started well but invariably developed 'into the usual American superficialities of mere "bilge" '; they sneered at one American's use of chewing gum and even suggested that Taussig was probably only interested in improving his own commercial contacts. Such was the mutual antagonism between the two Anglo-Saxon peoples that it became evident even to the Germans. Hitler sensed this Anglo-American tension. He tried to calm American apprehensions about German moves, by ridiculing rumours about German fifth columns in the western hemisphere, and repeating his theme of 'Europe for the Europeans and America for the Americans.'[27]

He repeatedly vowed that he had no designs on the French fleets in North and Western Africa and in Martinique. He was also sure that the Americans would not hand these fleets over to the English for the same reason that they would never supply Britain with destroyers: America, he told Mussolini, aspired to become the first naval power in the world.[28]

But, again, the Nazis seemed to have overplayed their hand in assuming that such social-cultural snobbery could translate into an ultimate clash of geopolitical interests. On 2 September, 1940 the US and Britain signed the 'Destroyers for Bases' agreement. Britain got 50 destroyers of World War I vintage, the US was granted 99-year leases to lands on which to build naval and air bases in The Bahamas, Jamaica, St Lucia, Trinidad, Antigua and British Guiana (Guyana). Bases in Newfoundland and Bermuda were 'free gifts'.

The seemingly unending string of US low cost and easy acquisition of new space was still unbroken. Who in the US could argue with such good fortune, for as R.A. Humphreys notes: 'Even the isolationists – and there were many of them – found it difficult to condemn so favourable a bargain.' Subsequently, the Americans demanded, and got, even more land than the 2 September Agreement called for. This led to vigorous protests from some of the colonial governors who took note of local resentment of the 99-year leases on some of the choice spots on the islands. There was opposition in the Colonial Office as well. In fact, it took the personal intervention of Winston Churchill to push through the additional agreements.[29] To Churchill the destroyers were essential but perhaps even more important was that the deal drew America even closer in as an ally. And, indeed, the agreement did move the US from a position of strict neutrality to one of non-belligerency. It also made the US the undisputed military power in the whole Caribbean-area and conferred on it the responsibilities that entailed. The idea was not – as it had never been in the Caribbean – to acquire territory or colonies, but to improve security. Race was still – as it had been in the nineteenth century – a factor. President Roosevelt was as clear on this as his predecessors had been: 'If we can get our naval bases', he wrote to his Secretary of State, 'why, for example, should we buy with them two million headaches, consisting of that number of human beings who would be a drag on this country and who would stir up questions of racial stocks by virtue of their new status as American citizens?'[30] Despite all the changes towards a Good Neighbour Policy, the old racial attitudes persisted, and Caribbean peoples were sensitive to this. The press in Trinidad got wind of Roosevelt's letter, and on 25 August, 1942 *The Trinidad Guardian* quoted Roosevelt as telling the British Secretary of State for the Colonies: 'Trinidad! No thanks. What a problem you have there – what a scrambled population! What an ethnic *pot pourri* . . . No, thank you . . . You people go right on ruling Trinidad.'[31]

The geopolitical nature of Caribbean defences had changed but not the racism of the Great Powers. For if Roosevelt's position reflected the historical US refusal to integrate non-whites into its federal system, the British were no less racist. In 1943 they opposed the American plan to replace white US troops in the Caribbean with Puerto Ricans. The Americans, while defending the fighting capabilities of the Puerto Ricans, could not escape the racial argument; they were not sending coloured troops to white countries, they were sending Puerto Rican whites to coloured countries. By 1945, two-thirds of the US troops in the Caribbean were Puerto Rican.[32]

Dealing with the Latin Caribbean involved no such racial clashes, yet it was more difficult for a variety of reasons. Panama became a test case of Latin resistance and US defence-oriented resolve since protection of the canal was the US military priority in the hemisphere. The election of Arnulfo Arias as President created difficulties for the negotiation of bases outside the Canal Zone. US intelligence was aware that as Panamanian Ambassador to Rome Arias had seen a great deal of Mussolini and met with Hitler in 1937. As a former US Ambassador to Panama put it: 'He returned to Panama in 1938 seemingly convinced that Fascism was the wave of the future.'[33] He certainly was a believer in the superiority of the white race and was strongly anti-American. Arias took a nationalist stance and refused to accept the US 'occupation' of bases outside the Canal Zone. The US wanted immediate approval of bases with the typical long-term lease (99 years). Arias insisted that leases should extend only for one presidential term plus one year. As Langer and Gleason noted: 'Panama constituted a test case for the Good Neighbour Policy in the eyes of all the other Republics . . .'[34] While the State Department counselled caution in dealing with Arias, the Defence Department and the military showed increasing displeasure and impatience with such moderation. The issue was solved with the connivance of the US when a *coup d'état* removed Arias from power and with him objections to American plans.

Clearly the diplomatic niceties of the Good Neighbour Policy were giving way to actions – unilateral when necessary – to shore up US defences. In early 1940 the threat was still limited to the North Atlantic. Passage of US supplies to Britain were the issue. By mid-1941, however, the Allies were defeated in Europe, the Mediterranean, and North Africa. It now appeared likely that the Germans would attack not only Iceland, but also Dakar, the Canaries, the Azores, and the Cape Verde islands. Even the bulge of Brazil (Recife-Pernambuco) seemed a possible target. President Roosevelt himself had decided that the greatest threat was posed to the Spanish and Portuguese islands in the mid-Atlantic and then to South America (see Figure 1, p. 55). All this amounted to what Langer and Gleason call the 'Crisis of mid-1941', an intense sense of threat, of vulnerability, of 'confusion and agitation in Washington' without any certainty as to how to confront it.[35]

In fact, so unprepared was the Administration that they had to engage in catch-up geography. It began with the President's 'Kitchen Cabinet' doing basic cartography, as Secretary of War Henry Stimson wrote in his diary on 10 April, 1941.

> We had the atlas out and by drawing a line midway between the westernmost bulge of Africa and the easternmost bulge of Brazil we found that the median line between the two continents was about longitude line twenty-five. By projecting that northward, it took into the western hemisphere most of Greenland.[36]

That the new geopolitical resolve had little time for niceties is evidenced when Stimson added that the President and his men 'were all in agreement that "every bit" of Greenland must be defended, line or no line . . .'[37] It was not until mid-1942, therefore, that the basic geography of the 'Command Zones' of the Allies had been agreed upon (see Figure 1).

Cartography followed geopolitics, driven as it was by the perception that the US – and by extension, Latin America – were vulnerable. By April 1941 Greenland was covered by the Monroe Doctrine and by May, the President was 'seriously contemplating drafting a message to Congress declaring West Africa within the scope of the Monroe Doctrine . . .'[38] As the President noted in his 'fireside chat' of 27 May, 1941: 'Anyone with an atlas, anyone with a reasonable knowledge of the sudden striking force of modern war,' knows that it is 'stupid' to allow a potential enemy to gain a foothold from which to attack. Old fashioned commonsense calls for 'the use of strategy which will prevent any enemy from gaining a foothold in the first place.' In 1941 US troops entered Suriname, and negotiations for a base in Recife, Brazil were under way. The US protested the British occupation of the oil refining islands of Curaçao and Aruba but were only too happy to have them there until Americans could replace them, as happened in February 1942. Similarly, they had protested about an English blockade of Martinique where pro-Vichy Admiral Georges Robert had what was in fact the most powerful fleet in the Caribbean at the time: one aircraft carrier with 125 US built planes, and six cruisers and auxiliary cruisers. He also had $250 million in gold bullion that the English were eager to get. Admiral Robert was not only following orders from the German-dominated Vichy government; he would later admit that more than anything he felt compelled to protect the French empire from the grasp of the US.[39] Eventually, the US persuaded Admiral Robert to remain neutral; the removal of vital ship parts guaranteed that Admiral Robert's

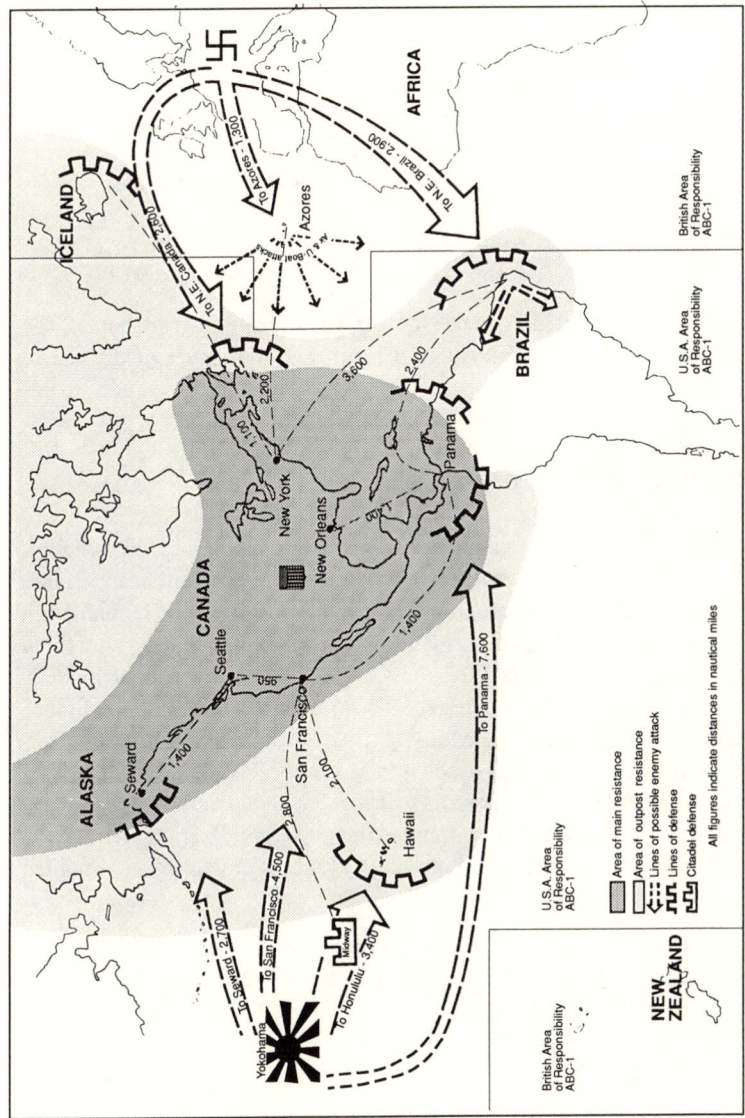

Figure 1: Logistics of hemisphere defence, 1941.

ships remained in Fort-de-France; not a trivial military gain for the Americans, given the paucity of their naval presence in the Caribbean.

Just before the Germans unleashed their U-boat wolf-packs on the Caribbean in 1942, the US 'Caribbean Sea Frontier's forces stood as follows:[40]

> *Total area*: 2½ million square miles.
> Headquarters: San Juan, Puerto Rico.
> Sector Commands (with great autonomy):
>   Guantánamo, Cuba; Willemstad, Curaçao; Chaguaramas, Trinidad.
> *Effectives*: 9 destroyers, 3 gunboats, 9 Coast Guard Cutters, 24 SC's, about 40 smaller craft.

This was hardly a force to make the Germans shake in their boots. The 'astonishing U-boat war', as Admiral Hoover, Commander of the Caribbean Sea Frontier, put it, was proof that the US was not prepared.

The audacious U-boats

Admiral Karl Doenitz, Commander of Germany's submarine forces understood very well the disadvantages of operating in the Caribbean.[41] First, there was the lack of support from Hitler and others of the German High Command. Acording to Doenitz, Hitler regarded war at sea as 'something strange and sinister.'[42] Secondly, the Germans had neither air reconnaissance nor surface ships in the area. Third, even with the fall of France ensuring the availability of the Bay of Biscay for submarine bases, Germany still had a monumental problem of logistics. These continental bases only slightly modified the German Doctrine that it was 'impossible to wage U-boat warfare successfully without Atlantic bases.'[43] Travel across the Atlantic from the closest base, 'Lorient' in France's Bay of Biscay, entailed the following:

To Bermuda	3,000 nautical miles	=	12.5 sailing days
To New York	3,000 nautical miles	=	12.5 sailing days
To Trinidad	3,800 nautical miles	=	15.8 sailing days
To Aruba	4,000 nautical miles	=	16.6 sailing days
To Galveston	4,600 nautical miles	=	19.2 sailing days

Doenitz was well aware that as early as 1915 Vice-Admiral Wolfgang Wegener had advocated the capture of French West Africa for the single purpose of establishing naval bases for naval warfare in the Atlantic.[44] It was precisely an appreciation of the logistics involved in operating in the 'virgin' Caribbean which led Admiral Raeder to recommend in mid-1942 that Dakar be seized and converted into a submarine area. This never happened, leaving Germany with a major problem.

Finally, there were the limitations of the submarine as a weapon. Of the three most telling limitations – low speeds once submerged, low surface speeds and its limited operational range – it was this latter which was the greatest drawback for operations in the Caribbean.[45]

While the larger U-boat (Type IXc) would consume 37 per cent of its range travelling from its base in the Bay of Biscay to a mid-Atlantic battle station (50° N, 30° W), a battle station off the coast of Aruba, for example, would require a 9,000 mile round trip or 67 per cent of the Type IXc's cruising range. But it was mostly the medium size Type VIIc submarine which operated in the Caribbean, and it consumed fully two-thirds of its fuel just getting there. Successful operations in the Caribbean, therefore, called for the innovative use of whatever resources – military and civilian – which Germany could muster.

From the military side, Admiral Doenitz temporarily solved the problem of fuel supplies by the use of submarine tankers, known as 'milch cows'. These beamy submarines carried enough fuel and supplies to keep a 10-boat wolf pack operating in the Atlantic for four months. There were 10 of these tankers built in 1942. Some 90 per cent of the submarines operating in the Caribbean used them to resupply, thereby adding 4,500 miles to their cruising range. Even so, the operational short-leggedness of the submarines curtailed their capacity to 'hunt'. This made it necessary for them to carry out ambushes from certain 'nodal points' along convoy routes or in specific areas of important activity. The Caribbean's 'narrow waters', those sea lanes discussed by Mahan in 1888, were the perfect nodal points, just as Elliot had predicted in 1938.

Despite the many evident handicaps, by late 1941 Doenitz had decided, that of all the seas, the Caribbean was the 'virgin area . . . the area in which U-boats could most economically operate.'[46] As Doenitz himself recalls, the Americans had not anticipated the presence of U-boats in the Caribbean and Gulf of Mexico. 'Once again', he concludes, 'we had struck them in a "soft spot" '.[47] Operation Drumbeat would begin.

Doenitz' strategy was simple in a way, it became known as 'tonnage': sinking the largest number of ships in the shortest space of time. This would cripple British and American war industries, and accomplish two other goals. First, it would pin down large numbers of Allied land, sea and air forces effectively with relatively few submarines, and, secondly, it would disrupt the actual Allied war capability by severing the vital oil lanes running from Venezuela and the refineries in Curaçao, Aruba and Trinidad to the US refineries. It was a daring strategy, given the limitations of the resources Doenitz had available. The initial results were nothing short of spectacular.

General George C. Marshall was not exaggerating when he noted on 19 June, 1942 that 'the losses by submarines off our Atlantic seaboard and in the Caribbean now threaten our entire war effort.'[48] Marshall and the Allies had plenty of reason to be concerned. With five U-boats operating, in December 1941 the Germans sank 116,000 tons, in January 1942 they sank 328,000 tons, and in February 1942 they sank 470,000 tons. Not a single U-boat was lost during that period. Among the 23 sinkings in February there were six light-draft oil tankers operating out of Maracaibo, Venezuela. During the first six months of what the Allies were now calling 'the Battle of the Caribbean', January to August 1942, 59 vessels were sunk in the Gulf of Mexico and 220 in the Caribbean. By 1943 they had sunk half of the 5,600 merchant ships existent in 1939, while 39,000 German U-boat sailors kept 800,000 Allied sailors and airmen tied up. Doenitz' submarines were so dangerous that from 1941 to mid-1943 the Allies had to commit 30 warships to each U-boat.[49]

In the Caribbean they were successful beyond Doenitz' most optimistic expectations. With only an average of five U-boats operational at any one time they controlled the whole Caribbean from 1941 to mid-1943. Especially relevant was the fact that over 50 per cent of the ships sunk were oil tankers, depriving the US of that vital resource. Although there were three key strategic areas: the Panama canal, the Venezuela-Trinidad-Curaçao-Aruba oil triangle and the Mexico Gulf States oil link, the most 'profitable waters' were the sea lanes between Trinidad and Curaçao, as Figure 2 shows.

If, as Doenitz, recalls, each U-boat operating in the Caribbean sank between six and ten ships, and the average was 9.2 worldwide,[50] the losses in the waters around Trinidad were 43.3 per U-boat.[51] Between eight and ten vessels, in convoys or unescorted, arrived and departed Trinidad every day, and about 60 bauxite freighters from Suriname and British Guiana off-loaded their cargoes for transhipment to the US.

So frequent were the sinkings off the north coast of Trinidad that the natives called it 'Torpedo Junction'. As a local history put it: 'The U-boats appeared to be turning the Galleon's Passage between Trinidad and Tobago into their private playground.'[52] The boldness of the Germans was astonishing. Ships were sunk in broad daylight and within eyesight of the airport in Tobago. In fact, on 18 February, 1942 two ships were sunk right inside the Port of Spain harbour. The boat responsible for that daring act, U-161 later performed the same deed in Castries, St Lucia. Its captain, Lt Commander Archilles, sank so many ships in that area that the Trinidadians gave him the nickname 'The Trinidad Well Borer'. Doenitz called him 'the ferret of Port of Spain and Port Castries.'[53] He later sank the British cruiser *Phoebe*.

US naval historian S.E. Morrison called it the period of the 'merry massacre'.[54] The area was so 'virgin' that there were even six Italian

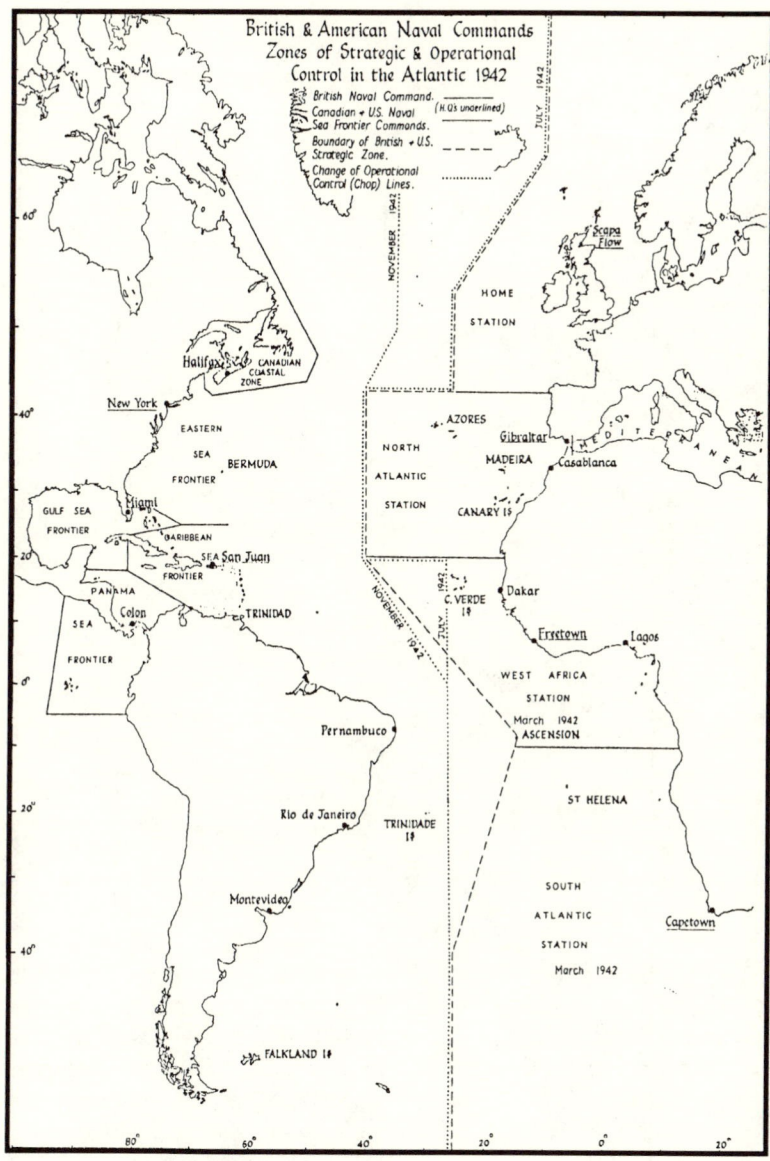

Figure 2: British and American naval commands: zones of strategic and operational control in the Atlantic 1942.

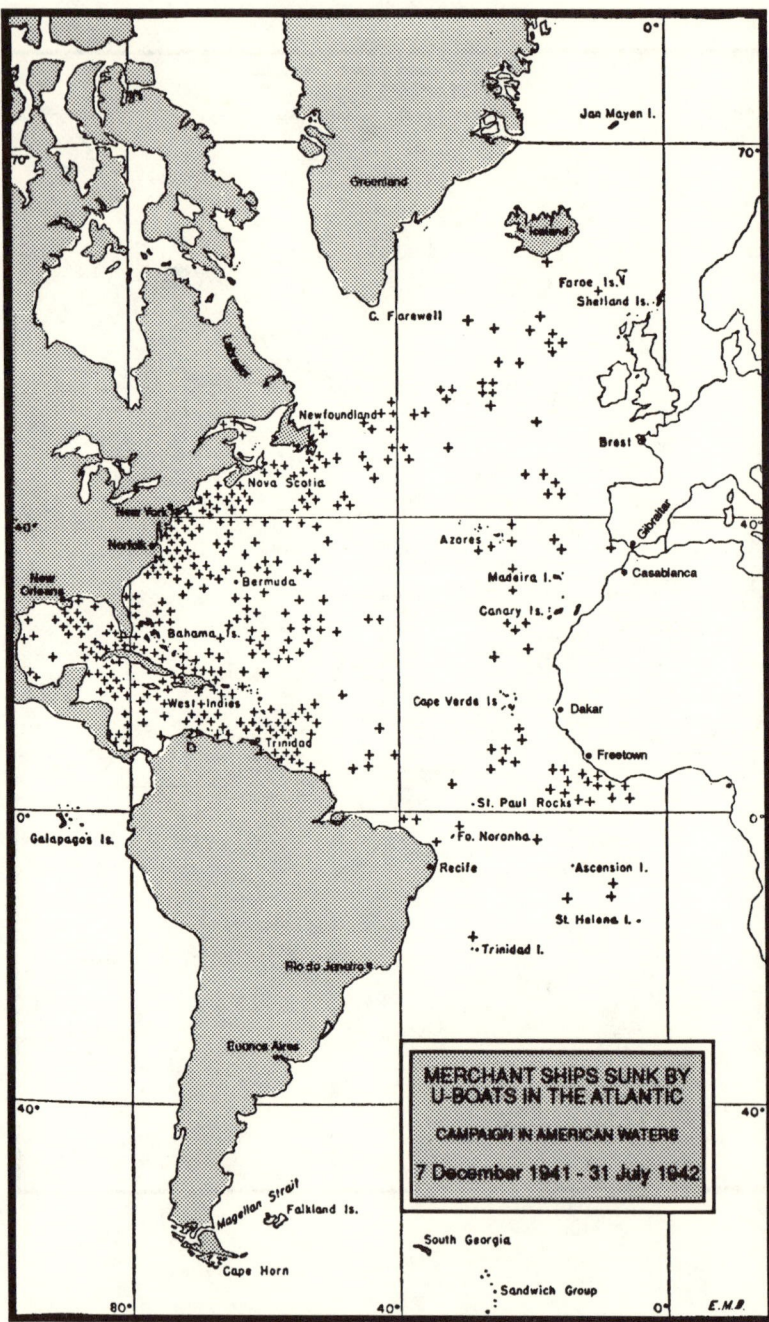

Figure 3: Merchant ships sunk by U-boats in the Atlantic.

submarines operating in this area with some success (34 ships sunk in six months). 'So wide was the choice of targets', wrote a German Commander, 'that it was quite impossible to attack them all.' One German Captain called it the 'American Turkey Shoot', another spoke with astonishment at the 'business as usual' attitude of citizens and merchants in coastal US towns. Their refusal to 'black out' denied Allied ships cover and encouraged the 'boldness' of U-boat captains even within sight of US shores.[55] In fact, even those US coasts were no longer impenetrable. In mid-1941 only luck led a coastal patrol to catch eight German infiltrators who had disembarked from a U-boat. They were all condemned to death by a military court.[56] Michael Gannon reports two other landings of saboteurs in the US: in Rhode Island on 13 June, 1942 and in Jacksonville Beach, Florida on 17 June of that same year.[57]

To Gannon, the 'Atlantic Pearl Harbour' as he calls it, was a greater strategic setback for the Allies than the loss of Pearl Harbour. While the latter destroyed US ships, in the Atlantic-Caribbean the U-boats came close to severing the vital lifeline to Great Britain as well as nearly crippling the US war industry by cutting off the supply of raw materials.[58] To Gannon, a major part of the blame lay with Admiral Ernest J. King, Commander-in-Chief of the US fleet. His Anglophobia, for instance, made him resist adopting the convoy method of protecting vessels urged by the British. It had worked in World War I, but fundamentally, according to Gannon, it was the long tradition of the US navy, unchallenged in its sphere of influence, which explains the American failure. 'One should not forget', writes Gannon, 'that King and his generation were shaped in the dream of great fleet actions and in the glory of single-ship enterprise.'[59] How this related to the geopolitical doctrines of A.T. Mahan is not clear. What is clear is that the easy victories over the Spaniards early in the century, as well as naval and marine actions against a group of weak Caribbean states, had led the US to overestimate its naval capabilities. This arrogance had near-tragic consequences.

'It can be argued', writes a student of submarine warfare, 'that the Allies could have lost World War II if the U-boat had not been defeated by mid-1943.'[60] This defeat was achieved by the occurrence of several events. First, there was an extraordinary English intelligence *coup* breaking the U-boat codes, the Enigma, through a cryptoanalysis operation called 'Ultra'. Operation 'Ultra' has been called 'the greatest secret in World War II after the atom bomb.'[61] If, up to April 1942, not a single U-boat had been sunk in the Caribbean, between June and August the Allies, aided by 'Ultra's capacity to decipher Admiral Doenitz' messages, sank five 'milch cows' and reserve tankers, and the hunt for the U-boat picked up pace.

With this capacity to decipher the German codes, came improved technology, especially of radar and sonar. Intelligence and technology combined to enhance the skilled use of the American's new presence in the Caribbean. The bases secured from the British made possible a strategy of 'double coverage', sea-air, both of defence and offence. The value of double coverage is definitely evident in the statistics: between September 1939 and May 1943, 1,541 merchant vessels or 71.7 per cent of all sinkings were of ships with no coverage. Of the sinkings 27.6 per cent (604 vessels) were in convoys with surface escort only, while the U-boats sunk only 16 ships or 0.7 per cent which had both air and surface escort while in convoy.[62] The systematic use of the convoy, now provided with air and sea cover, was critically improved.

Aside from these defensive and protective capabilities afforded by the bases, there was a striking offensive dimension evidenced in the statistics on U-boat kills: 31.4 per cent were sunk by surface vessels, 31.3 per cent were sunk by shore-based aircraft. It is an interesting thought that just as a sense of invulnerability had led to initial American unpreparedness, it was precisely German early successes which led them to complacency and to lag in U-boat technology. For instance, they did not make the Dutch-invented schnorchel or 'snort', which allowed prolonged underwater operation of diesel-driven submarines, operational until late 1943. It came too late, the tide of battle had already turned.

By the third quarter of 1943 the 'Battle of the Caribbean' had been won with the help of strategically-located bases, advances in technology and breakthroughs in human intelligence. The German submarine command's War Diary entry for 23 August, 1943 showed the following: 'Entire Caribbean area . . . strong to very strong air patrol . . . Isolated traffic protected by air and surface escort . . . Day and night (radar) location everywhere. Slight chances of success . . . Strength of crews taxed to utmost by heat and moist atmosphere.'[63] Facing insuperable odds, Doenitz shifted his few remaining U-boats to less threatening waters. For the Allies, the victory in the Caribbean had come none too soon, for in mid-1943 some 60,000 US troops were being ferried to England each month in preparation for the Normandy invasion and troops destined for the Pacific front were being trained in Trinidad and then transported through the Panama canal.

The 'Battle of the Caribbean' was more than a military affair, it was a grand rendering of geopolitical accounts. First and foremost, it established the importance of naval warfare. As Admiral Doenitz lamented: 'Hitler and the General Staff were determined to win *on land* a war in which our main opponents were the two greatest *sea* powers in the world.'[64] A German scholar who interviewed virtually all surviving major German naval officers, concluded that in rethinking 'the grand strategies of the future', it was critical to understand that 'Nothing has displaced or threatens soon to displace the sea ways as the indispensable routes . . . for the Western alliance.'[65] If this was German thinking, Americans were now more prone than ever to cite chapter and verse of Alfred T. Mahan's geopolitical doctrine that 'the Caribbean Sea is the strategical key to the two great oceans, the Atlantic and the Pacific; our own chief maritime frontiers.' US geopoliticians entered the post-war period with two deep-held convictions: beware of subversion from fifth columns and remember Mahan on the relationship between geography, politics and strategy. Both beliefs were critical to the development of the Caribbean as a more 'mature' American sphere of influence. Militarily this meant that Panama was most decidedly to remain the lodestone of the Caribbean defences and that the US would keep its bases in Puerto Rico, at Guantánamo, Cuba and in Chaguaramas, Trinidad.

Politically, it was evident that the 'Battle of the Caribbean' had an impact upon the nature of Caribbean society, both as it operated internally and as it related to the US. Internally, the search for fifth columnists tended to justify witch hunts. The hunts were often carried out with a very wide net, not so much to catch actual subversives but to snag political enemies. In the Dominican Republic, for instance, it was not only the government of dictator Rafael Leonidas Trujillo which pursued enemies in the name of the war effort, his political enemies constantly sought to gain American support for their goals by making allegations of Trujillo support for Nazis and U-boats. Such was the climate of accusations and counter-accusations that the Federal Bureau of Investigation strengthened its office there.[66] By 1942, J. Edgar Hoover and the FBI had taken control of counter-espionage in the western hemisphere. The Office of Strategic Services (OSS), the official intelligence service, focused on Europe, Asia and Africa.[67] In Cuba, Fulgencio Batista sought both local and US approbation by smashing pro-Falangist operations, banning the Cuban Nazi Party in September, 1940 and interning 700 Germans and 1,370 Italians. So thorough was Batista, in fact, that the only execution of a German agent by a Latin American government was carried out in Cuba.[68]

One legacy of the war on the Caribbean was a heightened sense that protection against external enemies as well as internal subversives, meant seeking US intelligence and military assistance. As Ronald Newton comments: 'both the Americans and the British were determined to spy on both the Nazis and the communists; the Americans, with the hubris which characterizes empires, carried the anti-communist crusade into the post-war period.'[69]

Interestingly enough, this anti-communism extended also to the non-independent islands of the Caribbean. In Jamaica, the initial opposition of the far 'left' of the Peoples National Party had made US military involvement in Jamaica a political issue: it would delay decolonization. While this position was held by only a very small part of the island's political classes, their concern over US racial policies did find an echo in a much wider sector of Jamaicans, at home and in the American diaspora.[70] Interestingly enough, some of the same Jamaican leftists appeared on English security dossiers as the intermediaries between Trinidad socialists and the Cuban communist movement. These dossiers were handed over to the Americans. The position and activities of these leftists was not forgotten in the post-war rendering of political accounts, both in local politics and by a US now thoroughly involved in the Caribbean. Indeed, throughout the Caribbean, American policy was to ensure that communist forces made no gains from the honeymoon which the war had forced between the western powers and Stalin. Even in the French Antilles, the US moved to ensure that anti-communist Gaullists gained control of Guadeloupe and Martinique. As Fitzroy Baptiste notes:

> In the European Caribbean, as in Western Europe and elsewhere by late 1943, the US was preoccupied with the post-war settlement. Washington was endeavouring to shape the Caribbean peace, that is, an anti-communist and pro-western peace.'[71]

Clearly there were frictions and resentments against the American presence. Local aristocrats found their historical overlordship now challenged, even their cherished beach and island homes sequestered. As a stanza in one of the popular Trinidadian calypsos of the time lamented, the Yankees 'broke down the pillars of our aristocracy'.[72] That same calypso also complained that the American influence had 'denationalized' the island. There were the usual complaints which accompany any concentration of troops: increased prostitution, venereal disease, fighting, in short, affronts to morality. Despite these complaints, however, the American presence was popular with the masses if not the English officials or local white aristocracy. Several reasons will explain this popularity and, collaterally, explain why the post-war anti-communist crusade was, if not popular, at least not resisted by the masses.

The first of these reasons was the fact that the menace of the U-boats was real and visible. Ships burning right off-shore was a common sight in many of the islands. Additionally, Doenitz' strategy of indiscriminate 'tonnage' led to the sinking of many inter-island schooners and small craft, creating intense resentment up and down the islands. All of which meant that, even if the contemporary research reveals that the reports of fifth columns and spies were often exaggerated, people tended to believe the rumours and stories of enemy activity. Perceptions of threat were so strong that the stories endure as a part of Caribbean folklore to this day.[73]

Not only did the Yankees (as they were called in the insular Caribbean) provide protection, they were generally seen as holding the ideological and moral high ground. American propaganda did not have to distort Nazi doctrines of Teutonic racial superiority, they were quite evident and thus repulsive to West Indians generally. Their opposition to fascism began when Mussolini invaded Ethiopia in 1935. As with so much else, popular sentiment can be traced through calypso lyrics. In 1935 Calypsonean 'Houdini' sang:

> Black men the bugle call. . . .
> Don't mind what Mussolini say
> Let us march in battle array.

By the time Germany had conquered France, 'Destoyer' won first prize with a calypso which expressed 'alarm, shock, anger, apprehension, defiance, hope' but then added:

> Adolph Hitler, Adolph Hitler
> You must be take Great Britain for Poland
> But you'll be a failure
> Britain is supported by America.

'Attila's' *Ode to America* spoke of that New World power as 'the veteran champion of democracy'. Calypsonean 'Tiger's' *The Best Place is the US* reflected the fact that early twentieth century West Indian immigration to the US had been a great success just as work with the Americans in the Panama canal had been. This explains the popular sonnet

> You can never be in a financial jam
> When you are working for Uncle Sam.

And Uncle Sam had plenty of work to give a population which had suffered through a severe depression throughout the 1930s. As the US Commander in Trinidad put it:

> We built piers, we built roads. We dredged new channels that
> led to new anchorages . . . We built an excellent hospital,
> developed repair facilities ashore that equalled about 2 ½ repair
> ships . . . .[74]

All the bases in the British colonies were built by US contractors. In Trinidad alone they spent $81,913,399 on construction of the port, the airfields and roads. Of the 44,899 men who worked on these bases, only 7,400 were American, the rest were West Indians who drew wages which were considerably higher than those obtaining locally.[75]

In short, the synergies between the US and much of the Caribbean was such that while the US was laying the fundamental transportation infrastructure of roads, ports and airports for the modern Caribbean, they were also generating goodwill. Even when the construction of the bases slowed down in late 1943 and 1944, West Indians were recruited as temporary workers in US agriculture. In 1943, 8,828 went to the American south-east and in 1944 that doubled to 16,574, plus 4,698 Bahamians. The program (H-2) has been so successful that it continues to date.

Certainly, the continued American military presence after the war would be a sore point in the developing nationalist movement. In the immediate post-war period, however, as the US and USSR struggled to gain adherents in the region, the US had a considerable advantage with all social classes. It would certainly need that goodwill given the nature of the challenges, but it would need something else: a Caribbean conviction that despite its racist practices and often uncouth entrepreneurial ways, the US was still the bastion of democratic hopes. A future West Indian leader, Eric Williams, would put it succinctly in 1942:

> With humanity at the crossroads, there are, for the Caribbean as for the rest of the world, for the Negro as for the rest of mankind, only two alternatives: greater freedom or greater tyranny.[76]

Notes

1   H.T. Beale, p. 49.
2   Cf. Capt. S.W. Roskill, *The Strategy of Sea Power* (London: Collins, 1962).
3   Saul Friedlander, *Prelude to Downfall: Hitler and the US, 1939–1941*. Translated from French by Aline B. and Alexander Werth (New York: Alfred A. Knopf, 1967), p. 41.
4   *The Memoirs of Cordell Hull*. 2 vols. London, 1948, Vol. I, p. 602.
5   On Bemis' influence and the classified work he performed, see Janet M. Mason, *Diplomatic Ramifications of Unrestricted Submarine Warfare, 1939–1941* (New York: Greenwood Press, 1990), pp. 157–8.
6   Samuel Flagg Bemis, *The Latin American Policy of the US* (New York: Harcourt Brace & Co., 1943), p. 355.
7   *Ibid.*, pp. 372–3.
8   Cf. Henry Myron Blackmer, II: 'Any attempt to erect a collective security system in the western hemisphere to maintain peace and security had to be preceded by the abandonment by the US of unilateral intervention in the affairs of neighbouring Republics. Co-operative participation of the twenty Latin American Republics could only be gained on this basis.' *Ibid.*, p. 11.
9   Cited in Robert Klein, *The Idea of Equality in International Politics* (Ambilly-Annemasse: Impremierie 'Les Presses de Savoie', 1966), p. 179.
10 Cf. R.A. Humphreys, *Latin America and the Second World War, 1939–1942*. Vol. I (London: University of London, 1981), p. 47.
11 *Idem.*, Vol. II, p. 529.
12 Cf. Louis De John, *The German Fifth Column in World War II* (Chicago: University of Chicago Press, 1956).
13 Cf. Investigation in Nazi Front Groups in the US: US Congress, House of Representatives, Special Committee/or the Investigation of Un-American Propaganda Activities in the US (Washington Government Printing Office).
14 Hubert Herring, *Good Neighbours* (New Haven: Yale University Press, 1941), p. 67. One

of the most popular of these journalistic writings was by Fernando Artucio H., *The Nazi Underground in South America* (New York, 1942).

15 *Ibid.*, p. 331.

16 For a convincing eyewitness account by a US social scientist see Carleton Beals, *The Coming Struggle for Latin America* (New York: J.B. Lippincott, 1938). On the Latin American perceptions, see R.A. Humphreys *Latin America and the Second World War, passim.*

17 One scholar who believed that the stories about fifth columns were exaggerated was Lewis Hanke, 'Plain Speaking About Latin America', *Harper's* (November, 1940).

18 For a review of the extensive German holdings see Albert E. Carter, *The Battle of South America* (New York: Bobbs-Merrill Co., 1941), pp. 261–72.

19 'Project No. 14' is discussed in Ladislao Farago, *The Game of the Foxes* (New York: David McKay Co., 1971), pp. 58–61. For various other Abwehr plots see R.A. Humphreys, *op. cit.*

20 Nicholas John Spykman, *America's Strategy in World Politics* (New York: Harcourt, Brace and Co., 1942), p. 238.

21 Cited in Edward N. Barnhardt, 'Citizenship and Political Tests in Latin American Republics', *Hispanic American Historical Review*, Vol. 42 (August, 1962), p. 313.

22 Elliott, *The Ramparts We Watch*, p. 91.

23 Richard M. Leighton and Robert Coakley, *Global Logistics and Strategy, 1940–1943*, Washington, D.C., The War Department, Office of the Chief of Military History, 1955.

24 Elliott, p. 91.

25 Elliott, p. 154.

26 Ken Post, *Strike the Iron. A Colony at War: Jamaica, 1939–1945*, 2 vols. (New Jersey: Humanities Press, 1981), Vol. I, p. 139.

27 Friedlander, p. 96.

28 Humphreys, *Latin America and the Second World War*, I, p. 77.

29 See the discussion in Eric Williams, *History of the People of Trinidad-Tobago* (Port of Spain: PNM Publishing Co., 1962), pp. 269–73.

30 Memo to Secretary Hull, 11 January, 1941 cited in William L. Langer and S. Everett Gleason, *The Undeclared War, 1940–1941* (New York: Harper, 1953), p. 262.

31 Cited in Michael Anthony, *Port of Spain in a World at War, 1939–1945* (Laventille: Ministry of Sports and Culture, 1983), p. 119.

32 Cf. Humberto García Muñiz, 'El Caribe Angloparlante: Desarrollo Histórico de la, Presencia Militar de EEUU en el Caribe' (Manuscript, Instituto de Estudios de Caribe, Rio Pedras, Puerto Rico, 1986), pp. 56–97.

33 William J. Jordan, *Panama Odyssey* (Austin: University of Texas, 1984), p. 21.

34 Langer and Gleason, p. 149.

35 *Ibid.*, pp. 452–55.

36 Stimson Diary, 10 April, 1941; cited in *Ibid.* p. 427. In early 1941 there had appeared an article recommending just such division of the western hemisphere on the grounds that it was 'rational from a geographical point of view and the same time strategically defensible.' (Vilhjalmuir Stefensson, 'What is the western hemisphere?,' *Foreign Affairs* (January 1941), pp. 344–6.

37 Langer and Gleason, p. 460.

38 *Ibid.*, p. 455.

39 Georges Robert, *La France aux Antilles de 1939 a 1943* (Paris, 1950). When the US blockaded Martinique and it was not until June 1943, when Free French sympathizers captured French Guiana that Robert relented his 'vigil' over French possessions and returned to France.

40 Cf. Richard M. Leighton and Robert Coakley, *Global Logistics and Strategy, 1940–1943*

(Washington, D.C.: The War Department, Office of the Chief of Military History, 1955).

41   Admiral Karl Doenitz, *Memoirs Ten Years and Twenty Days*. Trans. R.H. Stevens (Cleveland: The World Publishing Co., 1959).

42   *Ibid.*, p. 403.

43   Heinz Schaeffer, *U-boat 977* (N.Y. W.W. Horton & Co., 1953) p. 130.

44   Grand Admiral Karl Doenitz, Forward to Edward P. Von der Porten, *The German Navy in World War Two* (New York: Ballentine, 1974), p. 5.

45   The technical details discussed here are derived from Wolfgang Frank, *The Sea Wolves* (N.Y.: Ballentine Books, 1955) and Robert E. Kuenne, *The Attack Submarine: A Study in Strategy* (New Haven: Yale University Press, 1965).

46   Dr Jurgen Rohwer, 'The U-boat War against the Allied Supply', in H.A. Jacobsen and J. Rohwer (eds), *Decisive Battles of World War II: The German View* (New York: G.P. Putman's Sons, 1965), p. 270.

47   Doenitz, *Memoirs* p. 221.

48   Cited in Michael Gannon, *Operation Drumbeat* (New York: Harper and Row, 1990), p. XVII.

49   *Ibid.*

50   Doenitz, *Memoirs*, p. 221.

51   Cf. Fitzroy A. Babtiste, *War Cooperation and Conflict: The European Possessions in the Caribbean, 1939–1945* (New York: Greenwood Press, 1988), p. 144.

52   The Airports Authority, *The History of Aviation in Trinidad and Tobago*, 1913–1962 (Port of Spain: Paria Publishing Co., 1987), p. 79.

53   Wolfgang Frank, *The Sea Wolves*, p. 114.

54   Samuel Eliot Morrison, *The Atlantic Battle Won, May 1943–May 1945*. Vol. I. (Boston: Little Brown, 1956), p. 125.

55   Vice-Admiral Friedrich Ruge, *Sea Warfare, 1939–1945: A German Viewpoint*. Trans. by Cdr. M.G. Saunders, R.N., London: Cassells and Co., 1957, p. 198. According to Gannon on the refusal to have a general blackout: 'Civilian avarice and carelessness must take their places on the list of agents accountable for the U-boat triumphs' (p. 345).

56   Gannon, p. 379.

57   *Ibid.*

58   *Ibid.*, p. xxi.

59   *Ibid.*, p. 386.

60   Don E. Gordon, *Electronic Warfare* (N.Y.: Pergammon Press, 1981), p. 54.

61   See also Ursula Pows-Lybbe, *The Eye of Intelligence* (London: William Kimber, 1983).

62   The statistics are cited in Robert E. Keunne, *The Attack Submarine*, p. 21 and S.W. Roskill, *The War at Sea*, p. 264.

63   Quoted in S.E. Morrison, *The Atlantic Battle Won*, vol. x, p. 198.

64   Doenitz, *Memoirs*, p. 333.

65   Edward Von der Porten, p. 259. See identical views by Vice-Admiral Leland P. Lovette, foreword in Wolfgang Frank, *The Sea Wolves*, p. 9.

66   Cf. Bernardo Vega, *Nazismo, Fascismo y Falangismo en la República Dominicana*. (Santo Domingo: Fundación Cultural Dominicana, 1985).

67   Baptiste, *War, Co-operation and Conflict*, p. 166.

68   Cf Hugh Thomas, On German espionage in Cuba see Angel Tomás and Emilio Surí, 'El Hombre del Reich', serialized in *Granma* (Havana), March 1987.

69   Ronald C. Newton, 'The US, the German Argentines, and the Myth of the Fourth Reich', *Hispanic American Historical Review*, Vol 64 (February 1984), p. 103.

70   Cf. Ken Post, *Strike the Iron*, pp. 117–71.

71   Fitzroy André Baptiste, *War, Co-operation and Conflict*, p. 214.

72   See the revealing work by Gordon Rohleher and J. Cowley, 'Calypso and Society in Pre-Independence Trinidad', 2 vols. (Unpublished Ph.D., Warwick University, 1991).

73   For a vivid but somewhat fanciful account of German U-boat crew landings and visits to various islands see A.T. Gaylord and M. Kelshall, *The U-boat War in the Caribbean* (Port of Spain: Paria Publishing Co., 1988). Gannon points out that there is no evidence of boat crews ever leaving their craft (Gannon, p. 348).

74   Cited in Fitz Baptiste, 'Colonial Government, Americans and Employment Generation in Trinidad, 1939–1944. (Unpublished Paper, UWI, Trinidad, 6 December, 1985), p. 2.

75   Cf. Humberto García Muñiz, 'El Caribe Durante la Segunda Guerra Munidal' (Rio Piedras, Puerto Rico, n.d.).

76   Eric Williams, *The Negro in the Caribbean* (Westport, CN.: Negro Universities Press, 1942), p. 98.

Part II

The Marxist challenge and US responses

CHAPTER 4 | From anti-Fascism to anti-communism: Costa Rica and British Guiana

In his message to the US Congress of 1945, President Harry Truman noted that the American public was eager to put matters of defence and war behind them. Fearing the growth of an already evident isolationism, however, he warned that 'whether we like it or not, we must all recognize that the victory we have won has placed upon the American people the continuing burden of responsibility for world leadership.'[1]

The outlines of what that burden would be was provided by Winston Churchill on 6 March, 1946 in Fulton, Missouri. In what has gone down in history as the opening salvo of the Cold War, Churchill spoke of an 'Iron Curtain' which had descended 'from Stettin in the Baltic to Trieste in the Adriatic.' Everywhere else, except in the US and the British Commonwealth, communists and fifth columnists 'constitute a growing challenge and peril to Christian civilization.'[2] Churchill had discussed the speech with Truman and some of his closest advisers. Clearly, this was a western position.[3]

Indeed, such was the degree of public apathy with international affairs, that when it came to foreign relations government agencies fell into the temptation to 'act now and persuade later'. This, in turn, led to a propensity for secrecy. Secrecy was not, to be sure, a new phenomenon, but shortly after World War II it acquired a most impressive institutional capacity for its enforcement.

Although some of the agencies which carried over into the post-World War II period were important – the OSS for instance – the fact is that 1947 was a watershed year. It was the year in which the Truman Doctrine and the Marshall Plan were launched. In order to meet the Soviet challenge the National Security Act of 1947 made a series of fundamental changes which endure up to this writing. The National Security Council and the Central Intelligence Agency (CIA) were put directly under the President, under the Secretary of Defense, a newly-created Joint Chiefs of Staff, and under the Secretary of State, the Department of State's Policy Planning Staff. It was the CIA which would play a dominant role, surreptitiously of course, after 1947.

Among its many special powers the CIA enjoyed the proviso that the Director could spend the agency's funds without accounting for them. As was to be expected, neither did he ever have to divulge the size of the CIA staff. Employees were also exempt from civil service procedures as regards hiring, firing and personal checks.[4] The combination of a new isolationism at home, and increased responsibilities abroad, made this the ideal agency to carry out 'crisis' interventions.

Above and beyond its institutional-legal structure there were the recruits. They formed an elite, and like all elites they felt able to rise above their own rules. Rules to these men, notes Robin H. Winks, are like rules to academics, 'normative not binding.'[5] Not surprisingly, elite universities such as Yale, held much attraction to the intelligence community. The CIA, however, did not operate in a vacuum. It had as its context the geopolitical perceptions of the time.

This geopolitical thinking can be analyzed in terms of its general ideological thrust and of the specific international relations strategies which flowed therefrom. The general thrust was formulated by a series of scholars with close access to decision-making. The realist's argument, i.e., that his moral principles are limited because they are derived from reality rather than divorced from it, should not be confused with the jingoistic argument that nations ought to pursue only their own national interests. The basic dichotomy lies between those who approach foreign policy with the questions as posed by Hans Morgenthau: 'Is this policy in accord with moral and legal principles?' and those who approach policy with the question: 'How does this policy affect the power of the nation?' Morgenthau left no doubt as to where he stood. Realists are 'concerned with human nature as it actually is, and with historical processes as they actually are.'[6] From this assumption flowed the basic premise: power and the balance of power are the only true stabilizing factors in international relations. The influential George E. Kennan summed up the dominant intellectual influence in the US in the 1950s, as follows:

> The practice of government, after all, is a practical exercise and not a moral one . . . Morality as the foundation of civic virtue and accordingly as a condition precedent to successful democracy – yes . . . but morality as a general criterion for the determination of the behaviour of states and above all as a criterion for measuring and comparing the behaviour of different states – no . . .'[7]

Another major theorist of the period, Robert E. Osgood, aptly summed up the realist's position of the 1950s in terms of two beliefs or principles: (1) scepticism concerning any attempt to mitigate international conflict through sentiments or even written pledges and institutional devices, and (2) 'if power conflicts can be mitigated at all', this will occur only through 'balancing power against power' and through a circumspect diplomacy which also understands 'the uses of force and the threat of force as indispensable instruments of national policy.'[8]

Because of this, Morgenthau in particular saw American national interests as composed of three overarching goals: (1) a predominant position in the western hemisphere – a predominance to be guaranteed not by any collective security pacts but through the Monroe Doctrine; (2) a European balance of power, and (3) an Asiatic balance of power.[9] In the western hemisphere there was no question of a balance of power; there was only a question of American predominance through what was essentially a unilateral doctrine.

If this was the general geopolitical ideology, the specific strategic doctrines were defined in George E. Kennan's idea of 'containment'. This doctrine certainly influenced the policies of the early Truman administration. It involved three essential strategic points:[10]

1 The strategy of 'asymmetrical response': this was based on the perception that the US had limited resources and could not meet Soviet threats wherever they presented themselves. Rather, the US would respond only in those geographical areas and against threats directed at a set of predetermined, 'irreducible' US national interests.
2 The belief that there were only five centres of industrial and military power important to US national security: the US itself, Great Britain, Germany and Central Europe, the USSR and Japan. For the rest, and in order to protect US interests, secure spheres of influence were necessary. South America 'from the bulge North' was one of these.
3 The view that Marxist-Leninist ideology was a tool used at Stalin's whim. 'Ideology', Kennan wrote in 1947, 'is a product and not a determinant of social and political reality.' Stalin, as distinct from Hitler, had no fixed timetable for expansion; outside the USSR's sphere of influence, he was perfectly willing to wait for the 'right' conditions to develop. Subversion, i.e. fifth columns, not military conquest, according to Kennan, were Stalin's preferred weapons.

But if national security required a clear sphere of influence and spheres of influence were to be defended unilaterally if need be, what about all the agreements and declarations on sovereignty, self-determination and collective security signed over the years? Do legal commitments and treaties have any meaning? Here again, there was in the 1950s a substantial and important group of legal 'realists' whose writings cast some light on this question.[11] This group disputed two 'idealistic' stances. First, 'The view that verbal expression of a legal norm has only one 'true' meaning which can be discovered by correct interpretation', writes Professor Kelsen, 'is a fiction adopted to maintain the illusion of legal security . . .'. McDougal and Gardner concur: 'It should need no further emphasis today that the words of an international agreement cannot be taken as timeless absolutes.' A second idealistic position which they disputed was 'that it is possible for contemporary interpreters to divine in detail the "true" or "real" intention of agreement makers of an earlier day.' McDougal and Gardner sum up their position by agreeing with the legal journal *Harvard Research*, that interpretations involve 'giving' a meaning to a text rather than 'finding' that meaning. McDougal and Gardner recommend, therefore, that each generation, 'whatever its preference', interpret 'its legacy of agreements, as well as of other authoritative doctrine, in terms of contemporary conditions and objectives.' It is clear that this is what has been done with the Monroe Doctrine in the early part of this century. The Rio Treaty and the Charter of the Organization of American States would experience a similar fate as the turbulent Caribbean Basin politics of the post-war drew the US into its geopolitical vortex. An anti-communist 'corollary' to the Monroe Doctrine was about to be revealed. Like the original corollary, it was supposed to safeguard the Caribbean sphere of influence. In the post-war atmosphere, however, it had additional thrust provided by the sense of vulnerability to military threats and fifth columns.

One can speak of a 'rough geopolitical calculation', i.e. the assumption that the normal interactions which take place in any given country at any given time are accelerated if geographical proximity allows interaction with related events in other countries. Costa Rica became the 'cockpit' of the Caribbean of 1947–8. Axis submarine activity, suspected German fifth columns and the clash between a modernizing and nationalist bourgeoisie and a petty bourgeois communist party allied to a traditionalist landholding aristocracy was the heady brew which provided the broad ideological backdrop of the 1940s.

The story begins in February, 1941 when English submarines operating in the Pacific chased German and Italian warships, the *Fella* and the *Eisenach*, into the Costa Rican port of Puntarenas.[12] The initial Costa Rican instinct was to stay neutral since it had diplomatic relations with all three protagonists. Yet, afraid that activities in the port would be paralyzed by a naval confrontation, the government of Rafael Angel Calderón Guardia believed that if Costa Rica asserted its sovereignty by taking the ships, it would defuse the crisis. At that point the German and Italian crews burned their ships. The stage had been set for a confrontation between the Calderón government – which enjoyed strong support by the communists – and the German community. Because Calderón himself was a member of Costa Rica's oligarchy and that oligarchy sold much of its coffee to Germany, a break with Germany could come only upon grievous provocation.

The clash between the powerful German community and the government came to a breaking point on 2 July, 1942 when a German U-boat – following Doenitz' strategy of 'tonnage' – sank the banana boat *San Pablo* in Puerto Limón with a loss of 27 Costa Rican lives. The consequences of this incident were indeed far-reaching. Pressured by public indignation, including public demonstrations and attacks on German-owned property, the Calderón government decided to clip the wings of the politically active community of German descent. Calderón was sure that the pro-Americanism of the Costa Ricans would provide the support.[13]

First came the legal attack: on 9 July, 1942 the Legislature passed Law 79 which held that 'Costa Ricans who in any way manifest adherence to the political regime of countries at war with Costa Rica' would lose Costa Rican nationality. That same day five citizens of German descent (all born in Costa Rica) were denationalized in the 'interest of national security' and as contribution to the 'common work' needed to protect 'the political ends of the Allied Nations . . .'[14] These five would be the first of a total of 300 Axis nationals (mostly Germans) interned by the Costa Rican government and deported to the US.

In politics every move brings about a countermove. The government's punitive measures against the Axis nationals, its collaboration with the communists and its offer to the US to open bases in the country, all contributed to further antagonize a group of middle-class nationalists and technocratically oriented reformists. They had come together in early 1940 to form a group called the *Centro para el Estudio de los Problemas Nacionales.*[15] The important role of the Centro was that it promoted nationalist and radical reformist causes, providing an alternative pole of attraction to educated youth at a time when the communists were so openly pro-American that they entered into no-strike agreements with the foreign companies.

The opening salvo of the political battle took place when the young son of Spanish immigrants and member of the Centro, José Figueres Ferrer, went on radio in July 1942 to protest at the 'expropriation, ransacking and confiscation' of the property of Axis nationals. He was hastily arrested and deported to Mexico. It was there that the Costa Rican branch of an important Pan Caribbean geopolitical movement began to gestate: the social democratic, or as it is called in the literature, 'the democratic left'. In Mexico in 1943 Figueres met two individuals who would be crucial to his future: Raúl Haya de la Torre, exiled leader of the *Alianza Popular Revolucionaria American*a (APRA) and Rosendo Arguello, a Nicaraguan opponent of Somoza. The former, in particular, had a vision which transcended his native Peru; he had been influencing events in Central America since Sandino's revolution in the 1920s.

At a time when communists had turned pro-American, the APRA held notions of an Indoamerica, of nationalism and especially economic nationalism, and perhaps fundamentally, the idea that it would take a political party organized on modern US and European lines to bring reformist ideas to power.[16] It is entirely possible that the APRA also absorbed the idea that professional armies are natural enemies of such reformist parties; their only defence, therefore, lay in an armed civilian following. Together these ideas became the pillars of the fundamental tenet of the democratic left: political democracy, eternal enmity towards tyrants of the right or left.[17]

Another thinker who would contribute to this 'democratic' geopolitical vision of the 1940s was the Venezuelan Rómulo Betancourt. In his youth a fervent rebel, his career had a very Caribbean beginning. Exiled in 1928 to the island of Curaçao by Venezuelan dictator Juan Vicente Gómez, he spent his time reading and studying the oil industry. There he was first introduced to Marxist ideology. After a year, Betancourt, like Bolívar before him, left for Haiti and the Dominican Republic looking for arms. This was what he himself called his 'Garibaldian' period: the many attempts to invade Venezuela which took him all over the Caribbean in search of arms, men and ships.[18] He ended up in Barranquilla, Colombia where in March 1931, he proclaimed the 'Plan de Barranquilla' calling for hemispheric-wide political and social reforms. Despite Betancourt's Marxism, the language of the Plan was nevertheless devoid of Marxist language. In 1931 he went to Costa Rica, where he was a militant in the Communist Party until his departure in 1936. His break with that Party occurred for reasons which are still unclear but which probably had to do with the two visions which would dominate his political life: a Trotsky-like penchant for democratic revolutions which transcended borders, and a Pan-Latin American nationalism which made his relations with any major centre of power (Washington or Moscow) prickly. Like Haya, Betancourt realized the importance of a well-organized polyclass party with a capacity to back-up its power with arms if necessary. They had both had bad experiences with the Comintern and later both were deeply suspicious of communist 'penetrations' or subversions of democratic movements.[19] It is not surprising, therefore, that they perceived subversion in Costa Rica with an intensity which not even the Americans exhibited. Their vision was influential on the young nationalist aspiring to power.

During the period of the Hitler-Stalin understanding, the communists had contributed to the loss of popularity of Calderón Guardia by attacking his government's pro-Americanism as 'pro-imperialist.'[20] Suddenly they changed their position and began giving active and valuable support to the various reforms the Calderón government was legislating. While the founder and Secretary-General of the party, Manuel Mora, later insisted that the communists changed positions once they had to choose between Calderón and a pro-Fascist regime the German Costa Ricans were plotting to install,[21] the real shift in policy was probably mandated by Moscow.[22] Hitler's invasion of Russia on 22 June, 1941 had brought to an end the Ribbentrop-

Molotov 10-year non-aggression pact signalling the shift to an active pro-Allied stance by all communist parties.

Manuel Mora's fiery 'anti-imperialist' and anti-bourgeoisie speeches were changed to the trim of Moscow's mandated popular front. 'We are not now trying to build socialism', Mora told a radio audience in September 1942. And on another date: 'We have to unify, without regard to politics, without regard to class distinctions.' Perhaps most extraordinary of all was his allegation that: 'In these moments, not only are we not able to collaborate [to the war effort] with efficiency, but we are actually becoming a burden to the US and that is a disgrace.'[23] By 1943 the Costa Rican communists, like communists in the rest of the Caribbean, were under full 'Browderite' influence, i.e. mandated by the US Communist Party and its Secretary, Earl Browder, to support the US because of its assistance to Russia. Browder used the Cuban Communist Party (*Partido Socialista Popular*) as its Caribbean mouthpiece. This is a situation which lasted from 1938 until the abolition of the Comintern in 1943.[24]

The elections of 8 February, 1948 pitted ex-President Calderón Guardia as candidate of the governmental Republican Party supported by the communist, *Vanguardia Popular* party, against the anti-communist newspaper publisher Otilio Ulate with José Figueres' *Partido Social Democrático* in a coalition called *Partido Unión Nacional*. Anti-communism was at its height since in October 1947, *Vanguardia Popular* had openly announced its pledge of support to the newly-created PROFINTERN in Moscow. As one researcher put it: 'The declaration fell like a bomb in Costa Rica and all of Central America.'[25] The international Cold War reinforced the internal conflict, a fact the US was not alien to. In January 1948, just before the elections, stoutly anti-communist Nathaniel Davis was appointed US ambassador. This was a clear indication that Washington had recognized a communist threat in Costa Rica.[26]

After a violent campaign in which communist 'shock troops' were so out of control that the opposition called a general strike which lasted from 22 July to 3 August, the Picado government was forced to make significant electoral reforms. It took the Electoral Tribunal 20 days to declare Ulate the winner and three days after that the government-controlled Congress declared the election null and void. That was 1 March. On 12 March José Figueres took up arms at his farm, 'La Lucha' in the south central part of the country. His followers were some peasants but mostly youth from the large Costa Rican middle class. Their penchant for neck chains with a 'medallion of Costa Rica's "La Virgen de los Angeles" led to their nickname, "medallitas".'

By mid-April 1948, the land which authors like to call 'patriarchal', 'idyllic', or 'bucolic', was in flames, the national territory divided into several military 'zones', each controlled by a different army. Three of these 'armies' were serious contenders for power. In the south and east, the 'Liberación Army' of José Figueres had taken the second city, Cartago and the main Atlantic port, Puerto Limón. Through this port they received men and material from the friendly governments of Guatemala, Cuba and Panama. Most of the men were Nicaraguans and Dominicans – hoping to be in on what was thought to be stage one of the liberation of the Caribbean of dictators such as Trujillo and Somoza. In 1947 they had signed the Pact of the Caribbean vowing to combat all dictatorships. These international reinforcements would be given the name *Legión del Caribe*.[27]

San José, however, was in the hands of about 2,000 armed, working class followers of the communist *Vanguardia Popular*. They were nicknamed 'mariachis'. They had occupied the tallest building in town, put hundreds of political hostages on the top floors to ward off air attacks, and its leadership spent their time debating whether the national and international 'correlation of forces' warranted, or would permit, an independent grab of power. They had a few volunteers from other Central American countries, but mostly they had to content themselves with moral support from Vicente Lombardo Toledano, Mexican leader of the Soviet-oriented Confederation of Labour, and Blas Roca of the Cuban Communist Party, the *Partido Socialista Popular*. Other than that, they were on their own. The lame duck President of the Republic, Teodoro Picado, controlled what was left of the official national army while the defeated candidate, ex-President Calderón Guardia and his brother Francisco had the loyalty – though hardly 'control' – of another political army. Both Picado and the Calderóns were supported by their long-time personal friend, dictator Anastasio ('Tacho') Somoza of Nicaragua.

Hostilities lasted 40 days and took 2,000 lives; 1,933 of the government forces and only 67 of Figueres' forces. Obviously the middle-class 'medallitas' of Figueres and their Caribbean Legión friends were superior combatants to the working class 'mariachis'.[28]

Figueres headed up a provisional Junta which vowed to hand over power to the constitutionally elected Otilio Ulate within eighteen months, as, indeed, occurred. The Second Republic was declared with a new constitution which enacted the following reforms:

- nationalization of all banks;
- a 10 per cent levy on all property over $50,000;
- abolition of the army;
- prohibition of presidential re-election (8-year interlude);
- established an independent Supreme Electoral Tribunal;
- extended franchise to women and abolished literacy tests;
- conferred full citizenship on blacks born in Costa Rica and abolished all discriminatory laws;

- created multiple 'autonomous institutions' separate from government control;
- created independent civil service career; and
- bargained hard with the United Fruit Company, securing major gains for the workers.

What role did the US play in all this and especially in the defeat of the Picado-Calderón-Mora forces? Despite some revisionist histories,[29] probably, not much. The causes rather, lie in Costa Rican and Caribbean forces which were operating at the time.

First of these was the anti-communism of the Costa Rican middle class, a sentiment intensified by events at home and abroad. The communist take-over of Czechoslovakia came at a bad moment for the Costa Rican communists. It appeared to be the kind of 'inner subversion' which anti-communists feared communists were planning everywhere. Neither anti-communism nor containment were exclusively North American themes; much the opposite. Latin America was then agitated by ex-communists who had broken with the movement and were determined to keep the Marxists out of power, i.e. determined to avoid another Czechoslovakia.[30] Not surprisingly, it was not the Americans who provided Costa Ricans with the analogy to Czechoslovakia, it was the Peruvian Raúl Haya de la Torre whose battles with both the right and communist left in his native country had provided the particular framework with which he looked at Costa Rica. He called the situation there 'a second Czechoslovakia.'[31] The theme had already been picked up by a prominent *Figuerista*, Gonzalo Facio, who picketed the White House in Washington with a sign which read: 'Costa Rica: The Czechoslovakia of the Caribbean.'[32] The Americans, at least in this case, became an echo of Latin American sentiments. But the communists were also victims of their own political opportunism, dictated, it appears, by Moscow. Under the leadership of their educated, middle-class cadres, the communist party became a virtual co-initiator and co-administrator of the various social programs inaugurated by the Calderón Guardia government. In Costa Rica, the communists had carved out a most thankless role for themselves. They were the ones designing social programs and then defending them with their lives. At the same time their 'internationalism' – if not subordinate, at least adhering to Moscow – made them suspect by friend and foe alike. Fearing a Czechoslovak type *coup* the Picado government even refused to distribute weapons among the *Vanguardia Popular* stalwarts. What else could the communists expect from an alliance partner whose major international ally was Nicaragua's Anastasio Somoza? Political expediency and opportunism became the communist's own instruments of self-destruction. In 1943, seeking the approval of the Roman Catholic church, they had accepted Costa Rican Archbishop Sanabria's recommendation that they change their name to *Vanguardia Popular* (VP), even as Monsignor Sanabria was promoting and sponsoring the activities of his disciple, Father Benjamin Nuñez, who in that year created a competing, and anti-communist, trade union movement.[33] Nuñez would later be a major opponent and combatant against the Sanabria-supported Picado-Calderón-Mora coalition in 1948.

Another reason why the US did not feel inclined to get too involved in the Costa Rican case was that they, along with the rest of Latin America, were at the same time in Bogotá, Colombia hammering together the Organization of American States (OAS). It is true that in response to a journalist's question Secretary of State Marshall responded that the US had no intention of allowing Costa Rica to become 'a new Czechoslovakia', but when US troops stationed in Panama were mobilized, it was not for probable action in Costa Rica, but in Colombia. On 9 April, 1948 the assassination of Colombian *caudillo* Jorge Eliecer Gaitán led to a popular explosion which threatened to burn the whole city of Bogotá to the ground, including the building where the US and Latin American nations were meeting to give shape to the OAS. While this 'Bogotazo', as it would be called, contributed to the anti-communist mood and helped draw the US into the Caribbean imbroglio, the events of April 1948 in Costa Rica were proceeding without direct US involvement.

There was yet another fundamental reason behind the US neutrality in the Costa Rican conflict: the State Department's Manichean vision of the world. Specifically, they could not understand José Figueres. Wasn't he the one who in 1942 had attacked the government's clampdown on suspected fifth columnists? Wasn't the 1947 Pact of the Caribbean suspiciously 'socialistic'?[34] Walter La Feber reveals how State Department intelligence reports on Don Pepe were 'a revelation of the hidebound ideology and anti-communist preoccupation' of Washington officials. They were totally unable to deal with social democrats.[35] But if the US was suspicious of Don Pepe, the sentiment was heartily reciprocated. Far be it from a nationalist like Figueres to call in American assistance. In fact his dislike of the US State Department was second only to his dislike of the US banana companies. In an extraordinary letter in 1948 to radical Guatemalan Edelberto Torres, Figueres wrote at length about the need to force the US to change its attitude towards Latin America. In saying this Figueres made this characterization of the Americans:

> The Yankee, even though brutal, is at heart a child which one has to force to do what one wants by fooling him (*por medio del engaño*) . . . you have to use tricks because they have little cunning (*tienen poca malicia*) . . . I shall carry out more radical economic reforms than Mora and his whole party, and I shall

> win more battles against Yankee imperialism in shorter time
> than all those people have in twenty years, simply through a
> matter of tactics . . . Once [the Department of State] trusts me,
> I shall know what to do.[36]

In an earlier phase, such sentiments and the reforms Figueres actually launched, would have brought down the wrath of the 'Yankees'. By the late 1940s, with the Cold War turning hot in Berlin, Korea and other points East and West, social democrats like Figueres, while not supported, were left to battle against their enemies including the communists, on their own. By the end of the decade the US was involved in what James B. Reston of *The New York Times* called 'the single-minded determination not in catching Fascists but in stopping communists.'[37] It might be, as Jacobo Schiffer says, that Don Pepe was anti-capitalist, anti-oligarchy and anti-American,[38] but it is also patently clear that he was pro-democracy. The latter was his greatest contribution.[39]

If the US was willing to let the Costa Rican middle-class nationalists deal with the 'communist menace' in their own way, it showed no such moderation in the case of British Guiana in 1953. Several reasons explain why. First of all, anti-communism had grown into a veritable crusade in the US. Communist gains or actions in China, Vietnam, Czechoslovakia and other Eastern European countries, their aggressiveness in Greece, Korea and Berlin all led to a sense that no appeasement was allowable. The question in American political campaigns became 'Who lost China?', the dominant analogy, 'Munich'. Indeed, the latter became 'an iron law and a moral principle'.[40] In 1948 twelve members of the US Communist Party were arrested and jailed; an Internal Security Act was passed in 1950 and the Senate Internal Security Subcommittee became very active.

The rising tide of anti-communism evident in the behaviour of Senator Joe McCarthy and the Alger Hiss case reflected a shift in US strategy during the period 1950–3. The drawing up of what is known as National Security Council-68 (NSC-68) indicated the changed perceptions. Soviet power and intentions were judged to have global reach, through proxies. Because in the words of NSC-68, the USSR was 'inescapably militant', it 'mortally challenged' the US and the west and the Kremlin should be confronted wherever it showed itself. A major part of this aggressiveness stemmed from the fear of appearing weak in the eyes of allies who themselves were not fully recovered from World War II. 'Perceptions of power', says Gaddis, 'could be as important as power itself.' The fact that the USSR was interpreting the US attitude as a sign of weakness 'was being mirrored in many Latin American countries, where governments were losing their respect for the US for giving in to the Russians so frequently,'[41] warned the then Assistant Secretary of State Nelson Rockefeller.

The mood was clearly expressed by President Eisenhower in his 1953 Inaugural Address: 'As there is no weapon too small, no arena too remote, to be ignored, there is no free nation too humble to be forgotten.' Under a Secretary of State, John Foster Dulles, who believed that 'fear makes easy the task of diplomats' and that 'neutrality' was either 'obsolete' or 'an immoral and shortsighted conception', US foreign policy changed to a five-point strategy of defence.[42] The first three points were a combination of nuclear deterrence, alliances, and defence pacts. These were essentially defensive postures. The fourth and fifth points – psychological warfare and covert action – allowed the US to take the initiative. Finally, NSC-68 discouraged negotiation as a strategy until such time as the US had rebuilt its military strength.

The US view of the United Nations fitted this general approach. 'The United Nations', wrote Henry Cabot Lodge, 'is not able to involve the US in actions against our interests.' The Security Council was the only arm which could do anything more than recommend and there, noted Lodge, 'the US is protected by the veto power.'[43]

By 1950 unilateralism was back in the saddle, especially in the Caribbean. It was there that the US could still engage in what John Foster Dulles in 1952 called 'the modern way of getting maximum protection at bearable cost.'[44] British Guiana, a British colony on the east coast of South America, would find out just what Dulles had in mind. In 1945, an intelligent, US-educated dentist of Indian descent, Cheddi Jagan, organized a nationalist discussion group called the Political Affairs Committee (PAC). Decolonization was their goal and to that end they admitted anyone – liberal, Marxist, conservative – who shared that goal. British Guiana was being governed as a Crown Colony which meant that all important decisions were made in London. With the crucial elections of 1953 in mind, the PAC decided to consider becoming a political party. After a young lawyer of African descent, Forbes Burnham, joined PAC in 1950, the discussion group rapidly converted itself into a political party. The Progressive People's Party (PPP) was born in 1951. It had a decidedly Marxist orientation but was open to all.[45] Its basic support came from the trade union movement which Jagan and Burnham were leading. Each brought his own labour organization: Jagan the largely Indian sugar workers' Guiana Industrial Workers' Union (GIWU), and Burnham the largely black and urban British Guiana Labour Union (BGLU).

Perhaps reflecting its status as a British colony, removed, therefore, from the history of US interventions which the Hispanic Caribbean had long experienced, the British Guianese nationalists were explicit about their goals. There was a palpable naivete given the geopolitics of the region at the time. The PPP constitution, drawn up in 1951, stated specifically that its goal was to 'Promote the interests of the subject peoples by transforming

British Guiana into a Socialist country.'[46] One of the co-founders of the GIWU and PPP put its goals even more succinctly: 'We are fighting for national independence which leads to socialism and communism. We will have to do like the people of Russia.'[47]

In 1953 the PPP was the only organized party contesting the elections, the rest ran as independents. The PPP secured 18 or three-quarters of all seats, but did this with only 51 per cent of the votes cast. Only 37 per cent of the eligible electorate had participated. These statistics did nothing to dissuade Jagan, by now the political leader of the party, that he was leading a revolution. In one of his first speeches before the new House of Assembly (24 July, 1953), Jagan portrayed a world 'to all intents and purposes . . . divided into two camps: Fascism, imperialism and capitalism on the one hand and socialism and communism on the other.'[48] The PPP would side with the latter.

Throughout the English-speaking Caribbean, the liberal or at most Fabian-influenced politicians began to regard Cheddi Jagan and his wife Janet as 'subversives'. In 1952, Trinidad declared them 'prohibited immigrants.'[49] The British were not at all pleased. As they would later argue, the low turn out for the 1953 elections and the bare majority gained by the PPP hardly warranted the kind of radical changes Jagan was proposing.[50] The PPP government lasted 133 days. Following major labour disturbances and conflicts between the PPP and the British Governor, British troops landed, suspended the Constitution, and threw the PPP out of office.

Thomas Spinner puts the intervention in context. It is not difficult to understand why the British acted, he says:

> British troops were fighting communists in Malaya, Governor Savage feared for the safety of the entire English community in Georgetown, the United States government was agitating . . . and the violence in British Guiana might affect the entire British Caribbean and impede the planning for a federation of the British West Indies.[51]

The anti-communist hysteria had led to the violation of the most cherished principle of representative democracy: respect for the freely-expressed majoritarian will. As an eyewitness, R.T. Smith, later wrote: 'the election itself was absolutely free from violence or disorder. The order and discipline of the public reflected the responsible attitude of the party leaders.'[52] It is true, as the British White Paper on the issue stated, that the leadership of the PPP were professing communist principles.[53] How true was it, however, that British Guiana was on the path to becoming a 'totalitarian' society? The greatest concern of the Guianese at the time appeared to be the scheduled cricket match with Trinidad.[54]

In the Parliamentary debate on the crisis, Conservative Minister of

Housing and Local Government, Harold Macmillan, was at pains to justify his government's actions:

> It may be true, and I think it is true, that none of the separate accusations against the People's Progressive Party leaders could be held sufficient in itself to justify the serious course which Her Majesty's Government has had to adopt; but surely, taken together they are really conclusive.[55]

Anti-communism was hardly a purely American and British phenomenon. The anti-communist mood in the Caribbean was made evident when the governments of Trinidad, Barbados, Jamaica and the US refused to allow the Jagans entry. The Dutch in Suriname allowed them only 'in transit' status as they attempted to reach London to plead their case. This was the overt intervention; the covert intervention was being sponsored by the US. Most Guianese did not realize that what was unfolding was the first major anti-communist offensive by the US in the Caribbean – an offensive in which the US had substantial local support. In the early 1950s a major struggle was taking place between the Moscow-dominated World Federation of Trade Unions (WFTU) and the western-dominated International Confederation of Trade Unions (ICFTU). In the western hemisphere the anti-communist attack was led by the AFL-supported Inter-American Regional Workers Organization (IARWO).[56] In 1952 and 1953 the ICFTU and the IARWO scored major victories throughout the West Indies. In Jamaica, the Fabian-oriented People's National Party (PNP) led by Norman Manley expelled the major left-wing leaders of the Trade Union Congress. Both of Jamaica's major trade unions, the BITU and the NWU, became members of the ICFTU. In Barbados, Grantley Adams, first President of the WFTU-related Caribbean Labour Congress, called for the disbandment of that Congress, saying it was dominated by a Caribbean-wide clique of communists. In Trinidad, the Marxist trade unionists had been isolated even further from the evolving political arena. Even in British Guiana, Jagan's associate, Forbes Burnham, in 1952 joined his BGLU to the ICFTU. Burnham had thereby formally associated himself with such 'moderate' West Indian politicians as Manley, Bustamante and Adams – all subjects of virulent attacks as 'bourgeois labour unionists' in the PPP's paper *Thunder*. Clearly, not only was Jagan isolated in the Caribbean, he was setting the stage for a much more serious confrontation in British Guiana.[57]

It is quite evident that while the US was concerned about a potential Soviet ally in this hemisphere, it was the Conservative government of Winston Churchill which took the initiative in British Guiana. As in Costa Rica, where a strongly nationalistic middle class defeated any prospects of communist inroads, in British Guiana a series of internal factors were also critical. Leon Despres has argued that his detailed interview data of the early 1950s indicates that there were deep divisions within the PPP much before the 1953 elections. Three issues divided the party's elite: (1) ideology: a Marxist-Leninist vs. Fabian socialist split; (2) demography and race: rural Indians vs. black and coloured urban middle classes; (3) the West Indies Federation: Burnham favoured entering this federation of West Indian islands, Jagan opposed it. As Leon Despres relates, 'soon after the 1953 victory the radical wing of the PPP held a series of secret meetings at which the vacillating Burnham was one important topic. They concluded that he must either come to terms with the left wing or leave the party'.[58] Interestingly enough, that scholarly interpretation is not much different from the one given by British authorities.

In 1954, the Royal Commission investigating the causes leading to the 1953 suspension of the Constitution, concluded that six of the PPP's most prominent leaders were communists, including the two Jagans. Though 'ideologically ambiguous', according to the Commission, three others, including Burnham, were socialists. Burnham was perceived to be Jagan's main rival. The Commission concluded that they had no doubt that the socialists in the PPP were 'essentially democrats'. They did doubt, however, whether the democrats had 'the wit to see the essential difference between themselves and their communist colleagues or the ability to avoid being out-manoeuvered by them.' Repeatedly, the Commissioners asserted the belief that the more moderate PPP leaders were 'hardly a match for the extremists.'[59]

The fact is, as the official Burnham story tells it, he had long planned his split with the Jagans, using anti-communism as the dominant argument. Burnham knew, say his biographers, that 'Jagan's devotion to the communist cause transcended his commitment to his own country. . . . [by 1953] Burnham had made up his mind to part company with Jagan unless the latter was prepared to put Guianese nationalism above posturing as an international communist.'[60]

It is ironic that Jagan should have brought his pro-communist beliefs and sentiments from the US. He never was, therefore, influenced by British Fabian socialism as Burnham and virtually all the other West Indian nationalists were. Everywhere else in the English-speaking Caribbean these nationalists were working with allies within the British system to fulfill the promise of self-determination. It was first supposed to be in a federation and when that failed in 1961, as individual independent nations. Jagan would have no part of such 'colonialist' schemes. Independent Guyana would take a separate – and unfortunately destructive – path.

Between 1955 and 1958 several major splits occurred within the PPP. In 1956, the year of Khrushchev's attacks on Stalin and of the suppression of the Hungarian uprising, Jagan launched major attacks on 'deviationists' of the right and left within the PPP, citing 'Comrade Stalin' and 'Comrade

Mao' as authorities. Three Afro-Guyanese Marxists left the party soon thereafter, and by 1957 the Guyanese political scene reflected nearly perfectly the racial divisions existing in the society. The stage was set for the next dramatic round in Guyana. The US would then be a key player. For now, the Guyana crisis, like that of Costa Rica, was little more than a prelude to events which would bring full-scale US involvement and intervention. The successful containment of communist influence had become dogma. This meant putting the Good Neighbour Policy in mothballs and giving the Monroe Doctrine new life.

Notes

1   President Truman's message to the Congress, 19 December 1945 in Office of the Secretary of Defense, Historical Office, *The Department of Defense Documents on Establishment and Organization, 1944–1978* (Washington, D.C. 1979), p. 14.

2   Cited in Daniel Yergin, *Shattered Peace: the Origins of the Cold War and the National Security State* (Boston: Houghton Mifflin, Co., 1977), pp. 175–6.

3   *Ibid.*, p. 175.

4   This discussion is drawn from Harry Howe Ranson, *The Intelligence Establishment* (Cambridge, MA.: Harvard University Press, 1970).

5   Robin W. Winks, *Cloak and Gown: Scholars in the Secret War, 1939–1961* (New York: William Morrow, 1987), p. 24.

6   Hans J. Morgenthau, *Politics Among Nations*. Second Edition (New York: Knoph, 1954), p. 4.

7   George E. Kennan, *Realities of American Foreign Policy* (New Jersey: Princeton University Press, 1954), pp. 49–50.

8   Robert E. Osgood, *Ideals and Self-Interest in America's Foreign Relations* (Chicago: University of Chicago Press, 1953), p. 9.

9   Hans J. Morgenthau, 'What is the National Interest of the United States?' *Annals of the American Academy of Political and Social Science* (July, 1952), pp. 1–7.

10   This section draws heavily from John Lewis Gaddis, *Strategies of Containment: A Critical Appraisal of Post-war American National Security Policy* (New York: Oxford University Press, 1982).

11   Myeres S. McDougal and Richard N. Gardner are taken here as important figures in that group. See their essay on the interpretation of internal treaties, 'The Veto and the Charter: An Interpretation for Survival', *Yale Law Journal*, Vol. 60 (January 1951), pp. 262–92.

12   Cf. Juan Rojas Suárez, *Costa Rica en la Segunda Guerra Mundial* (San José: Imprenta Nacional, 1943).

13   After a year's research in Costa Rica, Irvin L. Child concluded that the individual Costa Rican 'seems in a very genuine sense to feel himself personally more closely connected with the US than with any other foreign nation'. 'The Background of Public Opinion in Costa Rica', *Public Opinion Quarterly*, Vol. 7, No. 2 (Summer 1943), pp. 254–55.

14   Edward Barnhart, 'Citizenship and Political Tests in Latin American Republics in World War II', *Hispanic American Historical Review*, 42 (1962), p. 304.

15   Oscar Aguilar Bulgarelli, *Costa Rica y sus hechos políticos de 1948* (San José: Editorial Costa Rica, 1983), p. 114.

16   Robert J. Alexander, *Prophets of the Revolution: Profiles of Latin American Leaders* (New York: The Macmillan Co., 1962), p. 96.

17   Cf. Harry Kantor, 'El Programa APRISTA para Perú y Latinoamerica', *Combate* (San José), Vol. I, No. 3 (1958), pp. 19–27.

18   For a detailed description of this period see Robert J. Alexander, *Rómulo Betancourt and the Transformation of Venezuela* (New Brunswick: Transaction Books, 1982), pp. 35–66.

19   For the influence of both Haya and Betancourt on Costa Rican 'independent' political thinking see Rodolfo Cerdas Cruz, *La Hoz y el Machete* (San José: Editorial Universidad Estatal a Distancia, 1986), pp. 363–97.

20   Jacobo Schifter, *Costa Rica-1948* (San José: Editorial Universitaria Centroamericana, 1982), pp. 94–5.

21   Cf. Manuel Mora Valverde, *Discursos, 1934–1979* (San José: Editorial Presbere, 1980), pp. 153, 163, 164.

22   *La Tribuna*, 19 August, 1943 cited in Rodolfo Cerdas Cruz, *La hoz y el machete* (San José: Editorial Universidad Estatal a Distancia, 1986), p. 348. Cerdas, a Costa Rican scholar argues that the Costa Ricans maintained great independence from the Comintern, from Browder, the Cubans and the Caribbean Bureau (under whose jurisdiction the Costa Ricans fell). While that might be so, their actions during this period are indistinguishable from what is known as 'Browderism'.

23   Mora, *Discursos*, p. 164.

24   Cf. Manuel Caballero, *Latin America and the Comintern, 1919–1934* (Cambridge: Cambridge University Press, 1986; by the same author, *Entre Gómez y Stalin* (Caracas: Universidad Central, 1989). See also, Stephen Clissold (ed.), *Soviet Relations with Latin America, 1918–1968* (London: Oxford University Press, 1970), pp. 77–9.

25   John Patrick Bell, *Guerra Civil en Costa Rica* (San José: Editorial Universitaria Centroamericana, 1985), p. 81.

26   Schiffer calls Davis' arrival a 'Watershed' between US indifference and fear of communism in Costa Rica (*Costa Rica*, p. 144).

27   For a good description of the labyrinthine Pan Caribbean origins of the Legion and its men, see Charles D. Ameringer, *The Democratic Left in Exile* (Miami: University of Miami Press, 1974), pp. 58–110.

28   Experiences in the Spanish Civil War and especially in World War II were important elements in the leadership of these 'liberation' armies. In Costa Rica on the government side Col. Rigoberto Pacheco Tinoco had served with the Spanish army in Africa; Figueres' main military adviser, Alexander Murray, had served with British Intelligence in Canada during World War II. For Spanish Civil War influences see Falcoff and Pike.

29   Cf. Miguel Acuña, *El 48* (San José: Editorial Lehman, 1974). In a 'revisionist' book, Jacobo Schifter, who had previously seen no such US involvement, agrees with Acuña. *La fase oculta de la Guerra Civil en Costa Rica* (San José: Educa, 1985).

30   For an account of the combative anti-communism of the many disillusioned communists see Eudocio Ravines, *The Yenan Way: The Kremlin's Penetration of South America* (New York: Charles Scribner's Sons, 1951). Ravines, a Peruvian, had been an important member of the Comintern.

31   John Patrick Bell, p. 207.

32   Ferreto, *Vida*, p. 90. Facio would later tell the press that he talked Haya into making that statement.

33   Cf. Victor Alba, *Politics and the Labour Movement*, pp. 192, 279.

34   Arnoldo Ferreto of the Costa Rican Communist Party claims that Figueres had 'planes fantásticos' to create 'the Socialist Republic of the Caribbean', *Vida Militante*, (San José: Editorial Presbere, 1984, p. 127). Elsewhere he characterizes Figueres as surrounded by 'gangsters and nazis'. (p. 135).

35   Walter La Feber, *Inevitable Revolutions. The US in Central America* (New York: W.W. Norton, Co., 2nd ed. 1993), p. 107.

36   First published in Rosendo Arguello, hijo, *Quiénes y cómo nos traicionaron*, (undated) pp. 126–30 and reprinted in several other books including Oscar Aguilar Bulgarelli.

37   *The New York Times*, 15 April, 1947, p. 16.

38   Jacobo Schiffer, *La fase oculta*, pp. 70–1.

39   Cf. John Patrick Bell, *Crisis in Costa Rica* (Austin: University of Texas Press, 1971), p. 161.

40   Daniel Yergin, *Shattered Peace*, (p. 198).

41   Yergin, *Shattered Peace*, p. 77.

42   Gaddis, *Strategies of Containment*, pp. 145–54 *passim*.

43   Henry Cabot Lodge, Jr., 'An Answer to Critics of the UN', *New York Times Magazine*, 22 November, 1953, p. 12.

44   *Ibid.*, p. 147.

45   Cf. Ralph R. Premdas, 'The Rise of the First Mass-Based Multiracial Party in Guyana', *Caribbean Quarterly*, vol. xx (1974), pp. 6–20.

46   For this background see Leo A. Despres, *Cultural Pluralism and Nationalist Politics in British Guiana* (New York: Rand McNally, 1967); Raymond T. Smith, *British Guiana* (London: Oxford University Press, 1962).

47   *Ibid.*, p. 179.

48   *Ibid.*, p. 179.

49   Cf. Thomas J. Spinner, Jr., *A Political and Social History of Guyana, 1945–1983* (Boulder: Westview Press, 1984), p. 31.

50   Report of the *British Guiana Constitutional Commission*, London: 1954, Cmd. 9274.

51   Spinner, *A Political and Social History*, p. 44.

52   R.T. Smith, *British Guiana*, p. 171.

53   *Suspension of the Constitution in British Guiana* (London: 1953). Command 8980.

54   Spinner, *A Political and Social History*, p. 45.

55   Cited in Raymond T. Smith, *British Guiana*, p.176.

56   Later the AFL gave birth to another even more interventionist arm, the American Institute for Free Labour Development, directed by Serafino Romualdi. Specifically created to challenge communist control of Latin American labour unions, it would be deeply involved in Guyana. See Sidney Lens, 'American Labour Abroad: Lovestone Diplomacy', *The Nation*, 5 July, 1965, pp. 10ff.

57   Much later Cheddi Jagan would write that the events of the early 1950s were 'catastrophic for the whole West Indian labour movement . . .' (not the least of which was the development of 'a strong right wing within [Jamaica's PNP . . .'). The one lesson learned was that 'while trade unions must have an active political outlook and interest, they must, under our multiparty political system, jealously guard their independence.' (*Trade Unions and National Liberation* [Georgetown, 1977], p. 27). How he reconciled this with his plans for a Marxist-Leninist state is not revealed.

58   Despres, *Cultural Pluralism*, p. 204.

59   *Report of the British Guiana Constitutional Commission* (1954), *op. cit.*, p. 37.

60   Cf. 'Introduction' by Kit Nascimento and Reynold Borrows to Forbes Burnham, *A Destiny to Mould* (New York: Africana Publishing Corporation, 1970), p. xix.

CHAPTER 5

The CIA unleashed: Containing communism in Guatemala and Cuba

Anyone even remotely familiar with how intelligence agencies work will know that secrecy has two functions: a national security one certainly but also a clear political purpose. In the ebullient American democracy, with its activist, investigatory press, the effort of intelligence agencies is invariably to provide cover for the President. This is called creating opportunities for 'plausible denial': burying deep anything which might embarrass the President and the country. This was not always possible given the crusade-like atmosphere of 'anti-communism' and the nature of American intelligence recruitment.

Robin Winks describes the sense of elitist adventurism of the Office of Strategic Services. 'The OSS was like the university: put itching powder into [enemy] safes, parachute drop thousands of pornographic pamphlets into the grounds at Berchtesgaden, so that Hitler might be driven mad with sexual desire . . . invent exploding donkey turds. The OSS was an elite which also individualized, which rewarded unusual, even frankly peculiar thought and, on occasion, action.'[1] The point is, that such elitist adventurism did not end with the OSS, it carried over into its replacement, the CIA. And it went against the grain of developments in the western hemisphere which was a growing opposition to interventionism.

The expansionism of the US in the nineteenth century and its self-appointment as the moral policeman of the Caribbean in the first decades of the twentieth century has not gone without response. More than anything else, the nations of the western hemisphere had sought during the early part of the twentieth century to avoid unilateral interventions through provisions guaranteeing collective security.[2] In its broadest sense collective security means the assertion of collective rather than individual action to contain aggression. The decisions on how and when to proceed, since they must be collective decisions, are made within an international organization set up to that end. Despite its failure in Europe, the principle of collective security was institutionalized by the nations of the western hemisphere, so strong was their fear of intervention by major powers, both European and American. They sought to ensure the principle of sovereignty through an overarching provision against intervention.

Since the Inter-American Conference at Montevideo in 1933 there had been a push in that direction. The question of non-intervention was again taken up at the conference in Buenos Aires in 1936 and in Mexico City in 1945. The Act of Chapultepec adopted at the meeting in Mexico provided the basis of the Pact of Rio de Janeiro, and must be regarded as the true cornerstone of the idea of collective security and non-intervention in the hemisphere – designed at that point to counteract Axis threats to the Americas. The pact declared that 'every attack of a State against the integrity or the inviolability of the territory, or against the sovereignty or political independence of an American State, shall . . . be considered an act of aggression against the other States.'[3]

This Inter-American Treaty of Reciprocal Assistance (known as the Pact or Act of Rio de Janeiro) was signed at the Inter-American Conference for the Maintenance of Continental Peace and Security in Brazil in 1947. According to Article 9 of the Treaty, 'aggression' was interpreted as 'an armed attack by one State against the territory, the people, or the land, sea or air forces of another state.' One year after the Pact of Rio de Janeiro institutionalized the concept of hemispheric collective security, the related concept of national sovereignty was given full recognition in the Charter of the Organization of American States (OAS) signed in Bogotá in 1948. Article 15 of the Charter reads: 'No State or Group of States has the right to intervene directly, or indirectly, for any reasons whatever, in the internal or external affairs of any other State.' Article 17 was even more specific. 'The territory of a State is inviolable; it may not be the object, even temporarily, of military occupation or of other measures of force taken by another State, directly or indirectly, on any grounds whatever.'

The categorical language of Articles 15 and 17 states the principle of non-intervention. Article 6, however, established the machinery, and the very language of that Article illustrates how geopolitics, by defining what or who belongs ('continental') and who does not ('extra-continental'), set important parameters for action. Article 6 is clearly a search for stability: 'If the inviolability or the integrity of the territory, or the sovereignty or political independence of any American State should be affected by an aggression which is not an armed attack, or by an extra-continental or intra-continental conflict, or by any other fact or situation that might endanger the peace of America, the Organ of Consultation shall meet immediately in order to agree on the measures which must be taken.'

Under the provisions of the Rio treaty, the Organ of Consultation of the OAS would decide on the measures to be taken. How, why, and when it should do so is left fairly open-ended by the language 'any other fact or situation' that might endanger 'the peace of America.' Between 1948 and 1953 the OAS Council met as the formal Organ of Consultation ten times; nine of these had to do with events in the Caribbean and circum-Caribbean. These nine cases concerned the general state of tension, intrigue, and enmity between the liberal-democratic forces in the Caribbean (led by José Figueres of Costa Rica, Juan José Arévalo of Guatemala and Carlos Prio Socarrás of Cuba) and the dictatorial regimes in Nicaragua and Santo Domingo. The tenth dealt with the dispute between Peru and Colombia over the exile rights of Peruvian leader Raúl Haya de la Torre. Law, and especially international law, is invariably a matter of interpretation. Its implementation is a matter of political will and physical capability.

The machinery for collective security seemed to work rather well when the disputes were not only intracontinental but, indeed, intra-Latin American/Caribbean. In none of the ten cases adjudicated during these years were US perceptions of its vital interests involved. It is fair to say, therefore, that the basic principles of collective security and non-intervention and the machinery so painstakingly assembled to enforce them had not really been put to the test by 1953. British Guiana, being still a colony, was not covered by this machinery. Since sovereign rights rested in Britain, the US did not violate them when it applauded the suspension of the Guianese constitution in 1953. The same cannot be said for the intervention in Guatemala only one year later.

In 1954, Guatemala, independent since 1824, was in its ninth year of democracy. The 13-year dictatorship of Jorge Ubico (1931–44) had been shorter than that of Manuel Estrada Cabrera (1896–1920) but equally retrograde and repressive. In the words of a journalist who travelled the whole region, Guatemala under Ubico was 'a vast game of the tin soldiers at which the Great Man amused himself.'[4]

Although both Ubico and important members of his cabinet sympathized with Fascist and Falangist causes, they were also very much in favour of expanding the privileges of one of the most notorious American-owned monopolies in Latin America, the United Fruit Company. The Company started operations in Guatemala in 1904, and in 1913 in Honduras. By the time Ubico was overthrown, the United Fruit's investments in Guatemala were valued at $60 million. The Company had more than 40,000 workers on its banana plantations, owned Guatemala's only railroad, administered its only Atlantic port and, as if to ensure total monopoly, it owned the country's telephone and telegraph companies.[5]

Through sheer size, and its influence with the US embassy, the United Fruit was like the gorilla who sat wherever it wished. It was this presence and preponderance that motivated a group of professional Guatemalans to overthrow Ubico and launch the 'revolution of 1944'. The ideology was very similar to that of Figueres' Centro in Costa Rica, a moderate form of social democracy.

Despite the intention to curtail the power of the monolith, the first democratically elected president in the nation's history, Juan José Arévalo, essentially left the United Fruit's lands alone. Ubico had confiscated much of the German-owned lands, thereby relieving pressure on the more desirable 'coffee highlands', while Arévalo observed that: 'In Guatemala, there is no agrarian problem.' The problems were psychological and political 'and it was to the solution of those problems – rather than the confiscation of land – that he would work.'[6] Unfortunately, the United Fruit was not ready to accept even the most modest changes: to have its workers unionized, to cede an inch on its monopolies or, in general, to come to terms with the 'new' Guatemala the 'revolution' of 1944 had promised.

The government of Colonel Jacobo Arbenz, democratically elected in 1951, had no intention of dealing with the United Fruit so benignly. It began challenging the Company's multifaceted monopolies with several major national projects. The highway to the Atlantic would destroy the Company's railroad monopoly; its port and dock projects, the Company's port monopoly; its promise to acquire ships, the Company's White Fleet; its project to construct hydroelectric plants, the Company's electrical monopoly. Finally, the government began to expropriate Company lands lying fallow.

Arbenz faced three formidable obstacles in carrying out his development plans. The first was capital. In 1953, Arbenz complained to the US Ambassador that the government had a budget of $70 million but collected only $150,000 in taxes. Clearly the Company was not providing Guatemala with the wherewithal to break the Company's monopolies. The second obstacle was that the influence of Guatemala in Washington paled in comparison to that of the Company. As Max Gordon noted, the antagonism in Washington was reinforced by a foreign policy staff, several of whose key members were or had been personally in the legal, financial, or political orbit of the United Fruit Company.[7] These included – through indirect contacts – Secretary of State John Foster Dulles, Assistant Secretary of State John M. Cabot, and Robert Cutler, presidential assistant for national security affairs.

This fact led numerous students of Guatemala to conclude that US actions in that country were basically driven by a desire to have the United Fruit Company's property restored; that the fear of communism was exaggerated, and was a virtual smoke screen for a business-rescuing operation.[8] Such an interpretation ignored the geopolitical realities of the Caribbean.

This geopolitical reality was the third and most intractable problem facing Arbenz. The 1954 view of a State Department official who had served in the CIA during 1953–4 comes closer to explaining the perceptions which were driving Washington: 'If the Guatemalans paid the United Fruit Co.'s full $16,000,000 claim tomorrow and decorated every last United Fruit official with the order of the Quetzal, we wouldn't be one whit less concerned with the danger of communism in Guatemala . . . [because] the strategy and tactics of the [Guatemalan] communists were clearly dictated by the Kremlin.'[9] The fact is that the national mood in the US had changed dramatically in a matter of years. While José Figueres in Costa Rica, after his victory in 1948, could put 'the squeeze' on the United Fruit with minor US protest, by 1954 Washington's 'geopolitical code' had changed. They had already acted to thwart the penetration of the PROFINTERN-allied labour unions in British Guiana and the Caribbean; they were certainly not about to be any more relaxed about Guatemala.

This was especially so since the President himself had candidly admitted to the US Ambassador that communists controlled the country's only labour federation, the National Agrarian Department, the Guatemalan Institute of Social Security, the directorate general of Radio Broadcasting, and the government financially supported the communist newspaper, *Tribuna Popular*. Arbenz even admitted to having a close friendship with the head of the Guatemalan Communist Party.[10] All the people, argued Arbenz, were loyal Guatemalans working for their country, not Moscow. It all seemed too disingenuous to the US Ambassador, John Peurifoy. He had been US Ambassador in Greece during 1950–3, the years of the Truman administration's battle to contain a communist take-over. He was hardly sympathetic or convinced by Arbenz' extraordinary openness and candour. 'I came away', he wrote to the State Department, 'definitely convinced that if the President is not a communist he will certainly do until one comes along, and that normal approaches will not work in Guatemala. I am now assessing the situation in this light and expect to submit recommendations in a few days.' What those recommendations were is evident in the statement made in 1963 by Senator Thurston Morton who recalled the following conversation he had with President Eisenhower:

> When the plans were laid to overthrow the communist government of Guatemala . . . the President said, 'Are you sure this is going to succeed?' – he was reassured it would, and said: 'I'm prepared to take any steps that are necessary to see that it succeeds. For if it succeeds it's the people of Guatemala throwing off the yoke of communism. If it fails, the Flag of the US has failed.'[11]

It is, of course, important to set the historical record straight on the actual degree of communist control in Guatemala at the time. The most recent literature dispels the notion that Arbenz was in any fashion either a communist or a captive of the communists. Neither do the reforms he proposed appear, in hindsight, to be that radical.[12]

Equally evident was the fact that the USSR played no major *overt* role in the Guatemalan process. Ronald Schneider points out two reasons for this Soviet caution: the internal struggle in the USSR following the death of Stalin in 1953, but even more importantly: 'the Soviet leadership was not inclined towards a major adventure so close to its principal Cold War adversary.'[13] There was no doubt a certain naivety about Arbenz and his generation.

As Robert Alexander explains, the 1944 revolutionaries came to power 'when everything seemed to be sweetness and light' between the democrats of the great western powers and the communists inside and outside the Soviet Union. 'The Guatemalan revolutionary leaders', Alexander concluded, 'never got over this wartime honeymoon.'[14] On what grounds should one logically expect perceptions of the Cold War which existed in Washington to be shared with equal intensity everywhere? The problem of 'quantifying' a process driven by both nationalism and strategic ideological goals is explained by Cole Blasier who points to the critical role of such strategically located groups. 'President Arbenz', says Blasier, 'found communist support useful and, as he grew weaker, he needed that support even more'. 'Additionally', said Blasier, 'all the . . . evidence left no doubt that Guatemalan communists had made substantial political gains in half a dozen years. They dominated the Guatemalan labour movement and had relatively free access to and influence with the President.' 'Influence is one thing; control is another', he concludes. 'It would be difficult to determine by quantitative methods whether the communists "controlled" or "dominated" the Guatemalan government.'[15]

Be all this as it may, the fact is that in the atmosphere of the Cold War, it was not necessary to cite specifics in order to generate perceptions of a threat. It bears repeating that policy is based on perceptions. As Schlesinger and Kinzer point out, this was a war fought mainly through the mass media. *Life, Time, Newsweek, Saturday Evening Post* and *New York Times Sunday Magazine* all ran stories about the 'communist penetration' of Guatemala. *The New York Times* editorialized that the US should make 'clear with finality' that all forms of communist activity are unacceptable in the western hemisphere. On 21 February, 1954 the *New York Times* asserted that 'the communists were about ready to assume outright control' of Guatemala. Earlier, (6 November, 1953) the *New York Times* correspondent Sydney Gruson had been expelled from Guatemala for writing that Arbenz was a captive of the communists in his government. In short, virtually every major US journal and magazine was calling for action in Guatemala. According to Schlesinger and Kinzer, a Clay Felker's story in *Life Magazine* on 5 July, 1954, summed up the prevailing mood among US journalists. Felker maintained that 'if the Arbenz forces are successful, the Kremlin will gain a *de facto* foothold in the western hemisphere.'[16]

Even the academic community seemed to feel that the communist menace in Guatemala had been real, not overstated. J.D. Martz[17] and Ronald M. Schneider,[18] for instance, wrote early accounts of this communist penetration. Even as cautious a scholar as Kalman H. Silvert documented communist moves and took the 'communist issue' seriously.'[19] Victor Alba, spokesman for the 'democratic left', claims that by 1952 'there were no independent unions' left in Guatemala and that any opposition to the communist controlled General Confederation of Guatemalan Workers (CGTG) 'were persecuted, beaten or exiled.'[20] Alba maintains that it was the communist's purpose not to take over Guatemala but rather to turn Guatemalan nationalism into a pro-Soviet, anti-American force.[21]

Is it any surprise, therefore, that the State Department was no less adamant about the issue? After all, they pointed out, there was Arbenz's Marxist Salvadorian wife and her Chilean advisers, only part of a whole community of foreign Marxists who made Guatemala their stamping ground; there was the labour link to Mexico's Vicente Lombardo Toledano, President of the Confederation of Latin American Labor (CTAL) since 1939, and since 1945, Vice-President of the Moscow-linked world Confederation of Trade Unions, already discussed.

This was the geopolitical reality, driven as it was by Cold War perceptions. However, what of the legality of the US actions? It was not that Guatemala had not been calling attention to the impending invasion from Honduras by the CIA-organized army of Colonel Castillo Armas. When the Tenth Inter-American Conference of the Organization of American States meeting in Caracas on 5 March, 1954 passed a resolution saying that 'the intervention of international communism' in any hemispheric republic was a threat to all, Guatemala's foreign minister noted that it was a blatant 'pretext for intervening in our internal affairs . . . .'[22] He should have taken a cue from US Secretary of State John Foster Dulles' claim at the same Conference that 'the threat which stems from international communism is a repetition in this century of precisely the kind of danger against which President Monroe had made his famous declaration 130 years ago.'[23]

In contrast to preceding cases where the Organ of Consultation of the OAS had acted promptly to resolve disputes between Latin American states, in 1954 they developed lead feet. The collective security instruments and mechanisms set up by the Organization of American States in 1948 seemed paralyzed as Guatemala pleaded its case. By the time they met the Arbenz government was in full flight. At that moment, US Secretary of State John Foster Dulles went on radio and television to inform the American public that: 'This intrusion of Soviet despotism in Guatemala was, of course, a direct challenge to our Monroe Doctrine, the first and most fundamental of our foreign policies . . . For 131 years that policy has well served the peace and security of the hemisphere. It serves us well today.'[24]

This stark restatement of the US right to unilateral action set the stage for an even more blatant use of covert action in the Caribbean: the invasion of Cuba in 1961. And, it was not only official Washington which was laying a 'bridge of perceptions' between Guatemala and Cuba. Academics did their part. This linking of Guatemala in 1954 and the later events in 1961 is evident in Lloyd Mecham. To him Guatemala was 'a case study of communist take-over' and as such was 'a significant preview of what occurred later in Cuba.' But Mecham's widely used textbook went beyond description and analysis to establish a 'principle': the right of US unilateral action:

> If we accept the Latin American argument that the Caracas declaration imposed on them [the Latin Americans] no binding obligation with respect to collective intervention, it likewise imposed no restraint on unilateral action by the US. The Monroe Doctrine still belonged to the US for ultimate resort in self-defence.[25]

An even more extreme position was that of the Thomases. The doctrine of non-intervention, according to the Thomases, applies only to 'democratic' nations. Democracy to them is not a set of institutions but rather a set of goals relating to human values – values which have as their base Christian doctrine. Only democratic nations in these terms are covered by international law.[26]

Accompanying the acceptance of unilateralism was the propensity for subterfuge. Note the thinking in a popular college text in international affairs, *The Instruments of American Foreign Policy*, in which Yale University's H. Bradford Westerfield discusses the Guatemalan case in a section tellingly called 'Overt and Covert Intervention in the Internal Politics of Foreign Lands.' Although he admits that 'the invasion from Honduran territory was a patent violation of international law . . .'[27] Westerfield proves to be quite a 'realist' when he contends that:

> In the specific case of Guatemala, assuming that the overthrow of Arbenz was essential to American interests because he would not rid himself of the communist penetration of his Administration, a significant question would be whether a *coup d'état* could have been engineered without requiring Americans to give assistance to a flagrant invasion from foreign soil . . . It is possible that more patient and skilful political intrigue and quiet diplomatic intervention, perhaps on a multilateral basis, could have sufficed to accomplish Arbenz' removal.

Westerfield answers his own question by stating that through a *coup*: 'The US might not afterwards have had available to it in the presidency as promising a leader as Castillo Armas seemed to be . . . Thus American policymakers' approach to the problem can be commended as appropriate.' So the US approached the critical decade of the 1960s as they had the 1950s, with a general theory of international politics which saw the world in terms of the balance of power. No one should have miscued the implications of this, for two principles were central to events in the Caribbean at this time. First, there was the concept of self-determination. Its value was deflated. The influential Dean Acheson put this in a US perspective. 'The vocabulary of morals and ethics', he noted, 'is inadequate to discuss or test foreign policies of states.' In that vocabulary one of the most 'delusive' of these moral maxims, according to Acheson, 'is the so-called principle of self-determination . . . [it has] a doubtful moral history.' In short, the criteria guiding foreign policy should be, in Acheson's words 'hard-headed in the extreme including the matter of the use of force.'[28] 'International communism', Dulles declared in 1957, 'is on the prowl to capture those nations whose leaders feel that newly-acquired sovereign rights have to be displayed by flouting other independent nations. That kind of sovereignty is suicidal sovereignty.'[29]

The second principle, spheres of influence, emerged restated and reinforced. George Ball – who had already warned the reader not to look in his book for 'noble sounding' sentiments such as 'world peace through world law' – maintained that the US national interests had to be reassessed in terms which were 'damnably difficult, requiring tough mindedness and the avoidance of moralistic mush.'[30] That reassessment should be done in terms of the functioning of the 'sphere of influence' principle as it operates between the US and the USSR. 'Thus wherever one side has had the overwhelming interest and military advantage, it has acted with strength and confidence . . . because both great powers have been reasonably sure that these actions would not challenge the other's most vital interests and thus trigger a nuclear response.'[31]

As Blanche Wiesen Cook notes, Eisenhower's use of the modern doctrine of counter-insurgency found swift and easy success, first in Guatemala and then against Prime Minister Mossadegh in Iran.[32] If one adds the case of British Guiana and the victory in the trade union struggle in the Caribbean, one understands why the theory was believed to have been fully vindicated. This explains why the failure in Cuba in 1961, came as such a shock. In fact, it represented a watershed. It is ironic, therefore, that the best summary of the forces operating in the Caribbean during this period was given by President Dwight Eisenhower in a letter to Senator Hubert Humphrey in which he acknowledged the role of nationalism in the world:

> It is my personal conviction that almost any one of the new-born states of the world would far rather embrace communism or any other form of dictatorship than to acknowledge the political domination of another government even though that brought to each citizen a far higher standard of living.[33]

Had Eisenhower acted on this undoubtedly accurate understanding of the dynamics of nationalism, he would not have acted with such a heavy hand in Cuba. If there is one interpretation which has received wide support in Cuban scholarship it is the theory of 'revolutionary continuity'. It certainly is not limited to the official Cuban interpretation that 1933 was a step toward 1959, the final culmination of a 'hundred year' revolutionary process. It is maintained by a substantial number of contemporary students of the Cuban revolution.

To Gellman, the revolution of 1933 set fires in Cuba which 'grew and spread during Batista's first era (1934–44), and from its live coals burst the flame of the Revolution of 1959.'[34] A somewhat modified version of this theory is sustained by Bonachea and Valdés who argue that in Cuba 'there always existed' a revolutionary tradition which sought guidance from José Martí. This tradition was nationalist and anti-imperialist, devoid of systematic ideology and above all, action oriented.[35] Even authors such as Bonachea and San Martín, who place Fidel Castro in a 'new generation of Cubans . . . the political generation of 1950', maintain that their ideological tenets 'seemed to have departed little from the ideals of the frustrated revolution of 1933 . . . .'[36]

Jorge Domínguez synthesizes this interpretation of the 1933 'revolution betrayed' by noting its place in revolutionary ideology. It was used throughout the 1940s and 'would become a far more powerful ideology of consolidation after 1959, when the need to avoid another 1933–34 would be crucial.'[37]

Perhaps it was too much to expect that in the context of the Cold War, great sensibilities about historical resentments and nationalist instincts would be entertained. Nor was there much interest in understanding the distinctly national nature of many Latin American communist parties. Even those, such as that of Cuba, which paid obsequious homage to Stalin and Moscow, had long coexisted in the political system precisely because they shared much of the political culture of the system. In Cuba that meant that the communists were the great opportunists, they were, says Domínguez: 'willing to shift and unite to anybody . . . .'[38] The Communist Party had done such manoeuvering so often that it was eventually weakened and discredited, 'spurned by everyone.'[39] Including, according to the most respectable scholarship, by Fidel Castro himself, at least until mid-1961.

It was the collective hysteria about communism in the Caribbean which led the US to help create the *Buró de Represión de las Actividades Comunistas* (*BRAC*) in 1954. Hugh Thomas calls it 'practically a branch of the CIA'[40] and relates US Ambassador Arthur Gardner bragging that he was 'the father of BRAC.'[41] With US Secretary of State John Foster Dulles, and CIA Director, Allen Dulles, putting on pressure, Cuban dictator Fulgencio

Batista passed an anti-communist decree in 1954. As Thomas interprets it, this was Batista's 'token of solidarity' with a US government about to overthrow the Arbenz regime in Guatemala.[42]

Not only was Batista being coerced into doing exactly the opposite of what he had done since 1940, accepting communist support, the communists were now being forced underground. They went from what Domínguez calls 'a known quantity, in votes, orientation, and willingness to bargain to preserve their access to power',[43] to being completely undecipherable to US intelligence.

Two journalists who have diligently reconstructed what they call 'An Embassy Divided' tell of an intelligence community, in Havana and in Washington, totally unable to agree on whether Fidel Castro, Raúl or even Ché Guevara were communists.[44] But, if the Americans were uncertain of Castro's ideological *bona fides* and ultimate intentions, so were the majority of Cubans. Sugar mill owners, bankers, industrialists, cattlemen, all financed the rebellion with millions of dollars in contributions. As Domínguez points out, given the unpopularity and corruption of the Batista regime, supporting Castro seemed a rational act.[45] Even the US understood that Batista was doomed and, exercising its enormous influence, contributed to the speed with which Batista fell.

The fall of Batista, however, was not the same thing as the arrival of the revolution. That revolution emerged in the course of early to mid-1959 and while there is a growing inclination to believe that Castro intended to turn toward Marxism-Leninism all along[46] there is general agreement on two things. First, Castro's single-minded determination to gain power and keep that power, and secondly his visceral dislike of the US. The two were linked in that Castro saw what he always considered to be American imperialism as the greatest threat to his plans. In fact, there is increasing evidence that he actively sought a confrontation with the US, both out of hubris and because he pragmatically thought this would serve his cause by triggering the always latent anti-Americanism of Cubans.[47] Like many others of his generation, he remembered 1933–34 well. 'He was', says Thomas, 'obsessed with the recollection of Summer Welles'. This affected his dealings with the well-disposed new US Ambassador, Philip Bonsal. He spoke of Bonsal as if he were Welles and expressed shock that any 'Cuban of honour' would treat Bonsal 'as a proconsul.'[48]

But if Castro showed hubris, so did many a US official. It often came down to a clash of egos. In April, the American Society of Newspaper Editors invited Fidel Castro to address them in Washington. Eisenhower, who was strongly impacted by the recent disastrous visit of his Vice-President Richard Nixon to Latin America, agreed with Nixon that the threat of communism in Latin America was greater than ever. He suspected Castro of being a communist and refused to meet him. He was 'more than irritated' with the editors' invitation 'and of Castro's acceptance.'[49] Castro refused to ask for assistance, the US offered none. Thomas is convinced that had it been offered it might have been accepted but: 'each side, proud and suspicious held back.'[50]

Be that as it may, it was a fateful visit because it was after his private meeting with Castro that Nixon – convinced Castro was either a communist or 'under communist discipline' – decided that the US should 'act accordingly'.[51] What that should be was revealed during the fourth Nixon-Kennedy presidential debate. 'What have you done about communism in Cuba?' asked Kennedy. Nixon, not able to reveal actual plans responded hypothetically. 'What can we do? We can do what we did with Guatemala [where] there was a communist dictator.'

What was being initiated is what President John F. Kennedy's Press Secretary at the time, Pierre Salinger, called 'the least covert military operation in history.'[52] It also has to be one of the most sloppily conceptualized policies ever, to be explained no doubt by the ease with which previous interventions had been carried out. Communism was the general nemesis accompanied by hubris, in the words of Neustadt and May: 'The classic case of presumptions unexamined'.[53] President Eisenhower, who as we saw earlier had shown great perspicacity about the forces of nationalism, now threw that caution to the wind. He would later write that his trip to Latin America (to make up for the damage of Nixon's) rekindled his understanding of historical Latin American resentment at US bullying and that he would uphold Franklin Delano Roosevelt's 'traditional policy of non-intervention'. In the very same paragraph, however, Eisenhower admits that less than two weeks after this trip, he ordered the CIA to begin training Cuban exiles in Guatemala.[54] This was ten months before the US would sever relations with Cuba.

The 1961 attempt to overthrow the Fidel Castro government through exiles goes by the name of the area where they landed: Playa Girón, known to historians as the Bay of Pigs, in the south central coast of Cuba. History now records it as 'the perfect failure' of US intelligence, military and political intervention. So crushing and humiliating was the defeat for the country and its young, recently inaugurated President, John F. Kennedy, that it is legitimately seen as a watershed incident. The era of the easy interventions ended in the Zapata swamps of southern Cuba.

There is general agreement in the serious literature on this incident that the Bay of Pigs revealed the nature of US official decision-making and the perceptions which underwrote that process up to 1961. Especially important were the historical analogies which the decision-makers got.[55] The major perception was that the Caribbean was an American 'can do' area. They had won the battles of the trade union affiliations after World War II, given vital support to British anti-Jagan policies in British Guiana in 1953, and, a year later helped bring down Arbenz in Guatemala. It was the Guatemalan case in particular which, in the words of an eyewitness, 'stirred dangerous longings for adventure in CIA breasts.'[56] In the words of Trumbull Higgins, by 1961 Guatemala was widely perceived as 'the successful practice run' for the Cuban intervention.[57] Images of a dapper US Ambassador to Guatemala, John Peurifoy – in military jump suit and 45 calibre colt prominent in evidence – must have been still vivid. He had personally taken charge of the 1954 operations. It would be wrong, however, to assume that Guatemala and the decade of 'easy' interventions affected only CIA 'operatives', the hands-on types; it had a pervasive influence on American foreign policy decision-makers in general.[58] What was operating is what Neustadt and May call classification according to analogical 'allure', a facile, opportunistic inclination to the obvious.[59] The point is, of course, that there was nothing in the history of US involvements in the Caribbean up to that point which had done anything to tarnish that allure.

Since it was generally agreed that something had to be done about Fidel Castro, when the outgoing Eisenhower administration presented President-elect John F. Kennedy the plans for an invasion by Cuban exiles, the arguments were about the details, not the principle of the matter. And they must both have gained additional comfort from the nature of these details. They reinforced the facile analogy between 1954 and 1961. First, there was a great continuity in the personnel used, starting with Allan Dulles, Director of the CIA – one of the few high officials whom Kennedy took over from the Eisenhower administration – but not ending there. The existing chief CIA experts on Latin American communism, a German refugee called Jerry Droller who knew no Spanish, was given the code name 'Frank Bender' and put in overall command. The major field operatives, Richard Bissell, Tracey Barnes and E. Howard Hunt, were all Guatemala veterans who also traced their intelligence careers back to the OSS of World War II. Not surprisingly in 1961, they were recruited to do exactly the same tasks they had performed in 1954. 'My job', wrote E. Howard Hunt, 'would be essentially the same as the one I had on that prior operation – Chief of Political Action . . .'[60] This was no low-level political job, it was, rather, nothing less than to organize the Cuban exiles 'into a broadly representative government-in-exile' that would form 'the new government in Cuba'. Shades of Guatemala! It appeared to be irrelevant that Fidel Castro was no Arbenz, that the old Cuban army, as distinct from the Guatemalan, had been destroyed and replaced with perhaps 100,000 eager men under arms, in short, that Cuba in 1961 was quite a different socio-political entity from the Guatemala of 1954. 'The nucleus of the project', says CIA operative Hunt, 'was already in being – a cadre of officers I had worked with against Arbenz.'[61]

The fact that in 1954 the rebel camps were across the border in

Honduras, while in 1961 they were across the sea in Guatemala and Nicaragua, were differences which were given little or no thought. In part this was due to arrogance but also because ignorance of geography was rampant. After all, both Guatemala and Cuba were 'in the Caribbean'.

Higgins relates that President Kennedy was 'startled' when told that Cuba was 800 miles long.[62] Yet geographical knowledge was central to the critical decision to change the landing site from the town of Trinidad, which had easy access to the Escambray Mountains, to the Bay of Pigs. The change was made with virtually no geographical knowledge. 'I don't think we fully realized', Kennedy adviser Arthur Schlesinger later acknowledged, 'that the Escambray Mountains lay 80 miles from the Bay of Pigs across a hopeless tangle of swamps and jungle.' In the words of one student, he and the others attending the White House meetings 'simply overlooked the geography of Cuba.'[63]

Other than the persistence of the alluring analogy, ignorance of geography and the carry-over of CIA personnel, what other significant body of information and knowledge about Cuba was brought into play? Apparently not much of any kind. Szulc and Meyer describe an Eisenhower administration resting on its Guatemalan laurels, and a Secretary of State who was 'frankly bored with Latin America.'[64] Additional evidence of this fatal indifference is found in the minimal amount of time dedicated to the project. 'The Bay of Pigs debacle occurred in part', say Neustadt and May, 'because President John F. Kennedy and his key advisers could never give it sustained attention for more than forty-five minutes at a time.'[65] Given such indifference and utter disregard of facts and context was it any surprise that CIA Director Allan Dulles could confess at the time that he had much greater confidence in the plans for the forthcoming Cuban invasion than he ever had before the Guatemalan one and that the Joint Chiefs of Staff should have concurred?

So sanguine was the mood in Washington that the record shows only one adviser openly dissenting from the operation: Senator J. William Fulbright. Urging a policy of containment, not invasion, Fulbright ended his objection to the plan with the celebrated phrase: 'The Castro regime is a thorn in the flesh, but it is not a dagger in the heart.' Fulbright's missive, Arthur Schlesinger would later admit, was 'a brilliant memorandum'. Kennedy, however, ignored it, because, says Schlesinger, he was in a 'militant' mood.[66]

The story of the failure of the operation which was 'too big to be a raid and too small to be an invasion' is now part of US Cuban and Caribbean history. Of the 1500 Cubans who managed to land, 80 were killed and the rest taken prisoner. Everything indicates they fought valiantly but with their airplanes shot down, and the ships carrying both munitions and communications gear sunk it was only a matter of time. There was no internal uprising. In fact, the anti-Castro underground had been kept in the dark; the diversionary landings planned for Pinar del Rio and Oriente never came off. Contrary to CIA predictions, Castro's militia fought well despite absorbing heavy casualties in the early fighting. What two journalists call 'the strangest tragedy of errors' in US history was over in 72 hours.

If, as is widely believed, the idea was for the Cubans merely to establish a bridgehead, set up the provisional government and have it call in US military intervention, it was totally unrealistic planning. An investigation by Lyman Kirkpatrick, Jr. of the CIA concluded that it would have taken '10,000 to 15,000 men with full and open American support, to seize the beachhead long enough to establish the rebel government.[67] This was not the kind of effort the US was ready to make in the Caribbean, in part because they had never had to do so before. Certainly World War II had led the Americans to understand the vulnerabilities of an enemy attack in the Caribbean. But Cuba was not seen in those terms, it was seen in terms more akin to being a fifth column in an American sphere of influence. It was perceived as communist 'infiltration', not populist, collective and nationwide nationalism. The point being, of course, that even if the former assumption were true – as it probably was – proper geopolitical planning should never have overlooked the possibility of the latter. But understanding nationalism must begin with respecting it and those who shape it. The US had not yet learned how to respect and trust Caribbean peoples. 'How can we have an alliance', said Costa Rica's José Figueres to Schlesinger after the fiasco, 'if even our friends will not believe that we can be trusted with secrets?'[68]

According to Irving L. Janis, the Bay of Pigs fiasco was a consequence of a particular 'chumminess' among men who felt comfortable with each other. This led to what he calls 'groupthink' which engenders an illusion of invulnerability based on two major presumptions: (1) 'We are a strong group of good guys who will win in the end', and (2) 'our opponents are stupid, weak, bad guys.'[69] Both presumptions were ethnocentric in nature. If not quite the arrogant Anglo-Saxon racism which accompanied the early US expansionism, it was at least a close approximation. This ethnocentrism was expressed in the way the Cuban enemy was misjudged and underestimated. The parallels with the indifference of coastal American cities during the early phases of World War II submarine warfare are evident. Higgins reveals that there were at least 200 Castro agents operating out of Miami,[70] and certainly on 4 January, 1961 the Cuban delegate to the United Nations, Raúl Roa, delivered a detailed – and, as it turned out, accurate – denunciation of CIA activities.[71] Cuban intelligence was far superior to that of the CIA.

If ethnocentrism was limited to the Cuban enemy, decision-making might have proceeded differently. Alas, it extended to America's Cuban allies. They were treated with utter disdain. As CIA operative Howard Hunt put it: 'Cuban [exile] plans, in any case, were not the ones that would be used on I-Day, but plans that were being developed by CIA and the Pentagon. . . . Cuban military planning, therefore, was a harmless exercise. . . . To paraphrase a homily: this was too important to be left to Cuban generals.'[72] The CIA excluded the groups with contacts in Cuba and 'isolated' the very Cuban Revolutionary Council created to govern a post-Castro Cuba. These gentlemen were put in 'friendly custody' in Opa-Locka, Florida where they were taken by surprise at the news of the exile landing. History repeated itself: the 1895 Cuban War of Liberation was brought to a conclusion by an American intervention which then locked the Cubans out of any role in the termination negotiations. As Louis Pérez notes, the revolutionary provisional government which had led the fighting for independence after 1895 was 'unrecognized by the US, ignored by the expatriate leadership, disregarded by the army command . . . .' They tried but failed to assert their constitutional authority. Similarly, the 1961 invaders were a valiant but forlorn bunch. As Johnson notes, the Cuban members and the Brigade responded to that disdain with blind trust. 'Virtually all the Cubans involved, believed much in the Americans – or wanted so desperately to believe – that they never questioned what was happening or expressed doubts about the plans.'[73]

The mood in the White House was summed up by the then US Ambassador to the United Nations, Adlai Stevenson, who called the fiasco the 'most humiliating experience' in all his years in government. US allies questioned the wisdom of the US, neutrals became more receptive to the Kremlin and Castro was stronger than ever. Castro was successful in getting Khrushchev to listen to his plans to install missiles. Despite all this, Arthur Schlesinger, Jr. returned from a February 1960 journey through Latin America convinced that Castro had few friends among the democratic leaders of the western hemisphere.[74] Cuban supported guerrillas were fighting in Venezuela, Colombia and elsewhere in Central America. In fact, both Rómulo Betancourt of Venezuela and Alberto Lleras Camargo of Colombia were soon to sever relations with Cuba. Social democrats like Raúl Haya de la Torre of Peru, José Figueres of Costa Rica and Juan Bosch of the Dominican Republic were by mid-1961 completely estranged if not outright enemies.[75]

Given this generalized opposition to the path Castro was taking so publicly towards Marxism-Leninism, why was there not more vocal support for the US anti-Castro position? In 1960 Arthur Schlesinger, Jr. discovered part of the answer by talking with Bolivia's Victor Paz Estensoro. Estensoro, who had led the Bolivian revolution in 1952, was quick to suggest that 'Castro must be eliminated' but when asked how, 'he trailed off into vagueness.' Schlesinger was perceptive about Paz Estensoro's attitude; it

was composed of equal parts of: (1) a strong fear of Castro, (2) a 'fervent hope that the US would rid the hemisphere of him' and, (3) a profound disinclination to identify himself publicly, except in the most marginal way, with anti-Castro action.[76]

A close aide and friend describes President Kennedy as irritated and disappointed by those Latin American governments which had urged him to intervention against Castro because they feared the Cuban leader, and then denounced the failed attempt also because they feared the backlash back home. 'President Kennedy recognized more clearly than ever', says Sorensen, 'that America's massive military superiority did not guarantee her success, much less respect, around the world.'[77]

That the largest of Latin American nations viewed the clash between the US and Cuba as a purely bilateral American-Cuban question rather than as a threat to the hemisphere, became evident when Mexico, Brazil and Argentina opposed the Colombian call for an Eighth Meeting of Consultation of the OAS in January, 1962. Colombia wanted to discuss Cuban behaviour. Even as the meeting was finally held in Punta del Este, Uruguay, Argentina, Bolivia, Brazil, Chile, Ecuador and Mexico refused to vote sanctions against Cuba. The US move to exclude Cuba from the Inter-American system was carried, however, by the bare two-thirds majority, a fact which involved submitting to the 'blackmail' vote of Haiti's François Duvalier's tyrannical government.[78]

Despite the quite generalized anti-communism of most Latin American countries, there was no unanimous or monolithic front against what Kennedy described as 'outside communist penetration'. Latin American neutrality stemmed from their traditional fear of US hegemony. The politics of geopolitical hegemony in a sphere of influence had created its own special burdens. One of these was that Cuba was perceived as an 'American problem'.

President Kennedy had warned right after the Bay of Pigs fiasco, that while the US had not used its own troops in Cuba, the record should show that 'our restraint is not inexhaustible'. Should it ever appear that the Inter-American doctrine of non-interference merely conceals or excuses a policy of inaction', said Kennedy, – if the nations of this hemisphere should fail to meet their commitments against outside communist penetration – 'then I want it clearly understood that this government will not hesitate in meeting its primary obligations, which are the security of our nation.'[79]

Kennedy, who had described Cuba and the Bay of Pigs fiasco as his 'heaviest political cross', was attempting to demonstrate that he could indeed act with resolution. He was much more willing now to accept the US military premise that interventions should go 'all out or get out.'[80] He also learned, however, to balance military threat with diplomacy and dialogue. 'Thank God the Bay of Pigs happened when it did', he told an aide, 'otherwise we'd be in Laos by now – and that would be a hundred times worse.'[81] Indeed, the record shows that it was. The Bay of Pigs, while teaching some lessons about decision-making, had in fact strengthened the US determination to contain communism through diplomacy preferably, through subterfuge if necessary, and militarily ultimately.

The Missile Crisis a year later would change many of the predispositions; it completed the process begun by the Bay of Pigs, bringing to an end the age of easy interventions in the Caribbean. The Kennedy administration had hardly recovered from the Bay of Pigs fiasco when they faced an even more grave crisis: Soviet missiles in Cuba. From the start there was the suspicion that Khrushchev was testing the new President's resolve and challenging him in his sphere of influence. This appears to be the most pervasive explanation: that Khrushchev put the missiles in Cuba, as Arthur Schlesinger, Jr. puts it: 'for Soviet reasons . . . a Supreme Soviet probe of American intentions.'[82] Not to act in Cuba would surely open the US to continued pressures elsewhere. This was also the conclusion of subsequent scholarship.

As Horelick and Rush put it: 'if deterrence of an attack on Cuba was the sole Soviet objective, . . . the plan backfired: the Soviet weapons provoked rather than deterred strong American action.'[83] They rejected the hypothesis that the Soviets intended the missiles for Cuban defence: ' . . . the size and character of the intended deployment', they maintained, 'indicate that it was meant to achieve some broader purpose.'[84]

The option, to somehow wean Fidel Castro away from the USSR through a secret deal, was quickly discarded.[85] The US wished to deal only with the USSR, since the missile sites were all under direct Soviet control. Even if they had not been, however, Kennedy did not wish to make the negotiations a three-way process, he did not want any Castro and Cuban participation in any negotiations. The crisis in the Caribbean was a Great Power confrontation, military and political. It was political because, as President Kennedy correctly appreciated, it involved questions of perceptions. The successful deployment of Soviet missiles in Cuba, Kennedy noted, 'would have politically changed the balance of power; it would have appeared to [change it] and appearances contribute to reality.'[86]

The eventual choice of policy – to 'quarantine' (i.e. blockade) Cuba – contained several desirable features: it was a middle course between doing nothing and an all-out attack, it put the ball in Khrushchev's court but under circumstances where the US had overwhelming military power. This was, in Alexander C. George's opinion, 'coercive diplomacy' at its best: avoiding bloodshed without appearing weak and indecisive.[87] Fundamentally, however, it was politically the most promising since it had the unanimous support of the OAS. This latter fact is generally regarded as critical to the outcome, it elated the Americans and staggered the Soviets. As a member of the ExCom, Theodore Sorensen, put it, Kennedy relied not on force and threats alone, but on 'a carefully balanced and precisely measured combination of defence, diplomacy and dialogue which "dazzled" America's allies.'[88]

The emplacement of missiles in Cuba was clearly the type of external threat the Monroe Doctrine was designed to confront. And yet, it was the only occasion when the Monroe Doctrine was explicitly excluded. 'The Monroe Doctrine', exploded Kennedy to an aide, 'What the hell is that?'[89] In other words, the Monroe Doctrine was for hemispheric use; the Missile Crisis was a global crisis which called for a different diplomacy. And yet, interestingly enough, the Kennedy-Khrushchev understanding meant a re-affirmation of straightforward sphere of influence thinking and contributed to the new era of US-Soviet *détente* which followed 1962. It came at a cost to the Cubans, however. It is indisputable that the peaceful termination of the crisis was achieved at the expense of the doctrine of absolute sovereignty in general and Cuban sovereignty in particular. Although Fidel Castro has given several mutually contradictory versions of why and on whose request the missiles were emplaced, the hypothesis advanced by Horelick and Rush, i.e. that the missiles in Cuba were part of a grand, global Soviet strategy – not to defend Cuba – appears the most plausible. They accept Fidel Castro's first major statement on the affair as being the closest to the truth: '[The Soviets] explained to us that in accepting them [the

Table 5.1: Chronology of CIA Involvements (1959–1973)

	1 9 5 9
December 11	[Allan] Dulles approves 'thorough consideration be given to the elimination of Fidel Castro.
	1 9 6 0
January 13	Special Group [of the National Security Council] considers Castro's overthrow.
April	President Eisenhower approves contingency plan for Dominican Republic – if situation deteriorates, US to take action to remove Trujillo when successor regime lined up.
August	Bissell [CIA Deputy Director for covert action], Edwards have discussion concerning use of underworld figures to aid in assassination of Castro.
August	NSC and Special Group discuss and Dulles orders 'removal' of Congo's Patrice Lumumba. Sometime after 8 November: Dulles and Bissell jointly brief President-elect Kennedy on details of planned invasion of Cuba.

1961

April 15–17	Bay of Pigs invasion fails.
November 9	President [Kennedy] tells Tad Szulc that he is under pressure from advisers to order Castro's assassination, but does not name advisers.
November	Operation 'Mongoose' created [a major new covert action program to overthrow Castro, headed by General Maxwell Taylor].

1962

January 18	Landsdale assigns 32 planning tasks against Castro regime.
October 22–28	Cuban Missile Crisis.
November	Operation 'Mongoose' ends.

1963

Early 1963	CIA Technical Services Division explores exploding seashell and contaminated diving suit schemes.
August 29	White House authorizes Saigon Station to support of anti-Diem coup.
November 22	President Kennedy assassinated. 'AM/LASH [code name for Cuban agent] given poison pen for assassinating Castro.

1964

March–May	Cashes of arms delivered to AM/LASH in Cuba.

1965

Early 1965	AM/LASH put in contact with leader of anti-Castro group and received weapon with silencer from him.

1970

September 15	President Nixon instructs CIA Director Helms to prevent [Chile's] Allende's accession to office. The CIA is to play direct role in organizing a military *coup d'etat*.
October 22	Three submachine guns delivered to Chilean Army officer by US Military Attaché.

1972

Helms issues directive against assassinations.

1973

Colby issues directive against assassinations.

Source: United States Senate, *Alleged Assassination Plots Involving Foreign Leaders*. An Interim Report of the Select Committee to Study Governmental Operations with Respect to Intelligence Activities (Published by W. W. Norton, Co., 1976) pp. 291–5.

missiles] we would be reinforcing the socialist camp the world over, and because we have received important aid from the socialist camp we estimated that we could not decline.'[90]

Cuba had invariably described its relationships with the Soviets in terms of the USSR's 'principled support of peace, self-determination of peoples and the independence and sovereignty of all countries . . .'[91] The unilateral Soviet decision to remove the missiles left very sore feelings and a damaged relationship.

During the decades which followed the Bay of Pigs and Missile Crisis, many new independent nations became part of the Caribbean family. The US faced a more complex environment in which to exercise the diplomatic, the covert or the military option. History records that they exercised all three.

Notes

1   Robin Winks, *Cloak and Gown*, p. 24.
2   Cf. Henry Myron Blackmer II, *US Policy and the Inter-American Peace System, 1889–1952* (Geneva: Institute of International Studies, Thesis No. 89, 1952).
3   For the text of the Treaty see O.C. Stoetzer, *The Organization of American States* (New York: Frederick A. Praeger, 1965).
4   William Krehm, *Democracies and Tyrannies in the Caribbean* (Westport, Connecticut: Lawrence Hill, 1984), p. 38. Krehm reported for *Time Magazine*; this book first appeared in Spanish in 1948.
5   Thomas McCann, *An American Company: The Tragedy of United Fruit* (New York: Crown, 1976), p. 13.
6   Cited in Stephen Schlesinger and Stephen Kinzer, *Bitter Fruit: The Untold Story of the American Coup in Guatemala* (New York: Anchor Books, 1983), p. 41.
7   Max Gordon, 'A Case History of US Subversion: Guatemala, 1954', *Science and Society*, Vol. XXXV (Summer, 1971).
8   Cf. Max Gordon, 'A Case History of US Subversion' Schlesinger and Kinzer; *Bitter Fruit: The Untold Story of the American Coup in Guatemala*.
9   Cited in Thomas W. Palmer, Jr., *Search for a Latin American Policy* (Gainesville: University of Florida Press, 1957), pp. 137 and 146.
10   Cf. 'Ambassador John Peurifoy: Impressions of Arbenz', Guatemala City, 17 December, 1953' (Secret), reprinted in Robert S. Leiken and Barry Rubin (eds), *The Central American Crisis Reader* (New York: Summit Books, 1987), pp. 106–8.
11   *Washington Post*, 18 February, 1963, p. 1. CIA participation in the overthrow of Arbenz is plainly described by the then Head of the CIA, Allan W. Dulles, in *The Craft of Intelligence* (Illinois: Harper & Row, 1963).
12   See especially the declassified documents revealed by Blanche Wiesen Cook, *The Declassified Eisenhower* (New York: Doubleday and Co. Inc., 1981), pp. 218–92. Richard H. Immerman, *The CIA in Guatemala: The Foreign Policy of Intervention* (Austin: The University of Texas Press, 1982) Schlesinger and Kinzer, *Bitter Fruit*.
13   Ronald Schneider, *Communism in Guatemala, 1944–1954* (New York: Praeger, 1959), p. 294.

14 Robert Alexander, *Communism in Latin America* (New Jersey: Rutgers University Press, 1957), p. 354.

15 Cole Blasier, *The Hovering Giant* (Pittsburgh: U. Pitt Press, 1976), pp. 156–7; cf. a similar interpretation in Schlesinger and Kinzer, p. 61.

16 Quoted in Schlesinger and Kinzer, p. 188.

17 John D. Martz, *Communist Infiltration in Guatemala* (N.Y.: Vintage Press, 1954).

18 Ronald M. Schneider, *Communism in Guatemala, 1944–1954* (N.Y.: Frederick Praeger, 1959).

19 Kalman H. Silvert, *A Study in Government: Guatemala* (New Orleans: Tulane University Press, 1954).

20 Victor Alba, *Politics and the Labour Movement in Latin America* (Stanford, California: Stanford University Press, 1968), p. 284.

21 *Ibid.*, p. 148.

22 See text of Foreign Minister Guillermo Torriello Garrido in Leiken and Rubin (eds), *The Central American Crisis Reader*, pp. 108–11.

23 Cited in *Ibid.*, pp. 112–13.

24 *Department of State Bulletin*, XXXI (12 July, 1954) pp. 43–4. Emphasis added.

25 Lloyd Mecham, *A Survey of US-Latin American Relations* (Boston: Houghton Mifflin, Co., 1965), p. 213.

26 Ann Van Wynen Thomas and A.J. Thomas, Jr., *The Organization of American States* (Dallas: Southern Methodist University Press, 1963).

27 H. Bradford Westerfield, *The Instruments of American Foreign Policy* (New York, 1963), p. 435.

28 These quotes are from Dean Acheson's speech 'Ethics in International Relations Today', reprinted in the *New York Times*, 10 December, 1964. See also 'A Realist's Advice on Foreign Policy', *Newsweek*, 21 December, 1964, p. 18. For an even more 'hard-headed statement of realism see Dean Acheson's special article in *Vision*, 4 October, 1963, pp. 24–7.

29 Dulles speech to Associated Press, New York, 22 April, 1957, in Gaddis, p. 181.

30 Ball, *The Discipline of Power*, pp. 3–4.

31 *Ibid.*, p. 10.

32 Blanche Wiesen Cook, *The Declassified Eisenhower*, p. 218.

33 Letter of 17 March, 1957 cited in Gaddis, p. 181.

34 Irwin F. Gellman, Roosevelt and Batista, *Good Neighbour Diplomacy in Cuba, 1933–1945* (Albuquerque: University of New Mexico Press, 1973), p. 3.

35 Cf. Luis E. Aguilar, *Cuba 1933: Prologue to Revolution* (Ithaca: Cornell University Press, 1972); James Suchlicki, *University Students and Revolution in Cuba*, 1920–1968 (Coral Gables: University of Miami Press; Hugh Thomas, *The Revolution on Balance* (Washington, D.C.: The American National Foundation, 1983); Rolando E. Bonachea and Nelson Valdés (eds), *Revolutionary Struggle, 1947–1958. Vol. I of the Selected Works of Fidel Castro* (Cambridge, Mass: The MIT Press, 1972), p. XIII.

36 Ramón L. Bonachea and Marta San Martín, *The Cuban Insurrection, 1952–1959* (New Brunswick, N.J. Transaction Books, 1974), p. 3.

37 Jorge Domínguez, *Cuba: Order and Revolution* (Cambridge: Harvard University Press, 1978), p. 120.

38 Domínguez, *Cuba*, p. 101.

39 *Ibid.*, p. 103.

40 Hugh Thomas, *Cuba: The Pursuit of Freedom* (New York: Harper and Row, 1971), p. 1009.

41 *Ibid.*, p. 855.

42 Thomas, *Cuba*, p. 855.

43   Domínguez, *Cuba*, p. 107.
44   Cf. John Dorchner and Roberto Fabricio, *The Winds of December* (New York: Coward, McCann and Gesghegan, 1980), pp. 144–63.
45   Domínguez, *Cuba*, p. 129.
46   Both Thomas (*Cuba*, p. 1214) and Domínguez believe Castro was still open to different options up to mid-1959; Tad Szulc believes he had decided on a course since 1953 (Cf. *Fidel: A Critical Portrait* (New York: William Morrow, 1986).
47   On Castro's extraordinary vanity and sense of destiny as the logical heir of José Martí see Peter G. Bourne, *Fidel: A Biography of Fidel Castro* (New York: Dodd, Mad and Co., 1986); Edward González, David Rondfelt, *Castro, Cuba and the World* (Santa Monica: RAND, June 1986).
48   Cf. Thomas, *Cuba*, p. 1200.
49   Dwight D. Eisenhower, *Waging Peace* (New York: Doubleday, 1965), p. 523.
50   Thomas, *Cuba*, p. 1207.
51   Richard Nixon, *Six Crises* 1962, pp. 351–2.
52   Pierre Salinger, *With Kennedy* (New York: Avon Books, 1966), p. 195.
53   Richard E. Neustadt and Ernest R. May, *Thinking in Time: The Uses of History for Decision-Makers* (New York: The Free Press, 1986, p. 140. Emphasis in original.
54   Eisenhower, *Waging Peace*, pp. 532–3.
55   Cf. Tad Szulc and Karl K. Meyer, *The Cuban Invasion: The Chronicle of a Disaster* (N.Y.: Praeger, 1962); Pete Wyden, *The Bay of Pigs* (N.Y.: Simon & Schuster, 1979); Haynes Johnson, *The Bay of Pigs* (New York: Bell, 1974).
56   Arthur Schlesinger, Jr., *A Thousand Days* (New York: Fawcet Premier, 1965), p. 396.
57   Trumbull Higgins, *The Perfect Failure* (N.Y.: Norton & Co., 1987).
58   In 1987 Jack B. Pfeiffer, former chief historian of the CIA filed a lawsuit under the Freedom of Information Act seeking copies of still-classified documents on the Bay of Pigs. It is Pfeiffer's contention that too much of the blame has been placed on the CIA; others – especially Kennedy's White House Staff – should also share the burden. (Cf. *The New York Times*, 30 December, 1987, p. 8).
59   Neustadt and May, *Thinking in Time,* p. 48.
60   E. Howard Hunt, *Give Us This Day* (New Rochelle: Arlington House, 1973), p. 23.
61   Hunt, *Give Us This Day*, p. 23.
62   Higgins, *The Perfect Failure*, p. 84.
63   Irving L. Janis, *Victims of Groupthink* (Boston-Houghton Mifflin Co., 1972), p. 29.
64   Szulc and Meyer, *The Cuban Invasion*, pp. 27–9.
65   Neustadt and May, *Thinking in Time*, p. 1. The figure comes from an analysis of President Kennedy's private calendar. This interpretation, say the authors, has not been disputed by those involved (p. 295).
66   Schlesinger, *A Thousand Days,* p. 236.
67   Lyman Kirkpatrick later published an excellent version of this secret report in the *Naval War College Review*, Vol. 25 (November–December 1972), pp. 32–42.
68   Schlesinger, p. 257.
69   Janis, *Victims of Groupthink*, p. 37.
70   Higgins, *The Perfect Failure*, p. 62.
71   See Roa's speech in Lester D. Langley (ed.), *The US, Cuba, and the Cold War* (Lexington, Mass.: D.C. Heath & Co., 1970), pp. 36–8.
72   Hunt, *Give Us This Day*, pp. 61–2.
73   Johnson, *The Bay of Pigs*, p. 29.
74   Schlesinger, *A Thousand Days*, pp. 167–76.
75   For details see Rollie E. Poppino, *International Communism, passim*.
76   Schlesinger, *A Thousand Days*, p. 174.

77   Theodore C. Sorensen, *The Kennedy Legacy* (New York: The MacMillan Co., 1969), p. 183.

78   The term is used by Arthur Schlesinger to describe the Haitian government's vote, (*A Thousand Days*, p. 717).

79   Department of State Bulletin, XLIV, 8 May, 1961, pp. 658–61.

80   Sorensen, *The Kennedy Legacy*, p. 183.

81   *Ibid.*

82   Schlesinger, *A Thousand Days*, p. 728.

83   Arnold L. Horelick and Myron Rush, *Strategic Power and Soviet Foreign Policy* (Chicago: University of Chicago Press, 1966), p. 135.

84   *Ibid.*

85   The following is reconstructed from Rober F. Kennedy, *Thirteen Days: A Memoir of the Cuban Missile Crisis* (New York: W.W. Norton and Co., 1969); Graham T. Allison, *Essence of Decision. Explaining the Cuban Missile Crisis* (Boston: Little, Brown and Co., 1971); Abraham Chayes, *The Cuban Missile Crisis*, (New York: Oxford University Press, 1974); Manuela Semidei, *Kennedy et la Révolution Cubaine* (Paris: Julliard, 1972).

86   President Kennedy cited in *The Washington Post*, 18 December, 1962.

87   See Chapter 3, 'The Cuban Missile Crisis, 1962', in Alexander L. George, *et. al.*, *The Limits of Coercive Diplomacy* (Boston: Little Brown, Co.).

88   Theodore C. Sorensen, *The Kennedy Legacy* (N.Y.: MacMillan Co., 1969), p. 188.

89   Quoted in Abraham Chayes, *The Cuban Missile Crisis* (New York: Oxford University Press, 1974), p. 23.

90   Interview with Claude Julie, *Le Monde*, March 22, 1963.

91   Jacinto Torres, 'El desarrollo de las relaciones soviéticas-cubanas', *Cuba socialista*, No. 10 (June, 1962).

CHAPTER 6 — The Caribbean plays the Cuban card: The US response

According to Arthur M. Schlesinger, Jr., communism had two types of targets in the early 1960s: those of 'priority' such as Venezuela and Brazil, and those of 'convenience'. In Schlesinger's opinion the main target of convenience in 1961 was British Guiana, less because of its intrinsic desirability than because 'it was there . . . .' In other words, the Soviets saw in Guiana an opportunity to create problems in the US sphere of influence.[1]

The US, says Schlesinger, was aware that the British wanted to get out of British Guiana as soon as possible and wished to 'dump the whole problem on us'. The 'problem' was Cheddi Jagan and his People's Progressive Party which had won elections in 1953, 1957 and again in 1961. As Schlesinger recalls, Jagan was 'unquestionably some sort of Marxist' yet he was also 'plainly the most popular leader in British Guiana'. The question was whether 'he was recoverable for democracy', should they attempt to 'wean' him away from Moscow as they were doing with Guinea's Sekou Touré? Geography, i.e. geopolitics, alone eliminated this option. 'The US could not afford the Sekou Touré therapy when it involved a quasi-communist regime on the mainland of Latin America . . . .'[2] That being the case, and despite the fact that it was generally perceived as a 'marginal problem', the 'problem' had to be addressed, especially since the solution appeared 'easy'. Given the mandate to keep the 'costs' low, the US came up with the perfect formula: convince the British to change the electoral system from the existing 'first-past-the-post' or single-member constituency to a continental system of proportional representation.

As late as 1954, the British Royal Commission empowered to recommend changes in the British Guiana Constitution noted that, 'if some system of proportional representation were now introduced it could hardly be represented as other than a device to mitigate the present dominance of the PPP. To enshrine in the constitution such a device would, in our view, be wrong and we, therefore, recommend no change in the present electoral system.'[3]

Under intense pressure from Washington, on October 1963 the system was changed. An easy victory over communism was on hand for, as Schlesinger noted, with the electoral change, British Guiana 'seemed to have passed safely out of the communist orbit.'[4] The US had achieved another easy victory. This allowed Jagan's political enemy, Forbes Burnham, to exploit successfully the racial tensions as well as introduce a much expanded system of overseas voting by proxy which was largely fraudulent. As ambiguous as Burnham might have seemed to the vested interests, he was clearly the lesser of two evils. In 1966, during independence celebrations, the *New York Times* reported from what was now called the Republic of Guyana, that in the foreign diplomatic and business community the outward attitude was much the same: they believed that the government of Premier Forbes Burnham, supported by the British, the US and by business, would 'remain stable and continue to be hospitable to foreign investment.'[5] It would be nothing of the sort. In fact, the Burnham years were secured through electoral fraud, were rife with corruption, economic decline and monumental ideological demagoguery. Only Cuba exercised greater control over the economy than Burnham's Guyana.

The role of US intervention is well recorded in Cheddi Jagan's autobiography.[6] But Jagan would have the last laugh when thirty years later he received a most extraordinary public apology from the architect of his electoral defeats, Arthur Schlesinger, Jr. His words throw light on a whole period of US-Caribbean relations:

> There was a great feeling after the Bay of Pigs, where the impression arose that Eisenhower had prepared an expedition to get rid of Castro, that Kennedy had lacked the resolution to follow it through. It was just politically going to look very bad if the dominoes began to fall in South America . . . The fear was that Congress might use aid to British Guiana as a means of attacking the whole aid bill then before it . . . Then of course what really happened was the CIA got involved, got the bit between its teeth and the covert action people thought it was a chance to show their stuff . . . I think a great injustice was done to Cheddi Jagan.[7]

Not every US intervention in the post-Bay of Pigs Caribbean was that bloodless. Fears of communist penetration and influence in a Dominican Republic torn by political confusion led to a US intervention with a force of over 25,000 US servicemen. The Latin Americans were informed after the invasion had started and the Monroe Doctrine invoked. The US was not taking any chances in its sphere of influence.

What has been called the 'Johnson Doctrine', was a combination of three elements: a determination never to relive the shame of the Bay of Pigs, a perception that Cuba was actively training and organizing leftwing revolutionary groups from around the hemisphere, and a resolution to meet this communist challenge with overwhelming force. When Guatemala-style counter-insurgency was thought ineffective, old-fashioned military intervention was the option. As the US Commander in the Dominican Republic in 1965 put it: henceforth the intervening army should have such superiority of forces that they could 'get in and get out as soon as possible.'[8] It is a fact that this is essentially what happened in the Dominican Republic, but for reasons which the Johnson administration ignored as it extended its doctrine to Vietnam, with the well-known disastrous consequences.[9]

The fact is that as distinct from Cuba in 1959, the Dominican uprising of 1965 was a highly circumscribed movement, limited to the inner core of the capital city, Santo Domingo. The divisions among the rebel leadership reflected the disparate and contradictory motivations and goals of the movement: the majority who favoured the return of deposed president Juan Bosch, those who wished to make the rebel commander – a nondescript officer of Trujillo's army – president, and the communists, a diminutive conspiratorial group divided into three factions, who hoped to establish a Marxist-Leninist state.[10]

It is hard to unravel the significance of this event for US-Carribean relations. It is one of the most remarkable historical facts that thirty years after this incident, Dominicans seem to have a severe case of collective amnesia about it. There is no significant impartial Dominican study of the event, its legacy and its significance for Dominican history, much less for the Caribbean. Events in the Caribbean evolved as if the Dominican crisis had never occurred.

While all this was unfolding in the Caribbean, the region was changing as new nations began to make their appearance. Independence, sovereignty, self-determination were in the air as Great Britain brought the curtains down on most of its empire in the region. Responsibility now shifted nearly completely to the US. What had begun with the bases for destroyers exchange in World War II had become US geopolitical dominance throughout the whole region. It would be the US, not Europe, which would oversee what we now know was the last act of the Cold War era, dominated as it was by anti-communist hysteria. During this last act, geopolitics would still hold centre stage but there was also evidence that there were those in Washington who held a more sophisticated understanding of the forces of ethnicity and nationalism. In the late 1970s the US confronted a renewed Cuban challenge in the Caribbean with greater diplomatic aplomb. Although not very obvious at the time, the basis for future Caribbean-US relations was being laid. The battleground was in the smaller islands of the English-speaking Caribbean.

In a footnote that in a different context would have been in the text, K.S. Karol related somewhat humorously his attempts to reach Cuba from Jamaica during the Bay of Pigs invasion. 'Our futile maritime adventures', he recalled, ' . . . taught me something about the unholy fear Cuban ideas inspired in the Caribbean.'[11] In the course of preparing for the trip he had dealings with both the Cuban Consul and the US Consul General. The former, Alfonso Herrera, occupied a room on the second floor of a 'dusty old house' and performed single-handedly all the tasks of the consulate. Karol had the clear impression that the times and the Cuban's lack of resources were such that his influence in Jamaica was extremely small.

The US Consul General, on the other hand, enjoyed luxurious accommodations both in the office and at home. This Consul General had previously been in the Belgian Congo where, to hear his wife tell it, the Belgians had done a splendid job. Jamaica he felt was different, and he appeared deeply concerned about the island's social unrest; it was, he claimed, reaching alarming proportions. 'According to the Consul', Karol recalled, 'the blame was entirely Alfonso Herrera's; it was only since the arrival of 'that revolutionary agitator' that the normal peaceful tenor of Jamaican life had become explosive.'[12] Karol, who had seen the poverty in the island, remembered having difficulty containing his laughter.

By the late 1970s the unholy fear of Cuban ideas had become not only more intense but also more widespread. Had Karol visited Jamaica then, he might have hesitated to laugh at stories of Cuban involvement. Rather than a dusty second-floor room, the Cuban mission in Kingston was now an impressive complex – complete with radio-transmitting antennas similar to those of their US and British counterparts. The Cuban Ambassador – not infrequently the centre of political controversy – presided over an ever-increasing network of Cuban activities in health, education, construction, agriculture, tourism, sports, and some would maintain, politics. And so it was in much of the rest of the Caribbean.

In Guyana, where the Cuban mission took up nearly half a city block, Cuba's multiple involvements had long been the talk of Georgetown. Across the sea in tiny Grenada, Cuba was represented at the highest level; it had the only resident Ambassador on the island, an island which had virtually no trade with Cuba, no Cuban citizens to represent, or any of the other traditional reasons for such high diplomatic representation. That Ambassador would preside over a growing Cuban presence. Cuban doctors arrived, some 15 of them, as did fishing trawlers and instructors; and on 19 November, 1979, Prime Minister Maurice Bishop told a rally that he expected 250 Cubans to start building a new international airport. As he had only just been in Canada seeking funds for a feasibility study for that same project, local surprise was understandable. Some Grenadians began to say that if it were only the fourteen bulldozers, six scrapers, twenty trucks, and thousands of tons of cement and steel that had arrived, it would have been all right. Rumour had it, though, that there were three truckloads of Cuban arms hidden somewhere on the island. Subsequent events proved that these rumours greatly understated the amount of weapons; a veritable arsenal was already on the island, and they kept arriving.[13]

What was not rumour were the new 'military zones', which were off-limits, and the presence of numerous military advisers; these were quite visibly on site. Grenadians were already laughing at the 'Chilean connection' of ex-Prime Minister Eric Gairy: three homesick Grenadian policemen training in Chile and two crates of World War II vintage guns that apparently were never opened and that certainly have never been seen publicly before or after the *coup d'etat* which overthrew Gairy.

This network of Cuban diplomats and involvements came under the aegis of the Caribbean section of the Cuban Ministry of Foreign Affairs. Unlike so many of the US diplomats sent to the area, these Cubans were professionals to be reckoned with. In Barbados (which had refused to allow a resident Cuban mission despite having diplomatic relations since 1972) high government officials already had a healthy respect for Cuban intelligence. They would note, for instance, that the man who headed the Caribbean desk in Havana was formerly posted in Guyana and before that was an important Directorio General de Intelligencia (DGI) agent; and that the Cuban Ambassador to Jamaica during the late 1970s was also a high-level DGI officer, well briefed in Jamaican and Caribbean affairs. Such was the Caribbean perception of Cuban skill and expertise in the late 1970s that in the Netherlands Antilles one heard that the Cuban Caribbean section had correctly predicted the outcome of mid-1979 elections in Curaçao, when even *antillano* pundits were at a loss to do the same.

It was not surprising, therefore, to hear moderate Caribbean leaders such as Antigua's Vere Bird warn the Venezuelans that Cuban 'intervention' was spreading everywhere in the area, aiding and abetting new radical groups in each island. Such warnings were eagerly received as Venezuela's relations with Cuba deteriorated and its interests in the Caribbean increased during the period.

How much of all this Caribbean perception of Cuban involvement and power was autochthonously arrived at and how much reflected US perceptions? It appears that both sets of perceptions were operating and reinforcing each other. After all, the Bishop coup in Grenada and his ridiculing of elections as 'rum and sardines' events, did not sit well with leaders whose whole decolonization struggle had been centred on the right to self-determination through universal suffrage and free elections. There was no reason, however, for hysteria. Clearly there was in the decade 1970–1980 at least a surface unity among the area's new Marxist-Leninist groups. This could be seen, for instance, at the public launching of Jamaica's communist party, Trevor Munroe's Workers Party of Jamaica (WPJ), formerly the Worker's Liberation League. In attendance were delegates from the communist parties of the USSR, Britain, Canada, the US, and Cuba; in attendance from the English-speaking Caribbean were Guyana's People's Progressive Party and the Working People's Alliance, the

Barbados Movement for National Liberation, Grenada's New Jewel Movement, St Vincent's Liberation Movement, and St Lucia's Worker's Revolutionary Movement.

Such was the mood in Washington that there was a tendency to see Cuban and Soviet machinations behind this unity among Caribbean radicals. Two factors should have cautioned against such a hasty judgment. First it ignored the long-standing ties among Caribbean radical groups – ties that pre-date the Cuban Revolution and that, more often than not, were the result of specific and independent decisions on each island. Secondly, it failed to separate Soviet and Cuban foreign policy interests. Even in the case of Grenada, as Mark Falcoff would later indicate, the Soviets were reluctant to make any commitments which they could neither fulfill nor defend.[14]

Be that as it may, it would be a mistake to underrate the significance of the political and ideological role defined by the Cubans and the capacity of their intelligence and diplomatic corps at the time. Art, science, sports, music, and everything else, were parts of this political thrust into the Caribbean. For instance, the Cubans astutely, albeit sincerely, understood the crucial importance of race in the Caribbean, took full advantage of the sad American past on this score and of the points built up by their popular and commendable anti-South African policies and actions. Less sincere, yet still effective, was the quite explicit use of black Cubans as diplomats in the Caribbean. An island where perhaps 25 per cent of the people were black and where few of these had achieved important positions in the Revolutionary government,[15] Cuba managed to be represented nearly exclusively by blacks in the Caribbean and in Africa. It was not surprising to note, therefore, the number of West Indians who believed Cuba to be a black Caribbean state. Unlike the Americans, who had played the racial diplomatic game since the beginning of their Caribbean contacts, the Cubans had the advantage of playing this racial angle while also emphasizing class and class conflict as the basic units of struggle. Such a strategy allowed a fundamentally pragmatic approach to the Caribbean area's complex politics in which issues of race and class interact in a bewildering fashion.

During the 1970s, then, the Cubans were clearly on the move in the Caribbean. Yet, despite this phenomenal expansion of the Cuban presence since Karol's Jamaican experience, it would be a mistake to conclude that the Cubans had it all their own way in the Caribbean. In part but not exclusively, this was due to US power and its capacity to contain Marxist advances in the area. Beyond that, however, there are other factors limiting Cuban policy and action. An important one was the political *savoir faire* of the region's leaders, most of them of Fabian socialist persuasion. They understood the limits of Washington's interests beyond geopolitics and were also wary of the stirrings on their left. They began to exploit the Cuban involvement. The 'Cuban card' began to be quite skilfully manipulated by some Caribbean politicians towards less than ideologically pure ends. The Cuban card was used as political leverage in some instances, as a protective shield in others, and in more and more cases as a straw man.

In the cases discussed here the Cuban role was fundamentally that of providing a mantle of revolutionary legitimacy to regimes that had both achieved and retained power through less than revolutionary means. And as every card has two sides (the other side is the actual or potential use of this same Cuban presence as a straw man), it is amazing how frequently some Caribbean politicians used both sides of this card. Some did so successfully; for others the tactic backfired dramatically.

In many ways both the Americans and the Cubans underestimated the toughness of the West Indian politician. They first tasted power during colonial days – defeating that noxious combination of racism and cultural haughtiness – and took a hearty appetite for it into independence. It can be argued, in fact, that few areas of the world have had more enduring practitioners of what Rexford Tugwell called 'the art of politics' than the Caribbean. Whether it is the old, traditional politician who stays in power by playing on the primordial attachments of race or religious fundamentalism, or the young 'revolutionary' seeking socialist modernization through extra-constitutional means, they all faced one dilemma: how to retain power in societies that are politically complex, restless and eager for better days, yet hardly revolutionary. The fact is that the masses in the English-speaking Caribbean have always tended to be politically radical but sociologically conservative. Call it 'false consciousness', 'fear of freedom', or whatever, they are a difficult lot to satisfy. Obviously the first task of those who would govern, whether they be conservatives or radicals, is to stay in power, and the Cuban card, played on both its sides, was proven to be of considerable value during difficult years. It involved a subtle and nuanced manoeuvering which often escapes those such as the CIA and others who think in categorical and Manichean terms.

During much of the 1970–80 decade, the English-speaking Caribbean divided into three distinct camps: those openly pro-Cuba (Jamaica, Guyana, Grenada); those retaining diplomatic relations with Cuba but privately critical of its role (Trinidad and Tobago and Barbados) and those openly hostile to Cuba and the 'leftist trend'. St Vincent's Milton Cato and Antigua's Vere Bird were the most outspoken leaders among the latter group. They would later be joined by St Lucia's John Compton, Dominica's Eugenia Charles and St Vincent's James 'Son' Mitchell.

As good as any player of both sides of the Cuban card was Jamaica's Michael Manley, an adept political practitioner in both national and international arenas. The multiple transformations of this erstwhile conservative son of Norman Manley were in the best tradition of political artistry.

Brought back from England in the early 1950s to do battle with the left wing within the People's National Party (PNP) – the so-called 4-Hs – Manley successfully cleaned out the radical elements from both the party and its labour branch.[16] As his father faded from the national picture, Michael began to transform his image as a conservative and partisan union leader into one of a more flamboyant charismatic figure of national and international dimensions. He became the bearer of two religious traditions: 'Joshua' to the Bible-reading Christians while to the large number of Rastafarians he became the man with the 'rod of correction', a reference to the imperial walking staff given to him by Haile Selassie, a god to the Rastafarians. This rod often made an appearance at political rallies. With it Manley would teach his opponents 'strict manners', an allusion to old-fashioned theories of 'proper' child rearing. This was in the first metamorphosis. The second was his socialist phase. In this phase, neither the biblical references ('comrade' replaced 'Joshua') nor the rod of correction was still relevant to Manley's new politics, the politics of 'principle'. In fact the noun 'principle' became the most common word in Manley's political vocabulary. Clearly he understood what is today axiomatic in political sociology: that expedient interests are more constant than principled interests and that in a conflict between the two, you always place your bet on expediency. Thus, Jamaicans heard Manley say that his relations with Cuba were 'principled relations'; his support for Cuba's right to have Soviet troops on its soil was based on 'a single matter of fundamental principle': that the Cuban people wanted them. Yet his support for independence for Puerto Rico was based on the non-aligned movement's 'principles' – even if through many votes the Puerto Rican people had shown that they did not want it. He was, of course, in favour of the US navy's moving out of the islands of Vieques and Culebra, not because the majority of Puerto Ricans wanted it but because it was a logical extension of his 'principled' stance on Puerto Rican independence. Despite this, it was evident that Manley understood that absolute and inflexible adherence to principle is the policy of political fools or fanatics, and he was manifestly neither.

Manley knew that outright communist movements had never fared well in Jamaica. This was seen in the defeat of the Marxists within the PNP in the early 1950s as well as the fiasco of Chris Lawrence's Communist Party of Jamaica of the 1960s. This was not surprising: both the major Jamaican parties emerged from trade union movements and both had been traditionally polyclass in composition from the inception of party politics and responsible government; also, both had been geared toward control by the state machinery – as tends to be the case in two-party systems. Both understood the circular operation of state patronage: power is dependent on patronage, continued patronage on continued power; patronage increases as the widening and deepening of power increases. In a political system such as this, third parties are for the disaffected, the alienated, or the ideologically 'pure', all of whom, in the final analysis, are equally irrelevant in the distribution of power in parliamentary systems.

Aside from this element of raw politics, there was the additional fact that there was, and still is, in Jamaica a deep-rooted fear of communism among both the urban and rural masses, as repeated surveys indicated.[17] As a consequence, both parties traditionally cast their programs in populist tones, the approach historically favoured by those who cater to popular grievances but fear the trap of excessive ideological dogma. How, then, to explain the shift to the left in Manley's second term (1976–1980)? The first thing to note is that this shift was more demonstrable in rhetoric than in actual programs or policies. But whether rhetorically or through actual policies, the shift responded to a series of complex changes in Jamaica that ran the gamut from urban growth and unemployment to a new generational struggle within the PNP.

Within the party, the leftward thrust came from a group of young PNP politicians clearly led by Dr D.K. Duncan, widely recognized as the party's best urban strategist. Although the young radicals within the PNP seemed to be committed to socialist principles, they were nevertheless more interested in power. If this had not been the case, many of them would have had a logical place in Dr Trevor Munroe's Marxist-oriented Worker's Party of Jamaica (WPJ). Ex-Rhodes scholar Munroe, an engaging and tireless organizer who, without any particular mass of labour union base at the time, consistently preached many of the 'principles' with which Manley had to play politics, often managed to capitalize on rhetorical support from the PNP's left. This support, however, could never be too overt, given the anticommunism of the masses of the PNP and of many of the party frontbenchers. One such was Finance Minister Eric Bell, who in early 1978 made it clear in the Jamaican House of Representatives that 'if any member of the People's National Party is a communist and avowed to be a communist then they are entitled to be expelled.'[18]

In the context of Jamaican politics during Manley's second term, the Cuban card came into play in the following fashion: it allowed Munroe to stick to Marxist ideological principle both in speech and in practice; Manley's intraparty opponents to emphasize these principles in speech while calling for the party to assert them in action; and Manley himself to assert the principles rhetorically. In other words, by providing legitimacy to all who asserted radical 'principles' the Cuban 'presence' blurred the distinction between theory and practice, an abandonment of the Marxist emphasis on praxis but one that nevertheless served all involved in the short term.

The point, of course, was that it served Manley even better because at any time he could play the other side of the card, which asserted – as his father had in the 1950s – that communists did not belong in the party and should therefore be either expelled or silenced. It is quite evident that this is precisely what happened to the radical Youth Wing of the party, silenced in 1977. This ability to play both sides of the Cuban card was especially convenient as the Cubans did not seem to be put off by it (at least not publicly). Thus the PNP – and by implication the system within which it functioned – continued to enjoy the support of the Cubans regardless of which way the card was played. This Jamaican case was in keeping with Cuba's policy of supporting friendly regimes no matter whether these were opposed by Marxist forces internally. Jamaica was no different from Spain, Peru, or Mexico in this regard. In exchange for this support, the Cubans benefited from Jamaica's (and Manley's) very real prestige in Third World, circles and not a few developed countries. After many failures in the Third World, the Cubans had learned that it paid to support friendly non-communist regimes rather than putting all their bets on small communist parties with little chance of coming to power, as had been the case in the Dominican Republic in 1965.

It was an arrangement that suited both parties and which, by the way, need not have affected North American multinational interests too adversely. The continued profits of the Jamaican bauxite sector and parts of the tourism industry, even while the Jamaican economy as a whole was (as of 1977) in a downward spiral of low productivity, unemployment, and inflation, stood as witness to that.

It was not only that the Jamaican economy was showing a real growth rate of minus 13 per cent for 1974–77 (compared to plus 20 per cent for 1969–73), for in some ways this could be attributed to external causes such as the increase in oil prices. Of more concern because they reflected purely internal causes were drops in productivity, notably in the agricultural sector. According to the Food and Agriculture Organization (FAO) figures, dry beans, corn and rice all showed substantial drops in output per acre during 1975–77 (as compared to 1969–75). Most disastrous of all was the brain drain, which even the Jamaican National Planning Agency called a haemorrhage of high-level manpower. But, were the educated fleeing from actual revolutionary change? Interviews with some of the 15,000 Jamaican 'exiles' in Miami in 1979 indicated that they were fleeing not from socialism but rather from unchecked crime, shortages of all kinds, and a general sense that no one was managing the economy. They saw Manley's pro-Castroism as a case of rhetorical radicalism gone berserk even as their view of the Cuban involvement in Jamaica was tinged with scepticism and not a little ethnocentrism. Cubans might be great revolutionaries but their technical and productive capabilities did not elicit admiration among educated Jamaicans. They pointed with incredulity to the fact that Jamaica was now importing milk from a country, Cuba, where milk was rationed and that received grants of milk from the FAO – milk produced originally in the US.

They noted that the dozen-odd general practitioners sent by Cuba were hardly substitutes for the mass exodus of Jamaican medical specialists.[19] As we shall see in the Conclusion, Manley was paying a high price for his pro-Cuban rhetoric. One source calculated that there were left on the island only thirteen dentists with specialized training, including one periodontist and one orthodontist.[20] The University of the West Indies Medical School was increasingly staffed with Indian medical professors, the Jamaicans and other West Indians having left in droves. And all this in a society where no socialist measures had been taken against the medical profession.

Far from being a socialist society, Jamaica during the second Manley period was rather what economists call a 'transfer society': resources were drawn from the few productive sectors and used up in an effort to acquire existing resources for others. In other words, more valuable resources were used to produce less valuable resources. The political advantages of such a system are obvious, but these are necessarily short-term as, economically, transfer policies result in a negative-sum game for the society as a whole. But in the short-term, there was a political advantage to the Cuban connection. It facilitated the rationalization that all this economic and social turmoil was a consequence of a 'revolutionary process'. Such a process pre-empted any 'ordinary' criteria of performance measurement or comparison with other, 'non-revolutionary', West Indian societies such as Barbados. With fewer resources, Barbados was managing at that same time a respectable pace of growth and development. Again, the Cuban connection operated as a sort of smokescreen covering up deficiencies and incompetence of all kinds. It was a significant element in the ability of the middle-class leadership of the PNP to defend its administrative performance with a degree of credibility it otherwise would have lost much sooner than it did. But lose it would. The two-term mandate which had already become traditional in Jamaican politics was up in 1980, and the PNP had little tangible to show. It lost the elections by the biggest margin in Jamaican history. In democratic, pluralist politics, such as Jamaica's, the Cuban card tended to lose its value much sooner than it did in dictatorial systems such as that of Grenada. It was in Grenada in particular that the coincidence between Cuban interests and the interests of radicalized middle-class groups bent on holding on to state power was clearly evident.

Grenada ranked with Haiti among the poorest of Caribbean societies. Its poverty had been only mildly ameliorated by the proximity of the neighbouring island of Trinidad, which traditionally provided an outlet for excess population as well as a source of remittances, historically an important part of Grenada's economy. Not surprisingly, relations with Trinidad had always been an important issue in Grenada's politics. All that changed when on 13 March, 1979, some 45 men (using arms smuggled in from Miami, Florida) carried out the first *coup d'état* in West Indian history. The victors, all members of the New Jewel Movement (NJM), promised a socialist revolution and even began talking as if they were in fact leading a social revolution. They were confusing middle-class relief at getting rid of the corrupt and incompetent Eric Gairy with support for socialist changes.

In fact, the situation facing the Revolutionary government of Grenada two years after the *coup* could be described as follows: significant sectors of the peasantry continued loyal if not to Gairy personally, at least to what is best called 'Gairyism' – black peasant populism; the coalition of urban forces that formed the backbone of the anti-Gairy movement (churches, Chamber of Commerce, Rotary, Lions, labour unions – the so-called Committee of 22) was not much given to revolutions; the civil service was interested in paychecks and security; and the traditional political parties were eager for elections and suspicious of the young radicals in the New Jewel Movement who had tried their hands at electoral politics before without much success.[21] On the other hand, the new government enjoyed the support of the largely unemployed urban youth, clearly a sector to contend with, and to some extent, of some big businesses whose profits had not been affected and who were totally disaffected with the incompetence and venality of the Gairy regime. Not surprisingly, the Grenada Chamber of Commerce declared after the *coup* that it did not 'anticipate any worrying changes in the methods and patterns of business or in the direction of the government's fiscal policy'.[22] Clearly, the chamber was basing its assessment on its acquaintance with the men involved rather than on the 1973 Manifesto of the New Jewel Movement, which called for a thorough socialist redoing of society.

Who, then, were these revolutionary leaders? To begin with the group that toppled Eric Gairy was fundamentally middle class in origin. Prime Minister Maurice Bishop was about five years old in 1950 when Eric Gairy returned from the oil fields of Aruba to begin the anti-colonial drive. Bishop was a graduate of Presentation College in Grenada and read for the law in London. He was clearly a member of the island's small but stable middle class. So were Bernard Coard, Ken Radix, and others in the regime. Richard Jacobs, Grenada's first ambassador to Cuba, and from mid-1982 to October, 1983 the USSR, although a citizen of Trinidad and Tobago, belonged to a prominent middle-class family which covered the Eastern Caribbean. This educated and well-travelled elite shared middle-class Grenada's dislike of Gairy's working-class origins, and he returned the favour.

Bishop once told an interviewer that he remembered Gairy's identifying and then rejecting him when he was nominated in the early 1960s to a commission of inquiry by the students of Grenada Boys' Secondary School. This incident probably had more social than political overtones, reflecting the strained relations between Gairy and his middle-class antagonists. Not surprisingly, Bishop's middle-class values were quickly apparent in his political positions. For instance, when he concluded that, although freedom of the press was appropriate for the British, who can weigh the points of view and choose one, this was not the case with Grenadians. His interviewer related his reasoning: 'He said that in the situation of Grenada with backwardness, illiteracy, superstition, rumour-mongering, certainly functional illiteracy, most people could hardly even fully appreciate the one statement in front of them'. 'How are they going to sift up three and four?' he asked.'[23] One could have expected such an attitude from a colonial Governor, but from a 'revolutionary'?

Similarly, for instance, was Deputy Prime Minister Bernard Coard's answer to a question on elections: 'We don't want to have only a "representative democracy" – which means that once every five years for five seconds you go to the polls and mark your X having been given enough rum and corned beef at the local rum shop. . . . We call this "five second democracy".'[24] Interestingly enough it was against such very attitudes that Gairy originally led his anti-colonial movement in the 1950s. But even beyond that, if Bishop's and Coard's description of the Grenadian people were to be accepted, one would not only have to agree with Marx's portrayal of the 'idiocy of rural life' but also to conclude most categorically that in such a population no socialist revolution was possible. What was possible, of course, was authoritarian state capitalism, not by the people but for the people by a self-elected elite.

The actions taken during the first two years of the revolution clearly reflected the secular rationalism of this educated middle-class elite. First to be combated were esoteric religious groups: Obeah (black magic) and Rosicrucianism, both skeletons in Gairy's political closet. A section of the Rastafarian movement came next. But in addition to those holding to 'superstitions' that had no place in a modern socialist state, others also had to fall in line. The only independent newspaper, *Torchlight*, was closed in 1979 on the pretext that it was largely foreign (Trinidadian) owned. In 1981 the government closed down as counter-revolutionary the totally Grenadian-owned *Grenadian Voice*.

That this authoritarianism suited well the nature of the radical middle-class leadership was the theme of a book by Archie Singham which, until the NJM coup, had been heralded as the most significant analysis of Caribbean politics in general and Grenadian politics in particular.[25] Singham identified two kinds of West Indian political heroes: the 'middle-class hero, and the hero who comes from humble origins.' Singham's sympathies were clearly with the latter, and Eric Matthew Gairy was the prototype. But Singham had enough sociological perspicacity to note that 'in spite of the differences in their class origins and their leadership style, however, these two types share certain similarities: they tend to develop personal organizations which are essentially authoritarian.' Singham was perceptive in his call for more studies on the 'anxiety-ridden' middle-class hero: 'His ideology is usually populist: for him the rhetoric if not the content of Marxism or radical socialism fulfills a very useful role by enabling him to sustain the vicissitudes of politics in the light of the sacrifices he has to make.'[26]

Be that as it may, there was good reason for the new Grenadian elite to be anxiety-ridden. As leaders of a political revolution, they had less time to deliver the goods than did leaders of social revolutions such as Cuba's. The latter preside over populations mobilized by nationalism and anti-Americanism, eager for change and prepared to sacrifice for that change. The former first have to secure their political positions, all the while engaging in redistributionist policies, policies designed to placate or even redress a sense of injustice rather than restructuring an unjust system. The problem in Grenada was that there was not much to redistribute: previous governments led a hand-to-mouth existence, and Gairy's past corruption and mismanagement virtually guaranteed the same for the New Jewel regime.

Here, though, is where the Cuban card came into play. First, and most important, was the immediate and efficient short-term Cuban aid – enough in fact to secure two requirements: to prop up the regime politically through military and security (including intelligence) assistance, and to shore it up economically where it counted by providing jobs, health services and technical advice. As noted above, so rapid were the Cuban moves that soon after Prime Minister Bishop visited Canada seeking funds for a viability study for a new international airport, he announced that some 250 men, together with a great deal of machinery, cement and steel, would arrive from Cuba to begin work on it. As other infrastructure projects were begun by the Cubans, the regime was freed to use its limited resources for what West Indians generally call 'make work', mostly unproductive public works employment on a piecemeal basis.

The Cuban connection also served to provide a mantle of revolutionary urgency for acts that were manifestly political: the closing down of the *Torchlight*, the banning of one branch of the Rastafarian movement, the suspension of students who led a protest, the arrest of opponents who were then held without formal charges, the sealing off of major areas for military reasons, and finally, the ridiculing of parliamentary politics as 'five-second democracy'. The Cuban card allowed Grenada's Minister of Security, Hudson Austin, to do all this and then explain: 'There are still some people in the country who do not realize there is a revolution in the country.'[27] Surely even the Minister should have recognized that his words contained an empirical truth as well as a rationalized political complaint.

The happenings in Grenada, and to a lesser extent Jamaica, were of deep concern to the governments of Trinidad and Tobago and Barbados. In the 30 April, 1979, 'Memorandum of Understanding of Matters of

Co-operation Between the Government of Barbados and the Government of the Republic of Trinidad and Tobago', Prime Ministers Eric Williams of Trinidad and Tom Adams of Barbados took note of the 'growing complexity of the security problems of the Caribbean region and agreed to consult from time to time thereon.' Among the issues they identified as of particular concern to their countries were 'terrorism, piracy, the use of mercenaries . . . and the introduction into the region of techniques of subversion.' Not unimportant was the April 1979 publication of the Trinidad government's 'White Paper on CARICOM [Caribbean Community and Common Market], 1973–1978,' a pessimistic assessment, especially of Jamaica's and Guyana's roles in the common market arrangements. The two documents were an indication that oil-rich Trinidad was at least intimating a shift in its regional policies, to favour its friends and shun its enemies. Barbados's Adams was in the former category; Manley, Burnham, and the other Caribbean leftists were in the latter. Eric Williams was playing the negative side of the Cuban card – Cuban subversion and interference as straw man. Thus the Trinidad case was further illustration of the West Indian art of politics, for few Caribbean politicians were more astute at playing the Cuban card than Williams; he remained the master political artist of the area until his death in mid-1981.

In a real sense Eric Williams's legitimacy as a politician was from the beginning based on his reputation for personal independence, even rebelliousness – first from the Caribbean Commission – created and dominated by France, Britain, the Netherlands and the US to guide the area after World War II – for which he worked, then as premier of autonomous Trinidad. During the years of the West Indies Federation, Williams led the battle for 'unit participation' in foreign policy, refusing to surrender any powers in this area to the federal government. His background included the writing of a classic in Marxist historiography, *Capitalism and Slavery* (1944), and a consistent battle to regain major parts of the US military base at Chaguaramas. Williams took good advantage of his reputation as a radical: he used it fundamentally to outflank the Trinidadian left represented within his party (the People's National Movement [PNM]) by C.L.R. James and outside it by the various leaders of the Oil Field Workers Trade Union (OWTU). When it was convenient, he played on the anti-colonial angle, British or American, as well as the racial one.

Williams's attitude towards Latin America in general and Venezuela in particular was always ambiguous. In 1963 Williams warned a high-level Venezuelan delegation that unless a Venezuelan 30 per cent surtax on goods from Trinidad was removed, he intended to initiate discussions in the United Nations on remaining colonialism in the Caribbean, 'and he wished to indicate that included the 30 per cent Antillean surtax, the importance of which should not be minimized.'[28] His hope had always been to integrate the Caribbean archipelago. 'Our stand on this', he wrote in 1968, 'has always been crystal clear from as far back as January, 1962. . . . It was to work towards the formation of a Caribbean Economic Community, beginning with, but not limited to, the Caribbean Commonwealth countries.'[29] Such an alignment, he argued, was warranted by a common history, geographical proximity, similarity of economic structure, and limited national markets.

In the early 1960s, however, Williams was not eager to push this idea far enough to include Cuba. In fact, it was the Cuban Revolution of 1959 that forced him to seek an understanding with Venezuela, which, as noted, gained Castro's ire. Good relations with that nation – which is separated from Trinidad by only seven miles of the Gulf of Paria – made good ideological and national security sense. With Cuba's Castro and Venezuela's Betancourt locked in a battle with hemisphere-wide ramifications, Williams placed Trinidad on the side of Venezuela and anti-communism in a clear anti-Castro stance. Faced with increasing opposition from leftist forces that had become disappointed in his middle-of-the-road policies, Williams had his eye on events at home and on the guerrilla movement just across the Gulf of Paria. The appearance in 1963 in Trinidad of a newspaper that carried news of Venezuela's guerrilla movement, including a verbatim reprint of a *Fuerzas Armadas de Liberación Nacional* (FALN) statement,[30] indicated some degree of transnational contact and co-operation among radical circles. Williams wasted no time.

That same year, 1963, the first anniversary of Trinidad's independence, Williams chose *Le Monde Diplomatique* of Paris to take his first public stance on the Cuban issue. He portrayed the significance of Trinidad and Tobago as an independent country in the modern world as representing a confrontation in the Caribbean of the dominant points of view that faced the world of the day: (1) active partnership between government and investors in Trinidad and Tobago as against the state direction of the economy of Cuba; (2) a direct democracy superimposed upon a parliamentary tradition in Trinidad and Tobago as against Cuba's one-party state dominated by its *caudillo*; (3) the vision in Trinidad and Tobago of a Caribbean economic community with some sort of independent existence as against the submerging of the Cuban personality behind the Iron Curtain. By 1967 the anti-Cuban line in Trinidad's foreign policy had reached a high pitch.

On 24 September, 1967, the position of Trinidad and Tobago *vis-à-vis* Cuba was put emphatically to the final session of the Twelfth Meeting of Consultation of Foreign Ministers of the Organization of American States (OAS):

> We have extended assurances to the government of Venezuela
> that we will not permit the soil of Trinidad and Tobago to be

used for purposes of subversion against the democratic regime
of the Republic of Venezuela.
. . . We propose to take all necessary action within our community to avoid the danger of communist infiltration. . . .
Finally, in the dispute between the government of Venezuela
and the totalitarian state of Cuba, and in all the circumstances
demonstrated at this meeting of Foreign Ministers, we wish to
state emphatically and unequivocally for public opinion in the
hemisphere and elsewhere in the world, we stand by Venezuela.

Again, only a few days later, on the occasion of Trinidad and
Tobago's presentation on 27 September, 1967, to the Twenty-Second
General Assembly of the United Nations, the Trinidad and Tobago position
on Cuba was made clear by its then Minister of External affairs, A.N.R.
Robinson:

I cannot end this brief review of areas of tension over which my
delegation is particularly concerned without reference to those
states which indiscriminately seek by force to impose a pattern
of government and of society on peoples outside of their borders. I refer particularly to the activities of the government of
Cuba in the western hemisphere. I say to the representative of
the government of Cuba: 'Unwarranted intervention in the affairs of other states cannot but justify intervention in your own.
Exporting revolution, be it remembered, is a two-edged sword.

Castro was incensed and disdainful. 'Isn't it ridiculous', he exploded,
'that even the spokesman of an English colony had the right to attack Cuba!
What are the merits of this colony except to have passed from British hands
to those of the Yankees?'[31] He was underestimating his opponent. In 1967
Trinidad imported TT$283,675,700 worth of goods from Venezuela
(primarily crude for refining and re-export); TT$298,137,900 worth of
goods was exported to the US; total imports from Cuba were TT$100 and
there were no exports to that island. These figures tell a story of Cuban
isolation, both ideological and economic. For Williams, keeping Cuba at a
distance was good politics. It helped mend fences with Venezuela, a major
supplier of crude for the island's refineries, at the same time making his
political moves against the left opposition in Trinidad easier.

By the end of the 1960s, however, Williams was preparing to use the
other side of the Cuban card, the 'positive' one. The shift began in 1969
with some ambiguous statements and positions. That year the Trinidad
government recommended that 'the door should be left open for the inclu-
sion of Cuba into CARIFTA [Caribbean Free Trade Association].' There
was no explanation of whether this meant with or perhaps after Castro. In

his 1969 book *From Columbus to Castro*, Williams noted for instance, that 'Castro's programme is pure nationalist, comprehensible and acceptable by any other Caribbean nationalist.' And in the field of race relations he saw Cuba as the only bright spot in the area. But Williams's old reservations were still there: 'Cuba has illustrated the basic weakness of West Indian countries – the tendency to look for external props. But the real tragedy of Cuba is that she has resorted to a totalitarian framework within which to profoundly transform her economy and society. This is the real point about the essentials of the political system in Cuba today.'[32]

The 'Cuban Model' as he called it, was not recommended for the Caribbean. Yet in 1970, Williams used the occasion of his chairmanship of the Economic and Social Council of the OAS meeting in Caracas to call for 'reabsorption' of Cuba into the OAS. Whether this was to counterbalance his call for the admission of Guyana (then locked in a border dispute with Venezuela) or an outright statement of conviction is difficult to tell. Two years later, Trinidad joined its CARIFTA partners in extending diplomatic recognition to Cuba.

It was not until June 1975, however, that Williams would make Cuba a central part of his foreign policy through a state visit to that island. 'In this mighty effort to achieve greater Caribbean solidarity', he told the students of the University of Havana, 'Cuba has a great role to play.' The search, Williams stressed, was for the Caribbean's fundamental unity and distinctive identity.'[33] Williams was now prepared to admit the island of Cuba into his conception of the Caribbean archipelago. Naturally this had to be justified somehow, and Williams was effusive in his reasoning. 'Cuba's progress', he wrote to Fidel Castro, 'is something that has to be seen to be believed.'[34]

What explained this dramatic shift in Eric Williams's foreign policy? Part of the answer lies in the changed context of the Caribbean. The 'subversive' threat seemed defeated in Trinidad as well as in Venezuela. To Williams, a new threat was posed by what he regarded as Venezuela's improper designs on the Caribbean area generally and Trinidad and Tobago specifically. Two speeches made in 1975 give a picture of Williams's concern with Venezuelan moves.

In the first speech (May 1975) Williams attacked the notion that Venezuela was a Caribbean country ('I expect next to hear that Tierra del Fuego is') and pointed to 'Venezuela's relations, territorial ambitions in respect of our area.'[35] The second speech was delivered to his party's convention on 15 June, just two days before his trip to Cuba (and to the USSR, Romania and the US, where he met with Henry Kissinger). In what amounts to one of the most scathing attacks by one Caribbean country on another during peacetime, Williams warned of Venezuela's 'penetration' of the Caribbean, berated that country for its 'belated recognition of its Caribbean identity', and chastised his CARICOM partners for falling for the new Venezuelan definition of the Caribbean (the 'Caribbean basin') and leading a 'Caribbean Pilgrimage to Caracas.'[36]

The sources of Williams's irritation with Venezuela were many, and some were certainly legitimate. For instance, contrary to the provisions of the CARICOM charter, which called for multilateral trade with non-members, Venezuela was encouraging bilateral deals. This was especially the case in bauxite and oil, both of which Williams had long wanted to dominate. But there were also differences regarding the law of the sea, objections to certain Venezuelan claims to islets in the Caribbean and to Venezuelan loans, tourism initiatives, and cultural 'penetration' through scholarships. Williams expressed the fear that Caribbean and Latin American primary products were 'jumping from the European and American frying pan into the South American fire' and that the net result would be the recognition of Venezuela as 'a new "financial centre" of the world.'[37]

Despite the weightiness of any one of these issues, however, Williams's most detailed analysis was reserved for an inventory of his attempts to get a fishing accord with Venezuela, a long-standing controversy that, by 1975, Williams wanted to put to rest, stating that 'one man can only take so much, and I have had enough. . . . As far as I am concerned, I have had my fill of this fishy business, and as Prime Minister I wash my hands of it . . . if we can't agree on fish, how can we agree on oil.'[38]

The truth was that the fishing dispute had spilled over into Trinidad's domestic political arena. It had become part of the racial political strife as the largely Indian opposition party, the United Labour Force (ULF), began to agitate for the rights of the predominantly Indian fishermen caught in the dispute with Venezuela. Williams felt that the Venezuelan government was siding with the Indians and thus interfering in internal Trinidadian politics. He feared that this was but a harbinger of what would follow once the question of oil in the ill-defined Gulf of Paria came up, as it no doubt would. It was time to play the positive side of the Cuban card on the international scene.

Williams gladly traded open praise for Cuba for Cuban neutrality in the struggle within Trinidadian politics, especially within the opposition party, in which a battle was unfolding between moderates and radicals. A radical victory could very well mean an end to the racial politics which was the best guarantee of continued power for Williams's black-based PNM. It paid off: in 1976 the ULF split with the radical faction remaining a clear minority isolated in every way. Once again, a radical group, not enjoying any mass base, had been outflanked by the traditional politician playing on the theme of friendship with Cuba. In this case, Venezuela adequately substituted as the straw man. In politics it is useful to have external enemies as well as friends; Williams knew how to manipulate both. After Williams's death, the PNM transferred power smoothly and proceeded to call an election in 1982, which it won easily. As the national budget for 1982 reached TT$10 billion, both Cuba and Venezuela faded as issues. Nothing had changed in Trinidad.

During the 1970s, however, politics in the Eastern Caribbean islands took a turn that caused a shift in the policies of both Trinidad and Venezuela. A renewed anti-Cuban alliance, similar to that which existed in the early and middle 1960s, was in the making.

By 1979, the islands of the Eastern Caribbean had clearly joined the ideological fray. The 30 April, 1979, 'Memorandum on Economic Co-operation Between Trinidad and Barbados' clearly illustrated the trends in the Eastern Caribbean: close links between oil-rich Trinidad and fast-growing Barbados, ranging from co-operation in defence and security matters, to support for the University of the West Indies, to energy. This was an obvious move to counter the activities of the 'radicals' in the Eastern Caribbean. And they in turn responded.

The July 1979 Declaration of St Georges (Grenada), signed by the Prime Ministers of Grenada, Dominica and St Lucia, was supposed to herald a dramatic shift in ideological orientation in the Eastern Caribbean. Bishop of Grenada clearly had the stellar role, followed closely by Deputy-Prime Minister George Odlum of St Lucia; a distant third was Oliver Seraphin from Dominica. Bishop and Odlum had previously revealed that they had met some ten years before on Rat Island, off St Lucia, to plan a revolutionary strategy for the Eastern Caribbean. The Declaration of St Georges was by all appearances the culmination of that process. With independence for St Vincent approaching, that island was fully expected to join the 'radical' alliance.

There can be no doubt that the political battle had been joined in the Eastern Caribbean. On the 'radical' side were the young intellectuals, scions of the area's middle classes, and on the other, the ageing veterans of the anti-colonial movements, the labour-union-based politicians. Events in St Vincent gave some indication of the way the battle went. It was predicted that the 1979 elections would be a toss-up between the traditional forces, which remained divided (Milton Cato's St Vincent Labour party, 'Son' Mitchell's New Democratic party (NDP), and Ebenezer Joshua's People's Political party – all three past premiers of the island), and the radical forces, recently united under the banner of the United People's Movement (UPM). This coalition joined one social democratic party (People's Democratic Movement) with two professing 'scientific socialism', ARWEE and the Youlou Liberation Movement (YULIMO).

YULIMO was led by a white Vincentian, Dr Ralph Gonsalves, at the time a professor at the University of the West Indies Cave Hill campus in Barbados. An intense and attractive public speaker, Gonsalves was representative of the new middle-class radicals of the region: impatient with parliamentary structures and procedures, moved by a profound conviction that they could provide better leadership than the old guard. The nearly eulogistic description of the radical UPM's principal leaders by *Caribbean Contact* is revealing: 'A roll-call of UPM's principal leaders is like a who's who of St Vincent's brighter and more dedicated sons and daughters. These include Oscar Allen, Simeon Greene, Dr Kenneth John, Carlyle Dougan, E. Dougan, Y. Francis, Robbie FitzPatrick, Renwick Rose, Adrian Saunders, Caspar London, Tysel John, Mike Browne, and Dr Ralph Gonsalves.'[39] The election results, however, indicated that Vincentians were not yet ready for what Dr Gonsalves called 'a broad theoretical programme of socialist orientation.' Cato's Labour party won eleven of thirteen seats and ex-Premier 'Son' Mitchell's NDP won the remaining two. Cato had run on virtually one theme: 'Stem the leftist tide.' It paid off, at least for the time.

The post-election uprising of Rastafarians on Union Island in the St Vincent's Grenadines and the quick dispatch of a Barbadian police contingent to assist the Cato government indicate that there might not be too many more Grenada-like surprises possible in the Eastern Caribbean. It was the first intra-regional intervention in the English-speaking Caribbean. It would not be the last as the West Indian leaders sought to remedy the tragedy of the murder of Maurice Bishop in October, 1983.

The American response to all this showed that the hysteria which had led to so many CIA operations was waning. Radical and dramatic shifts in the foreign policy of a major nation are rare occurrences. Not only do vital interests not change that readily, but the weight of the past continues to influence contemporary attitudes and predispositions. These international and internal constraints on West Indian government reforms became even more apparent during 1975 and 1976. They presented a unique opportunity for a foreign policy initiative such as the one the new Democratic administration had in mind. The Carter Administration in 1976 launched a diplomatic campaign, the intensity of which had not been seen since Kennedy's 'Alliance for Progress'. Critical was the level of travelling emissaries, which included his wife, his Secretary of State, his Under-Secretary of State for Political Affairs, his Assistant-Secretary of State for Inter-American Affairs, and his Ambassador to the United Nations (Andrew Young). Young's appeal and effectiveness cannot be overstated.[40]

Perhaps most important was the long-standing support from the House Sub-committee on Inter-American Affairs headed for many years by Democratic Representative Dante Fascell of Florida. Fascell has long held that relationshps with the Caribbean should subordinate military to political considerations and that the US should play a 'supporting' rather than hegemonic role, utilizing, where possible, multilateral and regional organizations. Though the US had not abandoned concern with military security (especially in view of Soviet naval activities), it is clear that US policy emphasis was no longer military, as Assistant-Secretary of State for Inter-American Affairs Terrence Todman explained:

> We no longer see the Caribbean in quite the same stark military security context that we once viewed it. Rather, our security concerns in the Caribbean are increasingly political in nature. The threat is not simply foreign military bases on our doorstep. It is possible an even more troublesome prospect: proliferation of impoverished Third World states whose economic and political problems bled with our own.[41]

Washington began on the one hand to downplay the significance of the radical threat in the area and on the other hand to emphasize the 'opportunistic' nature of the non-Marxist 'left'. As early as 1972, when asked about the significance of a Conference of Caribbean Revolutionary Groups in Guyana, the representative of the Defense Intelligence Agency (DIA) noted: 'It appears to have been a political image-building effort by the man in Guyana, Jagan. . . . It just seemed to be a lot of rhetoric and propaganda.'[42] The Agency, he told Congress, did not attach much significance to the meeting at all. Similarly, the Deputy-Assistant Secretary of State for Inter-American Affairs, after noting that Prime Minister Forbes Burnham of Guyana had declared Guyana to be a Marxist-Leninist state, had nationalized all large foreign-owned enterprises (and many local ones), voted against the US in the United Nations, and had very close ties with Cuba, could still conclude: 'But an independent Guyana seeking its own path to social progress is no threat to this country.'[43]

To Terrence Todman, Assistant-Secretary of State for Inter-American Affairs, there was a possible 'strategic' aspect to some Caribbean radicalism: 'A militant anti-US posture could appear to them as the only way to get our attention and realize their ambitions.'[44]

Washington had finally caught on to the contradictions inherent in the radical politics – both national and international – of the West Indian nations. Except for skilled nudges to the right, Washington appeared satisfied to allow these contradictions to work themselves out.

The shift in American foreign policy must be seen as a foreign policy ideal: the powerful should always exercise a degree of influence and force consonant with the effects sought and with the tenacity of opposition present or anticipated. The goal for the majority in both the Caribbean and the US had always been democracy. A major event in Nicaragua not only made this goal more possible than ever, it greatly contributed to bringing the era of the Cold War to a close.

The Sandinistas who defeated the Somoza dictatorship in 1979 had their origins in the guerrilla movement begun in 1959–60 under Cuban auspices. The Leninist nature of the Sandinista leadership was evident in statements such as Tomás Borges's rejection of electoral politics because: 'our working class in general is not spontaneously revolutionary. . . . It must be led to this role of vanguard of the revolutionary process.'

Clearly, an elite's determination to build a particular political system and its capacity and ability to do so are two different things. This is especially true in the case of Marxist-Leninist revolutions, which require major cultural changes.

While Nicaraguan historical anti-Americanism and nationalism served the Nicaraguans – as they had the Cubans – clearly this was not enough to sustain a revolutionary mobilization. It was enough, however, to contain the CIA-trained and financed irregular forces, the *contras*. The latter, secure in their Honduras encampments, could not be defeated, but neither could they win.[45] There existed a terribly bloody and destructive stalemate. Some comparative statistics will illustrate that there was nothing 'low intensity' (the favourite US military term for such wars) about the Nicaraguan situation. The ratio of war dead to population in Nicaragua between 1981 and 1986 was 1:100 while the ratio in the Vietnam War to US population was 1:4,233. Nicaragua was neither a purely CIA-created conflict as the Marxists wished to portray it nor a war against tyranny as US propaganda would have it. It was a fully-fledged civil war.

The war was brought to an end by two events which reflect the new reality in the Caribbean. First, the opposition in Washington itself to US assistance to the *contras*. From the moment when in December 1981, President Reagan signed the first National Intelligence Finding establishing US support for the Nicaraguan Resistance, there were voices of opposition in Congress. Evidence that the CIA had participated in the mining of the main Nicaraguan harbour, heightened the opposition. Congress responded in December 1982 with the Boland Amendment prohibiting Central Intelligence Agency (CIA) and Department of Defense (DoD) expenditures to promote overthrowing the government of Nicaragua. When, in October 1984, Congress voted to cut off all funding for the *contras*, the National Security Council staff, and especially Lieutenant Colonel Oliver North, moved to fill the void left by the CIA and the DoD. The complex legal, constitutional and political consequences of all this activity became a classic battle between the Executive Branch and the Congress. The resulting scandal, 'Irangate', has still not been totally unravelled but it is evident that the US was, officially at least, out of the fray.

By far the most important reason for the termination of the war, however, was the peace process initiated and concluded by Latin Americans themselves. It started with a meeting on Contadora island but when that initiative lagged, President Oscar Arias of Costa Rica carried a new process to a successful conclusion. His logic was clear, and had ample support in the literature:[46] the realization that in the face of an increasingly bloody stalemate that is likely to end in negotiations 'someday', it is best to begin negotiations now. This is so partly because of one well-studied advantage of pre-armistice negotiations: they tend to make it easier for either party to call for a ceasefire without losing face.

But Arias also understood that 'history' was on the side of a democratic opening. Three trends made this evident:

1 The new surge of democracy in Latin America, which not only converted the members of the 'Lima Group' (Argentina, Brazil, Uruguay and Peru) into living advocates of pluralist politics, but also tarnished the credentials of 'semi-democratic' Mexico to speak for Latin America.
2 The changing mood in Europe, especially in democratic Spain and France, as the Leninist nature of the Sandinista project became more evident.
3 The development of pluralist politics, which were in full swing in the rest of Central America by mid-1985.

The Sandinistas, said Arias, had to accept the principle of self-determination and let a democratic election decide the future of Nicaragua.

That the mood and trends in Latin America were not favourable to Leninist projects was made patently clear during the months of late 1985 and early 1986, as the electoral results from Honduras, Guatemala and Costa Rica became evident. Far from contributing to the continued official US position asserting the 'domino theory', the results of those elections showed that Sandinista and other Marxist-Leninist propaganda efforts in Central America had failed miserably. In Guatemala, Christian Democrat Venicio Cerezo won by the greatest landslide in that country's history, with 68 per cent of the vote; in Costa Rica, Oscar Arias received 52 per cent of the vote. Crucial was the fact that the Costa Rican Communist Party (under the banner of the Popular Alliance), which had undertaken a purge to put stoutly pro-Cuban and pro-Sandinista members on its Central Committee, received only 0.7 per cent of the popular vote.

The Sandinistas were persuaded, despite Cuban opposition, to accept the Arias plan and go to the polls. They were soundly defeated. With fully 86 per cent of the electorate voting, the opposition candidate Mrs Violeta Chamorro received 54.7 per cent while Comandante Daniel Ortega of the Sandinistas received 40.8 per cent. With the considerable intervention of former US President Jimmy Carter, the Sandinistas accepted their defeat. Carter, who initiated the politics of respecting Caribbean nationalism and demands for self-determination, returned to reap the fruits of what he had sowed.[47]

The whole Caribbean could now hope that the age of insurgency and counter-insurgency was finally over. There were other serious problems to attend to.

Notes

1 Arthur M. Schlesinger, *A Thousand Days* (New York: Fawcett Books, 1965), p. 709.
2 *Ibid.*, p. 713.
3 Report of the *British Guiana Constitutional Commission* (1954), p. 30.
4 Schlesinger, p. 713.
5 *New York Times*, 24 May, 1966, p. 14.
6 Cheddi Jagan, *The West On Trial* (London: Seven Seas Books, 1966).
7 The meeting between Jagan and Schlesinger took place in the offices of *The Nation* in New York (cf. Editorial *The Nation*, 4 June, 1990).
8 General Bruce Palmer, Jr., *Intervention in the Caribbean: The Dominican Crisis of 1965* (Lexington: The University Press of Kentucky, 1989), p. 150.
9 Cf. Lawrence A Yates, *Power Pack: US Intervention in the Dominican Republic, 1965–1966* (US Army Command and General Staff College: Leavenworth Papers No. 15, 1988), pp. 178–9.
10 The best study on the Dominican 'left' is Piero Gleijeses, *The Dominican Crisis: The 1965 Constitutionalist Revolt and American Intervention* (Baltimore: The Johns Hopkins University Press, 1978). For an account of the mistakes made by the communist leadership see the amazingly candid essay by J.I. Quello and N. Isa Conde, 'Revolutionary Struggle in the Dominican Republic and its Lessons', *World Marxist Review* (Pt. One, December, 1965, pp. 71–81; Pt. Two, January, 1966, pp. 33–36).
11 K.S. Karol, *Guerrillas in Power: The Course of the Cuban Revolution* (New York: Hill & Wang, 1970), pp. 19–20.
12 *Ibid.*, p. 20.
13 See the various studies and documents in Jiri Valenta and Herbert J. Ellison (eds), *Grenada and Soviet/Cuban Policy* (Boulder: Westview Press, 1986).
14 Mark Falcoff, 'Bishop's Cuba, Castro's Grenada', in Valenta and Ellison (eds), *Grenada*, p. 71.
15 Cf. Carlos Moore, *Castro, The Blacks, and Africa* (Los Angeles: Centre for Afro-American Studies, 1988). Moore believes that blacks are a solid majority in Cuba today but grossly under-represented in authority positions.
16 For a fuller discussion of this point, see A.P. Maingot, 'The Difficult Path to Socialism in the English-Speaking Caribbean', in Richard Fagen, (ed.), *The State and Capitalism in US-Latin American Relations* (Stanford, Calif.: Stanford University Press, 1979), pp. 254–301.
17 These surveys by Carl Stone appeared periodically in the *Daily Gleaner* (Jamaica), 30 January, 1978, and 6 February, 1978. Carl Stone has also made the point in his study *Electoral Behaviour and Public Opinion in Jamaica* (Mona: ISER, 1974).
18 *Weekly Gleaner* (Jamaica), 10 April, 1978.
19 Interviews by the author with Jamaican 'exiles' (Miami, Florida, August 1978).
20 *New York Times*, 30 September, 1979.
21 Cf. by this author, 'Political Analysis and Contemporary History', in Peter A. Gonzales, *et. al.*, (eds), *Independence for Grenada* (St Augustine, Trinidad: Institute of International Relations, 1974), pp. 21–35; 'Options for Grenada: The Need to be Cautious', *Caribbean Review* (Fall 1983), pp. 24–8.
22 *Caribbean Insight*, Vol. 2, no. 4 (April 1979): 4.

23 Interviewed by Alister Hughes and John Redman, *Caribbean Life and Times*, Vol. I, no. 2 (December 1979): 39.

24 *Miami Herald*, 27 November, 1979.

25 Archie Singham, *The Hero and the Crowd* (New Haven, Conn.: Yale University Press, 1968).

26 *Ibid.*, p. 152.

27 *Miami Herald*, 16 October, 1979.

28 This section is more fully analyzed in A.P. Maingot, 'National Policies and Regional Definitions: The Caribbean as an Interest Area', in Basil Ince *et. al.* (eds), *Issues in Caribbean International Relations* (Lanham, M.D.: University Press of America, 1983) pp. 309–37.

29 'Feature Address and Official Opening', in *Seminar on the Foreign Policies of Caribbean States* (St Augustine, Trinidad: Institute of International Relations, 1968), p. 9.

30 *The Circle* (Port of Spain, Trinidad), Vol. 1, no. 11 (November 1963).

31 Cited in Moore, *Castro*, p. 269.

32 Eric Williams, *From Columbus to Castro* (London: André Deutsch, 1970), pp. 486, 510.

33 *Guardian* (Port of Spain, Trinidad), 21 June, 1975, p. 1.

34 *Ibid.*, 24 June, 1975, p. 1.

35 *Ibid.*, 13 June, 1975, p. 9.

36 *Ibid.*, 18, 19 and 20 June, 1975 (all p. 1).

37 *Ibid.*, 20 June, 1975, p. 9.

38 *Ibid.*, 16 June, 1975, p. 1.

39 *Caribbean Contact* (Barbados), September 1979. The arbitrary and selective nature of radical sentiments in the Caribbean is patent in this weekly. Although financed by US, Canadian and Western European monies, this weekly has been a vocal supporter of Cuba and the radical movements in the Caribbean – except Guyana, from where the editor was expelled.

40 See *The New York Times* coverage of Andrew Young's trip: 'There really has been a change Mr Young has been saying throughout the tour, and the responsiveness of the Caribbean leaders . . . has seemed at times to be more than the visitors expected.' (14 August, 1977, p. 15). 'During the trip, hosts and guests sometimes seemed to be bursting with eagerness to cement the new relationship with praise.' (18 August, 1977, p. 3).

41 *Hearings, House Sub-committee on Inter-American Affairs*, 28 June, 1977, p. 30.

42 Soviet Activites in Cuba, Part 3, *Hearings, SIAA* [Subcommittee on Inter-American Affairs], 26 September, 1972, p. 18.

43 Soviet Activities in Cuba, Parts 6 and 7 *Hearings*, SIAA, 15 June, 1976, p. 2.

44 *Hearings*, SIAA, 28 June, 1977, p. 30.

45 Cf. Anthony P. Maingot, 'Why Not a Diplomatic Political Option in Nicaragua?' in David Ronfeldt and Brian Jenkins (eds), *The Nicaraguan Resistance and US Policy* (Santa Monica, CA.: RAND, 1989), pp. 48–71.

46 Paul R. Pillar, *Negotiating Peace: War Termination as a Bargaining Process* (Princeton, N.J.: Princeton University Press, 1983).

47 A lively account of President Carter's multiple involvements in democratic elections around this period are recorded by one who was a major architect of that initiative, Robert A. Pastor, *Whirlpool: US Foreign Policy Toward Latin America and the Caribbean* (Princeton, N.J.: Princeton University Press, l992.)

Part III

Problems of the modern Caribbean

CHAPTER 7

Threats to social and national security: The internationalization of corruption and violence

The shift from geopolitics, with its emphasis on containing communism, to geoeconomics had come none too soon for the Caribbean. Even a cursory survey of the literature on the region in the early 1990s reveals the outlines of a monstrous new menace to the survival of these small democratic societies. There are the accounts of the corrupt banking practices which stretch throughout the hemisphere,[1] detailed accounts of region-wide organizations smuggling drugs and weapons and laundering money,[2] and there are case studies on corruption in Antigua, the Dominican Republic, Venezuela and Colombia.[3] A recent visit to the island of Dutch Sint Maarten reveals society-wide concerns over Italian Mafia involvements in casinos, hotels and yacht havens.[4]

Despite evidence that American intelligence services have not yet switched out of the Cold War mode to confront the new threats,[5] throughout the region the sense of threat is so great that governments are showing some flexibility with an otherwise strict adherence to state-centric principles of self-determination. They are calling for outside assistance in sensitive investigations. This certainly was the case in the Bahamas and in Trinidad. One of the first measures taken by the new Bahamian government of Hubert Ingraham's Free National Movement (FNM), was to set up a commission to enquire into corrupt practices during the 25-year rule of Lynden Pindling's Progressive Liberal Party (PLP). Not only did the new Bahamian authorities bring in a Jamaican-born judge from Bermuda to head the commission, they sought the active participation of Britain's Scotland Yard, the US FBI and the Royal Canadian Mounted Police. When questioned whether this was not a political vendetta, Prime Minister Ingraham responded that the elections of 19 August, 1992 had been fought on a promise of returning 'an acceptable level of accountability' to public officials including the Prime Minister. Democracy had worked, and Pindling was dismissed by the public. 'As far as I am concerned', Ingraham concluded, 'that was very adequate punishment for the abuses which he was guilty of while in office.'[6]

In Trinidad, the new Peoples National Movement (PNM) government of Patrick Manning was not having as easy a time of it. He admitted that one of the first things which struck him when he took office 'was the extent of corruption in the society.'[7] At that point, let it be said, he was not yet informed of the full extent of the rot. The following chronology describes what is at this time of writing still unfolding as a dangerous crisis in the island:

31 March, 1992	Assistant Police Commissioner Rodwell Murray states on television that his dismissal from the Police Service was because of his refusal to co-operate with a gigantic 'drug cartel' operating in the Police Service.
3 April, 1992	The Minister of National Security says the government had launched an investigation using members of the island's Police Service.
4 April, 1992	The Leader of the Opposition, Basdeo Panday, calls for an independent, foreign commission to do the investigating. He relates the fate of previous investigations (*Scott Drug Report*, *Report on the Latinta Affair* – all relating to police corruption).
18 April, 1992	The government appoints an Appeal Court judge and a pastor of the Seventh Day Adventist Church as a Commission of Enquiry.
8 May, 1992	On the eve of his departure for the US, Prime Minister Manning announces that the island's inability to handle the crisis has led him to call on the UK's Scotland Yard (SY) and that he would ask the US to establish a DEA office in Trinidad. 'This is an international problem that cannot be handled by one country alone.'
24 June, 1992	The SY officers arrive.
30 August, 1992	Ex-Commissioner criticizes the move, calling it 'The recolonialization of the Police Service.'
17 September, 1992	The Prime Minister says that he is 'amazed' at what the SY uncovered and asks for a larger team. There is a drug cartel operating, murders and millions of dollars are involved going back to 1984.
21 September, 1992	'What is being unearthed by the SY detectives is a sad and demoralizing reflection on our country.' (Editorial, *Trinidad Guardian*).
29 November, 1992	Police Chief Sagram Bhagwandeen is suspended for hampering SY investigations. 'In one instance the [SY] detectives were threatened with a gun by a senior police officer,' says the Prime Minister.
5 February, 1993	Some 200 police officers picketed Parliament demanding the resignation of the Minister of National Security and protesting the presence of the SY officers. At

the same time, the government was announcing the retrenchment of 2,000 civil service jobs; a national strike was threatened.

In Jamaica, drug seizures in 1992 were breaking all records and a serious heroin link, Nigeria-Jamaica-US, was uncovered. Meanwhile, US-Jamaica relations were strained when a US bounty-hunter attempted to kidnap a Guianese who had jumped bond in Florida where he was under indictment on cocaine smuggling charges. Foreign Minister David Coore announced that Jamaica would review its extradition treaty with the US. 'Jamaica', said Coore, 'could not accept the US Supreme Court's finding that US courts could try criminals kidnapped out of foreign countries.[8] In early November, 1992 the new Prime Minister, P.J. Patterson, declared 'war' on crime, much of it drug related, which had already taken 500 lives that year.[9]

Throughout the region corruption was engendering violence and un-certainty about the loyalty of forces of law and order. The word 'com-munist' seemed to have disappeared from the vocabulary, replaced by 'czar', 'don', 'Kingpin', 'big man' – however each island referred to the new breed of pirates. It was a challenge which demanded greater co-operation with the US, in part because the US was the source of much of the problem.

In many ways Robert Vesco is prototypical of the modern-day pirate operating in the Caribbean. A fugitive from US justice, his status as a 'felon in flight' in no way prevented him from establishing the closest of relation-ships with political elites, first in Costa Rica, then in the Bahamas, Antigua and, finally, as a guest of Fidel Castro in Cuba. In September 1989, a Federal Grand Jury in Florida accused Vesco of collaborating with Medellín Cartel *capos* Pablo Escobar Gaviria, José Gonzalo Rodríguez Gacha, and Jorge Ochoa Vásquez and of trafficking drugs from Colombia through Nicaragua, the Bahamas and Cuba.[10] Clearly, aside from money, Vesco has talents and skills which a variety of elites of diverse ideology find useful. There are, in the Caribbean Basin and elsewhere, no shortage of sovereign states ready to give such pirates safehaven. Indeed, there are even states which purposefully encourage and facilitate the granting of safehaven as a significant source of income in convertible currency. Panama under the Noriega dictatorship was one such case. Citizenship, passports, visas, all were for sale and governments as diverse as the US and Cuba found the Panamanian 'arrangement' quite suitable to their wider geopolitical goals. It is now revealed, by the Director of Panama's Technical Judicial Police (PTJ) that 75 per cent of the criminals sought by INTERPOL had entered or settled in Panama at some point.[11]

It is the awareness of this reality that led Jamaican Prime Minister,

Michael Manley, to tell the United Nations that drug traffickers and criminals 'have the globe to play with':[12]

> You are dealing with a level of international criminal organization that is probably without precedent. Those who manipulate production, transport, distribution and marketing operate in a global framework.

What Manley was addressing was the internationalization of corruption which made such a 'global framework' possible. What makes this corruption international is the fact that it invariably involves actions and transactions in more than one national jurisdiction. A whole series of actions, generally referred to as 'layering', make the tracing of money flows and principal actors virtually impossible. This type of corruption is beyond the control or supervision of any one state. Manley's concern was, of course, with how this process would affect his native Jamaica. 'I certainly can't conceive', he told the press, 'of what kind of Jamaica our people could build on the basis of a drug culture or a society massively corrupted by drug trafficking.'[13]

Neither traditional (viz. nepotism) nor bureaucratic-administrative (viz. jobbery) corruption are new to the Caribbean. From the Bahamas through Cuba, all the way down the island chain to Trinidad, the region has had a reputation for both. Nor is it a case that the region is necessarily more corrupt than other areas. When Walter Lippmann noted that in the US corruption was 'endemic', he could well have spoken for many another country.[14] Lippmann also made a universally valid methodological point when he maintained that no history of corruption was possible, only the history of the exposure of corruption. Exposure, he maintained, invariably was merely one sequence in a cycle which alternated between 'unsuspecting complacency and violent suspicion.' Clearly, however, empirical and conceptual elusiveness should not deter attempts at a more systematic understanding of the phenomenon. It is the central argument of this chapter that the greatest menace to the security of the states in the Caribbean Basin stems from a new form or level of corruption which should best be called the internationalization of corruption and violence.

The Caribbean Sea acts both as a barrier and as a bridge. Both functions favour the new internationalization of corruption and violence. By balkanizing the region into relatively weak nation states while at the same time facilitating the flow of international commerce and transnational activities of some of the world's great producers and exporters, this sea puts many an international activity beyond the reach of nation states. The result is often an asymmetry in manoeuvering capabilities between national and international actors. This asymmetry is augmented and perpetuated by the technical and electronic revolution which gives even private parties enormous capacities of communication, including the electronic transferral of capital. The international cartels tend also to have preferential access to human talent. Indeed, as ex-President Lopez Michelsen of Colombia has noted, the transferability of skills and technology from legitimate industry to the drug trade, has made the latter a truly modern and transnational industry.[15] The Caribbean not only provides the bridge between the producer and the consumer in that industry, its modern banking system provides virtually impenetrable shelter to its profits.

The importance of all this is that the drug trade both contributes to and is facilitated by widespread and enduring corruption which permeates key elements – though certainly not all – of both the public and private sectors. Combating specific aspects of the drug trade (cultivation, transportation, distribution), difficult as that is, is a great deal simpler than uprooting corruption. The problems are both conceptual and practical.

The central methodological difficulties in discussing security in the post-Cold War era are two. The first problem is that the bulk of the literature has concentrated on Cold War issues, i.e. the threat from communist subversion. The role of Cuba in this has been amply covered. Secondly, the preference of the behavioural sciences to 'measure' and quantify behaviour, leads necessarily to a focus on discrete events or 'incidents' which fit into fairly clear conceptual categories. As such, the *coup d'état* (an internal action to overthrow a regime) and the *coup de main* (an overthrow attempt by invasion or, at least, by external forces), lend themselves very neatly to quantification. Once quantified, social scientists can 'measure' degrees of instability.[16] Using the *coup d'état* and the *coup de main* as the dependent variables, for instance, the first major study of security in the Eastern Caribbean concluded that population size is 'the best explanation of how size affects the probability of security incidents occurring.'[17] The smaller the population, the greater the instability. Destabilizing incidents in small states, however, tend to be over quickly. The minuscule size of the political, social and economic institutions in microstates 'simply makes it difficult to sustain prolonged divisions in the body politic.'[18]

Neither of the above approaches, however, are adequate to an understanding of the *ongoing* threats to the security of small Caribbean states. Neither versions of a communist menace nor enumerations of discrete – and short lasting – incidents of violence address the true nature of the contemporary threats. Much more promising is the approach of Peter Calvert who divides the threats to small states into four categories:[19]

1   Attack by external forces, including mercenaries;
2   *Coups d'état*;
3   Subversion by narcotic traffickers;
4   Generalized corruption in government and/or the private sector.

It is not that there has been no awareness that the threats of the Cold War have been displaced by a new type of threat. Note the exchange between Senator John F. Kerry (D-Mass.), Chairman of the Sub-committee on Terrorism, Narcotics and International Operations of the Senate's Committee on Foreign Relations, and Nestor D. Sanchez, former Deputy Assistant Secretary for Latin American Affairs, Department of Defense:[20]

Senator Kerry: You are familiar with the assessments that General [Paul] Gorman made . . . that the national security of the US was threatened by Latin drug conspiracies dramatically more successful at subversion in those areas than the subversion efforts from Moscow.

Mr Sanchez: Absolutely, it's a national security threat to one (*sic*) country, because of the countries and individuals involved.

Senator Kerry: Now, General Gorman also testified that if you want to move weapons or munitions in Latin America, the established networks are owned by the cartels.

Senator Kerry could have mentioned that the cartels not only control networks of gun-running but also of illegal aliens. While the vast majority of illegal aliens are law abiding,[21] there are key 'pipelines' used by the cartels to bring in distributors, 'enforcers' and others into the US. Much attention has been focused on the Jamaican 'posses' (called 'yardies' in the UK) but the so-called 'Sandoval Pipeline' brought into South Florida some 175 illegals a week, at US$1700 per head, via Panama, Nassau, and Bimini.[22]

The critical methodological point, however, is that events in the Caribbean demonstrate that hardly ever do Calvert's four points operate as discrete or 'independent' events; they are interconnected and related. Nevertheless, it is the assumption here that they all have to be understood in the context of a widely practised type of corruption: a corruption which is 'functional' to the internationalization of capital, labour and labour movements which characterize the region's (and the world's) economy. In other words, it suits the logic of the market place. 'A corrupt civil servant', writes Jacob van Klaveren, 'regards his public office as a business, the income of which he will . . . seek to maximize.' The office then becomes a 'maximizing unit'. The size of his income depends 'upon the market situation and his talents for finding the point of maximal gain on the public's demand curve.' The definition is similar to that of Robert Tilman's which sees corruption in terms of a rational choice, a 'free market' type calculus: they may 'decide that it is worthwhile to risk the known sanctions and pay the higher costs in order to be assured of receiving the desired benefits.'[23] It should be evident that in the context of a new corruption, fostered by the enormous amounts of drug related monies, the concept of 'maximization', or any other utility function, cannot be measured in 'normal' terms. Even if historical standards of corruption are incorporated in the calculation, the phenomenon defies measurement. Robert Klitgaard's sound recommendation that administrative corruption should be combated through material and other incentives, clearly fails on the material (i.e. wages) side; and up to now, no one has figured out which 'other' incentives will work.[24]

Interestingly enough, the 'rational' corruption of the individual civil servant operates with the same logic as the foreign policies at certain periods of major state actors. What else, if not the maximizing of geopolitical advantages, would lead an administrator to 'marry' a corrupt dictator such as General Manuel Antonio Noriega?[25] Again, the calculus might not be financial gain but rather an attempt to avoid the discomfort of being called 'colonialist' or imperialist by a corrupt 'Third World' tyrant such as Suriname's Colonel Desi Bouterse.[26] What, then, do we know about Caribbean Basin elites' perceptions of threat?

The decades of the 1970s and 1980s were convulsive ones for the then newly-independent countries in the Caribbean. An array of violent challenges to legitimate authority seemed to find, if not direct causes, at least fertile ground in the area's propensity to both traditional and bureaucratic corruption. In the process, both the nature of corruption and violence changed.

There can be no doubt that the present attempts to 'structurally adjust' the various economies of the Caribbean Basin have put these governments under tremendous strain. The pressures are all the more threatening because these attempts at creating 'open' economies follow decades of centralizing tendencies and growth in the public sector. Pressures from the newly-enfranchised masses and formerly marginalized elites, forced the state into the economic field. A 1972 Trinidad White Paper made government's role in promoting jobs quite clear:[27]

1   The public sector must be expected to play the role of a prime mover in the economy;
2   It is important to make optimum use of private foreign capital to develop the country in a manner consistent with the emergence of local initiative and local enterprise;
3   A complex of financial and non-financial corporate bodies under public control is being progressively developed, each with terms of reference which give it greater opportunity and facility for participation in the equity of private enterprise in order to stimulate new activity.

Indeed, given their oil resources and the jump in revenues from the 'OPEC shock' of the 1970s, Trinidad had the wherewithal to enter into a state-led development program. The other societies in the Caribbean had no such source of wealth but the expectations of jobs and 'localized' development were equally strong. This was the impetus behind the calls for a 'mixed economy' which were particularly well articulated by Michael Manley and the PNP in Jamaica.

With governments throughout the region involved in negotiating contracts, from oil refining to tourism and casino gambling, it was not surprising that opportunities for malfeasance increased. The 'Commission of Enquiry' into this or that 'deal' became a fixture of West Indian political life.

By the end of the 1970s there was a clear perception in some quarters that the threats to national security were more varied than just those related to the Cold War. Indeed, the geopolitical perceptions of some Caribbean elites were being shaped by a series of events, many not directly related to the basic structural problems of the society. These are summarized in Table 7.1. The important fact is that during this radical decade, it was this array of events rather than apprehension over mass revolutionary movements which generated the local perceptions of threat.

The differences can be appreciated in the changing nature of the declarations by Barbados's Tom Adams. In 1976 he visualized no threats and thus no need to establish an army or enter into any foreign defence pacts. By 1979 he had established the Barbados Defence Force and what became known as the 'Adams Doctrine' was in full evolution. Adams's Barbados Labour Party Manifesto for 1981 made it clear that events 'within Barbados and the Caribbean' made it necessary to create 'a limited defence force with a capacity to withstand the immediate assault of potential marauders, terrorists and mercenaries.' The language was similar to that of the 1979 Memorandum of Understanding between Barbados and Trinidad which spoke of the threat of 'terrorism, piracy, and the use of mercenaries.' In the face of such a variety of threats, it was Adams's belief that a policy of 'wait and see' was akin to a policy of no assistance. The Adams Doctrine called for good intelligence so that the small but well-trained defence forces could nip conspiracies in the bud.[28]

As is evident in Table 7.1, the threat did not come from one country or one ideology. 'In 1982', wrote Prime Minister James F. Mitchell of St Vincent, 'although the US might be single-minded in its position, the Caribbean with its political diversity cannot agree on a common enemy'.[29] 'Not that West Indian leaders were innocent about Cuban actions', wrote Mitchell, 'but there were other threats'. 'Those who disparage the menace posed by the Mafia', he noted, 'are already victims'. And then, there was white collar crime. 'In St Vincent's case', he noted, 'more money is swindled through our offshore banks from US accounts than our total annual budget.'[30]

Prime Minister Mitchell's description of one of the shady sides of the growing offshore banking industry (see Chapter 8) was a rare official Caribbean statement about that business. Easily one of the fastest growing

Table 7.1: Specific events leading to a Caribbean sense of threat

---

1969   Massive urban riots in Curaçao.

1970   Black Power movement and mutiny of the army in Trinidad.

1975   Transhipment of Cuban troops (to Angola) through Barbados.

1976   Bombing (by Cuban exiled terrorist group) of Cubana Airlines plane out of Barbados.

1976   Barbados PM Tom Adams reveals that mercenaries under Sidney Burnett-Alleyne (and supported by South Africa) were preparing to invade. French in Martinique intercept Burnett-Alleyne and he is convicted of arms smuggling out of Martinique.

1978   The SRC corporation operating out of Barbados and Antigua found to have links with Israel and shipping arms to South Africa through Antigua.

1978   British intelligence reveals a second Burnett-Alleyne attempt at invading Barbados.

1979   Marxist *coup* in Grenada.

1979   St Vincent's Prime Minister Milton Cato requests (and receives) Barbadian military assistance with an invasion of Union Island by a group called Movement for National Liberation.

1980   *Coup d'état* in Suriname by l6 NCOs.

1980   Cuban airforce MIGs sink Bahamian Coast Guard cutter.

1981   Two separate *coup* attempts against government of Eugenia Charles in Dominica. The recruitment of mercenaries in the US was revealed by French intelligence in Martinique.

1982   The Regional Security System created in the OECS.

1983   The OECS requests and receives US, Jamaican and Barbadian military intervention in Grenada.

Source: A.P. Maingot, *Some Perspectives on Security of Governing Elites in the English-Speaking Caribbean*, (Claremont McKenna College: Essays on Strategy and Diplomacy No. 4, 1985).

sectors in the Caribbean, the offshore tax havens have attracted increased attention from British and US law enforcement authorities.[31]

The upshot of this series of concerns was that by the early 1980s the leaders of the small states of the Eastern Caribbean had reached the conclusion that security was to be found in collective action. On 30 October, 1982 the governments of Antigua, Dominica, St Lucia, St Vincent and Barbados created the Regional Security Systems (RSS). At this point the perceptions of threat to the Caribbean leadership came closer in line with those of the Reagan Administration. The alignment was not total, however. While the actions of Marxist-Leninist Grenada and its Cuban ally certainly were instrumental in giving shape to the new Caribbean geopolitical perspective, this was only part of the story. Many Caribbean leaders – though certainly not all – emerged from the radical period fully aware that 'pirates', 'mercenaries' and 'terrorists' responded to more than just Marxism-Leninism, that the issue of security was broader than the North-South confrontation which had taken up so much intellectual attention and energy in the Caribbean.

The fact is that Caribbean leaders' perceptions of threat were not grounded in any broad ideological or theoretical conception of national security but on hard experiences. None of the important politician-writers of the Caribbean in the 1960s, 1970s and even early 1980s had ever intimated that the threat to Caribbean security would come largely from corruption, internal and external. Even the prolific Michael Manley was totally absorbed by the North-South issue. Elected in 1972, he published a book in 1973 in which he advocated national control of the 'commanding heights of the economy' plus a 'non-aligned' foreign policy,[32] and another in 1975 which took an even more strident 'democratic socialist' stance.[33] In his decade out of power, Manley published an explanation of why they lost the 1980 elections (US 'destabilization' was a major cause),[34] a new call for his idea of 'self-reliance' through a New International Economic Order and South-South co-operation,[35] as well as a monumental book on cricket. Nowhere is the issue of a criminal threat to Jamaica seriously discussed prior to his return to government in 1989.

Academic scholars tended to follow suit; their concern was with issues of 'revolution' and dependency. Even one as moderate and well-informed as Carl Stone refused to confront the issue of the international criminal threat. As late as April 1988, Stone wrote that he found it distressing that in a year when Jamaicans were electing a new government, 'we are spending as much time agonizing over petty US gossip about supposed mafia-type links between local politics and drug dons.' He called for a discussion of 'the real issues'.[36]

Exactly one year later, after the Jamaican electorate had elected a new government without any serious debate or discussion of the Jamaican drug problem, Stone demonstrated a dramatically changed perception of the threat. The drug dealers, he wrote, were 'crippling' Jamaica: 'the very future and livelihood of this country and its people are at risk.' Such was his sense of threat that he urged that steps be taken 'in a hurry' to stop this trade, including 'any constitutional changes necessary.'[37] So what had happened, and how does it illustrate the nature of the threat to the security of Caribbean countries?

Between 1987 and 1989 several major shippers stopped shipping goods out of Jamaica: Evergreen Lines had already paid US$137 million, and Sea-Land Services, US$85 million in fines to US customs; the Kirk

Line had one of their ships confiscated in Miami (released after the payment of a fine); Air Jamaica was suffering from constant fines, and the Free Zone manufacturers were said to be in a 'tailspin' because of the use of the port by drug lords.[38]

The discovery on 6 January, 1989 of a container in the port of Kingston with US$8 million in arms, illustrated that the problem had wider ramifications. Of West German manufacture, the weapons were shipped from Portugal on a Panamanian registered ship and were destined for an unspecified group in Colombia. It took a joint effort of Jamaican, British, US and Colombian intelligence to break the Jamaican link of what was called 'an international network of drug traffickers and terrorists.'[39] The Panamanian ship was owned by Bluewater Ship Management Inc. of Panama. Both the company and its British (naturalized Panamanian) President had previously been linked to illegal arms shipments, cocaine distribution, and the laundering of drug-related monies.[40]

What was happening in Jamaica was symptomatic of a regional crisis. The region-wide alarm over the links between the corruption wrought by the drug trade and violent threats to the region, was heightened by three events in 1989 and 1990 which put a frightening new gloss on the region's problems. By far the most dramatic was the mid-1989 trial of Cuban General Arnaldo Ochoa and thirteen other high-ranking co-defendants. The most serious of the various charges was: 'engaging in hostile acts against a foreign country' through involvement in the drug trade. Ochoa and three co-defendants were sentenced to death on the basis of the prosecutor's arguments that their involvement in the drug trade had resulted in Cuba's humiliation:

> The shower of insults, infamies, and slanders that are currently
> falling upon our country is basically motivated by the imperial-
> ist press agencies, using as an excuse the actions perpetrated by
> the accused . . .[41]

Following the trial and execution, the Minister of the Interior, José Abrantes and numerous other high-ranking officers of the Ministry of the Interior were either arrested or reassigned. It was by far the largest purge in Cuban revolutionary history. Certainly no other country in the Caribbean Basin had ever confronted a drug-related crisis so deep as this one. The self-congratulatory, not to say self-righteous, tone of the Cuban media reflects the severity of the crisis:

> It would be difficult to find a country in the world where a vice-
> president [Torralba] is sent to prison for corruption . . . where a
> man with a distinguished record such as Arnaldo Ochoa's is the
> subject of a trial . . . or where a group of relatively high-ranking

officers of MININT also is sent to trial . . . and where the crime of drug trafficking is exposed in front of national and world opinion . . . To do this, a great deal of moral fortitude, honesty, and political integrity is required . . .[42]

It might very well be, as Enrique Baloyra has indicated, that in that trial *'no son todos los que están, ni están todos los que son.'*[43] It is not that one has to accept the Cuban version of the trial; certainly, the guilt of General Ochoa is much in doubt.[44] The important point is that the US had long been accusing Cuba of being involved in the trade.[45] Cuba's admission that not only were the accusations correct (despite the shift in characters involved), but that the involvement went to the highest reaches of the government, was startling. No one can read Andres Oppenheimer's journalistic *tour de force, Castro's Final Hour* without sensing that Fidel Castro himself was in on the trade. Most frightening, however, are the implications for the US and the Caribbean of a possible alliance between the underworld and state institutions. Oppenheimer cites from a secret DEA recording of a major drug smuggler regularly making the Colombia-Cuba-Miami run:

> We've got two torpedo boats!. . . . And they clear, they can scan the whole fucking [US] coast! And they tell you: go this way, go that way.[46]

The critical point for leaders in the Caribbean was that: if a tightly controlled society such as Cuba could be so deeply penetrated and threatened by the drug cartels, was any society in the Caribbean immune? To read the various testimonies presented before an ever-more alarmed US Congress, few seemed to have escaped the reach of the cartels.[47]

Further evidence of the difficulties facing the region was provided by two other dramatic events which shook Caribbean leaders and their societies. The first occurred in Trinidad in July and August, 1990: the taking as hostages of the Prime Minister and much of his government by a group of black Muslims. According to their pronouncements, they were motivated to combat the 'rot' which rampant corruption had engendered in the society. Here, then, was a case – not unknown in the Caribbean – where allegations of corruption were used as a justification to disrupt constitutional government. And yet, the very preparation and execution of this plot demonstrates the intimate links between the labyrinthian world of international finance, the world trade in weapons, and violence. The fundamental factor in this event, from the point of view of security, is the realization of the ease with which a terrorist group, regardless of 'cause', can carry out a military operation in the Caribbean. Neither Trinidadian nor US authorities appeared to have learned much from the already well-developed concern with threats to existing democracies. In the US case, it appears to demonstrate a feature evident in the past: lack of preparation and even basic information about the Caribbean.[48]

Since 1983, Trinidad papers had been reporting that Muammar Ghadafi's money was splitting the Muslim movement on the island. The papers also contained reports of the purchase of weapons by the Ghadafi-supported group, Jamaat-Al-Muslimeen.[49] Calls for the Trinidad government to sharpen its intelligence skills through Scotland Yard assistance were rejected as being 'too colonial'.[50] From the US side there appeared to be no intelligence failure, only a very evident failure to take action on the known intelligence. Between 21 October, 1990 and 7 April, 1990 US agents in Miami recorded all the purchases of assault rifles and ammunition, their storage, and the purchase of a large shipping container. They recorded the tens of thousands of $100 bills used in the purchases, brought into Miami and declared to US-customs from Trinidad, or in traveller's cheques from a Bahrain bank. The terrorists did not assume false names; they even shipped the container directly to the Jamaat-Al-Muslimeen headquarters in Port of Spain,[51] a location which had been placed under 'surveillance' by the Trinidad Special Branch since 1986.

The capacity of the terrorists to collect weapons, train their men in Libya, and in broad daylight capture a whole government, leads to several conclusions. First, Miami, not Moscow or Havana, is today the centre of subversion of Caribbean states. The flow of illicit drugs and monies, and the freedom of the arms market, all make it an ideal city in which to plan terrorist actions.[52] Secondly, despite the heightened perceptions of threat with which they emerged from the previous phase, there is no evidence that all West Indian governments have taken the necessary precautions to safe-guard their national security. There is, in fact, a certain sensitivity about accepting foreign assistance in the area. Criticisms about the 'militarization' of the Caribbean – often terribly superficial and naive – might have contributed to that sensitivity.[53] Fortunately, as we saw in the Bahamas and in the discussion of corruption in the Police Service of Trinidad in 1992, this sensitivity is beginning to change.

As grave as the Trinidad events were, they pale in comparison to the implications of the second event which came more fully to light in 1990: the Antigua guns scandal. The fundamental difference between that and the Trinidad case was that while the guns in Trinidad were privately bought for domestic terrorist use, the Antigua guns were government purchased for international terrorist use. The latter borders on turning the state into an agent of international terrorism. The Antigua case – as revealed by the Official Commission of Inquiry – exposes the depth and spread of corruption, indeed, its internationalization.[54] It also clearly reveals the links between internationalized corruption and violence.

The charges were that 10 tons of arms were bought in Israel, the end-user to be the Antigua Defence Force (less than 100 men already armed by the US), but the weapons ended up on the farm of Medellín Cartel henchman, José Rodríguez Gacha. It was proven that some of the guns were used in the assassination of popular Colombian presidential candidate, Luís Carlos Galán. Among the many terrifying details revealed by the Commission of Inquiry are the following:

1   While Antigua had 'a heavy moral duty' to Colombia and the world to pursue this matter, its meagre diplomatic and police capabilities meant that it could not alone pursue the investigations which had to cover 'over four continents'.
2   Despite the wider conclusion that small Caribbean states cannot confront the cartels on their own, 'Intellectual collaboration to elicit the truth about Israeli firearms finding their way into the hands of Colombian drug barons was not to be easily achieved.' (p. 40) 'The British government', said Blom-Cooper, 'have turned a blind eye' to evidence that their nationals, operating as skilled mercenaries, 'turned untrained killers into trained killers'. (p. 34)
3   On the central role of the city of Miami: 'This conspiracy was, in my judgment, hatched in Miami and developed from that city.' (p. 37)
4   On the role of the banks: 'I find it wholly unacceptable that banks in America, whose services were used to facilitate what can without exaggeration be described as a crime against humanity, should be permitted through the inaction of the American authorities to hide evidence of that crime behind the cloak of confidentiality.' (p. 37)
5   Finally, and critically, the Report called attention to the role of wider, more enduring corrupt relationships between the principals in the scheme and high officials of the Antigua government, which called for 'further investigation.' (p. 83) Two questions in particular required urgent investigation: (1) what, if any, were the roles of Israeli and British mercenaries in establishing a training camp for terrorists in Antigua, and (2) were there plans to train Tamil guerrillas in that camp in exchange for access to the East Asian heroin trade?

These questions were answered by an investigation undertaken by the Permanent Sub-committee on Investigations of the US Senate. In a hearing held in February, 1991 the Sub-committee established conclusively that: (1) British and Israeli mercenaries, under contract to Colombian drug cartels, had been operating in Colombia since 1988; (2) that because of pressure from the Colombian government, they decided to shift operations to Antigua; (3) Antigua would serve both as a training base and conduit of guns for the cartel; (4) that the Antigua deal was only one part of a much deeper and wider operation. As the Sub-committee noted:

This transaction provides a case study of the multinational nature of arms trafficking. In this case, we had weapons made in Israel purportedly going to a Caribbean nation which wound up with the drug cartels in Colombia, financed through banks and individuals in Panama, the US, Israel, Antigua and, probably, Colombia.

The Sub-committee was adamant that any effort against such international networks had to be multinational in scope. It came as no surprise, then, that by the 1990s there were few who doubted that the most serious threat to the security of the Caribbean stemmed from the drug trade and its links to violence. Those who formerly ignored it or regarded it as merely a local nuisance, now raised voices of alarm. Michael Manley, who had spent little time on the drug threat up to that point, declared that combating the drug mafias would be one of his top priorities upon taking office in 1990. 'We are threatened', he told an audience in Toronto, Canada in April, 1990, 'by an international criminal network in drug trafficking that has no precedent in history.' Manley's words were being thoroughly corroborated by investigators[55] and by events in the Caribbean. Not only did Manley make the war on drugs priority number one of his administration, he carried his call for collective action to the United Nations. Similarly, Trinidad's Prime Minister, A.N.R. Robinson, called for the establishment of a special international court to try drug dealers. Unfortunately, not everyone was ready for Manley's or Robinson's ideas on how to combat the trade: traditional conceptions of sovereignty had still to be overcome in the Caribbean.

That world awareness about the threat posed by the drug trade, the internationalization of corruption, and violence has reached new levels is evident in the language of the 1987 UN Draft Convention Against Illicit Traffic in Narcotic Drugs and Psychotropic Substances. It is a multinational agreement designed to increase the effectiveness of law enforcement efforts against illicit drug trafficking. That Convention's language demonstrates that the threat is perceived in quite broad terms. It calls for seven areas of action:

1 Eradicate illicitly cultivated narcotic crops;
2 Monitor chemicals and equipment used in the processing of drugs;
3 Identify, seize, and forfeit illicitly generated proceeds;
4 Improve international legal co-operation by such means as extradition, mutual legal assistance, and exchange of information relating to trafficking activities;
5 Improve 'controlled delivery' procedures (a term referring to law enforcement co-operation whereby the movement of an illicit drug consignment can be monitored so that arrests are made at the time of ultimate delivery);

6 Require commercial carriers to take reasonable precautions to avoid use of their facilities and means of transport for illicit trafficking; and
7 Prevent illicit traffic by sea, through the mails, or by abuse of special rights prevailing in free trade zones and free ports.

As broad as these seven areas are, they do not fully address the problem. In fact, they omit any reference to the underlying structures and practices which make the drug trade possible: corruption, national and international.

Quite evidently, as aware as the leaders of the world are of the threats posed, they still resist any outside 'interference' with 'internal' political and administrative affairs. Any notion of extra-territorial jurisdiction being located in an international body is stiffly resisted. The state-centric view predominates. It is still regarded as an absolute precept that each nation should be left to govern its own territory and apply its own laws within that territory, never outside it. Corruption – to the extent that it is so regarded and punishable by a nation's laws – is clearly a national matter. Yet, can any major inroads against the cartels be made without effective, and worldwide, sanctions against it? It is to the credit of the US Senate's Caucus on International Narcotics Control that they believe not. As their report on the UN Draft Convention notes, the absence of any charge on corruption is a major weakness:

> Official corruption and complicity in the drug trade by some governments, particularly the laundering of illicit drug profits, has been one of the biggest obstacles to effective bilateral and multilateral drug enforcement efforts. The draft Convention, however, contains no language addressing this aspect of the international drug control problem, nor have any proposals been seriously discussed by any participating nation. There are several options that could be considered to address the gap in the draft Convention's language: (a) including sanctions similar to those included in the 1961 Single Convention and the 1971 Convention on Psychotropic Substances against governments found participating in the drug trade, and (b) prohibiting any such government from participating in co-operative drug enforcement efforts with all signatory countries. While this Convention may not be the most appropriate vehicle to address the corruption problem, *international narcotics control efforts will never adequately attack the trafficking problem until official government corruption in the drug trade is eliminated*, so that the efforts of the international community can be focused solely on prosecuting the criminal syndicates directly involved in the international drug trade.[56] (Emphasis added)

The US, for instance, wants money laundering to be considered as serious a crime as narcotics trafficking. In a region where, as will be discussed subsequently, offshore tax havens are thriving, and where their fastest growth is still in colonial or semi-colonial territories, there is great resistance to any such suggestions. In short, the Caribbean, like much of the rest of the world, knows what the poison is and many have ideas about what a possible antidote might be; they are not yet prepared to take the full dose of any remedy.

While solutions to the new threats to small Caribbean states appear nowhere in the offing, there is no reason for total despair. These are not what Gunner Myrdal called 'soft states': where corruption, brigandage and venality are parts of a total way of life. The profoundly conservative nature of most Caribbean societies means that there are deep sources of moral indignation ever ready to flow.

Even so, it is not evident why new leaders such as Trinidad and Tobago's Patrick Manning, quoted above, repeatedly express surprise at finding such levels of corruption once they assume office. Three tentative explanations suggest themselves: the first is political. The very nature of the party system means that political parties are much better equipped for fighting elections and taking power than they are for exercising power once in office. Even in otherwise admirable systems such as the Westminster-like parliaments with their 'loyal opposition' and 'shadow cabinet' traditions, actual cabinets tend to result from intra-party bargaining, not specialized expertise. Thus, there is very little institutional memory.

The second explanation is cultural: high levels of patronage and favouritism are expectations ingrained in the society and culture. The worst reputation anyone in a position to 'help out' can earn is that of 'ingrate', 'selfish' or 'cold-hearted'.[57] Finally, the rapid centralization of both political and economic decision-making and ownership which occurred in the 1970s, compounded the effects of the political and socio-cultural predispositions. It converted corruption from what James C. Scott calls a 'parochial' to a 'market' type. As a major conference on fraud and corruption in government concluded: 'The centralized nature of government financial management concentrates the authority to make decisions, and this leads public officials to sometimes put 'a price' on their privileged services.[58]

The fact is that corruption has been a theme in Caribbean politics since time immemorial. In Cuba in 1922, the US forced the government of President Alfredo Zayas to create what was called the 'Honest Cabinet'. Under US pressure, the 'moralizing program' turned into somewhat of a US puritanical witch hunt, as Charles E. Chapman recalls:

> The implication of possible [US] intervention had the effect
> both of stimulating the [honest] legislative program and of

inducing a general clean-up of Havana; scores of undesirable persons were hastily deported, Marianao gamblers were subject to more rigorous sentences, and suggestive African dances were forbidden at campaign meetings.[59]

Such externally imposed campaigns, especially those which reflected the racial and moral haughtiness of the hegemonic power at the time, do not endure. Cuba became, in the 1940s and 1950s, a centre of criminal activity. So corrupt was its political system that a candidate, Eduardo Chibás, with a one-theme campaign, '*Verguenza contra el dinero!*' shook the system and arguably paved the ground for Fidel Castro's own attacks on the system.[60]

No one who has followed the issue of corruption in Trinidad will forget that it was a major theme in the campaign of Eric Williams and the PNM as early as 1955. Yet two decades later the same Eric Williams had to appoint an 'Integrity Team' to do something about the corruption which, in the words of the Chairman of the team, had given Trinidad the reputation abroad of being 'Corruption Country'.[61] To hear a Jamaican journalist put it, corruption in Jamaica since independence in 1962 has become 'the norm' and the costs to development so high that it dictates the need for a 'national crusade' against it.[62]

Raymond Aron warned that corruption in the state machinery is one of the main causes of revolutions against that state. Gunnar Myrdal noted the detrimental effects of what he coined, the 'soft state'. It is important that Caribbean leaders heed the Arons and Myrdals rather than those who regard corruption as 'functional' to rapid development.[63]

On an issue such as this, the Caribbean has to develop a region-wide perspective and learn from each other's history. If that is done, the case of Cuba will take centre stage. In 1950, a high-level mission from the Internatonal Bank for Reconstruction and Development was prescient when it warned Cuban officials that: 'If leaders have neglected to prepare Cuba . . . they will be held to blame by the people. And, if that should happen, control may well pass into subversive but specious hands – as it has done in other countries whose leaders have ignored the trends of the times.'[64]

The target has to be 'market' corruption, which today has an international dimension. It is the former also which threatens the very structure of Caribbean societies. They need international and especially US cooperation, since much of it is linked with an offshore type of development now widespread in the region.

Notes

1   Cf. Jonathan Beaty and S.C. Gwynne, *The Outlaw Bank* (New York: Random House, 1993) and Rachel Ehrenfeld, *Evil Money* (New York: Harper Collins, 1922).

2   Cf. David McClintock, *Swordfish: A True Story of Ambition, Savagery, and Betrayal* (New York: Pantheon Books, 1993).

3   Cf. Robert Coran, *Caribbean Timebomb: US Complicity in the Corruption of Antigua* (New York: William Morrow and Co., 1993); M.A. Velazquez-Mainardi, *Corrupcion e impunidad en la Republica Dominicana* (Santo Domingo: Editora Tele-3, 1993); *Diccionario de la Corrupcion*, Vols. I and II (Caracas: Consorcio de Ediciones Capriles, 1989, 1990); Hector Mario Rodriguez, *Los piratas de la bolsa* (Bogota: Peyre, 1988).

4   Observations and interviews by this author on Sint Maarten, 1–6 September, 1993.

5   Just how dated thinking about intelligence and counter-intelligence tends to be is evident in Roy Godson, *Intelligence Requirements for the 1990s* (Lexington, KY.: Lexington Books, 1989) which summarized the thinking in intelligence circles up to 1989. There is one paragraph devoted to narcotics traffic even though it is admitted that in the Caribbean it represents 'a force with enormous potential for disruption' (p. 206).

6   Interview with Don Bohning, *The Miami Herald*, 8 February, 1993, p. 6.

7   *Trinidad Guardian*, 17 September, 1992, p. 1.

8   *The Jamaican Weekly Gleaner,* 21 August, 1992, p. 6.

9   *The Jamaican Weekly Gleaner*, 6 November, 1992, p. 1.

10   Rachel Ehrenfeld, *Evil Money*, (New York: Harper Business, 1992), p. 27.

11   *El Nuevo Herald*, 30 December, 1990, p. 2.

12   Speech made available by The Office of the Prime Minister, 9 June, 1989.

13   *The Miami Herald*, 10 June, 1989.

14   Walter Lippmann, 'A Theory About Corruption', *Vanity Fair*, vol. 35 (November 1930), p. 61.

15   Alfonso López Michelsen, 'Is Colombia to Blame?' *Hemisphere*, Vol. 1, No. 1 (Fall, 1988), p. 35.

16   Cf. Steven R. David, *Third World Coups d'État and International Security*, (Baltimore: Johns Hopkins University Press, 1987); Michael Nacht, 'Internal Change and Regime Stability', International Institute for Strategic Studies, *Adelphi Papers*, 166.

17   Wade Parrish Hinkle, 'The Security of Very Small States', (Unpublished Ph.D. dissertation, University of Maryland, 1990), p. 99.

18   *Ibid.*, p. 138.

19   Peter Calvert, 'Problems and Policies: An Agenda for the 1990's', in Peter Calvert, *The Central American Security System: North-South or East-West?*, (Cambridge: Cambridge University Press, 1988), p. 195.

20   Hearings. One Hundredth Congress. Second Session. Part 4 (11, 12, 14 July, 1988), p. 196.

21   Robert E. Fenton, 'Illegal Immigration to the US: A Growing Problem of Law Enforcement' (Centre for Advanced Research, The Naval War College, March 1983), pp. 85–8.

22   El Paso Intelligence Centre. *The Maritime Smuggling of Aliens*, Report No. SR–09–81 (31 August, 1981).

23   See these and many other approaches to the issue of corruption in Arnold T. Heidenheimer (ed.), *Political Corruption* (New York: Holt, Rinehart and Winston, 1970), *passim*.

24   Robert Klitgaard, 'Incentive Myopia', *World Development*, Vol. 17, No. 4 (1989), pp. 447–59.

25   Cf. Frederick Kempe, *Divorcing the Dictator: America's Bungled Affair with Noriega* (New York: Putnam, 1990); John Dinges, *Our Man in Panama: How General Noriega Used the US and Made Millions in Drugs and Arms* (New York: Random House, 1990).

26 Note Gary Brana-Shute's questions in a recent essay on Desi Bouterse: 'What exactly is the agenda of the military? Would they again call upon Libyan assistance or strike financial deals with drug cartels? Clearly they have abandoned ideology and now maintain power through pragmatic thuggery'. ('Suriname: Years of Living Dangerously', *The Times of the Americas*, 28 November, 1990, p. 11). For an essay of the Dutch 'pandering' of Bouterse's corruption see Peter Meel, 'Money Talks, Morals Vex', *European Review of Latin American and Caribbean Studies* (June 1990, pp. 75–98).

27 *White Paper on Public Participation in Industrial and Commercial Activities* (Government Printing Office, 1972), pp. 7–8.

28 Cf. F.A. Hoyos, *Tom Adams: A Biography* (London: Macmillan Caribbean, 1988), p. 110.

29 J.F. Mitchell, *Caribbean Crusade* (Waitsfield, Vermont: Concepts Publishing, 1989), p. 155.

30 *Ibid.*, 159.

31 On 7 March, 1991 the newly-appointed Financial Secretary to the Government of Montserrat revoked over 300 bank licenses on that island (cf. *The Financial Times*, 3/7/91, p. 15). For an account of the role of such 'Offshore' Operations see A.P. Maingot, 'Laundering Drug Profits: Miami and Caribbean Tax Havens', *Journal of Inter-American Studies and World Affairs*, Vol. 30, Nos. 2 and 3 (Summer/Fall, 1988), pp. 167–88, and A.P. Maingot, 'Does the Caribbean's Future Lie Offshore?', in Anthony Payne and Paul Sutton (eds), *Caribbean Politics: A Comparative Analysis* (Baltimore, MD.: Johns Hopkins University Press, 1993).

32 Michael Manley, *The Politics of Change* (London: André Deutsch, 1973).

33 Michael Manley, *A Voice in the Workplace* (London: André Deutsch, 1975).

34 Michael Manley, *Jamaica: Struggle in the Periphery* (London: Writers and Readers Publishing Cooperative Society Ltd., 1982).

35 Michael Manley, *Up the Down Escalator* (London: André Deutsch, 1987).

36 *Jamaican Weekly Gleaner*, 18 April, 1988. For a similar attitude by the then Minister of Labour, see *Jamaican Weekly Gleaner*, 18 July, 1988.

37 *Jamaican Weekly Gleaner*, 17 April, 1989.

38 Cf. A.P. Maingot, 'The Drug Menace to the Caribbean', *The World and I* (July 1989), pp. 128–35.

39 *Jamaican Weekly Gleaner*, 16 January, 1989.

42 Dr Edward C. Ezell's Testimony, Hearings, Permanent Sub-committee on Investigations of the Senate Governmental Affairs Committee (Washington, D.C. 28 February, 1991).

41 *Informe Oral del Fiscal, Granma*, 5 July, 1989, p. 4.

42 *Granma*, 3 July, 1989, p. 1.

43 Enrique Baloyra, unpublished paper on the trial presented to the American University research group on civil-military relations, 26 July, 1990.

44 For a serious legal analysis of the trial see 'Cuba Situation Report', (May–August 1989), Washington, D.C.: Radio Martí, February 1990.

45 The first story linking Cuba to the drug trade appeared in *The Miami Herald* on 24 January, 1982. Between that date and 6 April, 1983 *The Herald* published nine more stories on the subject.

46 Andres Oppenheimer, *Castro's Final Hour* (New York: Simon and Schuster, 1992), p. 49.

47 The number of congressional hearings on the drug trade in the Caribbean Basin is so great that a special bibliography has been produced. Cf. Edith Sutterlin, *Narcotics and Illicit Drug Trafficking: Selected References, 1986–88* (Washington, D.C.: Congressional Research Service, August 1988).

48 A good assessment of the US lack of preparation and totally inadequate intelligence prior

to the invasion of the Dominican Republic, 1965, and Grenada, 1983, is provided by General Bruce Palmer, Jr. *Intervention in the Caribbean* (Lexington: The University Press of Kentucky, 1989). General Palmer's startling conclusion is that the US is in a weaker position in the late 1980s than it was in the 1960s (p. 179).

49   Cf. *Trinidad Guardian*, 15 August, 1983 and 3 September, 1983, p. 1.

50   See the account of John Babb, *Trinidad Guardian*, 12 August, 1990, p. 13.

51   These events are compiled from the US District Court, Southern District, Florida: *USA vs. Louis Hanee, Yasin Abu Bakr, Bilaal Abdullah and Riad Ali*, Criminal Complaint, 13 September, 1990.

52   In a recent book, Rachel Ehrenfeld documents the range of skulduggery and scams which have the Miami-Bahama connection as major centres of operations, *Evil Money* (New York: Harper Business, 1992).

53   Dr Dion E. Phillips, co-editor of *Militarization in the Non-Hispanic Caribbean* (Boulder: Lynne Reinner Publishers, 1986), gave this definition of 'repression' at meetings in Venezuela and Barbados: 'Repression occurs when legitimization fails or is peeled away. It involves preventing people from taking actions that would harm or are perceived as having the potential to harm the state in major ways.' ('Defense Policy and Planning in the Caribbean: the Case of Barbados', presented 23–26 March, 1989 and 23–26 May, 1989, p. 36).

54   'Guns for Antigua', Report of the Commission of Inquiry into the Circumstances Surrounding the Shipment of Arms from Israel to Antigua and Transhipment on 24 April, 1989 en route to Colombia, Commissioner: Louis Blom-Cooper, Q.C. 2 November, 1990.

55   The extent of the Italian Mafia's reach into the Caribbean and Latin America is documented by Claire Sterling, *Octopus, The Long Reach of the International Sicilian Mafia* (New York: W.W. Norton, 1990). Sterling maintains that Caracas, Venezuela is the Latin American 'headquarters' of the Mafia, (pp. 130–44).

56   *A Report on the Status of the Draft Convention, the US Negotiating Position, and Issues for the Senate*, Senate Caucus on International Narcotics Control, 100th Congress, 1st Session, October, 1987, p. 10.

57   What Dominican Juan Bosch said about Cuba applies to the rest of the area: 'It is a moral transgression of the highest order to be ungrateful'. Not giving favours (*coba* in Cuba, *bobol* in Trinidad) would be such a transgression. (Cf. Juan Bosch, *Cuba: la isla fascinante*, (1955), p. 190.

58   First Inter-American Conference on the Problems of Fraud and Corruption in Government. Final Report. (Miami, Florida 4–6 December, 1989), p. 7.

59   Charles E. Chapman, *Republican Hispanic America: A History* (New York: The MacMillan Co. 1937), p. 175.

60   Cf. Luís Conte Aguero, *Eduardo Chibás, El Adalid de Cuba* (Mexico: Editorial Jus, 1955). On corruption in Cuba generally, see E. Viguier G. Alonso (ed.), *La corrupción política-administrativa en Cuba, 1944–1952* (Habana: Instituto Cubano del Libro, 1973).

61   Cf. Government of Trinidad and Tobago, *Integrity Team Report* (Port of Spain: Government Printing Office, 1979). The chairman was then Justice of the Supreme Court, Karl de la Bastide.

62   Basil Buck of *The Daily Gleaner*, in *First Inter-American Conference*, p. 21.

63   See the range of theories on the role of corruption in Arnold T. Heidenheimer (ed.), *Political Corruption* (New York: Holt, Rinehart and Winston, 1970).

64   IBRD, *Report on Cuba* (published for International Bank for Reconstruction and Development by Johns Hopkins Press, 1951), p. 13.

CHAPTER 8

The 'offshore' development strategy: Is it for everyone?

The internationalization of corruption cannot be discussed in isolation from one of its most cherished privileges: the safehaven for its proceeds, dirty money. As a recent account puts it: 'If drug trafficking is vilified and punished, the proceeds of this crime – drug money – are welcomed with open arms everywhere.'[1] The amount of this money is astronomical, perhaps $1 trillion worldwide, of which 40 per cent, or $400 billion, is laundered in the US. Much of the rest goes into banks offshore. This business is often too good to resist, especially for those societies with few other sources of income.

The US is impacted by money laundering in several interlocking ways: it funds criminal enterprises, it deprives the government of legitimate tax revenues and it undermines the societies of its allies. But even the US has not been able to get a grip on the practice. In response to the apparent inefficiency of the Bank Secrecy Act as a mechanism to impose criminal liability on money launderers, Congress enacted the Money Laundering Control Act of 1986.[2] Additionally, the Racketeer Influenced and Corrupt Organizations Law of 1970 (RICO), was originally intended to go after organized crime, but was expanded to prosecute a wide range of white collar crime, including securities and commodities fraud.

None of this stopped what has been called the largest bank fraud in world financial history, the collapse of the Bank of Credit and Commerce International (BCCI). All this has enormous implications for those small countries which, confronted with a lack of natural resources, have cast their lot with a three-pronged approach to development: export-driven manufacturing, offshore financial services and tourism.[3] It is believed that this combination serves these small societies well in that they employ both blue collar and white collar labour, bring in hard currency and use their strategic geographical location to ensure the relative permanence of these industries. For very small countries, the financial services and tourism sectors are particularly attractive. They can exist in productive symbiosis. Because the financial service industry is 'environmentally clean', it coexists nicely with the tourist-attracting natural resources of many of these mini-states. Monaco is often cited as a case where a small country successfully combined both approaches, taking full advantage of its geographical location.

There can be no doubt about the compelling 'logic' in this development thrust, a logic made more evident by the question: what are the alternatives, not theoretical or ideological, but actual, 'living' ones? A kind of economic 'law of necessity' is exercising a strong influence on development thinking in the insular Caribbean. Decades of excessively ideological and partisan attacks on any offshore activity, whether it be tourism, medical schools, free trade zones or even straightforward foreign investment, has exhausted the tolerance towards virtually any criticism of offshore development.[4] This situation is especially lamentable in the Caribbean where the offshore approach is fraught with dangers and potential pitfalls. There is a need to scrutinize this chosen path, to reveal how it has performed elsewhere in the past, and attempt to discern some of the danger signs already in evidence. One way to formulate the problem is as follows: the Caribbean region is experiencing a dramatic increase in a wide array of transnational or 'offshore' activities at a time when its capacity for collective, region-wide responses are at a low point. Certainly, not all offshore activities are nefarious or detrimental. It is a plausible hypothesis, however, that those activities which are detrimental to the well-being of these small societies tend to take full advantage of the arrangements and 'milieu' created by the bulk of offshore activities. In fact, the very characteristics which make the islands attractive to one set of activities, make them attractive to the more nefarious other part. The offshore activities described here – the drug trade, offshore banking and tax havens – illustrate this point.

A first question relates to the issue of state capabilities *vis-à-vis* the enormity of the tasks involved. Capabilities have to include the capacity to discriminate the good from the bad – a task not even major societies seem capable of performing – and then both promote and defend healthy development initiatives from the nefarious ones. Since by definition transnational and offshore activities are largely beyond the authority of states or international agencies, policing such activities is not easy. It is even more intractable and slippery when geopolitical factors favour those who place a premium on secrecy and evasion. This is clearly the case in the Caribbean, where three elements of transnational development are present: (1) a sending society with the clients (whether as tourists or drug users) and the money, (2) a receiving society with the geographical location and commodities (sun, sand, and relaxed banking and company laws), and (3) native elites with the will and the talent to exploit one or the other – and in some cases both (1) and (2) – above. The issue is not an absence of public opinion, it is the fragmentation of that opinion typical of archipelagal areas. While the existing region-wide agencies limit themselves to the technical or legal side of 'development', none concern themselves with the creation of a 'climate of opinion' or regional consciousness raising. Certainly there are, in the mid-1990s, no Caribbean leaders with the region-wide moral influence or even audience to address some of these weighty issues. The days of influential and broad gauged models, viz. the Puerto Rican, the Cuban, or the 'democratic socialist', have vanished with surprising speed.

What is evident today in the area is a variety of responses to the threats created by many of these offshore activities, responses which go from the draconian measures taken by the Cuban authorities to the much more relaxed approach of most of the others. Whatever the response, the reality is that none – not even supposedly puritanical Cuba – has escaped the ravages wrought by many of these offshore activities, the most dangerous of which is the drug trade and the ease of laundering monies derived from criminal activity.

Indeed, in the Cuban case money laundering has become a virtual necessity because of the US embargo. They created a Moneda Convertible department run by members of the old oligarchy who knew their way around western finances. Andres Oppenheimer describes the activities of its director:

> In 1975, Tony de la Guardia was in Switzerland laundering $60 million that Argentina's Montonero guerrillas had obtained in the sensational kidnapping of industrialists, Jorge and Juan Born. Shortly thereafter, the Cuban secret agent was transporting millions in precious stones and gold from Lebanon to Czechoslovakia – the take from a series of bank robberies by the Palestinian Popular Democratic Front. In 1976 he was stationed in Jamaica, as head of the Cuban Special Troops contingent that provided military support to leftist Prime Minister Michael Manley.[5]

As the analysis in this chapter of the Panamanian banking system will show, it should come as no surprise that the Cubans decided on Panama as a location for their offshore activities. The Cuban CIMEX Corporation and dozens of others used Panama to circumvent the US embargo by exporting Cuban goods (even to the US) and importing US and other western commodities. If Panama was a blatant case of a state organized to promote corruption, it was not the only one. Haiti, as we shall see in Chapter 10, is run by many in the military for similar purposes. Suriname is similarly engaged since the *coup d'état* by a supposedly left wing group of non-commissioned officers grabbed power on 25 February, 1980. These officers immediately established close ties with the region's radical governments in Cuba, Nicaragua and Grenada. Its leader, Sergeant Desi Bouterse was especially close to Maurice Bishop. The collapse of the Grenada revolution and the murder of 15 major civilian leaders by Bouterse, which upset the Cubans,[6] brought any pretence of 'revolution' to an end. Bouterse and his regime were now in the most profitable offshore business: smuggling drugs to Europe.[7] The route used is usually Suriname to French Guiana to France. The murder of four Brazilians in Suriname also shows a link with the booming Brazilian trade.

Up to the time of the US invasion (December 1989), Panama was a country where it was not the state authorities who were pitted against illicit groups, but against each other for the spoils which those groups produced. There appeared to be no evident good-versus-bad guys dichotomy. The sums involved were so large that it was not at all surprising that corruption was rampant.[8] The point is that the drug trade is enormous and diversified in terms of its sources, conduits and markets. The amount of money generated is astronomical. Operation Pisces, a sting operation against only one of the estimated 30 groups involved in money laundering, illustrated this fact. In one day, the operation impounded $5.6 million in cash from 56 bank accounts and $21 million in assets. But as the DEA spokesman told the US Senate, this was only 'a snapshot of any weekly activity of one money-laundering operation in the US pertaining to only one drug, cocaine.'[9] Fortunately, Caribbean governments are becoming aware that the corrosion is deep-rooted, not epiphenomenal, and that there are potentially very serious consequences to their political cultures. Examples abound: in the Dominican Republic – the trial for corruption of former President Jorge Blanco; in the Turks and Caicos Islands – the arrest in Miami on drug running charges against a sitting Premier; the Netherlands Antilles – the use of the Free Zone to tranship drugs. The list could be augmented but the case is made about the widespread corruption in the region. [10] Such enormous amounts of money are in constant search for safehavens which is where the offshore centres come in.

Offshore banking is not a subject taught in Caribbean classes in banking and finance, yet the flow of what is now called grey and black market money, seeking safe and anonymous financial havens, caught the attention of a select number of 'forensic' investigators at least two decades ago. It is not, therefore, an unstudied topic even though it remains a difficult one. To Ingo Walters, for instance, the flow of monies to tax havens is a topic of enormous qualitative and quantitative importance. He laments, therefore, that there is so little hard evidence available on the subject. According to Walters, the reason for this secrecy is that the offshore tax haven business is 'of great value to some, yet positively bad for others . . .' An additional obstacle to its study is that the business thrives on schemes of 'almost diabolical complexity',[11] a complexity made possible by sophisticated technology. As the Chief Executive Officer of one of Canada's largest banks told a Canadian Senate committee: 'I can hide money in the twinkle of an eye from all the bloodhounds that could be put on the case, and I would be so far ahead of them that there would never be a hope of unravelling the trail.' The secret, he concluded, was electronics.[12]

The sources of the money are various and certainly not all illegal. For instance, it appears to be a growing practice across the globe that an ever increasing army of specialized and legitimate 'investment advisers' are available to recommend which of an estimated 45 tax havens you should choose from. It certainly is not a new phenomenon, though the amounts involved have been growing steadily. In fact, it is known that the tax haven is one of the fastest growing areas for US investment abroad. In 1968, the total assets of US-controlled corporations held in these havens stood at 12.1 per cent of worldwide assets of US corporations; by 1976, this had grown to 17.6 per cent. It is also known that this growth has been particularly rapid in tax havens located in the western hemisphere. Growth of foreign holdings in western hemisphere tax havens increased 40 times over – to 108.1 investments per 100,000 population – between 1970 and 1979, compared to a growth rate of 2.0–2.11 per 100,000 population in non-tax haven areas. In 1979, banks in tax havens held some $385,000 billion.[13] The trends continue today and for the same reasons. As Sara West of *The Financial Times*[14] put it: 'More investors are showing an interest in offshore asset management, either for fear of a change of government or because they want to minimize their tax bills by using offshore trusts.' Those planning national economies in the Caribbean know that the offshore financial services are a growth industry and that they have the location, the communications infrastructure and the educated workforce to be competitive. They intend to get their share of this international river of money in the same fashion that Switzerland, Liechtenstein, Luxembourg, Monaco and so many other financial centres have. In the Caribbean, however, there is an additional and major source of these offshore funds: laundered drug money. The link between the criminal drug trade flowing through the Caribbean and the presence of money laundering facilities there is in part explained by R. Thomas Naylor when he notes that: 'The ultimate objective of the criminal is to enjoy his gains, perhaps in a tropical haven, more likely within the same geographic milieu in which his criminal enterprise operates.' [15]

Despite its secret and largely inscrutable nature, there are some facts which are known about the offshore tax havens in general and those in the Caribbean in particular. Referring to the 'staggering' amount of actual cash which moves through the Caribbean, Ingo Walters outlines a typical laundering process:[16]

Step No. 1: Money transferred (occasionally wired) to secrecy haven abroad.

Step No. 2: Lawyers there create a shell corporation using 'boiler plate' documentation (for a fee).

Step No. 3: Funds are deposited in the name of this dummy corporation in

a co-operative local bank – usually an offshore bank author-
ized to conduct transactions only with non-residents.

Step No. 4:   Money is then transferred to a larger international bank.

Step No. 5:   The corporation then borrows money from this bank (secured
by the deposits) for legitimate use in the original country.

It is evident to all who have studied the offshore banking business that
its growth has been fuelled by the phenomenal increase in cash from the US
drug trade as well as capital flight. One estimate of the interest earned on
drug profits stored in 'safe' banks is $3 million per hour. [17] As new to the
game as some of these Caribbean financial centres are, they are hardly
new to the role of flight capital and laundered monies. The vast majority of
the criminal cases identified in the criminal investigations of the Internal
Revenue Service (IRS) in the late 1970s and early 1980s occurred in the
Caribbean. Between 1978–83, there were 464 such cases, of which 45 per
cent represented illegal transactions with legal income. Of the other 55 per
cent, illegal income was involved (161 cases of which dealt with the drug
traffic). Of these, 29 per cent involved the Cayman Islands, 28 per cent
involved Panama, 22 per cent the Bahamas, and 11 per cent the Netherlands
Antilles. These four offshore sites alone accounted for 85 per cent of the
cases involving transactions with illegal income.[18] The actual movement
of large amounts of cash throughout the Caribbean made a mockery of
official statistics on the nature of the economy.

The Caribbean, however, was not the only place where big money
was moving in the area. In fact, it is critical to an understanding of the
growth of Caribbean offshore centres to know that in many ways they are
part of a larger financial region of which Florida is an important part.
Indeed, by the late 1970s, Florida had become the banking centre for the
Caribbean and, perhaps, Latin America. As figures reveal, the climate for
banking in Florida was clearly propitious: in 1982, Florida banks held 33
per cent of all commercial bank deposits and an extraordinary 51 per cent
of all savings and loan deposits in the south-eastern part of the US.

One Florida banker (William H. Allen Jr., Chairman of Pan American
Bank) calculated that Florida received some $5–6 billion in one year (1982)
in flight capital.[19] Another (J.S. Hudson, Executive Vice-President of Flag-
ship Bank) calculated that 'roughly 20 per cent' of the total deposits of
his own banks were from non-nationals.[20]

It is believed, however, that the amounts involved in capital flight
pale by comparison to those stemming from the illegal drug trade. A report
from the Group of Seven calculated that in the late 1980s the retail proceeds
of the drug trade were $122 billion, $85 billion of which 'is available to be
laundered through the banking system' every year.[21] Such movements have
long been part of the Florida-Caribbean connection. With the drug traffic of

the early 1980s amounting to some $50 billion per year, $7 billion of which was believed remained in Florida, it was clear that this trade represented, by far, the largest single financial link between Miami and the Caribbean. It takes monumental disingenuousness not to question the fact that, in 1983, Miami's Federal Reserve District bank showed a cash *surplus* of $3–4 billion while New York's Federal Reserve District showed a *deficit* of $4 billion.[22] Miami's banks were taking in so much cash that they began to charge a fee just to accept a deposit! US Customs Commissioner William Von Raab provided an interesting calculation of what only $74 million in cash represented to one who wished to avoid the reporting requirements of US banking law: 7,500 deposits (of under $10,000) in US banks, and 15,000 trips abroad (to avoid the $5,000 reporting limit). The commissioner made it clear that moving so much money required the active collaboration of banks both in the US and offshore.[23] Within this situation, the Miami banking system was the crucial link between the financier, the seller and the market. One must assume, charitably and legally, that in the majority of cases such collaboration was unwitting.

However, by the mid-1980s the social and political climate in the US changed. A 'war on drugs' was declared and with it came greater controls and supervision on the operation of the banking system. New standards on 'flagrant organizational indifference' and 'collective knowledge' were exacted from the banks as part of the Anti-Drug Abuse Act of 1986. The traditional distinction between 'deliberate intent to violate the law' and 'indifference to legal requirements' were for all practical purposes abolished. It might well be, as one legal scholar put it, that the new provisions against money laundering of that Act placed an impossible burden on the banks and that Congress had 'simply dropped the problem in the lap of the financial services industry and walked away.'[24] Whatever the legal arguments, the fact is that despite the existence of anti-laundering legislation since 1970, the mid-1980s was a watershed in terms of public and political concern about the link between drugs and 'hot' money and the role of the banks in their capacity to move and to hide. Not surprisingly, the mid-1980s was when the offshore centres really began to boom and proliferate. With the US declaring war on drugs, there was an even more obvious role for offshore centres not controlled by the US which could serve not only as tax havens, but also help launder dirty money. Much of the money came out of the US and often went back into the US as legitimate real estate and business.

The business is so lucrative that today Caribbean states are no longer content to interact with Miami, they are determined to become 'world class' offshore centres in their own right. Of course, they have not all made it, but at one time or another, virtually every island in the Caribbean has tried. St Vincent had its own little book on how it was 'today's most desirable haven to protect your money and assets from inflation, from dollar devaluation, from the tax collector, from creditors, and even from your spouse in the event of divorce.' It really never took off.[25] Little Anguilla, on the other hand, which had three banks in 1980, had 96 by 1983, only one of which even had a vault. In the Turks and Caicos, things were going well until several senior government ministers were jailed for running drugs. It is now recovering as a haven for companies, especially US credit life assurance companies. In early 1989 there were 6,729 companies registered on these minute islands.[26] The activity had been just as feverish in Montserrat which came to be ranked by a known authority on establishing offshore banks as 'a wise jurisdictional choice.'[27] It contained the vital characteristics for the easy establishment of a bank: (1) good communications between the island and the rest of the world, (2) no taxes on any banking activity, (3) a very low licence fee ($7,600), (4) tight secrecy laws, (5) very low requirement for paid-in capital ($300,000) which 'can sometimes be waived or postponed', and (6) no monetary ties with or supervision by the US. Within a short time the situation of corruption surrounding the establishment of offshore banks had created a political-constitutional crisis which led to a situation of constitutional 'devolution', i.e. recolonization. The Governor exercised 'colonial regulatory control' over the Montserrat Ministry of Finance and imposed a moratorium on the granting of new bank licences and also closed several suspicious banks.

The outrageous and region-wide nature of the problem was illustrated by the headline in a major business daily: 'Con Men Are Raking in Millions by Setting up Own Caribbean Banks'. The essence of the story was that a multitude of islands (Montserrat, St Vincent, Anguilla) had become, in the words of the *Wall Street Journal*:

> A spawning ground for dozens of small, shadowy private banks whose main activity seems to be turning out phony financial documents that are used in this country as collateral for loans and other illegal purposes.[28]

The *Journal* cited an unpublished study of offshore banking, commissioned by the Ford Foundation, which concluded that the Caribbean had become 'a playground for fraudulent and other criminal bank users'. The situation had become so bad that there was not even a semblance of shame left, as evidenced by the following exchange between a US senator and the former president of the bank in Montserrat:

Senator Rudman: Didn't it bother you travelling around the Caribbean with one-half million dollars in a suitcase?

Mr Stocks: Now that I have had more time to reflect on it, I guess it was a little bit ridiculous . . .'[29]

Various factors contributed to such situations in some of the islands: the absence of a central bank, of trained personnel, of regulations, and of a willingness on the part of government officials to provide information on their dealings. 'There is no question', concluded the *Wall Street Journal*, 'that the buccaneer forays into banking . . . will continue. Once established on a Caribbean isle, the pirates are difficult to dislodge'.[30] One of these modern-day pirates single-handedly sold 'over one hundred' banks in the Caribbean before switching operations to the Pacific. Nevertheless, the record just might be held by Interseco of Panama which, over a 15-year period, created and sold some 2,000 Panamanian corporations. Almost all its employees, even the errand boys, took turns at being an officer or director of one of these tax shelters. The then head of the Panamanian Bankers Association seemed happy to describe his nation as a 'tropical wheeling-and-dealing paradise'.[31]

Clearly much of the Caribbean continues to be involved in this offshore business. The fact that so much of it takes place in British dependent or colonial territories has concerned the UK's Department of Trade and Industry enough to commission a study of these offshore financial centres in the Caribbean. The report, by Rodney Gallagher of Coopers and Lybrand, indicated that there were many grounds for concern if for no other reason than the virtual absence of local inspection and investigation of financial activities. Most of the local effort and talent goes into the process of attracting and registering firms.[32] British concern grew over the patently illicit activities of banks in the dependencies of Anguilla and Montserrat. In the latter, two-thirds of the 350 local banks were closed down after a 1989 Scotland Yard investigation, and a moratorium on new banks was mandated in Anguilla in May 1990. By that time this little island of 7,000 inhabitants had 3,500 companies – including 42 banks – registered.[33]

Four cases, which tower above the rest in this area, will illustrate some of the benefits and many of the dangers and risks which accompany this rush into the offshore business: the older centres, Panama, the Bahamas and the Cayman Islands, and the new kid on the block, the British Virgin Islands.

Panama is one of the oldest offshore banking and service sectors in the Caribbean. Its destiny as such a centre was arguably determined in 1904 when the new Republic signed a monetary agreement with the USA.[34] The US dollar was adopted as local currency and Panama agreed not to establish any exchange restrictions of any sort. In 1927 Panama took a page from the Delaware and New Jersey corporation laws and passed its first General Corporation Law in order to attract offshore financial business. It provided favourable tax treatment for any capital invested, it guaranteed confidentiality and it established that any two people of legal age – whether Panamanian or not, whether present in Panama or abroad – could establish a corporation. The basic elements of the offshore centre were in evidence. To these were added coded bank accounts, allowed by law 18 of 1959. Both the 1927 and the 1959 legislation were consolidated and added to by the Banking Law of 1970. Not only did the law further lower taxes and make the movement of funds free, it also provided complementary legislation in the Criminal Commercial and Labour codes to enforce bank secrecy obligations and guarantees.

It is evident, as a report put out by the US Embassy in Panama in January 1989 notes, that 'Panama's banking sector has flourished in part because certain banks are actively involved in the laundering of drug money, primarily Colombian drug money.' Panama did make some efforts to improve its image as an offshore centre. Law 23 of 30 December, 1986 provided the first definition of 'money laundering' and recognized crimes committed abroad as a basis for action in Panama. It does not appear, however, that such legislation made much difference to the money launderers; Panama continued to be a favourite destination. It was the political crisis caused by the indictment by a Miami Grand Jury of strongman, General Antonio Noriega, which finally led to the flight of many – not all, according to the US Embassy – of the big laundering banks and their capital. The following figures (Table 8.1) illustrate just how much of the funds deposited in Panama were scared off by the pressures applied by the US against Noriega.

The interesting thing is that only five 'general licence' and two 'international licence' banks abandoned Panama during that period.

Most of the money fled to other offshore centres in the Caribbean. Whether it will return to Panama is a matter of great speculation. Panamanian bankers along with most other Panamanians welcomed the US invasion which rid them of General Noriega. They are much less enthusiastic, however, with what they perceive as US attempts to penetrate the country's bank secrecy laws.[35] In fact, they are resisting any efforts by the US to

Table 8.1 Removal of funds deposited in Panama, December 1987–September 1988

Date	Internal Deposits (000,000)	Off-Shore Deposits (000,000)	Total Deposits (000,000)
December 1987	$4,275	$28,947	$33,222
June 1988	2,967	7,704	10,671
September 1988	2,763	7,382	10,146

Source: US Embassy, Panama, January 1989.

change banking laws at all. Part of the problem is that more than ever, Panama needs the capital. Another part is that, as Stephen Labaton of *The New York Times* points out:[36] 'It is difficult to find any senior officials here who do not have important ties to banks.' Indeed, both the President and the Second Vice-President have had ties with banks tied to the laundering of Colombian drug money. Many of the investment and banking firms in Panama are not betting on the major money returning soon, they are moving much of their activities to the Caribbean islands to which the money fled.[37] In 1990 it appears that Panama's loss has been and will continue to be for a long time, the gain of many an offshore centre in the Caribbean.

One of the few offshore centres not to benefit from the fall in Panama's offshore fortunes was the Bahamas. In fact, among the world's major financial centres, the Bahamas and Panama were the only ones which have shown no growth since 1987. Certainly part of the explanation is the fierce competition coming from a plethora of new offshore centres in the Caribbean, and the Atlantic. But another reason points to the double-edged sword that much of the offshore business represents. Rachel Johnson of *The Financial Times*[38] explains that among the most important reasons for this decline have been, 'publicity about alleged drug-trafficking, endemic corruption, bureaucratic delays and inefficiency, and growing drug-related crime and violence in Nassau.'

Banking is the second industry in the Bahamas after tourism. The initial expansion of the banking sector occurred while the Banks Act of 1909 was operational. This was not brought up to date until 1966. By then, over 600 companies were, in the words of an official publication: 'transacting banking or trust business . . . including a number of "so called" banks that created an unfavourable image.'[39]

In analyzing the forces behind the rise of the Bahamas as an offshore banking and trust centre in 1968–70, one is made aware of how little depended on Bahamian actions themselves. The three weighty causes were: (1) US Federal Reserve Board restrictions on export of capital for foreign lending or investment, (2) the expansion of the pool of Eurodollars, and (3) the fact that the Federal Reserve did permit US banks to set up foreign branches with little regulation. With these factors as impetus, the Bahamas proceeded to open the door even further, removing the requirements for either separate premises or a full-time staff or the establishment of a corporation in the Bahamas.

By the late 1980s the Bahamas had some 380 banks, only 180 of which had more than a nameplate and a post office box.[40] There are those in the Bahamas who question the overall benefits – compared to the toll in corruption and bad reputation – derived from this offshore operation. They note that the banking sector provided 10 per cent of the GDP in 1988 but directly employed only 3,000 or 2 per cent of the labour force plus an additional 2,000 jobs which depend on that sector.[41] Such criticisms appear to be very much of a minority opinion. The offshore sector appears to be politically well-established, rooted institutionally and socially; in other words, an integral part of the Bahamas' conception of themselves as a nation. All efforts in 1990 were to improve the image of its financial centre, expand and facilitate the registration of International Business Companies, and improve its ranking as an offshore ship registration (flag of convenience) centre. It presently ranks tenth in the World Shipping League. Bahamian officials, like their counterparts in the other offshore centres, are hoping that Hong Kong's problems and the standardization and stricter reporting in the EC in 1992 will send new monies their way.[42]

For many years, no amount of charges of corruption against Prime Minister Sir Lynden Pindling and various members of his Cabinet and personal inner circle have thus far made a dent in their political fortunes. The high standard of living of the population (the per capita GNP of US$10,560) was certainly one reason for such tolerance. Another was the collective memory of black nationalism which still recalled the contributions of Pindling and his Progressive Liberal Party. But, perhaps more important might be a kind of resignation about national capabilities, an awareness that the Bahamas had done much to fight the drug trade but to no avail. Could anyone else have been expected to do better? There was much to be said about the Bahamian assertion that, on a per capita basis, the contribution to the anti-drug effort 'was unequalled anywhere else in the world'.[43] This combination of reasons seemed to make Prime Minister Pindling a safe bet for the 1992 elections. But there were dark clouds on the horizon, as tourist arrivals declined and investors began to shy away from the island's bad reputation. The fact is that increased US pressure on the drug interdiction side, plus pressures stemming from increased indebtedness and unemployment, had the Pindling administration worried. A Central Bank economist admits that 'what we are seeing now is the real economy emerging'. 'That real economy', says a journalist, 'stripped of its drug-related froth, is in difficulties.'[44] Certainly the opposition had an attractive leader in Hubert Ingraham, who is untainted by any charges of corruption and nepotism and is highly sceptical about too heavy a dependence on offshore activities. Sceptics said that Bahamas' political history indicates that honesty and good intentions have never been enough to wrest power from the wily Sir Pindling. In fact, Pindling was, as already noted, soundly defeated by a party promising a total cleansing of the system.

One archipelago where there are no dissenting voices on the issue of its offshore activities is the Cayman Islands, one of the three remaining British colonies in the Caribbean. This is the Switzerland of the Caribbean. It is an interesting fact that it is this colonial status which provides the Caymans with an edge over areas such as Panama and the Bahamas. This was the calculation behind the 1963 Caymans Legislative Assembly's petition to Britain that it be allowed to break away from Jamaica and revert to a Crown Colony Status. If constitutional devolution was used in Montserrat to dismantle an offshore centre gone awry, in the Caymans it was used to better promote one. Three years after the return to Crown Colony government, the Caymans began their move towards becoming the number one tax haven in the world, especially after 1973. Independence for the Bahamas and the behaviour of its Prime Minister, caused many banks to seek the safety of British colonial rule.

In 1987 the Cayman Islands had more than 18,000 companies on the register. There were 520 banks and trust companies with assets in excess of US$200 billion.[45] By early 1992 there were 23,500 companies and 548 banks with assets of US$400 billion, however, only 68 of these actually have offices and personnel. Of the world's 50 largest banks, 46 are present in the Caymans. It can boast of having the highest density of banks in the world.[46]

Certainly the Cayman Islands, through the UK connection, has made efforts at maintaining banking respectability. In 1984 the US and the UK signed the Cayman Islands Narcotics Assistance Agreement, but according to well-placed investigators, that Agreement merely slowed down, it never stopped the flow of illicit cash.[47] While continually denying any role in laundering dirty money, the Cayman Islands has never been reticent about admitting that it benefits from the travails of others. Note the language of its Financial Secretary, Tom Jefferson, in a 1984 interview:

Look around us. The US has $200 billion of debt and a loss in purchasing power, per dollar, of almost 50 per cent in 15 years. Canada is in a similar position. Mexico has been having serious financial problems despite the vast oil reserves and, additionally, has to provide jobs for a massive labour force.

The economies of El Salvador, Guatemala and Nicaragua are unfortunately depressed from falling production due to political turmoil. Costa Rica's inflation continues on an upward trend. Venezuela has imposed major exchange controls as a possible solution to its problems. Brazil is on the verge of a real currency crisis and Argentina faces years of economic turmoil ahead. Haiti has the worst unemployment situation in the hemisphere and the population continues to grow at about 3 per cent. Jamaica is rebounding well in the face of adversity.

As you can see, the economic stability of our region is questionable. Yet, in Cayman, in the midst of it, we enjoy a very stable economy and marginal inflation – a mere 5 per cent per annum over the last two years.[48]

As early as 1984 there was talk in Cayman about capturing flight capital from Hong Kong, showing in the process some keen political insights: 'We can now observe the waning of investor confidence in Hong Kong as the New Territories lease nears determination in 1997 . . .'.[49] The British Virgin Islands did not send a mission to Hong Kong until July, 1990.

By the late 1980s they were benefiting from the turmoil in Panama and again picking up more nervous money from the Bahamas. Again, their Financial Secretary showed the self-confidence characteristic of the Caymans when he noted in 1988 that other competitors for the offshore business – the British Virgin Islands and Turks and Caicos – were 'gaining ground' but none could come even close to the Cayman operation.[50]

It is evident, of course, that much of what the Cayman Islands and the other offshore centres do is legitimate by any nation's laws. Another part of their services is illegal elsewhere but legal in the offshore centre, while another part of their activities, laundering monies, is illegal by any country's laws. It does not appear, however, to be the business of offshore centres to figure out which is which. The Financial Secretary of the Caymans made this quite plain in a 1984 interview:

Q: Cayman has been portrayed by some as a major component in drug trafficking, money laundering and tax evasion. Respond to that please.

A: As others have stated: 'we are a tax haven, not a crime haven. That statement is irrefutable. Our drug laws are harsh and justice is swift for violators. As for money laundering, in any financial centre, New York City, Chicago, etc. you can find illegal dealings. Their financial screening of clients, etc. has not been perfect and they have been in the business for many more years than ourselves. Therefore, why is it that, whatever we do in Cayman, perfection is expected of us? Tax evasion is not a crime under our laws and we have no jurisdiction over US, Canada or any other country's tax matters.'[51]

Whatever the shortcomings of the Caymans may be, it appears that is the most one can hope for in terms of regulation at this point. A major survey for the British government recently termed it 'an example for all in regard to the efforts made to introduce sensible and relevant procedures for regulations and supervision of the offshore financial sector.'[52]

The attitude is not much different in the fastest growing offshore in the Caribbean, the British Virgin Islands (BVI) which came on line in 1984. That year the favourable double tax agreement between the UK and the US was terminated. The BVI's response was an innovative International Business Company (IBC) ordinance which proved to be a boon. In 1988 there were 13,000 ICBs established on the island and a year later (in part reflecting the flight from Panama), there were 22,000. Other centres, most recently the Bahamas, have begun to adopt similar ICB-type legislation.

Despite the fact that the BVI adopted model legislation for drug trafficking offences and does co-operate with US authorities in narcotic related investigations, they are as casual as are the Cayman islanders about the provenance of the funds. 'There is no such thing as a clean money market', says Robert Mathavious, the BVI's Financial Secretary. 'There is no way to know whether the companies registered in the BVI represent drugs profits.'[53] Even the lawyers profess to depending on 'bigger legal firms in the US and the UK to weed out the bad apples.'[54] And, as in the other centres of the Caribbean, both regulation and inspection, especially for the trust companies, were found to be at a 'bare minimum' by the Coopers and Lybrand investigator.

Meanwhile, the reports by the mid-1990s are of a growing drug trade, local drug use and increasing crime, the importation of between 55 per cent and 70 per cent of the work force, and growing inflation.[55] It sounds in many ways like the Bahamas a few years into its establishment as an offshore financial centre. Is this the fate that awaits these offshore centres in the Caribbean?

Offshore centres are now an integral part of the world's economy with as much as half of the world's money deposited in these centres or transiting through them. This reality leads to a certain resigned 'realism' among those who have to administer these offshore banking havens. 'I wish I could put my hand on my heart and say we won't have any more trouble', said the Governor of Anguilla after an official crackdown on illicit banking. 'But the crook will always be one step ahead of law enforcement. And how much clean business is there out there?'[56]

This risk appears to be in the nature of the beast itself, and not necessarily in any particular 'Caribbean propensity' to corruption. As Barry Riley notes about the British Crown-owned Channel Islands, being offshore is not the same as being onshore: 'The regulations are not usually quite as tight, and there may be unregulated as well as regulated sectors.' He illustrates this by noting that 'what goes on in the shadowy offshore trust business in the Channel Islands is still largely unknown.'[57] But Riley quite correctly notes that there is a new European consciousness about the dangers of this dirty money business, especially as national regulatory barriers are dropped after 1992. Because of the developing banking legislation in anticipation of 1992, there is a 'search for respectability' among major offshore centres. If at first it was the absence of regulations which was the bait, today the appeal tends to be the opposite: security through tight – 'but understanding' – supervision and regulation. In April, 1990 eight major banking centres famous for their tight secrecy laws, joined the Group of Seven industrialized countries in proposing a broad set of new banking regulations. Their target was specifically the laundering of dirty money. There were no Latin American or Caribbean countries at that April meeting. This led some observers to speculate whether such European measures would make the Caribbean secrecy havens even more attractive to the laundering business.[58] The Caribbean was not long in responding to the newly-developing concern with ethics. In a meeting organized by 20 Caribbean islands in Aruba in June, 1990 they discussed the North American and European concerns and concluded with the signing of the same 40-point anti-money laundering program of the Group of Seven as well as a 21-point plan trimmed to Caribbean circumstances. But, as the Business Writer for *The Miami Herald* reported: 'the dominant tone in Aruba was: if you want us to give up our lucrative offshore banking business, you will have to pay for it.'[59] Quite evidently, what is presented is a developmental Hobson's choice: the reason why these states have chosen this offshore enterprise is because of the absence of viable or sufficiently rewarding alternatives. It is a utility, not a moral, calculation. This leaves us with the empirical question: what are the risks and benefits of this offshore development strategy?

The independent states argue that the industry provides employment and sources of capital for local development. Independence allows them the flexibility to pursue innovative strategies of development which maximize the linkages between the offshore banking and other sectors. These claims are not upheld by those who have studied the issue independently. The small economic gains in white collar employment and stamp and tax revenues do not seem to outweigh the degree of risk involved. The most serious risks have proved to be the danger of corruption of state institutions and personnel and, deriving from this, the loss of respectability of the state and society. Panama under Noriega and to a lesser extent the Bahamas under Pindling were examples of such 'pariah' states.[60]

The remaining colonies or dependencies have a different perspective. To them colonialism represents a guarantee of political and social tranquillity and protection against snooping US authorities. Both ensure the kind of confidentiality, predictability and secrecy which are the hallmarks of a good offshore haven. In the new climate of concern over the role of dirty money, the colonial tie also provides a barrier to runaway corruption. It is doubtful, therefore, that the Cayman Islands, the BVI and the Turks and Caicos will go the corrupt way of the Bahamas and Panama. British actions in both Montserrat and Anguilla illustrate this reality. On 7 March, 1991, for instance, the Colonial Financial Secretary of Montserrat announced the cancellation of some 400 bank and company licences. They were listed by name in the press.[61] This was surely a response to the very critical Gallagher Report on both Anguilla and Montserrat.

All this reveals the role of paradox and irony in the contemporary Caribbean. Independence was meant to bring liberation from the evils of colonialism and, in many ways, it did. But independence also resulted in a dangerous, because insidious, type of vulnerability: threats built into certain routes to development made logical by the islands' geographical location, educational standards and political systems. It makes no sense to have to spend enormous resources to protect the rest of the society from the potential ill effects of an industry which is not exactly bountiful in its developmental returns. Ironically, to small nations venturing into the offshore business in this nefarious sea which serves as the bridge between some of the largest producers of illicit drugs and the greatest market for those drugs, colonialism is a protection against rampant corruption and mafia-type threats to a way of life.

And, yet, there might be an ultimate irony to all this. It is quite evident that since the BCCI scandal rocked the financial centres of the US and Europe, pressures towards stricter and more uniform banking regulations will be forthcoming. Senator John Kerry (D-Massachusetts) has recently warned that there will be penalties for those unregulated offshore centres which 'do not play by the rules.'[62]

Should the rules get too strict it could result in a detrimental situation for those still colonial areas in the Caribbean, and they might then opt for independence. On the other hand, should they remain colonial and regulated from the metropolis, then we can expect much of the dirty money to seek out 'safer' havens in independent, and more 'relaxed' Caribbean islands. There will be plenty of candidates in the Caribbean, not many of whom have the capacity to police either the drug trade or its financial networks.

As long as there is money to be made from the sale of drugs there will be havens where the profits can be safely tucked away. The mismatch between the instruments of the 'law' and those of the criminals is only quantitatively larger in the islands than it is in industrial countries. In the final analysis they all face a task chillingly described by R. Thomas Naylor when he says that given the present laws and technology, a state trying to catch financial wrongdoers is: 'a little like trying to capture a laser-beam in a cardboard box.'[63] It is precisely this situation which led the task force on money laundering initiated by the Group of Seven to state, in the words of the UK representative, that money laundering 'is an international problem which cannot be tackled by individual countries in isolation. The commitment by the major industrialized countries to strengthen international co-operation in the fight against money laundering is therefore all the more welcome.'[64] The US, along with the ex-colonial powers have a very real responsibility to help the newly-independent countries sustain civil and democratic societies. These, in turn, should realize that state-centric sovereignty will not protect them from the potential dangers involved in the offshore business.

Notes

1   Rachel Ehrenfeld, *Evil Money* (New York: Harper Business, 1992), p. 240.

2   John K. Villa, 'A Critical Review of Bank Secrecy Act Enforcement and the Money Laundering Statutes', *Catholic University Law Review*, Vol. 37, No. 4 (1988), pp. 489–509.

3   Cf. Robert C. Efros (ed.), *Emerging Financial Centres* (Washington, D.C.: International Monetary Fund, l982).

4   Perhaps typical of the over-ideologized objection to any type of foreign presence in the Caribbean is Tom Barry, Beth Wood and Deb Preusch, *The Other Side of Paradise: Foreign Control in the Caribbean* (New York: Grove Press, 1984). This point of view was also (in the 1970s and 1980s) that of the bi-monthly *NACLA Report on the Americas* and its Canadian twin, *Latin American Working Group Letter*. In the Caribbean the journal of the Caribbean Conference of Churches, *Caribbean Contact*, was generally critical of the tourist and assembly industries. In the UK, the publications of the Latin American Bureau have been systematically critical of foreign investment, from oil to bananas.

5   Andres Oppenheimer, *Castro's Final Hour* (New York: Simon and Schuster, 1992), p. 39.

6   There has been a persistent rumour that the Cuban Ambassador to Suriname, one of those Cuban intelligence officers mentioned in Chapter 6, had a major role in the murders. In fact, a solidly researched new book reveals that the Ambassador was shocked and angered by the events, saying: 'This man [Bouterse] is a goddamned butcher!' (Cf. Harmen Boerboom en Joost Oranje, *De 8 - december moorden* (s-Gravenhage: BZZToH, 1992), p. 95.

7   On the military involvement in drugs and money laundering see, Rudie Kagee, 'Het vergeefse gevecht van de wet legen de corruptie militairen', *Vry Nederland*, 5 January, 1991, pp. 12–14; Bert Bommels, 'Alles danst om Desi', *Elsevier*, 24 February, 1990, pp. 12–24; Bert Bommels, 'De Paramaribo-connection', *Elsevier*, 3 March, 1990, pp. 20–2.

8   Cf. Frederick Kempe, *Divorcing the Dictator: America's Bungled Affair with Noriega* (New York: Putman, 1990); John Dinges, *Our Man in Panama: How General Noriega Used the US and Made Millions in Drugs and Arms* (New York: Random House, 1990).

9   Committee on Banking, Housing and Urban Affairs, 'Banks and Narcotics Flow in South Florida', 95th Congress, 1st. Session (Washington, D.C.: Government Printing Office, 1988), p. 11.

10   Cf. Committee on Foreign Affairs, 'US House of Representatives, US Narcotics Control Efforts in the Caribbean', 100th Congress, 1st Session (December 1987).

11   Ingo Walters, *Secret Money: The World of International Financial Secrecy* (Lexington, MA.: Lexington Books, 1985), p. 22. For some early studies see Thurston Clarke and John Tigue, *Dirty Money* (New York, 1976); Robert C. Efros, (ed.), *Emerging Financial Centres* (Washington, D.C.: International Monetary Fund, 1982).

12   Canada, Senate's Standing Committee on Banking, Trade and Commerce, Proceedings, 2 October, l985, p.24.

13   The figures are taken from R. Gordon, 'Tax Havens and Their Use by US Taxpayers', (Washington, D.C.: US Internal Revenue Service, January, l981).

14   *The Financial Times*, 30 June/1 July, 1990, p. 21.

15   R. Thomas Naylor, 'Drug Money, Hot Money, and Debt', *The European Journal of International Affairs*, Vol. II, No. 3 (Winter, 1989, p. 62).

16   Walter, *Secret Money*, pp. 81–82.

17   Naylor, 'Drug Money, Hot Money', p. 58.

18 US Treasury, Tax Havens in the Caribbean Basin (Washington, D.C.: US Government Printing Office, January, 1984), p. 34.
19 *The Miami Herald*, 3 January, 1983, p. 19.
20 *The Miami Herald, ibid.*
21 *The Financial Times*, 20 April, 1990, p. 30.
22 J. Schneider, 'Crime and Secrecy: The Use of Offshore Banks and Companies'. Testimony before the Permanent Sub-committee on Investigations of the Senate Committee on Government Affairs, 98th Congress, 1st. Session. (Washington, D.C.: US Government Printing Office, 1983), p. 66.
23 *Ibid.*, p. 60.
24 John K. Villa, 'A Critical View of Bank Secrecy Act Enforcement and the Money Laundering Statutes', *Catholic University Law Review*, Vol. 37: 465, 1988, p. 502.
25 Jerome Schneider, *How to Profit and Avoid Taxes by Organizing Your Own Private International Bank in St Vincent*, Revised Second Edition (Los Angeles: WFI Publishing Co., 1979), p. 1.
26 Cf. *The Financial Times*, 27 November, 1989, p. 29.
27 Jerome Schneider, *Using an Offshore Bank for Profit, Privacy and Tax Protection* (Los Angeles: The Word Foundation Inc. Publishing Co, 1985), p. 129.
28 Walter, *Secret Money*, p. x.
29 Investigations of the Senate Committee on Government Affairs, 1983, p. 36.
30 Walter, *Secret Money*, p. x.
31 *The Wall Street Journal*, 17 April, 1986, p. 1.
32 Cf. *The Financial Times*, 29 June, 1990, p. 13.
33 *The Observer* (London), 27 May, 1990, p. 28.
34 This historical section is taken from Enrique M. Illueca, *Is Panama Still an Iron-Clad Secrecy Jurisdiction?* (Panama, 1989).
35 Cf. *LDC Debt Report*, 23 February, 1990.
36 *The New York Times,* 6 February, 1990, p. 1, C5.
37 Interviews in Panama, 10–17 May, 1990.
38 *The Financial Times*, 10 July, 1990, p. 16.
39 The Central Bank of the Bahamas, *150 years of Banking in the Bahamas, 1836–1986* (Nassau: The Communicators and Associates Inc., 1986), p. 35.
40 Cf. interview with James H. Smith, Governor of Bahamas Central Bank, *Business Monday*, Miami, Fla., Oct. 24, 1988, p. 21.
41 Interviews in the Bahamas, June, 1989.
42 See the interview with the Governor of the Central Bank of the Bahamas, Mr James Smith, *The Financial Times*, 10 July, 1990, p. 16.
43 See the letter from the Bahamian High Commissioner to the UK, *The Financial Times*, 14–15 July, 1990, p.7.
44 Tim Coone, *The Financial Times,* 10 July, 1990, p. 16.
45 Cayman Islands Bankers Association *Newsletter*, Issue No. 2, Summer 1988.
46 Steve Lohr, 'Where The Money Washes Up', *The New York Times Magazine*, 29 March, 1992, p. 27 ff.
47 Cf. National Narcotics Intelligence, Consumers Committee Report, April, 1988, cited in *American Banker* (New York, NY) 24 July, 1989, p. 23.
48 *Cayman Horizons*, Vol. I, No. 4 (January–February 1984), p. 36.
49 Martin Connolly, 'Property Investment in the Cayman Islands'. *Cayman Horizons*, Vol. 1, No. 4, January, February 1984, p. 65.
50 Cayman Islands Bankers Association *Newsletter*, Issue No. 2, Summer 1988, p. 2.
51 *Cayman Horizons*, Vol. I, No. 4, p. 37.

52 Report of Mr Rodney Gallagher of Coopers and Lybrand on the Survey of Offshore Finance Sectors in the Caribbean Dependent Territories (London: HMSO, 1990), p. 3.
53 Cited in *The Financial Times*, 29 June, 1990, pp. 11, 13.
54 *The Financial Times*, 29 June, 1990, p. 11.
55 See the report by Rachel Johnson, *The Financial Times*, 29 June, 1990, p. 11.
56 *The Observer*, (London), 27 May, 1990, p. 29.
57 See *The Financial Times Survey*, 'The Channel Islands', 19 December, 1990, p. 29.
58 *The New York Times*, 20 April, 1990, p. C-1.
59 *The Miami Herald*, 10 June, 1990, p. 28.
60 On this see the very thorough analysis by Ramesh Ramsaran, *The Commonwealth Caribbean in the World Economy*, Warwick University Caribbean Studies (Basingstoke: Macmillan Publishers Ltd, 1989), pp. 95–114.
61 Cf. *The Financial Times*, 7 March, 1991, p. 15.
62 Lohr, 'Where The Money Washes Up', *The New York Times Sunday Magazine*, p. 52.
63 Naylor, 'Drug Money, Hot Money', p. 69.
64 Quoted in *The Financial Times*, 20 April, 1990, p. 30.

CHAPTER 9 — Migration and development: All roads lead north

Jamaicans, like all West Indians, have a long history of migration.[1] In the mid-nineteenth century they went to Panama, later to the US, and then to Cuba. The man who led the island into independence left Jamaica as Aleck Clarke and after a long stay in Costa Rica, Cuba, and the US returned as Alexander Bustamante. To that young man, migration had meant opportunity. As his biographer noted, even though he was socially 'heir to an upper-class tradition', his other avenues seemed blocked at home.[2] This was the case of many others. For instance, in Cuba, Bustamante met Marcus Garvey, who, being black and belonging to the artisan class, was much more representative of the Jamaican migrant of the early twentieth century; however, he seemed driven by the same political aspirations.

Marcus Garvey established the United Negro Improvement Association (UNIA) in New York, which eventually became the largest black-based organization in the US. Several aspects of the Garvey story provide the broad outline by which to illustrate not only British West Indian migration to the US but also the socio-cultural area and its multidimensional system of status. The essence of the story is well-presented by Robert A. Hill:

> At the simplest level, Marcus Garvey and the UNIA symbolize the historic encounter between two highly developed socio-economic and political traditions: the social consciousness and drive for self-governance of the Caribbean peasantry and the racial consciousness and search for justice of the Afro-American Community. . . . Garvey came to America endowed with this Caribbean ideology.[3]

Leaving aside the psychological aspects of Garvey's struggle to become a personality, we see him as representing a type who, failing to succeed in Jamaica, transfers his energies and ideas to what Hill called 'the emerging capital of black achievement in America' – Harlem. Not having the political limitations of a colony, the US provided space for development for the likes of Garvey.

Marcus Garvey indisputably was only one of a type of Caribbean man and so was his pattern of integration into US society. This capacity to organize was not limited to Jamaicans nor was it directed solely toward economic ends. The political activities blocked in the colonies seemed to spark new activity in the US, and many of these new organizers had links with Garvey and the UNIA. For instance, Trinidadian Charles Augustus Petioni, was an English-educated doctor whose political aspirations could be fulfilled neither at home nor in England. He migrated to Philadelphia where he immediately established the Trinidad Benevolent Association and later the West Indian Committee in America; the latter was specifically geared to using its US base to fight for West Indian political rights.

Similar men were Eliezer Cadet, a Haitian who first migrated to London where his contacts with black soldiers radicalized him, and Arden A. Bryan, originally from Barbados but with a three year interlude in Panama, who after breaking with Garvey, founded the Negro Nationalist Association. Along with these political types were also the artists; by far the most important of whom was the Jamaican, Claude McKay. In an American milieu still permeated with racism, the West Indian was superb at bridging the gap between the liberal elements of the establishment and the oppressed. His education, language skills but perhaps especially, what David Reisman calls his 'inner directness' (a goal-oriented and determined sense of self) were valuable attributes in the American context. How then, beyond their personality traits, can the obvious synergies between these migrants and their hosts be explained?

In 1955 the Jamaican anthropologist M.G. Smith sampled opinion among 2,050 rural Jamaican youths between the ages of 10 and 15.[4] He discovered that only 3 per cent wished to be farmers while 23.8 per cent wished to be professionals (11.3 per cent of these, doctors), and 31.1 per cent desired high-skill occupations. Smith noted that since such occupations could be secured in such numbers only in urban Jamaica *and* abroad, there existed a lamentable gap between reality and desire. He postulated that this revealed a potentially high degree of anomie. Smith placed the blame on the educational system, which he said presented 'a curriculum . . . designed for urban populations in industrial countries.'

Very similar findings about student ambitions were being revealed in Trinidad, leading to some harsh words from one of the Caribbean's outstanding writers, Vidia S. Naipaul.[5] Naipaul found the grand ambitions of the black and East Indian students a 'fantasy . . . part of the carnival lunacy of a lively, well-informed society which feels itself part of the great world, but understands at the same time that it is cut off from this world by reasons of geography, history, race'.

The fact is, of course, that the island and its people have never been cut off from the 'great world'. Naipaul himself admits that the island was 'fully part of the advanced consumer society of the West . . .'. He ends by noting that 'Trinidad is simply small . . . what is needed, is access to a society, larger in every sense, where people will be allowed to grow'. His vision of Venezuela being that larger society was palpably illusory; to Trinidadians and other West Indians, the US and Canada were and are it.

West Indian education, thus, has prepared West Indians for the migration so many would eventually make. Under those circumstances, it was pragmatic and not anomie-producing, certainly not some form of lunacy. The criticisms levelled against the educational system for engendering aspirations which can be fulfilled only in larger societies, take on greater salience when joined with the criticisms about the impact of this predisposition to migrate on development. Not untypical are the arguments of Jamaican sociologist Orlando Patterson. Patterson argues that in Caribbean societies, migration 'dominates and defines the social structure' and has created a 'model personality syndrome devoid of trust and seemingly incapable of compromise'.[6] As such, migration is an obstacle to good government, because the elite is willing and able to 'use migration as a weapon against any progressive policy' to correct the very conditions which make migration both possible and necessary.

The problem with the M.G. Smith and Orlando Patterson type critiques is that they present no alternatives to the culture of migration. Since this culture is today a recognized West Indian – indeed, a Caribbean-wide – reality, it has to be incorporated into any policy recommendations on development. In fact, it represents one of the most fertile sources of US-Caribbean synergies.

Taken as a whole, the Caribbean Basin has experienced one of the fastest population growth rates in history: from 55 million in 1940 to 166 million in 1980. This has been an annual growth rate of 3 per cent for four decades. The explanation lies not so much in increasing birth rates as in declining mortality rates, what demographers call the 'death dearth'. Improved standards of health account for much of this change. This has been especially true for the island societies.[7]

In the Caribbean Basin, the insular Caribbean grew much slower than Mexico and Central America. In 1936 Mexico had 36 per cent of the Caribbean Basin's population; this had risen to over 42 per cent in 1980. By contrast, the proportion of the insular Caribbean fell from 25 per cent to 18.5 per cent of the total. As the data in Table 9.1 illustrate, the share of the West Indies specifically is expected to drop from the present 4.15 per cent of the total Caribbean Basin population to 3.3 per cent by the year 2000. On some islands, populations are projected to actually decrease. One explanation is the increased use of birth control methods. (In Trinidad 52 per cent of women of childbearing age use contraception; in Jamaica the figure is 51 per cent.) Another part of the explanation, however, lies in the fact that

Table 9.1: Population projections, Caribbean Basin, insular Caribbean, Mexico and Central America and West Indies ('000)

	1985	2000	2025
Caribbean Basin Total[1]	133,690	185,971	–
Mexico and Central America	104,935	148,838	222,274
Insular Caribbean	28,755	37,133	53,195
West Indies	5,554	6,135	–
W.I. Countries[2]			
Antigua/Barbuda	81	101	
Bahamas	234	–	
Barbados	253	260	
Belize	169	215	
Dominica	78	81	
Grenada	102	98	
Guyana	794	795	
Jamaica	2,336	2,800	
Montserrat	11.9	12	
St Kitts/Nevis	46	44	
St Lucia	139	128	
St Vincent	111	108	
Trinidad/Tobago	1,199	1,259	

Sources: (1) The World Bank, *World Development Report, 1986* (New York: Oxford University Press, 1986); (2) Commonwealth Secretariat, *Caribbean Development to the Year 2000. Summary Report* (London, May, 1988).

emigration trends are calculated into projections. Most West Indian development scenarios are calculated according to projections of migratory flows. The joint Commonwealth Secretariat and Caribbean Community Secretariat study of the Caribbean in the year 2000 is no exception. The dramatic impact of emigration flows on the rate of job creation is described in that study (see Table 9.2). Case 'A' indicates the increases in the supply of jobs which the study believes will be necessary to reach full employment if emigration is eliminated. Case 'B' shows the increases necessary to keep 1980 employment rates if emigration rates remain at the 1980 level.

Without calculating in emigration rates, it is evident that the growth rate of the labour force will be substantial. It is difficult, indeed, to conceive of the economies of these countries – given their present structure – generating that many new jobs over the next decade.

Table 9.2: Labour force projections to the year 2000 ('000 workers)

	CASE A		CASE B	
COUNTRY	WORKERS	% ON 1980	WORKERS	% ON 1980
Barbados	129	33	115	18
Belize	103	157	62	54
Dominica	41	93	29	38
Grenada	49	85	34	29
Guyana	405	115	235	25
Montserrat	6	43	5	23
St Kitts/Nevis	22	54	18	23
St Lucia	65	101	45	40
St Vincent	54	106	36	37
Trinidad/Tobago	624	93	43 (*sic.*)	34

Source: Caribbean Development to the Year 2000, op. cit., p. 11.

Accompanying this increase in the labour force will be a qualitative change in the demographic and economic composition of the population: urbanization is, and will continue to be, a dominant trend in the West Indies. The annual rural growth rate will have decreased from 1.35 per cent in the 1950–60 decade to 0.71 per cent during 1980–90. The urban growth rate, on the other hand, will have risen to 3.18 per cent in 1980–90 from 2.93 per cent in the decade of the 1950s.[8] The upshot is that an area which is already 54 per cent urban will become even more so, some countries faster than others. Jamaica, for instance, already 78 per cent urban, will experience a phenomenal 7.1 per cent annual urban growth rate. Can these societies provide the jobs in the cities for these new hands? Any answer which analyzes the projected growth of the work force in the context of the present rates of unemployment and the probable rates of growth of the newly liberalizing and restructuring economies, would have to conclude that they can not. The trend everywhere in the Caribbean – including Cuba since 1991 – is to reduce government spending by reducing public sector hiring and the subsidizing of money-losing state enterprises. It is doubtful that the relatively underdeveloped private sectors of these islands will be able to absorb significant numbers of the 25 to 30 per cent of the workforce which traditionally has been in the public sector. This explains the keen concern of societies with deep ethnic divisions with the hiring practices of both the public and the private sectors. Unemployment – especially when it is given an ethnic twist – is always an explosive issue.[9]

In this context, migration, in addition to being a traditional practice, is a fundamental safety valve. American policymakers have always understood this and acted accordingly. One of the arguments undergirding the Caribbean Basin Economic Recovery Act (CBERA) adopted by the US Congress as part of the Reagan Administration's 1982 Caribbean Basin Initiative (CBI) was to enhance the productive, and thus employment, capabilities of non-traditional sectors of the economies. The expectation was that this would also reduce the flow of migrants to the US. The position implicitly accepts the idea that there is a linear relationship between levels of development and numbers of migrants. The assumption was that CBERA was, if not the solution, at least a major step in that direction.

The facts do not support this assumption; while the CBERA has certainly been a generous attempt to assist the Caribbean Basin secure greater private investment and to increase exports to the US market, it has not had the overall impact it was expected to have. The following trends illustrate this:[10]

- While US imports from all other parts of the world increased during 1980–86, imports from CBERA countries decreased by an annual average of 8.2 per cent over 1980–86 and even faster (11.8 per cent) if we measure it for 1983–86.
- CBERA-eligible countries are losing out to other areas in exports to the US: in 1980 their exports accounted for 4.3 per cent of total US imports, in 1986 it was 1.7 per cent.
- From 1985 to 1992, US imports from the Caribbean did grow by 1.7 per cent, reflecting the growth of the manufacturing and apparel industries. US exports, however, grew by 6.9 per cent during that period making the Caribbean one of the few areas with which the US has a favourable balance of trade.
- Exports of primary products to the US, traditional areas of employment, declined by 6.2 per cent during 1985–1992.

Part of the explanation lies in: (1) the decline in oil and sugar exports, and (2) the nature of the investments encouraged by this development strategy. Of US imports from CBERA countries, 95 per cent come from three areas: apparel, electronic machinery and SIC-39 'miscellaneous manufactures'. All require heavy importation of US raw or partly-manufactured materials. The result, as the US Department of Labour indicated, has been that while in 1986, US content value comprised 17 per cent of the customs value of US imports from all sources under TSUS 807.00, 'for imports from CBERA beneficiaries, the share of US content was 70 per cent'.[11]

The availability of '936' funds from Puerto Rico has been limited because of high wages and the failure of many West Indian governments to sign the mandatory Tax Information Exchange Agreement (TIEA). Up to 1987, only Jamaica, Dominica, Grenada, Barbados and St Lucia had signed.

While CBERA has not had a significant overall effect on development trends in the area, it has created new employment in non-traditional sectors of the economy. In Jamaica, for instance, employment in the garment industry exporting under US 807.00 went from 6,500 in 1983 to 29,500 in 1987. While Caribbean exports of garments grew by 37 per cent during that period, Jamaican exports grew by 89 per cent.[12]

Several aspects of this garment industry are worth analyzing.

1   Ninety-five per cent of the workers are women. The entry of these women into the labour force explains why the unemployment rate in Jamaica has lingered between 25 and 30 per cent.
2   They draw the second lowest wages (after Haiti) in the Caribbean Basin. Because the wage is based on piecework, it is calculated that wages are 'as low as' J $67 and 'as high as' J $300 per week.[13]
3   The Jamaican government calculated that of every $100 in garments they exported to the US, $80 of the value originated in the US. Deputy Prime Minister Hugh Shearer calculated that the employment in the US directly attributable to 807.00 exports went from 5,000 in 1980 to 74,500 in 1986.[14]

This latter claim would be hard to document. It is a fact, however, that between 1985 and 1992, US imports of apparel from the Caribbean increased by 20.2 per cent but US exports of apparel components to the region increased by 21.8 per cent.

What, then, can be expected from the traditional sectors? In some, such as bauxite, there is a new lease of life which will benefit Jamaica and Guyana. But the most traditional sector of all, sugar, is in crisis. It is still by far the largest employer, as indicated in the list of number of workers below:

Jamaica	45,000	Trinidad/Tobago	15,000
Belize	20,000	St Kitts	17,000
Barbados	10,000		

An example of the effects of any attempt at rationalizing this industry is St Vincent where the government of James ('Son') Mitchell closed down the money-losing industry at a cost of 2,000 jobs. This at a time, 1986, when the unemployment rate was 35 per cent. The situation is not as dramatic in the other countries but the prospects are not encouraging. The situation of sugar in these countries is starkly summed up by the US Department of Commerce: 'Generally speaking, the sugar industries of these five countries are in a state of disarray'.[16] The situation in other agricultural sectors is not much better.

World Bank statistics[17] show that while employment in agriculture has dropped drastically, so has agricultural output. In Jamaica, agricultural employment went from 39 per cent of the labour force in 1960 to 25 per cent in 1991; its output from 12 per cent to 8 per cent. Similar or larger drops in both agricultural employment and output are being experienced throughout the area.[18] Visits to any farming or fishing community in the region will immediately reveal a dramatic demographic picture: virtually all the people in the field or fishing are older, the young are simply not entering agriculture.

Except in some of the smaller islands, land hunger or scarcity is not the central problem. This can be seen from the case of Guyana, or indeed Trinidad, where the government holds large tracts of 'Crown lands'. The move away from the land results from very complex forces which have yet to be fully analyzed in the region. Caribbean leaders have long been concerned with the low degree of self-sufficiency in foods of the region but at a loss to find solutions.[19] The result is that every country in the Caribbean is today heavily dependent on food imports.

Thus far we have discussed investments under the CBI and Puerto Rico's 936 twin plant initiatives. These have tended to draw new workers into the labour market – women, pay low wages, require little infastructural investments and create few backward linkages.

There is another type of development strategy which bears analyzing: the capital intensive industries. The purposes of these investments was to diversify the economy, earn foreign exchange and provide employment in a series of 'linked' industries. It has not worked that way.

The oil transhipment operation owned by Amerada Hess Oil Co. in St Lucia illustrates this case. Its operations spread over 500 acres and it is the island's largest source of tax revenues. It directly employs 60 people and few, if any, others. The most dramatic attempt to diversify the economy and reduce the dependence on any single market through industrialization was that of Eric Williams in Trinidad. It is now studied as an example of what *not* to do in the West Indies.[20]

Williams was certainly one of the most independent-minded leaders in the English-speaking Caribbean. A man with very definite ideas about colonialism, he was also one of the few with the financial opportunity to implement the development plans of his choice. Despite internal and external criticisms (his critics, he would say, wished to keep Trinidadians 'colonialized'), Williams enacted these choices: capital intensive development. The IMF reported that of a total of TT $11.5 billion in surplus revenues deposited in the Development Fund between 1974 and 1981, TT$8.6 billion were disbursed in this attempt to convert the island into a major energy-based industrial country, TT$3.8 billion (US$1.4 billion) in capital and TT$1.26 billion in infrastructural investments. By 1987 the project had generated 1,694 jobs. This represented an investment of TT$2.3 million per job. It was not a good investment. There is evidence that the aggregate loss of Point Lisas between 1982 and 1986 has been some TT$1.48 billion. To this has to be added payments on TT$1.64 billion in outstanding loan commitments.[21]

There are definitely some positive trends in most of the other islands which will ameliorate the pressures on employment. The most important is the declining rate of population growth: from 2 per cent in the 1960s to 1.5 per cent in the 1980s. The overall figures, however, are not encouraging: unemployment in Trinidad among the age group 15–19 stands at 50 per cent; age group 20–24, 36 per cent; 25–34, 22.2 per cent; and 35–44, 17 per cent. These are candidates for jobs (and a potential migratory pool). Additionally, the employment pressure will be augmented by two significant West Indian-wide trends:

1   The increasing entry of women into the labour force taking jobs made available by US 807.00-type investments. There is ample room for growth here since only 33 per cent of the women of working age are presently in the work force.

2   A reduction of state support for tertiary education will hasten the entry of more young adults into the job market.

3   The unpredictable impacts of three developments, one concluded and the others objects of serious speculation. Foremost is Mexico's entry into the North American Free Trade Agreement (NAFTA). Will the elimination of tariffs, combined with its proximity and low wages, redirect US trade and investment capital from the Caribbean to Mexico? Certainly, the concessions made by the CBI for certain non-traditional manufactures will be negated by the NAFTA provisions. Secondly, will the US Congress rescind Puerto Rico's '1936' program, denying the Caribbean that source of investment funds? Finally, and most speculatively, what will be the consequences of the re-entry of Cuba as a competitor for tourism and offshore manufacturing as well as investment capital? All three cases illustrate the need for the Caribbean to increase its negotiating efforts in the US not just for markets but also to keep avenues of immigration open.

There is little optimism, therefore, that the Caribbean, and the West Indies in particular, has found the 'right' development strategy for the longer term. However, even if the West Indies managed a balanced growth development strategy, will this keep West Indians from migrating? That economic growth in itself will not keep West Indians at home can be illustrated with the Jamaican case during the 'boom' years 1953–70. Stephens and Stephens describe the situation: 'Unemployment remained at 17.5 per cent from 1953 to 1957, despite a growth rate of 11.5 per cent per annum and a labour-force growth rate of only 0.9 per cent'. Between 1953 and 1970 unemployment declined to 13.5 per cent, but as the Stephens note: 'only because the labour force actually declined in this period, apparently because of migration'.[22] In fact, Jamaican emigration began to escalate precisely during these boom years. Pressures to migrate appear constant in the West Indies. What are the implications for the US?

In 1985 the 22 island states in the Caribbean, with a combined population of 29 million sent 83,000 *legal immigrants* to the US. This was 14.5 per cent of the total legal immigration into the US that year from a group with 0.5 per cent of the world's population. Jamaica sent 15,797 legal immigrants to the US in 1986, 0.7 per cent of its total population, but that same year there were 60,000 Jamaicans on the waiting list for US visas, or 2.6 per cent of its population. Table 9.3 describes the numbers coming to the US on immigrant and non-immigrant visas from the most populous West Indian islands. Not listed in the table is the Bahamas, which in 1986 received 36,577 non-immigrant visas for travel to the US – 15.6 per cent of its total population. When money is available they travel: in 1981, 6.5 per cent of the Trinidad population received a non-immigrant visa to travel to the US. Aside from the drain in hard currency this implies, the figures also reflect destination preferences plus the degree and frequency of interaction and acquaintance with the US.

The critical aspect is that these large numbers represent legal migrants, carefully screened by US consular agents on each island. The available evidence indicates that illegal entry or stay-over is a relatively small part of the West Indian movement to the US.

Although extremely difficult to assess, some approximation to the numbers of illegals can be made. One way is to look at illegals in the 1980 census figures. Estimates on the high side are those of Passell and Woodrow who calculate that Haitians, Jamaicans and Trinidadians were 4.9 per cent of all illegals counted in the 1980 census.[23] The General Accounting Office, on the other hand, placed the figure for that 3-nation group at 2 per cent.[24] If we realize that Haitians are probably the largest number in that group, we have an approximate sense of the West Indian numbers (see Table 9.4).

Another window is provided by the statistics on legalization applications under the provisions of the 1986 Immigration Reform and Control Act. Table 9.5 shows the comparatively small numbers of West Indians seeking amnesty as of 20 May, 1988. The total from Jamaica, (15,100) was equal to the legal migration to the US from that island in 1970 alone (15,003). Even these illegals seem to have done well: those seeking legalization under I-687 (in the US prior to 1982) were mostly employed or students. Only a very small minority were listed as 'unemployed or retired'. And, yet, there are some worrying trends.

The rise in criminality among some West Indian residents, evident in the rise of the Jamaican 'posses' and 'yardies', is a recent phenomenon tied

Table 9.3: Visas to selected West Indian countries

Country	Immigrant visas				
	1977	1979	1981	1983	1986
Barbados	8,191	4,835	5,333	4,962	4,816
Guyana	5,345	5,723	5,679	7,473	9,491
Jamaica	10,876	14,840	18,739	15,029	15,797
Trinidad/ Tobago	3,832	4,222	3,442	2,120	2,071

Country	Non-immigrant visas				
	1977	1979	1981	1983	1986
Barbados	26,254	24,894	20,768	20,500	21,770
Guyana	4,980	5,559	5,949	7,182	9,865
Jamaica	29,130	48,170	47,131	36,519	39,173
Trinidad/ Tobago	20,675	37,719	65,238	47,476	22,133

Source: US Consular Service, Port of Spain, Trinidad, September 1988.

Table 9.4: Estimates of illegal aliens from Haiti, Jamaica in seven states

US States	Estimates: based on 1980 census[1]				Legalization Applications I–687 I–700[2]	
	Haitians, Trinidad/ Tobago Jamaicans	Total	Haitians	%	Jamaicans*	%
California	3,000	513,486	45	–	105	–
Florida	6,000	74,482	28,526	38.30	4,672	6.27
Illinois	2,000	50,634	81	0.15	61	0.12
Massachusetts	3,000	4,233	949	22.40	100	0.36
New Jersey	4,000	10,596	749	7.06	233	2.20
New York	70,000	49,781	4,637	9.30	2,337	4.70
Texas	1,000	146,468	18	–	109	–

* Only West Indian Group listed
Sources: (1) J.S. Passel and K.A. Woodrow, 'Geographic Distribution of Undocumented Aliens Counted in the 1980 Census by State', Washington, D.C.: Population Division, Census Bureau, 1984; (2) Immigration and Naturalization Services, Statistical Analysis Branch, 1988.

directly to the increase in the drug trade in the US. Jamaicans are now part of a much wider group of criminal aliens operating in the US.[25]

Generally speaking, one can conclude that West Indian migration to the US has historically been largely legal and productive.[26] Up to now also, most West Indians would argue that it has been productive for the West Indies, Orlando Patterson and Vidia Naipaul notwithstanding.

All this might change, however. Increasing criminality and fraud, as discussed in Chapter 7, might be harbingers of changing trends. With the US and Canada virtually the only remaining outlet for a people accustomed and historically predisposed to migrate, pressures might lead to behavioural changes. The pressures for migration to the US, for instance, are evident not just in the backlog of those applying for legal migration but also in the number of illegal immigration schemes revealing themselves throughout the Caribbean. In Jamaica, fraudulent US immigration visas are known to cost on average J$10,000,[27] in Trinidad up to US$5,000 and in Haiti the assassination of the head of airport security has been linked to his interruption of a ring peddling fraudulent US visas and passports.[28] Criminality is one dimension of the problem, fraud another. Large numbers of Jamaicans,

Table 9.5: Estimated legalization applications, I-687, I-700 (as of 5–20–88) by select CBI and WI citizens

	Total	%	I-687	%	I-700	%
Mexico	1,581,800	73.0	1,138,400	71.1	443,400	81.3
Haiti	50,400	2.3	16,800	1.0	33,700	6.2
Dominican Republic	24,700	0.7	13,100	0.8	1,600	0.3
Jamaica	15,100	0.7	10,800	0.7	4,300	0.8
Belize	4,900	0.2	4,900	0.3	100	—
Guyana	3,400	0.2	2,800	0.2	600	0.1
Trinidad/Tobago	2,900	0.1	2,500	0.2	400	0.1
Bahamas	2,100	0.1	2,000	0.1	100	—
Antigua/Barbuda	1,300	0.1	1,300	0.1	—	—
Barbados	1,000	—	900	0.1	100	—
Grenada	1,000	—	900	0.1	100	—
St Vincent/ Grenadines	800	—	700	—	—	—
Dominica	600	—	500	—	100	—
St Kitts/Nevis	600	—	500	—	100	—
St Lucia	500	—	500	—	—	—

Source: Provisional Legalization Application Statistics', Statistical Analysis, US Immigration and Naturalization Service (20 May, 1988).

and especially Trinidadians, have recently been claiming 'refugee' status, an outrageous claim given the human rights records of those countries. While these trends should be – and are – worrying to West Indian and US officials alike, they are a minor part of the link between migration and development in the West Indies. The most important aspect of that link is the effects of the West Indian 'brain drain'.

The loss of talent is certainly not a new phenomenon in the West Indies. Between 1962 and 1968, Trinidad lost 143 doctors and dentists, 170 engineers, 629 nurses, 784 teachers and 909 other professionals, mostly in the productive 20 to 34 age group.[29] It was calculated that in the 1970s the West Indies were losing some 14,000 skilled personnel per year.[30]

In 1982 it was calculated that 50 per cent of the output of Jamaica's training institutions for 1977–80 had migrated. Some 70 per cent (150,000) had gone to the US and 30 per cent (64,000) to Canada. Jamaica has always been able to do without those with few skills since, as the National Planning Agency admitted, their leaving 'relieved unemployment' pressures. It was the highly-trained and skilled ones they could hardly afford to lose. The level of development was 'adversely affected'.[31] The Agency concluded that: 'it is the cream of the country's labour force which emigrated to North America during this period'.[32]

The frustrations created by this brain drain, even after such heavy investments in industrialization such as those made by Trinidad, were clearly evident in the last presentation made by Eric Williams, Prime Minister of Trinidad and Tobago, before his Party's Annual Congress. Noting the massive loss of skilled personnel and professionals, he lamented that 'there will soon be no West Indians left in the Caribbean . . .'.[33] This was more an expression of his frustration, though, than a statement of reality, given the rate of population growth. Is it the numbers of migrants or the nature or quality of the migration that Williams and other West Indian leaders bewail? How different is this West Indian situation from that in Great Britain, for instance, where it is calculated that 25 per cent of the fellows of the Royal Society – the United Kingdom's most prestigious scientific organization – have migrated?[34] Whatever the factual answer might be, present West Indian perceptions are that they are confronting a crisis.

Two considerations seem to undergird the increasing West Indian concern over the brain drain. First, it impedes their planned shifts towards service and higher technology economies; second, and related to this, is the growing sense that West Indians are bearing the costs of a part of US and Canadian skilled labour needs. They see a loss of talent and of investment monies at a time when they can afford neither. So bad has the situation in certain fields become that concerned officials have been tempted to ask the US to deny visas to particular technicians. The 'flight' of nurses is particularly serious in Jamaica and Trinidad.[35] US active recruiting is directly related to what a US Federal Commission called the 'pervasive' shortage of registered nurses in the US. While in 1987 the overall US shortage was 11.3 per cent, in the inner city public hospitals – where West Indians have traditionally gone – it stood at 15 to 20 per cent.[36] So great was the demand for trained nurses that in 1989 the US Congress passed the Immigration Nursing Relief Act (INRA), scheduled to expire in 1995. INRA simplified the processes of securing a temporary work permit and for converting temporary visas into permanent ones. An American hospital had to prove a vacancy rate of at least 7 per cent before it could hire foreign nurses. But in Jamaica, for instance, nursing vacancies were 31 per cent in 1987 and reached 50 per cent in 1991. Fully 80 per cent of the nurses' resignations were attributed to plans to migrate.[37] Accompanying this US 'pull' is the West Indian 'push': low pay and poor working conditions.[38] The West Indian joke that if a medical doctor wishes to migrate to the US he should marry a nurse, does not humour West Indian health authorities. A government which spends US$5,000 per year for three years in basic nursing training plus another $5,000 for a year's midwifery training only to see them migrate, rightly feels that they are subsidizing US health care.

The problem is that short of an outright ban on travel and an effective closing of foreign borders, everything indicates increases in the pressure to migrate. Illegal migration will probably increase but in terms of West Indian development it will be the loss of skilled and technical people which will hurt the West Indies most. These people, in their vast majority, are legal migrants. To the extent that 'solutions' are possible, they will have to be in the area of legal migration.

The Immigration Reform and Control Act of 1986 is fundamentally an attempt to control the flow of undocumented aliens into the US. As such, it deals with a minor part of the West Indian issue. Relatively few West Indians come to the US illegally but large numbers of legal immigrants do. To the extent that one is concerned with the relationship between development and migration, it has to be admitted that there is no evidence that even sustained and respectable rates of economic growth have stemmed the flows from the West Indies. A culture of migration generates its own impetus and collective rationale for migrating. But the recent history of the West Indies indicates it is an area in structural economic crisis. These are transfer economies attempting to sustain employment in areas which are no longer viable. New employment opportunities are in low-wage, assembly-type industries which make few inroads into the armies of unemployed. These new developments certainly appear to be doing little for the middle classes.

Observing the nature of economic development in Jamaica, the late

Carl Stone concluded that those most eager to move were 'the victims and casualties of white-collar poverty':

> Never in the history of this country have so many qualified people just packed their bags and moved on to New York, Toronto or Miami . . . because they see no hope of ever buying a car, owning a house, or just enjoying the modest lifestyle [of] 20 years ago . . .'.[39]

Again, observing the statistics on this middle-class migration, he noted their high training, their language proficiency, their marketable skills and their determination. 'And there is no force of any sort', Stone concluded, 'that can prevent them from leaving our shores and seeking out greener pastures'.[40] These migrants are not unemployed; they do not dislike their countries, they are frustrated by the lack of *opportunities*. They know, like all past generations did, that migration is the widely accepted avenue for dealing with those frustrations.

The central questions have to be: what are the consequences to future development of the loss of the broad middle and lower middle classes? Are there any policy recommendations which not only address that trend, but which are grounded in the realities of US needs and West Indian social, economic and cultural predispositions? There are certainly many interesting suggestions.[41] In other words, have there been programs which have shown synergies which have worked to the advantage of both societies – the US and West Indians – and can they serve as contemporary models?

The H-2 program, for West Indian cane cutters as it existed in the 1970s and early 1980s, might be just such a model. Not that that program, and all guestworker programs, do not have their critics. What is interesting, however, is how few of the basic criticisms of guestworkers' programs apply to the Caribbean case.[42] The first objection is to admitting workers who enjoy restricted rights. West Indian H-2 workers are represented in the field by the West Indian Central Labour Organization; in the 1980s the WICLO had twelve liaison officers located right in the sugar cane areas of Florida. There are specific grievance and bargaining provisions built into their contracts. Additionally, the Constitution of the State of Florida specifically guarantees the right of H-2 workers to join a labour union or to strike.

The second criticism is that guestworkers have a negative impact on local labour, especially among disadvantaged groups such as refugees; in the case of Florida, Haitian refugees. None of the studies, thus far, has been able to pinpoint a group, including the Haitians, who could do the kind of skilled yet arduous work West Indians can. All experiments with non-West Indian cane cutters have been less than successful.[43] Since this is the case, critics raise a third objection: guestworkers perpetuate the physically exerting and unpleasant jobs Americans won't take. Cutting cane is certainly one of those but the only way to 'raise the standard' of cane cutting is by mechanizing it. In Florida soil conditions have made this impractical. The success of this H-2 program[44] is the story of a felicitous match between economic needs and soil conditions in Florida and the cultural orientations of West Indians.

Florida cane is grown under conditions which do not allow full mechanization; it needs skilled and dependable manual labour. And here is where nature shapes economics, for if a machete-wielding man in Florida is to compete with a harvesting machine in Hawaii, he has to be skilled. But cutting cane manually is unpleasant, backbreaking work that no one in the world engages in unless the rewards are real, as indeed they are to the West Indians, even though the major element of this reward is monetary – the difference between what the workers make abroad and what they would have made staying at home. In 1980–81, the US Department of Labour set the hourly minimum rate at $4.09, but a piecework formula allowed these skilled workers to make an average of $5.10. In 1981, the average wage, not including bonuses, was $202.57 per week. But there was another incentive which explains the popularity of the H-2 program: the worker is not locked into the 'cane culture', i.e. the complex and demeaning lifestyle associated with the West Indian sugar plantation which affects not just the worker but his whole family.

Aside from subsidized room and board, they get a 50 per cent subsidy for travel to the job and upon completion of contract, free travel back. Workers receive a medical exam before travelling, are covered by their own group hospitalization insurance as well as state mandated worker's compensation for job related injuries. The goal in negotiating these subsidies was of course to fulfill the whole purpose of migratory work: sending major parts of the earnings back home.

The fourth objection to guestworkers – that they tend to 'overstay' their contractual periods – has never been documented for the West Indians. Part of the explanation might be that usually up to 64 per cent of the H-2 workers in Florida are full-time farmers back home; they have families and occupations to return to. The final objection, that it is unclear whether exporting workers is economically beneficial to the sending countries, is worth further exploration, as the case of the migration of nurses illustrates.

Clearly, the H-2 workers have been content with the pay off. An 8,000-man force, working five months, managed to generate the following monies for the 1980–81 season: (1) mandatory savings (24 per cent of wages), US$7.7 million; (2) mailed remittances, $4.7 million; (3) value of foods purchased in US, $4.5 million; (4) cash in hand upon return, $1.9 million – totalling nearly $19 million. Table 9.6 shows how these monies were invested and, as is to be expected, housing was the most important item.[45]

None of this, of course, fully answers objection number five. It is not at all evident that what is good for the few thousand workers is good for the broader sending society's development, but is this the appropriate question? Should the question be: has this particular experiment in legal and institutionalized labour flows worked for both the West Indian and the particular sector of the US economy which hired them? The answer has to be a categorical yes, for the US as well as Canada.

In Canada the program was established much later than in the US.[46] First came the Jamaicans in 1966, then in 1976 workers from the Eastern Caribbean and Mexico. By 1982 there were some 6,000 working on fruit, vegetable and tobacco farms. Over half of these were Jamaicans. In Canada, as in the US, the economic rationale was the same: the inability to recruit sufficient native workers.

There are some important differences between the guestworker program in Florida and the one in Canada, which serve to make the model even more flexible and attractive.

As in the case of those going to Florida, nearly all going to Canada had jobs back at home when they were recruited, but those going to Canada tend to come from a different labour pool: over half were skilled or semi-skilled workers. This explains why, as can be seen from Table 9.6, the educational level of the workers going to Canada tended to be considerably higher than those going to cut cane in Florida. This might be explained by their background: 63.8 per cent of the H-2 workers in Florida were full-time farmers by occupation and 37 per cent did farming as a second occupation; only 30 per cent of the Eastern Caribbean workers in Canada were farmers back home.

As is to be expected, West Indians indicated that they travelled for the increased pay, yet fully 22 per cent of those in Canada indicated that they travelled for the experience of being overseas. Since 63 per cent of these workers first heard about the Canadian job opportunity from friends, the interest in migrating tended to be self-sustaining and in keeping with the history and culture of migration and work abroad. Another indicator of satisfaction on the side of employers and workers is the fact that between 1974 and 1981 the average worker had made five trips to Canada, most of them to the same farms.

In a region where there is a culture of migration with well established patterns of movement, social networks and collective expectations, can an H-2 type program work in other, non-agricultural, areas? Can similar programs for middle-class professionals and skilled labour be designed? A tentative yes is worth exploring and has, indeed, been previously suggested.[47]

Table 9.6: Main investment strategies of earnings brought home by farm workers

FLORIDA[1]	%	CANADA[2]	%
Housing	66.8	Housing	35.0
Farming	15.1	Land	8.3
Livestock	11.0	Vehicle	1.3
Schooling	2.2	Schooling	10.3
Living expenses	13.0	Family support	31.3
Business	9.1	Clothes	1.0
Personal expenses	3.2	Appliances/furniture	0.6
Savings	14.5	Savings	6.3
		Other	3.3

Educational levels of guestworkers, Florida and Canada

FLORIDA[1]*		CANADA[2]
No schooling	13.0%	0.3%
Average years primary school	3.9	7
Some secondary school	4.4%	21.0%

* Note: Includes Jamaicans

[1] Workers from Barbados, St Vincent, St Lucia, Dominica, (1981), *Source*: Terry L. McCoy, 'The Impact of Seasonal Labour Migration on Caribbean Development' (Paper, American Political Science Association Annual Meeting, Chicago, IL, September, 1983).

[2] Anne V. White, 'The Experience of New Immigrants and Seasonal Farm Workers from the Eastern Caribbean to Canada'. Unpublished ms., Institute for Environmental Studies, University of Toronto, July, 1984.

The point is that synergies between countries with such asymmetries of power and wealth should be sought and encouraged whenever and wherever found. The ultimate criteria have to be those of rights, both human and economic: they should not be psychologically demeaning nor economically exploitative. The H-2 program has met those criteria, if not perfectly, at least to the satisfaction of both sides. It should be looked at as a model.

Notes

1 Because the largest group of Caribbean immigrants, Cubans and to a lesser degree Haitians, have been coming to the US as political refugees, this chapter focuses on people from the English-speaking Caribbean. They are mainly legal immigrants.

2 George E. Eaton, *Alexander Bustamante and Modern Jamaica* (Kingston: Kingston Publisher, 1975), p. 13.

3 Robert A. Hill (ed.), *The Marcus Garvey and Universal Negro Improvement Association Papers* (Berkeley: University of California Press, 1983), Vol. I, pp. XXXVI–XXXVII.

4 M.G. Smith, *The Plural Society in the British West Indies* (Los Angeles: University of California Press, 1965), pp. 196–220.

5 In 1957 and again in 1961, Vera Rubin and Marisa Zavalloni studied Trinidadian high school students' 'expectations, plans and hopes for the future'. (Cf. *We Wish to Be looked Upon*, New York: Teachers College Press, Columbia University, 1969). Naipaul's review appeared in *The New York Review of Books* (3 September, 1970).

6 Cf. Orlando Patterson, 'Migration in the Caribbean Societies', in William H. McNeill and Ruth S. Adams (eds), *Human Migration* (Bloomington: Indiana University Press, 1978), pp. 125–38. For a similar interpretation of the negative consequences of 'the ease with which the decision to migrate is taken' see Evelyne Huber Stephens and John D. Stephens, *Democratic Socialism in Jamaica* (Princeton, New Jersey: Princeton University Press, 1986), pp. 33–4.

7 Leon Bouvier and David Simcox, *Many Hands, Few Jobs*, (Centre for Immigration Studies, November 1986; CIS Paper 2), p. 14.

8 Kempe Ronald Hope, *Urbanization in the Commonwealth Caribbean* (Boulder: Westview Press, 1986), p. 40.

9 Cf. *Employment Practices in the Public and Private Sectors in Trinidad and Tobago*, 2 vols (Port of Spain: Centre for Ethnic Studies, UWI, 1993).

10 US Department of Labour, Bureau of International Labour Affairs, *Trade and Employment Effects of the Caribbean Basin Recovery Act* (Washington, D.C., August, 1987); *Latin America and the Caribbean: Selected Economic and Social Data* (Washington DC: US Agency for International Development, May 1993), pp. 137–50.

11 *Ibid.*, p. i.

12 Cf. *The Jamaican Weekly Gleaner*, 25 April, 1988, p. 3, and 6 June, 1988, p. 2.

13 Statement by Free Zone Operators Association, *The Jamaican Weekly Gleaner*, 28 March, 1988, p. 5.

14 *The Jamaican Weekly Gleaner*, 25 March, 1988, p. 3.

15 *Trade and Employment Effects of the CBERA*, *op. cit.*, p. 47.

16 US Department of Commerce, International Trade Administration, *US Sugar Policy: An Analysis* (Washington, D.C.: US Printing Office, 1986), p. 63.

17 Cf. The World Bank, *The Commonwealth Caribbean* (Baltimore: The Johns Hopkins University Press, 1978), p. 119.

18 The World Bank, *World Development Report – 1986* (New York: Oxford University Press, 1986), pp. 190–91.

19 Cf. UN Caribbean Regional Integration Advisors' Team, 'Planning to Meet the Caribbean's Growing Food Needs' (Port of Spain, Trinidad and Tobago, 1975).

20 Cf. De Lisle Worrell, *Small Island Economies. Structure and Performance in the English-Speaking Caribbean since 1970* (New York: Praeger, 1987), pp. 143–62.

21 Cf. Dennis A. Pantin, 'Whither Point Lisas? Lessons for the Future', in Selwyn Ryan (ed.), *Trinidad and Tobago: The Independence Experience, 1962–1987* (St Augustine: ISER, University of the West Indies 1988), pp. 27–45.

22 Evelyne Huber Stephens and John D. Stephens, *Democratic Socialism in Jamaica*, *op. cit.*, p. 32.

23 Jeffrey Passell and Karen A. Woodrow, 'Geographic distribution of undocumented immigrants: estimates of the undocumented aliens counted in the 1980 census by state', US Bureau of the Census. Population Division, Washington, D.C. A paper presented at the Annual Meeting of the Population Association of America, Minneapolis, MN, 3–5 May, 1984.

24 Cf. GAO, 'Illegal Aliens', (Washington D.C.; GAO-PEMD-86-9BR, April 1986), p. 7.

25 Cf. US General Accounting Office, 'Criminal Aliens', (Washington, D.C.: GAO/GGD-86-56 BR, March, 1986).

26 For some interesting examples of this productivity see Thomas Sowell, *Ethnic America* (New York: Basic Books, 1981), and Dolores M. Martinez and Roy S. Bryce-Laporte (eds), *Female Immigrants to the US* (Washington, D.C.: RIIES, 1981).

27 Cf. *The Jamaican Weekly Gleaner*, 24 October, 1988, p. 12.

28 Cf. *The Miami Herald*, 12 November, 1988, p. 5A. In October and early November, 1988 the INS was reported to be returning 20 Haitians per flight from Haiti because of fraudulent documents (Cf. *The Miami Herald*, 21 November , 1988, p. 6).

29 Trinidad-Tobago, *The Emigration of Professions, Supervisory, Middle Level and Skilled Man-Power from Trinidad-Tobago, 1962–1968* (Port of Spain; Government Printing Office, 1970).

30 *Report of the Caribbean Task Force* (Port of Spain, Trinidad: Government Printing Office, 1974), p. 91.

31 National Planning Agency, *Emigration to North America from Jamaica, 1970–1980* (Kingston, January 1982), p. 1.

32 *Ibid.*, p. 4.

33 Eric Williams, *Forged From the Love of Liberty. Selected Speeches of Dr Eric Williams* (Port of Spain, Trinidad: Longman, 1981), p. 443.

34 Cf. Malcolm Gladwell, 'The British Elite in Exodus: "We're Losing our Captains," ' *Insight,* 29 June, 1987.

35 Jamaican Minister of State in the Ministry of Health, Karl Samuda, called for the measure in order to stop a flow which would 'plunge the whole country into a deep crisis . . . the likes of which we had never seen before'. *The Daily Gleaner*, 30 October, 1987, p. 3. In Trinidad, open recruiting by US and Saudi Arabia is said to have resulted in a 'crisis' 50 per cent reduction in trained nurses. *Trinidad Guardian*, 12 September, 1988, p. 1.

36 Cf. *The New York Times*, 13 December, 1988, p. 14.

37 Cf. Rush E. Levine, 'Assessment of Health Manpower Development in Jamaica' (Washington, D.C.: Urban Institute Research Paper, February, 1992); Ruth E. Levine and Gerard La Forgia, 'Resource Allocation in the Health System in Belize', (Washington, D.C.: Urban Institute Research Paper, April, 1992).

38 Joan Rawlins, 'Why are Nurses Leaving?' *The Jamaican Weekly Gleaner*, 15 February, 1988, p. 10.

39 *The Jamaican Weekly Gleaner*, 7 March, 1988, p. 8.

40 *Ibid.*, 6 June, 1988, p. 10.

41 See especially the imaginative suggestions by Robert A. Pastor in the Introduction, Chapters 15 and 19 of his edited book, *Migration and Development in the Caribbean* (Boulder: Westview Press, 1985). Also David S. North and Judy A. Whitehead, 'Policy Recommendations for Improving the Utilization of Emigrant Resources in Eastern Caribbean Countries', in Anthony P. Maingot (ed.), *Small Country Development and International Labour Flows*, pp. 15–54.

42 The arguments against guestworkers are presented approvingly, by D.G. Papademetrion,

P.L. Martin and M.J. Miller, 'US Immigration Policy: The Guestworker Option Revisited', *International Migration*, XXI (1983), pp. 39–54.

43 Cf. US House of Representatives, Sub-committee on Labour Standards, *Job Rights of Domestic Workers: The Florida Sugar Cane Industry* (Washington, D.C.: US Government Printing Office, 1983).

44 This argument reflects the West Indian view of the H-2 program. For a full discussion of the arguments surrounding that program see Terry L. McCoy, 'The Impacts of US Temporary Worker Programs on Caribbean Development: Evidence from H-2 Workers in Florida Sugar', in Robert A. Pastor (ed.), *Migration and Development, op. cit.*, pp. 178–206.

45 Cf. David S. North, *Non-Immigrant Workers in the US: Current Trends and Future Implications* (Washington, D.C.: Employment and Training Administration, US Department of Labour, May 1980), p. 53. Cf. Terry L. McCoy, 'The Impact of Seasonal Labour Migration on Caribbean Development' Paper, American Political Science Association Annual Meeting (Chicago, IL, September, 1983).

46 Cf. Anne V. White, 'The Experience of New Immigrants and Seasonal Farm Workers from the Eastern Caribbean to Canada', Unpublished ms., Institute of Environmental Studies, University of Toronto, July 1984.

47 Cf. Patricia Y. Anderson, 'Migration and Development in Jamaica', in Robert A. Pastor, *Migration and Development, op. cit.*, pp. 134–36.

CHAPTER 10 | Haiti: Intractable problems, shifting commitments

'Democracy', said the President of Haiti to the United Nations, 'has won out for good, the roots are growing stronger and stronger.' This was on 25 September, 1991. One week later, President Jean-Bertrand Aristide ('Titide' to his followers) was deposed by a *coup d'état*. The regime of the only internationally-certified freely-elected president of Haiti had lasted seven months. The 70 per cent or so of the Haitian electorate who cast their votes for the changes Aristide promised had been robbed of their hopes. What are the chances that these democratic hopes can be restored by internal changes? Can this occur without international, especially US, pressures?

Any response has to begin by admitting that it is an impossible methodological task to answer this question responsibly by attempting an analysis of Haitian politics and society within given chronological parameters. Periodizing contemporary Haitian history – if we mean by that distinct changes in political behaviour, not just institutional or formal changes – is difficult. The task for those who would study Haiti, therefore, is not so much to identify momentary formal changes, but to understand structural continuities in political cultures.

In his refreshingly original 1989 book, *Quand la Nation demande des comptes*, Alain Tournier reviews the reprisals and confiscations which historically have followed each period of dictatorship in Haiti. Noting that sometimes Haitians, and nearly always foreigners, tend to think of the most recent crisis ahistorically, Tournier asks: 'Is the present political reality merely the rebeginning of history?'

Without being naively sanguine about man's ability to learn from history, the fact remains that one ignores Haitian history at terrible peril to contemporary policymaking. The need to explore and reflect on the lessons of Haitian history holds true generally. It is especially relevant, however, in understanding the failure of third parties, especially the US and the Inter-American system's attempts to force political changes on the island. One should keep in mind what was discussed in Chapter 2: that Haiti was under US military occupation longer than any other country in the Caribbean. This nineteen-year occupation did little more than leave a bad memory which all Haitian groups use to their own advantage. As one sympathetic author expressed it, the problems of 1915 were still the problems of 1935; 'No power on earth could have solved them in a dozen years . . .'[1] There is a minimum of three features of Haitian history which should be kept in mind as one ponders on the intractability of Haiti's political problems.

First and foremost is the uniqueness of Haiti's struggle for independence. While the struggle for individual freedom certainly reflected a commonly-shared sentiment, there was unity on pitifully little else. Independence – so heroically and bloodily fought for – hardly brought about unity. Haitians opted variously for republicanism (both democratic and authoritarian), monarchy, empire, and presidencies for life under different institutional arrangements. Regardless of the form chosen, the outside world considered the island an outcast and kept it in tight political isolation.

Such actions certainly contributed to the second important feature of Haitian history: the evolution of a fierce sense of independence and autonomy among Haitian elites. This obstinate determination to safeguard independence of action was a blend of pride, resignation to a world they could not change, and logical resentment at those – such as the Venezuelan Liberator, Simón Bolívar – who refused to acknowledge the debts they owed Haiti. A consequence of this attitude was and is the historical capacity of Haitian political elites, of whatever persuasion, to utilize successfully every known technique of negotiations with foreigners. Attempts to dictate Haitian affairs are invariably confronted with strategies which go from avoidance to procrastination, and, if felt necessary, even a suicidal 'scorched-earth' approach. The lack of repect with which they were treated has left its mark. In the 1880s nationalist President Salomon realized that not dealing with foreigners constrained Haiti but he preferred it to 'the extortions, to the humiliations of every minute.' Or as a local paper put it in 1887: 'Our desire for progress must not lead us like Egypt to shame, to servitude, to death.'[2] If they ever enter into negotiations, they are grandmasters of the stall-and-outlive tactic. History tells them that the rest of the world has little staying power when faced with the intractability of Haitian problems. Dictator François Duvalier believed that the US was a 'paper tiger' when it came to toughing it out; that, he believed, was Haiti's trump card.

The third feature which in many ways not only made the first two possible but, indeed, intensified their inflexibility, was the nature of the post-plantation economy. Since independence, the radically reformed landholding system has been characterized by generalized peasant ownership and subsistence agriculture. This system certainly spared the Haitian peasant the horrors of the typical Latin American *latifundio*. It was, however, harsh on the ecology and not conducive to surpluses which could be invested elsewhere. The Haitian economy was characterized by a very few pockets of tightly (i.e. family) controlled wealth based in coffee or commerce. Opportunities for employment were largely in government; governments which, crucially, were sustained and financed by squeezing the peasants and the few concentrations of wealth.

The consequences of this economic situation began to be manifested with alarming clarity after World War II. The growth of Port-au-Prince allowed politicians to use the masses as veritable 'steam rollers' (*rouleurs compresseurs*) to intimidate their enemies. This rural-to-urban migration has accelerated as Table 10.1 shows. By the 1980s, Haiti was dotted with small urban areas, all in direct contact with the all-important capital city which Haitians call 'the Republic of Port-au-Prince'.

It is not that the cities have that much to offer in terms of jobs, schooling, health services; rather, there has been an accelerating deterioration of the rural, peasant economy. Haiti's situation is bad by any comparative standards: the annual growth of Haitian agricultural production during the early 1980s was 1.2 per cent; for South America it was 3.3 per cent; while the total for the Third World was 2.9 per cent.[3]

Haiti is quickly shifting from being a rural and agricultural country to a country where the rural sector cannot sustain life, of those in the cities or, indeed, even their own. *Minifundio*, or as the French call it, '*une paysannerie parcellaire*', describes a situation where 72 per cent of the landowners possess less than one hectare. The traditional, and usually partly optimistic, studies of the peasantry, have been replaced by a pessimistic literature which engages in debates over the residual value or lack thereof of the 'atomization' of the peasantry. Atomization refers to the system of *multi-culture* or mixed cultivation for family consumption, local needs, and

Table 10.1: Changes in rural and urban populations, 1950–1982

	Population (000)			Annual growth rates (%)	
	1950	1971	1982	1950–71	1971–1982
Total	3,097	4,330	5,053	1.6	1.4
Urban*	255	707	1,042	5.0	3.6
Port-au-Prince	152	507	720	5.9	3.2
10 towns over 10,000 in 1982	98	180	235	2.9	2.5
Other towns over 5,000	5	26	97	8.2	12.7
Rural	2,831	3,623	4,011	1.2	0.9

* Defined as towns over 5,000.

Source: The World Bank, 'Haiti: Policy Proposals for Growth', 26 April, 1985, p. 5.

external markets. Paul Moral, for instance, saw this as promoting 'disorder'; he called it a system of *grappillage* (*grapiye* in Creole) which means literally: 'grab wherever you can'. George Anglade, on the other hand, sees Haitians turning necessity (i.e. survival) into a virtue. Whatever the merits of this *minifundio* may or may not be, there is one consequence with which no one argues: Haiti now has to import more and more of its food needs. Importation of foodstuffs increased 300 per cent between 1973 and 1980 and continues to grow.[4]

The decline of the Haitian countryside goes beyond food cultivation. The pressure on the land and its wood resources continues its inexorable march towards total ecological disaster. Table 10.2 describes this desperate reality with frightening clarity.

It is evident that this deteriorating resource base of the island is an ongoing structural situation which can be redressed only with a dramatic reduction in population pressure on the land. Migration, mostly to the Dominican Republic, certainly relieves the pressure but cannot be regarded as a structural solution. Structural improvements can come about in only two ways: in the short-term, by an urban industrialization program which would absorb the 'excess' rural workers, or, in the long-term, by a dramatic reduction in the birth rate. Neither appears likely to occur soon, especially not the latter. The trend is clear. The population is growing at an annual rate of 1.7 per cent, certainly not extraordinary in Third World terms. There is no evidence, however, that either of the two factors which bring down fertility is presently operating: natural birth control resulting from substantial increases in the standard of living or widespread and effective artificial birth control measures. Only 19 per cent of married Haitian women (who, additionally, make up only 20 per cent of the total in the procreation age

Table 10.2: The deteriorating Haitian resource base

Year	Population	Arable land (in hectares)	Arable hectares per person	Consumption of fuel wood* (in thousand cubic metres)
1938	2,500,000	540,000	0.216	NA
1954	3,400,000	370,000	0.109	8,869
1970	4,300,000	225,750	0.052	13,125
1980	5,500,000	225,750	0.041	20,000

* Represents 75 per cent of all wood consumption
NA   Not available
Source: Compiled by author from AID Library, Port-au-Prince, Haiti, 1980.

group) practise artificial birth control. This compares poorly with the 55 per cent who do so in neighbouring Jamaica.

The known demographic facts are that Haitians will not reach a net reproduction rate of 1 until the year 2030 and, even after that, actual population size will not become stationary until the year 2145, at which point it will stand at 17 million. In the West Indies, Arthur Lewis had constructed a theory of urban industrialization needed in order to absorb the excess labour of the rural areas. However, the dimensions of the problem in the West Indies pales in comparison to the situation facing Haiti. Another look at Table 10.1 helps to explain what a growth of these dimensions implies in the context of a shrinking land base. What, then, can one expect from the peasant in terms of action towards social change?

Alain Rocourt speaks for many social scientists in saying that the Haitian democratic process cannot advance without the participation of the peasantry, who make up 80 per cent of the population. Yet, how to get them involved? 'It was the city', he says, 'which brought about the fall of Duvalier. It was as though the peasantry had not really been concerned, as though it had been on the sidelines of history, solemnly watching the events.'[5] This is not an exclusively Haitian problem but it certainly does require an exclusively Haitian solution. There are quite a few projects being tried in the rural areas but they are invariably based on small-scale or 'pilot' projects. One particularly candid author, Marie-Michele Rey, admits that these rural projects are like 'a drop of water in the sea.'[6]

It is evident, therefore, that the crisis in Haiti's countryside affects the whole country, including the urban areas. These urban areas have been the epicentres of Haitian politics, and still are today. The difference is that virtually all significant political activity used to take place in Port-au-Prince while now it is taking place in every town of over 10,000 people. Control of Port-au-Prince, however, continues to be the key to power. The reality, therefore, is that a mobilized peasantry can vote and as such is a democratic resource. However, there is no evidence that they can either overthrow dictators or defend democrats.

Locating the sites of politics, therefore, is not the same as explaining the political culture which drives it. This latter is not easily done for Haiti, but in order to try to understand the political culture the nature of Haitian politics will now be explored.

In September 1986, the Woodrow Wilson Centre in Washington invited twelve of the best-known Haitian 'leaders' to analyze their homeland's prospects.[7] This was seven months after the fall (the *dechoukage*) of the Duvalier dynasty, and thirteen months before the first attempt at a democratic election (see Table 10.3). Some were pessimistic and others optimistic about Haiti's chances for democracy and civilian rule. None of the twelve, however, came even close to predicting what would take place between the time they met to discuss Haiti's future and the date their book was actually published. Between the conference and the publication of its proceedings, the army contributed to the slaughter which stopped the November, 1987 elections, 'elected' Leslie Manigat president, overthrew Manigat, put their commander in, overthrew that general and put another in. This last general, Prosper Avril, survived two major *coup* attempts before being forced to leave the country.

The problem is one which Haitian sociologist Pierre-Raymond Dumas has singled out with great sociological insight.[8] Dumas anticipates that democratic transitions are fundamentally different from democratic consolidations. In Haiti this is a problem within a dilemma: you cannot have a democratic consolidation without a viable democratic transition. The problem is that in Haiti only the army is in a position to guarantee the latter.

Table 10.3: Calendar of Haitian political instability

1957–1971	Rule of François (Papa Doc) Duvalier.
1971	Jean-Claude (Baby Doc) inherits rule.
7 February 1986	President Jean-Claude Duvalier overthrown by General Henri Namphy.
29 November 1987	General elections called off after massacre of voters.
17 January 1988	Leslie F. Manigat is 'elected' president. General Namphy installs himself as commander of the armed forces and General Regalá as Minister of Defence. Manigat makes attempts at reducing corruption in military and civil service. Attempts to counter moves by General Namphy by siding with Colonel Paul.
19 June 1988	General Namphy overthrows President Manigat, with critical support of General Lhérisson and Colonels Avril, Augustin, and Charles.
17 September 1988	General Namphy is ousted by a *coup* ostensibly led by non-commissioned officers under Sgt Joseph Hébreux. General Prosper Avril is declared President.
1 April 1989	Attempt to overthrow Avril fails.
March 1990	General Hérard Abraham overthrows the Avril government.
November 1990	Free elections won by Aristide.
January to October 1991	Aristide governs for seven months.

Whatever the army's proclivities might be, it is evident that it does not operate in a vacuum and that any 'guarantees' will involve a *quid pro quo.* Under those circumstances, there can never be a transition totally removed from military interests or at least, from significant segments of that military.

How then does one analyze a political context within which the military might be the final arbiters but not the sole actors? Surely there must exist a 'common' sense to the Haitian 'system'; all societies systematically perform some minimal essential political functions and all cultures carry out even a minimum of political socialization. The latter creates one or more political cultures. In other words, the very concept 'Haitian society' implies some acceptance of a 'goals-means' behavioural scheme, for politics as well as in other areas. That we, or anyone else known to be in print, have not been able to unravel that system or scheme for Haiti speaks more to our intellectual shortcomings than to the absence of a Haitian system or political culture.

This failing is not limited to non-Haitians. Few men were more respected for their written, and, presumably, actual intimate knowledge of Haitian politics than Professor Leslie F. Manigat. Similarly, once in the presidential palace, his cabinet was a veritable repository of Haitian talent. And, yet, as we shall note, he and they, showed a singular incapacity to sustain power or gain popular credibility once they came into authority.

Based on the notion that there are indeed one or more political cultures in Haiti (even though the totality of which is beyond our conceptual reach), the following 'problems' or characteristics can be presented as hypotheses, not certainties.

In Haiti, politics has traditionally been perceived as a competition intended for narrowly private, not public, benefit. There has never been either the context, or the encouragement, to bargain collectively, to engage in the associational behaviour which is generally regarded as the foundation of pluralist, democratic politics. This does not, of course, mean that selfless, patriotic politicians have been lacking in Haiti. What it does mean is that, without the institutionalized mechanisms requisite for collective action, political individualism became the norm. Individuals could achieve their aspirations only through access to the one office which allows maximum individual action and national power: the presidency. This explains why most prominent Haitians perceive themselves as 'presidential'; there are no second prizes in Haitian politics. Even as selfless a person as the ethnologist Jean Price-Mars hoped, with what one author calls 'almost childlike faith', to be president.[9] His dream was to minister to his black brothers of rural Haiti, or, in Price-Mars' words: 'to rouse him from his long slumber, from his rut and from his dejected resignation.' And so it is for most of the literary luminaries, from a Jacques Roumain, who founded the

Haitian Communist Party, to René Dépestre, a world-class poet who also viewed Marxism as the political route to be followed at one time.[10] An extreme example of this individualism is the following explanation given by Dr Sylvain Jolibois, Coordinator of the 'Jean-Jacques Dessalines Sector' and a contender for the presidency in the 1980s:

> We ourselves are not followers of any one man. We are not even followers of any one party. We are both autonomous and in the [democratic] front simultaneously . . . I think that it is characteristic of a political leader to see how things feel day by day, to see what is going on.[11]

This individualism was further aggravated after 1986 by what can be called 'the law of large numbers'. If the system was segmented for most of Haitian history, and political participation limited, the sudden opening up of this system in 1986, including, very importantly, the return of numerous exiles, created a reverse problem: too many contenders. A partial listing of parties, associations and groups which have been politically active during 1986–89, provides more than 30 presidential 'candidates'. The consequence of such a multiplicity of individuals participating was that the impact of the actions of each individual was perceived as insignificant. Even under the best of circumstances such a 'dilution' would result in little mutual co-ordination or assessment of the actions of the others. Haiti represented the worst of circumstances, a situation where there is no strategic interaction based on factual knowledge, where politics becomes an unreal game. In such a context predictable politics are non-existent since 'positions' are little more than smoke and mirrors.

The post-1986 situation illustrated also how difficult it is to influence domestic affairs from exile. Not one of the exile political groups proved to have had significant operations during or after the Duvalierist period. Clear evidence of this is the nearly complete absence of effective machinery for the articulation and dissemination of factual knowledge and information about the system and its main actors. Yet Haitians, like political actors everywhere, engage in some form of strategic interaction, i.e. they behave according to their perception of their environment, human and social. The problem is that perceptions in Haiti are based almost entirely on guesswork rather than on factual information. Because the society is still at least 75 per cent illiterate, radio is the most influential means of information. Yet the fact that in mid-1989 there were over 40 radio stations for some 120,000 radio receivers, as well as numerous newspapers and two television chan-nels – all using Creole, which had already become the operative language of Haitian politics – tended to confuse things even more. All of which combined to create what ex-President General Namphy called a *bamboch democratik*, a democratic festival or fling. Contributing to this euphoric but short-lasting 'festival of confusion', if you wish, was another characteristic of post-Duvalierist Haiti: the presence of a large number of risk-free participants, actors who were exogenous to the system and had relatively little to lose in the struggle. This included, of course, not only the American embassy but also foreign private sector organizations, France, international ideologically-based groups such as Social Democrats, Christian Democrats, and Marxist-Leninists, liberation theology advocates organized by religious orders, viz. the Jesuits or Salesians, and also, in many ways, Haitian exiles permanently residing abroad. They invested money, published newspapers,[12] sent delegations to the island, and generally tended to get more attention than did most local actors.

It is evident, therefore, that the post-Duvalier conjuncture involved numerous individuals and groups with high expectations but no general framework, information or mechanisms for collective interaction and bargaining. It was the kind of turbulence which was ripe for manipulated outcomes. Manipulated, that is, by the one group with a modicum of cohesion and agreed agenda: the military. How these problems operated and played themselves out in the rise and fall of two Haitian presidents demonstrates the intractable nature of Haitian politics as well as the constantly shifting commitments and loyalties of the major players.

The multiple personal and petty clashes and enmities, especially those built up during 30 years of Duvalierism, are beyond the scope of social analysis. One is cautioned, therefore, against attempts at uncovering the 'true' reasons why individual X or Z behaved in a particular way *vis-à-vis* the President. What is possible is a general outline of the problems these presidents faced, the way they interpreted them, and some assessment as to any possible generalizable understanding about the Haitian system which can be derived from their short tenure and fall from power. The first President we shall discuss in this context is Leslie F. Manigat.

The old canard that the Haitian people are not prepared to participate in electoral politics had been laid to rest in the months before Manigat's investiture in February, 1988. The referendum of 3 March, 1987 on the new constitution had gone off without a hitch and 72.55 per cent of the eligible voters had enrolled to cast their ballots in the elections of 29 November, 1987. A team of some 600 international observers were on hand and a total of 16 parties were participating. There were 5,721 voting stations set up for that election, and, as a hundred pictures and eyewitness accounts testify,[13] the people were out *en masse* as early as 6.00 a.m. on election day. Manigat had withdrawn from the race the day before claiming that the electoral process was rigged against him. Whatever the truth of that assertion might be, the fact is that it was a wilful act of violence and bloodshed against innocent citizens standing in line to vote which brought the democratic process to a halt. Obviously, Manigat did not condemn the cancellation of

Haiti's first attempt at universal, direct elections. He was subsequently 'elected' on 17 January, 1988 in an election totally manipulated by the military.

The structures Manigat faced were those of the Duvalier tyranny which were never dismantled after Jean-Claude fled in early 1986. This left the following institutions very much active and operational:

1 A national army which had been thoroughly 'sanitized' by 28 years of Duvalierist purges. Although it is evident that Manigat must have had some initial support in the military, it does appear that in the final analysis his power depended on whatever terms had been set by the existing power elite in the military.
2 A population which had been disarmed and controlled by new groups of armed, semi-private armies, the *ton-ton macoutes* and the *Volontaires de Securite National* (VSN). These groups, during Manigat's term, and to this day, have the arms and appear to be co-ordinating their actions with elements of the military and police. Manigat is not known to have had any ties to these groups; logically, he could not count on their support.

Not only were the same Duvalierist military forces in existence, there had been a compounding of their vested interests since the departure of the Duvaliers. This process resulted from the changes in governmental economic policy, largely compelled by multilateral lending agencies and the US AID mission. The policy involved the dismantling of the state-controlled (read Duvalier) monopolies in consumer staples and utilities as well as the opening of the market to outside goods. One result of this was, and continues to be, heavy smuggling. Goods come across the Dominican border and through the ports and are largely controlled by the military. Together with the control of the illicit drug transhipments discussed in Chapter 6, this contraband provided individual military men with substantial funds. Some military commanders were reputed to supplement the salaries of their men out of their own pockets. It was said to be the only guarantee of their loyalty.[14]

These economic and marketing changes also led to two other changes, both vital to an understanding of the situation Manigat faced: (1) a dramatic drop in the cost of staples for the masses, and thus a removal of the 'microeconomic' dimension of any conjectural political crisis; and (2) a serious division in the nation's economic elites between commission-agent importers, those in import-substitution manufacturing and those in manufacturing for export. This division removed the old *quid pro quo* arrangement between the Duvaliers and the business elites in which the latter were left alone in return for their neutrality in politics. Manigat never had this luxury: every sector wished to influence state policy on their terms. After

1986, the various sectors lined up behind different contenders for power, thereby considerably diluting their potential effectiveness as an opposition to any new dictatorship-in-the-making. Taken together, these economic conditions gave the military more operating space in the short-term. Nothing indicates that Manigat actually achieved any restructuring of this state of affairs. How could he? Surely Manigat knew his Hobbes, who as early as 1651 cautioned us that while military men redeem honour through war, politicians compensate for bad games by constantly reshuffling the cards. In Haiti the military were trained and disposed toward politics, not war. Honour is a fancy word, not an intrinsic value. They, and no one else, do the reshuffling because they virtually own the deck.

Manigat certainly knew this: he condemned it in a 1964 monograph called *Haiti of the Sixties: Object of International Concern*. But he compromised. The military, he kept repeating, has to be negotiated with . . . like you do with the business community or the church. But was it negotiating or simply compromising? His own Minister of Foreign Affairs and close friend, Dr Gerard Latortue, recalls how Manigat thought of the army as 'a kind of *grand electeur*'. He understood that 'in order to get in power in Haiti there is no way not to make a compromise with the army.'[15] 'Not to participate in the military-run elections', he told a Haitian journalist, 'would be like the best football team ceding the championship by default'. He was the one who could best negotiate with the military.[16] But negotiation implies a *quid pro quo* which Manigat did not have. Once his academic and international prestige did not translate into new foreign aid and investments, Manigat was an emperor without clothes. That he was an honest, well-intentioned statesman surrounded by the best cabinet ever assembled in the history of Haiti was so many pearls cast before military swine. And yet, Manigat was human and ultimately Haitian. He too was 'presidential'. 'When they reach their forties', overthrown military President Paul Magloire once said, 'all good Haitians have a higher objective than a seat in the Senate.' Manigat certainly did.

It is not that the military is enormous. With about 7,000 men in a population of 6 million, Haiti has one of the smallest military-to-civilian ratios in the hemisphere. That said, and also that it is very poorly armed, one should quickly note that it does not need more. Simply stated: Haiti has been an unarmed society since the US occupation which means the army has the only firearms in the country. The Uzi – a weapon suitable for interpersonal violence but hardly for national defence – is the preferred sidearm of the officer corps and is bought through Miami dealers. Cancellation of US military assistance does not affect the military's power capabilities. Additionally, military political influence is enhanced by their concentration not only in the capital but, indeed, right around the Presidential Palace. Manigat depended on the support of the 'Battalion Caserne

Dessalines' which had the advantage of location: a well-fortified garrison right behind the Presidential Palace. It also had good intelligence based on its traditional ties to the police force and to the *ton ton macoutes*. Its commander up to November 1988 was Colonel Jean-Claude Paul. He had become something of a household name in South Florida because of his indictment in a Miami court on drug smuggling charges. Paul was the closest thing to a General Noriega (of Panama) that Haiti had, and as such was no push-over. Manigat was counting on his support, so in return he defended him against the drug-running charges. He would say that it was Paul's Haitian nationalism that antagonized the Americans.[17]

Whoever may or may not have been involved in drugs in Haiti might be hard to discover. What is not hard to discern is the fact that Haiti had become – at least since 1983 according to the DEA[18] – a major transhipment point for Colombian cocaine. President Jean-Claude Duvalier's brother-in-law was jailed in Puerto Rico, accused by the Carter administration of transporting drugs. Haiti did not become a major centre of US concern, however, until 1987.[19] By that year, the pressure was turned on President Manigat to rid his regime of one officer in particular, Colonel Jean-Claude Paul. The Haitian situation had gone beyond personalities; it was now believed to involve systematic and well-organized links between the Colombian cartels and Haitian gangs operating in the US. The Miami river appears to have been their main point of entry into the US. An analysis of Haitian vessel activity on the Miami river alone, according to a high US customs official, revealed that approximately 45 per cent of the vessels, and 60 per cent of the vessel agents were documented for alleged involvement in alien and narcotics smuggling activities.[20]

This, then, was the history and the context; these were the players that Manigat had to deal with. They put him in the Palace, it was only a matter of time before one or more of them would decide that the game was not to his liking and profit and attempt to shuffle the cards. Who initiated the fatal round of intrigues, who promised what to whom and, then, who betrayed who when, is all for present speculation and subsequent history books. The general context, however, was all too clear: shifting personal loyalties. The one who actually led the *coup* was General Henry Namphy who had put Manigat in power and whom Manigat attempted to dismiss, assuming that Colonel Paul and the Battalion Casserne Dessalines would back him up. He had badly miscalculated his own political culture. Note the shifting commitments in the following interview conducted by Radio Canada (RC) with Leslie Manigat (LM) immediately upon his overthrow:

RC: If Namphy made your election possible, why did you dismiss him?

LM: The greatest number of officers felt that Namphy was an obstacle to the democratization of the military; they were very happy with the dismissal of Namphy.

RC: Why, then, did those same officers rally to Namphy when he moved
       to overthrow you?

LM: They did not want to break military ranks.[21]

General Namphy was himself removed on 17 September, 1988. The
one doing the removing this time was General Prosper Avril, Commander
of the Presidential Guard. Soon thereafter, Colonel Paul was no longer. His
mysterious death on 6 November, 1988 was never investigated further than
an analysis of the pumpkin soup he was eating at the time. Clearly, the
stakes of having access to the business of governing Haiti were now worth
killing for.

Later, from his exile in the Dominican Republic, General Namphy
would claim that he was overthrown because he was 'struggling against
drug trafficking and putting a stop to the conflicts of interest going on
within the Haitian army.'[22] As it turns out, Avril was just then also claiming
that it was his policy of 'cleaning up the nation' of politicians and officers
'implicated in drug trafficking' which led him to move against the Namphy
government.[23] It is not at all evident that this was the cause. The fact is that
the *coup* which brought down General Namphy was led by one, Sargent
Joseph Hebreaux and his non-commissioned officer colleagues. Avril appeared to have joined the winning side, making appropriate noises about
fighting corruption to impress the American Embassy. Sergeant Herbreaux
was not another Fulgencio Batista who as a sargent in Cuba overthrew the
officer corps and gave rise to the reformist government of Grau San Martín.
It was the entry into Haitian politics of the *Ti soldats* (the little soldiers)
which gave the more populist-oriented some hope,[24] though it should not
have. What was occurring in Haiti was the slide into anarchy – a *bamboche
tyrannique*.

An attempt to overthrow General Avril on 1 April, followed his
dismissal of four high-ranking officers accused of involvement in the drug
trade. These expelled officers, in turn, accused Avril of buying the loyalties
of the Presidential Guard through weekly 'extra payments' made from his
ill-gotten wealth. They spoke of Avril's 'corrupting' of the armed forces.[25]

Indiscipline and greed are fatal to any organized body, and perhaps
even more so to one which has a monopoly on force. Parallelling the
collapse of military discipline was the rise of a series of para-military
groups, again without any known central command but all 'in business'.
Haitians called them variously *grupes sans maman* (groups without
mothers), *zenglendo* (bandits) or simply *escadrons de la morte* (death
squads). While it can safely be assumed that many former *ton-ton macoutes*
and variously purged officers and soldiers formed part of these bands, it
would be wrong to believe that they were limited to such types. Two other

sources of possible recruits were: (1) groups of hired-guns employed by disgruntled wealthy Haitians and, (2) any number of *chefs-de-section*, the traditional rural section chiefs who are laws onto themselves. With 565 rural sections in Haiti, each calculated to have some 100 armed lieutenants, they represent a number substantially greater than the 7,000 man army. Almost certainly, they were part of the massacre of over 300 peasants of the *Tet Ansamn* (Heads Together) movement in rural Jean Rabel on 23 July, 1987.[26]

Despite this dreary scenario, hope springs eternal among those who follow Haitian events, even though that hope invariably flies in the face of incontrovertible experience. 'Of the four governments to rule Haiti since the departure of Jean-Claude Duvalier', said a senior US official, 'we judge the Avril government as offering the best, and perhaps the last real chance for democratic reform in Haiti for the forseeable future.'[27] This official spoke too soon.

In March 1990 the pattern of apparently uncontrollable anarchic behaviour – strikes, crime, roving gangs and especially a brutal attack on the parish of a radical priest called Aristide – brought down the Avril regime. This time it was General Hérard Abraham who was the saviour of the moment. Hérard appeared all the more appealing because, contrary to tradition and expectations, he did not put the presidential sash on himself. Rather he put it on Madame Ertha Pascal Trouillot, a Supreme Court Justice now elevated to Provisional President. Despite such uncharacteristic self-effacement, who could blame *The Washington Post* for editorializing on 14 March, 1990, 'Haiti has been at this place before'.

It is a fact that General Abraham gave the green light to the holding of new elections and in so doing won the respect of a wide array of foreign human rights groups from the OAS to President Jimmy Carter's special observation team. The state machinery, however, was in an advanced state of decomposition. Military units in outlying towns were refusing to accept the officers General Abraham was assigning, labour was agitating for higher wages, the elite was calling for 'law and order'. Howard French of *The New York Times* reported a generalized 'anything goes' attitude among military and police. President Pascal Trouillot admitted that her government was unable to collect taxes and pay its employees.[28]

Even the Security Coordinating Committee for the elections set up by General Abraham – to which the Carter group gave high marks and was led, fatefully, by Colonel Raoul Cedras who would be part of the overthrow of Aristide – was said to be penniless.[29]

The upshot of all this was that Haiti entered into its second attempt at truly democratic elections in three years in a state of near anarchy in terms of authority and with a bankrupt government. The long and the short of those elections were that they were carried out with foreign monies (an estimated $40 million), under foreign supervision (over 1,000 civilian and military observers and electoral experts), and, even, foreign management.[30]

These were the elections which Father Jean-Bertrand Aristide swept with a movement called *Se Lavalas* (we will wash away). He had ridiculed the elections of 1987 and all the efforts which preceded them; now he was ready to join his undisputed popularity to the machinery others had pains-takingly hammered together.

Born in 1954, Aristide was the son of an educated and devoutly Catholic Haitian family. After joining the Salesian teaching order he did advanced studies in the Dominican Republic, Israel and Canada. Thoroughly influenced by the more radical wing of the Latin American Theology of Liberation, Aristide was an early member of what came to be known as the *Ti L'egliz* (Little Church). His antagonism to the established church hierarchy was equalled only by his dislike of the local bourgeoisie and of the US. To Aristide, the US was always the 'cold country' which he blamed for most of Haiti's ills. Preaching from St Jean Bosco church in the slum *La Saline*, Aristide frequently used biblical passages to preach rebellion. On the right of the common people to defend themselves, Aristide would quote from the Gospel of St Luke (Luke 2:36) 'And he that hath no sword, let him sell his garment, and buy one.'[31]

Neither Aristide nor his followers seemed to have accumulated any swords. They defended Aristide through a willingness to die for him. A human shield appeared to be his only protection. No one can read Amy Wilentz' account of Aristide and not be moved by the apparent total and unconditional devotion of Aristide's followers, even as he seemed to welcome martyrdom.[32]

On 11 September, 1988 armed thugs attacked his services at St Jean Bosco church killing thirteen and wounding over seventy. Father Aristide had to be forcibly moved to safety by his parishioners. Whether due to raw courage or some irrational side of his personality, Aristide's many brushes with, and miraculous escapes from death have become part of his charisma. *Msieu Mirak* (Mister Miracles) they call him. It would be a true miracle, indeed, if such constant confrontations with brutality and death did not affect his personality. It appears to have done just that. The following account in *Newsday* (the foreign journalist group closest to Aristide) has been corroborated by others. 'Nervous by disposition, Aristide suffers from periodic prostrations that leave him virtually out of touch with the world around him. He has on occasion appeared catatonic, almost haunted, as if totally overwhelmed by some frozen image of the most recent blood-letting.'[33]

It is important that Aristide never gave the appearance of being one of the conventional seekers of formal political office. In fact, he made a distinct point of dismissing constitutional and party politics as irrelevant. Asked as late as May 1990 whether he had political ambitions he responded, 'I do not suffer from that sickness.' And yet, he constantly advocated and called for political changes. In an interview in Mexico in June 1990, Aristide portrayed the call for elections as an imperialist US scheme, 'a farce'. The candidates who had decided to run were all 'on their knees at the feet of the US.' General Abraham who promised to respect the results, was 'a faithful dog of any imperialism.' Citing events in Nicaragua and Mexico, Aristide said that the struggle was an international one to unmask US imperialism.[34] So sudden and unexpected was Aristide's entry into the 1990 electoral campaign that he was not listed in the 29 May, 1990 election handbook prepared by the National Democratic Institute for International Affairs, nor does he appear as a significant candidate in the most used Haitian electoral handbook.[35] Indeed, even the left-of-centre Catholic human rights organization, Puebla Institute, thought that the attention Aristide was getting in the foreign press could be explained by the priest's flamboyance. In any case, Puebla thought that it was 'far disproportionate to his importance in Haiti.'[36]

His was more of a messianic movement than a campaign. When the head of the Salesian order attempted to have Aristide sent to the Dominican Republic, the *Movement despaysans de Papaye* (MPP) sent him a petition on 12 January, 1989, bearing 18,552 signatures which read as follows:

> *Nous declarons de toute notre force, de toute la force de notre foi que la parole du Pere Aristide, c'est la parole de Dieu de la Vie, c'est celle due prophete Isaie, C'est celle de Jesus-Christ, Fils du Dieu de la Vie.*[37]

'You see', Aristide told a veteran Haiti-watcher, 'I don't have to campaign. It's the people who will do the campaigning.' 'He had', he said, 'accepted this rendezvous with history.' He was 'one with the Haitian spirit'.[38] 'Titid's not like the others', exclaimed a marketwoman, 'he does not have any woman, so he wouldn't be spending the country's money on fancy cars and diamond necklaces. He's pure.'[39] Nothing here, therefore, of the traditional Haitian-Caribbean *macho* man. Not even the red cock they adopted as their symbol could dispel the aura of purity and cleansing the *Se Lavalas* movement invoked. He won close to 68 per cent of the vote with 85 per cent of the electorate voting. He swept every section of the island. It was a national victory.

The elections had gone remarkably smoothly. This fact alone, and despite the situation of near anarchy in the society and bankruptcy of the state, gave Aristide several advantages in addition to his massive popular support. To wit:

1 The 7 January, 1991 attempted *coup* by former Duvalierists under Roger Lafontant was squashed by loyalist troops and massive public protests. His most dangerous known enemy now sat in jail, and many others were in flight.

2 The international community responded enthusiastically to his victory. President François Mitterand received him in Paris (the first Haitian President so invited); the US restored, and doubled, its direct aid to the Haitian government, suspended since the aborted elections of 1987. Carlos Andrés Pérez of Venezuela had received him in Caracas with promises of substantial future assistance.

3 The leading opposition figures, Marc Bazin and Louis Dejoie III had pledged loyal opposition.

Problems, however, became evident from the start. Surrounded by ideologues and idealists, all equally amateurish, Aristide never seemed able to distinguish friend from foe. Worse, he never seemed interested in the profane art of political manoeuvering, the only way to increase one's allies and reduce or neutralize one's enemies. 'He is not a natural strategist. He is not much of a team player . . .' remarked one who knew him well.[40] In fact, he seemed to exult at turning allies into opponents. Midway through the Aristide administration, a source in the Presidential Palace told the press: 'An adversary you can argue with is better than a blundering ally.'[41]

Five early acts of commission or omission weakened Aristide's hand in the beginning.

1 His failure to speak out forcibly against mob violence by his followers. The practice of *pere lebrun* (placing a burning tyre around an enemy's head) was never sufficiently condemned. Over one hundred perceived Aristide enemies were killed after the failed Lafontant *coup*, the Papal Nunciature and Haiti's oldest cathedral were burned to the ground, the Papal Nuncio and his Zairean deputy were beaten and made to walk nearly naked down the street. Aristide's already strained relations with the church's hierarchy deteriorated dramatically.

2. His 4 April arrest of ex-president Pascal Trouillot on vague and unsubstantiated conspiracy charges. Fear of arbitrary arrest spread through the already uneasy opposition ranks.

3 His sweeping purges of the army top command, including the retirement in July of Brigadier General Hérard Abraham who had managed the peaceful transfer of power. Another case of shifting commitments? Traditional Haitian military apprehensions about civilian intentions intensified.

4 His sudden, and some say, intemperate and threatening request that the 'monied classes' contribute millions of dollars to the state. He gave

them four days to do so. It reminded some of Duvalier's notorious *contributions voluntaires* (voluntary contributions) campaigns.

5 All of this, however, could have been managed or at least explained away if Aristide had not committed his most costly error: marginalizing, then antagonizing, and eventually attacking, his own political party and its followers within the Legislature.

It was this final behaviour which best revealed not only Aristide's *modus operandi* but indeed how soon and completely he had picked up the very conventional Haitian emphasis on the presidency as the only significant office. In fact, the post-Duvalier Constitution of 1987 had specifically reduced the office to a purely ceremonial one. Aristide ignored this, which set Congress against him. Although holding only 40 of the 110 seats in parliament, Aristide's National Front for Change and Democracy (FNDC) initially controlled the presidency and other significant posts in that legislature. It is with this group that Aristide had his major confrontations as they attempted to exercise the checks and balances on the executive which was the single most important feature of the 1987 Constitution. Many parties had participated in drawing up that Constitution and took their role in the new politics seriously. They were indignant with the way in which they were being ignored in appointments, policies, or, indeed, even informal consultation. Not surprisingly, it was Aristide's own FNDC legislators who began calling for the resignation of Aristide's Prime Minister, René Preval, and it was this sector which was violently threatened with individual *pere lebrun*'s if they proceeded with their plans. Under pressure from the executive, the FNDC lost control over parliament, control shifting to minor opposition parties. One of these, the miniscule National Patriotic Movement – November 28 (MNP-28) – secured the presidency of the Senate; its leader, Dejean Belizaire, soon turned into a formidable opponent of Aristide's. Later, Belizaire would emerge as one of the legislative leaders opposing Aristide's return to the presidency.

By early May the complaints about Aristide's style was becoming a chorus. He was, they said, surrounded by incompetent 'yes men', he did not 'trust people'. Others spoke of a 'Jekyll and Hyde' approach to issues. Human rights activist, and Aristide supporter, Jean-Claude Bajeux summed up the situation: 'Aristide', he lamented, 'has established himself as the parish priest of the National Palace.'[42]

Be all this as it may, no one was predicting a significant political crisis. Don Bohning spoke of an army 'brought under civilian control', control over the feared chiefs of section, and general optimism among business people. Similarly, Howard French of the *New York Times* described the Haitian success in securing US$442 million from a consortium of lenders led by the World Bank, and quotes the US Ambassador: 'He has gotten off to a very credible start. The process is well begun.' Even members of the formerly sceptical business community were cheered by what they thought was a new realism in Aristide's actions.[43] In September, Vice-President Quayle's wife visited Haiti.

It all seemed to corroborate the ratings given Haiti by a major US risk analysis service, Political Risk Services. In April 1991 they ranked Haiti less risky than the Dominican Republic and equal to Jamaica in the following areas: turmoil risk, financial transfer risk, investment risk, export risk.[44]

In September Aristide made a triumphal trip to the UN and received the keys to the cities of New York and Miami. On 30 September, the day after his return to Haiti, Aristide was overthrown by what appeared to be a rabble of soldiers and police. The *Ti soldats* brutally suppressed public protests and the President was courageously freed from detention and escorted to the airport by the French and American Ambassadors. He had been in the Presidential Palace for seven months.

It is a fact that few countries of the Caribbean have been as studied as Haiti.[45] Invariably the quest, of Haitians and outsiders alike, has been to explain the island's lack of progress. What is evident from this often excellent literature is that in the Haitian case, an accurate diagnosis does not guarantee a solution. In his classic treatise *The Haitian People* (1941), James Leyburn expressed a common despair: 'How conceivably might this problem be dealt with?' His solution: the 'moral imperative' of US and European assistance. To Mats Lundahl (*Peasants and Poverty: A Study of Haiti*, 1979) the solution lies in changing the elite's anti-peasant bias. He concludes by asking, however, whether that bias would ever change. This tendency to end studies on Haiti with a rhetorical question is evident also in Robert and Nancy Heinl's *Written in Blood* (1978): 'Are the Haitian people living endlessly in a perverse continuum, oblivious of their past, doomed always to repeat a history that has been written in blood?' This is also the position of Alain Tournier with whom this chapter opened.

Is the explanation to Haiti's intractable problems to be found in the island's culture? Accurately or not, that is precisely where many scholars have located the problems. One of the earliest of the serious outside scholars to point to cultural imperatives of the Haitian status was the anthropologist Melville Herskovits. Herskovits took his cue from Haitian J.C. Dorsainvil's comment that Haitians 'to an astonishing degree . . . live on their nerves.'[46]

Herskovits concluded that what was involved was a need to reconcile two cultural traditions which often were in inner conflict: the African and the French. To indicate its structural nature, he called it 'socialized ambivalence': rapid shifts in attitude toward people and situations. 'The same person', wrote Herskovits, 'will hold in high regard a person, an institution, an experience or even an object that has personal significance to him, and simultaneously manifest great disdain and even hatred for it'. 'In its broader implications', he concluded, 'as a matter of fact, it is entirely possible that this socialized ambivalence underlies much of the political and economic instability of Haiti . . . .'[47]

Many others have noticed this tendency to rapid shifts in loyalty. Robert Rotberg attributed it to the pervasive attitudes of rivalries, suspicion and intrigue which characterized rural and urban Haitians alike.[48] Lawrence Harrison, citing Rémy Bastien, puts the blame squarely on Vodun, its promotion of irrationality and cultural listlessness and inaction. 'Vodun', say Bastien and Harrison, 'is the great bulwark of the status quo'.[49]

Two problems immediately suggest themselves. First, Vodun is a peasant religion, and peasants do not and never have conducted Haitian politics. Secondly, if Vodun favours the status quo, how does one explain Aristide and the *Se Lavalas* movement for structural change? Indeed, how to explain the truly impressive post-1986 political mobilization of the Haitian countryside which made the electoral registration, the Constitution of 1987 and the enormous voter turnouts in 1987 and 1990 possible?

It is clearly not the mass of Haitian peasants who brought the great democratic political experiments of post-Duvalierist Haiti to a halt; it was the elites, military and civilian, the 15 per cent urbanites who live off the government budgets, and the rapacious *chefs de section*. All were inadvisably threatened at once by Aristide's proposed sweeping reforms. For 200 years the meagre yet amazingly munificent cow called the state has nurtured a small elite and a much larger middle sector. The Kingdom of Heaven might well belong to the 85 per cent who are Aristide's beloved poor, but the key to power is held by the 15 per cent who use the state to avoid joining the great unwashed. This key eluded Aristide.

In Haiti the problem is one of political economy, not culture. Those who would assist that island should not begin by attacking the cultural and religious beliefs of the masses, but rather concentrate on overcoming the resistance of those who fear for their livelihoods. Contrary to the claims of more radical thinkers, this includes many more than the 'capitalists' and the military. It also includes a political culture which is shared in one form or another by most Haitians, urban and rural.

Two formidable, because entrenched, paradoxes represent serious obstacles to outsiders attempting to contribute to political change. The first paradox consists of those very features we so admire about the Haitians – their heroic struggle for independence, their love of the land and relatively egalitarian distribution of that land. These are the very things which make their political attitudes not only implacable but also stubbornly resistant to third party involvements. The point is, all sides play on this nationalism; Duvalier did, Aristide did, his opponents in Haiti certainly did.

A second paradox is that in Haiti the most effective type of power (i.e.

such as is necessary for political survival) is hardly ever a positive resource: the ability to make people do what you wish them to do. It is rather, a negative resource: stopping others from doing what they wish to do. It is the ability to negate, not create. From that perspective strategies of decision-making are hardly ever related to choosing a desired path but rather choosing an alternative, any alternative, which does not involve elements one disagrees with. This explains why Haitian politicians, be they Duvalier or Aristide types, have extraordinary difficulty agreeing on the idea of broad coalitions, much less actually creating them. As such they can never fight the war (against poverty, against gross injustice), they are only geared towards fighting the next political battle. Manigat's and Aristide's behaviour while in power are clear examples of this political culture.[50]

Paralleling this paradox is the fact that, given the incessant struggle-without-quarter for possession of the government, any form of authority in Haiti – democratic or authoritarian – requires the protection of an armed force. The built-in problem is that the armed forces have never been neutral towards the virulent struggles for power, and seldom if ever, sympathetic towards democratic government.

The final paradox, and clearly the most intractable, is the one Aristide himself constantly alludes to: there can be no progress without democracy, and both require mass participation. The problem is, as Aristide found out, the masses can assist in the *transition* to democracy, they are less purposeful in the consolidation of that system. The reason is perhaps evident: they have never had occasion to experience the benefits of a consolidated democracy. In his superbly revealing study of Haitian politics, David Nicholls cautions that when Haitians quote the proverb, '*Aprés bon-dié sé l'eta*' (after God comes the state), 'it is not the goodness or the benevolence of God that people have in mind; it is rather His remoteness, unpredictability, and power.'[51] If this is true of God, how much truer it must be of the state, which is especially feared by that mass of dispossessed, and increasingly displaced, peasants. To them the state is still represented by the *chef de section*; in fact he is still referred to as *l'état*, the state. Bringing these self-sufficient autocrats under central control is a question of power, state budget and even terror capabilities which no democrat has.

In light of this history and these paradoxes, the question is: how can third parties intervene in such a political system? The answer has to be: forcefully or not at all. No half measures such as embargoes have ever worked to bring about a desired course of events in Haiti. The first thing that is already patently evident is that the incapacity to move the usurpers who overthrew Aristide has dealt a very severe blow to the credibility of the Inter-American system. The international community's response to the criminal sabotage of the 1987 elections were timid to the point of being pusillanimous. The US Senate's resolution of 7 December, 1987 noted that it 'deplores' the failure of the Haitian government to bring about democratic elections and supported the US government's decision to embargo the Haitian government. The OAS also 'deplored' the acts of violence and disorder and expressed its 'solidarity' with the Haitian people. In the same breath, however, the OAS telegraphed its irresolution to the enemies of democracy in Haiti by stating that they reaffirmed the principle 'that states have the fundamental duty to abstain from intervening, directly or indirectly, for any reason whatever, in the internal or external affairs of any other state in accordance with Article 18 of the Charter.'

The response to the 1987 crisis laid the foundation for the response to the 1991 crisis: statements of regret but reassertions of the principles of state sovereignty as an absolute prohibitor of effective international action. Effective in this case has to be defined in terms of the political culture of Haiti which, as already noted, is not susceptible to half-measures, certainly not verbal threats and ineffective embargoes.

The legacy of US interventions in the Caribbean now haunt those who would assist Haiti in two ways. First, it crystallized an absolute and categorical principle of sovereignty which lies, not in the people, but in the state no matter who governs or misgoverns that state. This has been overcome only when US vital interests are perceived to be threatened and Haiti is no longer such a case. Secondly, it left a lingering resentment against intervention among the people, which the enemies of democracy manipulate to their benefit. As we will discuss in the Conclusion, nothing in Haiti will change fundamentally as long as these sentiments remain.

Notes

1   Ludwell Lee Montague, *Haiti and the US, 1714–1938* (Durham: Duke University Press, 1940), p. 276. Hans Schmidt notes the stimulus given to a new black middle sector but also agrees that even the substantial material accomplishments 'proved to be largely ephemeral'; *The US Occupation of Haiti, 1915–1934* (New Brunswick: Rutgers University Press, 1971), p. 233; see also David Healy, *Gunboat Diplomacy in the Wilson Era* (Madison: University of Wisconsin Press, 1976), p. 229.
2   Cited in Montague, *Haiti*, pp. 22–3,
3   Ramón Barceló, 'Changements techniques et paupérisation dans les campagnes; dix ans d'agriculture en Amerique Latine', *Amerique Latine*, No. 14, avril–juin, 1983, p. 14.
4   Pierre-Jacques Roca, 'Agriculture et dépendence: la paysannerie haitiénne dans l'impasse', *Amerique Latine*, No. 21 (Jan–March, 1985), pp. 12–16.
5   Richard M. Morse, (ed.) *Haiti's Future: Views of Twelve Haitian Leaders* (Washington, D.C.: The Wilson Centre Press, 1988), pp. 73–8.
6   *Ibid.*, p. 86.
7   *Ibid.*
8   *Ibid.*, pp. 13–20.
9   J. Antoine, *Jean Price-Mars and Haiti* (Washington, D.C.: Three Continents Press, 1981), p. 163.

10 For a revealing analysis of the meshing of literary and artistic and political careers in Haiti, see J. Michael Dash, *Literature and Ideology in Haiti, 1915–1961* (Totowa, N.J.: Barnes and Noble Books, 1981).

11 Broadcast on Radio Soleil, 2/23/89 (FBIS, 2/27/89).

12 It is an interesting fact that some of the most influential newspapers presently circulating daily on the streets of Haiti are edited and printed in Miami and New York: *Le Progres* on the Left and the Centrist *Haiti Observateur*.

13 This author's eyewitness accounts of the 29 November, 1987 elections are contained in two essays: 'The Heroic People of Haiti', *The Miami Herald, Viewpoint*, 12/6/87, p. 6C and 'The Haitian Situation: Short, Medium and Long-Term Implications and Policy Options', a paper prepared for the Inter-American Dialogue, 22 December, 1987.

14 These problems are discussed in greater detail in Anthony P. Maingot, 'Haiti: Problems of a Transition to Democracy in an Authoritarian "Soft State" ', *Journal of Inter-American Studies and World Affairs*, Vol. 28, No. 4 (Winter, 1986–87), pp. 75–102.

15 Interview, *Caribbean Review*, XVI, No. 2 (Winter, 1988), p. 9.

16 Carlo A. Desinor, *De Coup d'Etat en Coup d'Etat* (Port-au-Prince: L'Imprimeur II, 1988), p. 66.

17 Author's interview with President Manigat, Port-au-Prince, 19 March, 1988.

18 Cf. Maureen Taft-Morales, 'Haiti: Political Developments and US Policy Options', CRS Issue Briefs, 14 March, 1989 (Washington, D.C.: Congressional Research Service).

19 Evidence of this was the fact that Haiti was not among the Caribbean States touched by a 1987 investigation. Cf. 'US Narcotics Control Efforts in the Caribbean', Report of a Staff Study Mission to the Caribbean, 23 August – 6 September, 1987 to the Committee on Foreign Affairs, US House of Representatives. December 1987 (Washington, D.C.: US Government Office, 1987).

20 Cf. Testimony by George Heavey, Regional Commissioner, S.E. Region, US Customs Service, in 'Haitian Narcotics Activities' Hearing, Caucus on International Narcotics Control of the US Senate. One Hundredth Congress, Miami, Florida 21 May, 1988 (Washington, D.C.: US Printing Office, 1989).

21 Desinor, *De coup d'état*, pp. 191–2.

22 Interview with Radio Soleil, 4/13/89, FBIS, 4/17/89, p. 8.

23 See Official Government Release on 1 April, 1989, *coup* attempt, Radio Nationale, 8 April, 1989, FBIS, 4/11/89, p. 8.

24 See, for instance, the hopes expressed in Catholic Institute for International Relations, *Haiti* (London, June 1989).

25 See interviews on Radio Metropole, 4/5/89, FBIS, 4/6/89, p. 18.

26 Cf. Organization of American States, Inter-American Commission on Human Rights, *Report on the Situation of Human Rights in Haiti* (Washington, D.C., May 1990).

27 Richard Melton, Deputy Assistant Secretary of State for Caribbean Affairs to Congress, 14 March, 1991. Cited in the *Miami Herald*, 6 May, 1989, p. 8.

28 Cf. Howard French's in-depth story in *The New York Times*, 15 May, 1990, p. 5.

29 National Democratic Institute for International Affairs, Report of the Visit of the Carter Delegation to Haiti, 25–26 July, 1990.

30 This author was an observer to the 1987 and 1990 elections.

31 Jean-Bertrand Aristide, *In the Parish of the Poor. Writings from Haiti*. Translated and edited by Amy Wilentz, (New York: Orbis Books, 1990), p. 15.

32 Amy Wilentz, *The Rainy Season: Haiti Since Duvalier* (New York: Simon and Schuster, 1989).

33 *Newsday*, (New York, 14 May, 1990), p. 15.

34 Cf. Gregorio Selser, 'Haiti: el drama permanente de su pueblo. Entrevista al sacerdote

Jean-Bertrand Aristide', *El Caribe contemporaneo*, (Mexico), No. 22 (enero-julio, 1991), pp. 41–63.

35   *Haiti 1990: Quelle Démocratie* (Port-au-Prince: Haiti Solidarité Internationale, 7 November, 1990).

36   The Puebla Institute, *Haiti: Looking Forward to Elections. An Interim Report* (Washington: D.C., July 1990), pp. 7–8.

37   Reprinted in Paul Dejean, *Dans la tourmente* (New York: Bohiyo Enterprises, 1990), p. 199.

38   Don Bohning, *The Miami Herald*, 26 November, 1990, p. 4.

39   *Ibid.*

40   Amy Wilentz, Foreword in Aristide, *In the Parish of the Poor*, p. XX.

41   *Haiti Insight,* October 1991, p. 2.

42   Cf. Don Bohning, *The Miami Herald*, 2 May, 1991, p. 1 ff.

43   *The New York Times*, 4 August, 1991, p. 6.

44   'Business Risks in the Americas', *The Miami Herald*, Special Report, 22 April, 1991, pp. 28–9.

45   See the monumental bibliography compiled by Michel S. Laguerre (ed.) *The Complete Haitiana: A Bibliographic Guide to the Scholarly Literature, 1900–1980* (New York: Kraus International Publications, 1982).

46   Melville J. Herskovits, *Life in a Haitian Valley* (New York: Alfred A. Knopf, 1937), p. 297.

47   *Ibid.*, p. 299.

48   Robert Rotberg, *Haiti: The Politics of Squalor* (Boston: Houghton Mifflin Co., 1971), pp. 17–19.

49   Cf. Rémy Bastien, 'Vodoun and Politics in Haiti', in Bastien and Harold Courlander (eds), *Religion and Politics in Haiti* (Washington: Institute for Cross-Cultural Research, 1966); Lawrence E. Harrison, 'The Cultural Roots of Haitian Underdevelopment', in Anthony P. Maingot (ed.), *Small Country Development and International Labour Flows* (Boulder: Westview Press, 1991), pp. 223–46.

50   There is no reason to expect that Haitians will be much different from the Lasswell and Kaplan definition of political man as 'one who demands the maximization of his power in relation of all his values, who expects power to determine power, and who identifies with others as a means of enhancing position and potential.' H. Lasswell and A. Kaplan, *Power and Society: A Framework for Political Inquiry* (New Haven, Ct.: Yale University Press, 1950), p. 78. The question is, however, power to what end? This is where Haitian elites have failed, first politically, and then developmentally, as Mats Lundahl pointed out in 1979. Mats Lundahl, *Peasants and Poverty: A Study of Haiti* (New York: St Martin's Press, 1979).

51   David Nicholls, *Haiti in Caribbean Context* (New York: St Martin's Press, 1985), p. 220.

Conclusion

The challenges of sovereign consent in US-Caribbean relations

'Liberty without hatreds'. This was José Martí's recommendation on 17 April, 1884, for the theme of the Cuban Revolutionary Party. As was noted in the Introduction, Martí, who knew America well and disliked its racially-tinged imperialism, always argued for a working relationship with the US. He did not argue for a 'special relationship' such as the US had with Great Britain. That special relationship was based on common race, language and institutions, attributes Cuba did not share with the US. Martí argued, instead, for a *strategic* relationship: a pragmatic and sincere search for those interests which Cuba and the US had in common and the possible synergies which would come from that. Certainly a love of liberty was one such shared interest, though not always defined in the same terms. The pursuit of a common definition, however, required that the hatreds generated by US' bullying be set aside. By his pragmatism and generosity of spirit, Martí had set the example for the modern Caribbean. As they face the perplexing post-Cold War international environment, Caribbean leaders are well aware of the global nature of the problems they face. Confronting them requires co-ordination, between themselves and also with the US. The politics of hatred, resentments and symbolic differences are obstacles to such co-ordinated action. It creates what sociologists call non-realistic conflict.

Despite this awareness, however, two very powerful forces militate to make the path recommended by Martí difficult. First is the weight of history. The burden of past US behaviour, especially as that behaviour offended national and ethnic pride, is not readily overlooked. This is especially the case when it combines with the second contentious element: enormous asymmetries in power. It is the latter especially which has become one of the overarching questions of our age. In a world with one superpower, is it possible for archipelagic regions of small states to formulate and execute their own definitions of national interests? In this specific case, the issue is whether the small states of the insular Caribbean have the autonomy to decide and then implement their own strategies of development and security. Granting that all international politics – of small as well as of large states – invariably involves trade-offs, manoeuvering and often compromise, are the trade-offs of the small Caribbean state *vis-à-vis* the US so one-sided as to make a mockery of the concept and principles of sovereignty and self-determination?

The emphasis of many recent theories of international relations is on the inequalities or asymmetries which characterize those relations. Whether they be straight Marxist interpretations or various theories of dependency, the argument is that most claims to reciprocity and equivalence in today's international relations are, in fact, rhetorical façades hiding gross or subtle domination and exploitation. Independence under such circumstances is mythical. This perspective is considerably sharper when it comes to small-state/superpower relations. Even one as non-ideological as the late Dudley Seers tended to describe small states as characterized by 'a small population, serious ethnic divisions, location close to a superpower, few natural resources, a culturally subverted bureaucracy, high consumer expectations, and a narrow technological base.'[1] Quite an accurate description of most Caribbean small states. Under such conditions nationalism – which Seers defined as self-reliant development or autarchy – is near impossible. In the same vein, all the talk of 'internationalism' and 'interdependence' is really camouflage for global superpower – and especially US – domination.

If this interpretation holds for the whole range of state-to-state relations, how are the bilateral relations on questions of greater national interest such as military security and trade to be characterized?

This Conclusion addresses this issue by first attempting to establish what the underlying or basic assumptions and policy preferences of both the US and West Indian actors are. It does so by following the analytical schema presented in Figure 4. It is easy to imagine the schema as a scale or balance with the US (country 'B') on one side and the small Caribbean country ('A') on the other. The natural and logical question is, how could anyone who has read the history of US-Caribbean relations presented here conceivably argue that the reciprocity between country 'A' and the US is based on any equivalence? 'US concerns' start with 'US global objectives', pass through 'US regional objectives' before reaching 'US country objectives' which is the stage at which 'dialogue' with country 'A' theoretically begins. But it is not just that 'US concerns', both empirical and symbolic, are so much weightier, there are also the issues of state capabilities: the purely administrative and bureaucratic dimension through which any eventual country program will have gone. Even the budget process through which all US procurement planning goes is complex and protracted. And this is but one element in the enormous administrative network which deals with matters of interest to the US. The small state has nothing even approaching such a bureaucracy. It is often at a loss as to how to even

Figure 4: A model of small state – US bilateral negotiations for a country program in the small state

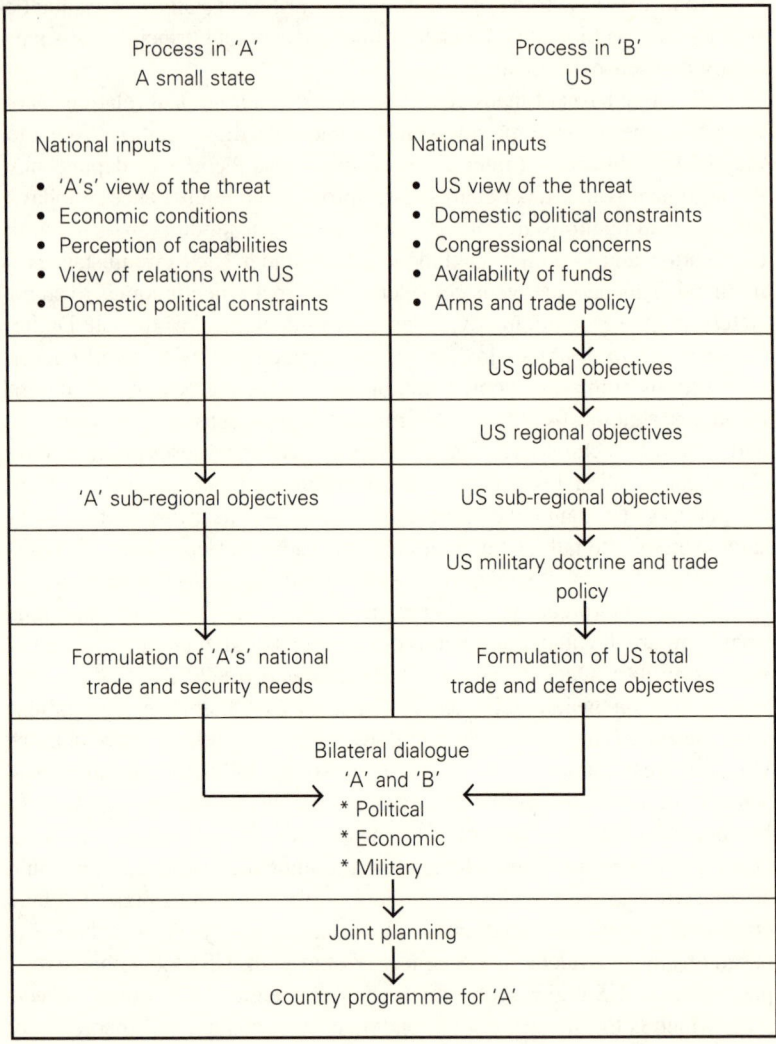

Source: A. P. Maingot, 'The US in the Caribbean: Geopolitics and the Bargaining Capacity of Small States', in Anthony T. Bryan, J. Edward Greene and Timothy Shaw (eds), *Peace, Development and Security in the Caribbean* (New York: St Martin's Press, 1990), p. 59.

approach or engage the Americans in a bargaining mode. It is clear that the purpose of this political-administrative process and machinery is to ensure a good interface between domestic considerations, multilateral and bilateral relations and the global and regional defence and trade postures decided upon. It is quite properly said that in the US domestic policy is foreign policy, and *vice versa*. How does actor 'A' understand, much less influence this? One can conclude from Figure 4 that from a purely administrative perspective, the 'dialogue' and 'planning' stage has input from 'A' and 'B' of quite different types which tend to leave the analyst with few illusions about the term 'common' in the scheme.

But, having said this, do we have to settle for the theoretical despair of a Seers, for the idea that even to speak of relations is to opt for hope over experience? This study argues not.

Clearly elites in these small nations operate within much narrower decision-making parameters and constraints than do those in larger states. But to say this is hardly to accept the position that they are automatically or by definition bereft of any options and, indeed, even autochthonous preferences. Theoretically, the only productive approach to understanding international relations is to assume that all national elites behave with what can be called strategic rationality, i.e. they will always attempt to maximize the benefits from any exchange.[2] The elites of even the smallest state will take the choices and actions of others into account but they behave with as much self-interest as circumstances – and their opponents – permit.

Thus, what is in question is not the strategic rationality of the elites representing small states, but the limits placed on that rationality through curtailments of their autonomy. Having said that, however, the issue of the degree or margin of sovereignty and independence in small state decision-making should be approached as an empirical question to be answered through the analysis of specific historical and contemporary cases, not argued *a priori* by ideologically-driven paradigms.

None of this is meant to minimize the problems which flow from the monumental asymmetry in power between the US and the small Caribbean state. It is merely to force systematic empirical analyses of specific cases. Two Caribbean examples – Jamaica under Michael Manley in 1975–80 and Grenada under Maurice Bishop 1979–83 – illustrate both the ability to make autochthonous choices and, most decidedly, the costs which certain choices incur. Interestingly enough, these costs had more to do with internal island opposition than direct US actions. The two cases also illustrate a feature of Caribbean relations with the US which José Martí discovered over a century ago: that assistance for a national cause – from liberation to development – is best achieved by working with, and often within, the US. As we shall see, neither Manley nor Bishop learned this lesson until it was too late for them.

The Michael Manley who emerged victorious, for a third time, in the 1988 elections was not the same one who in 1976 began playing the Cuban card as we saw in Chapter 6. His defeat in 1980 had, in his own words, 'matured' him. Part of that 'maturing' was realizing the limits of radical rhetoric both in small countries and in the Caribbean. In the 1970s Manley sought to confront the US rather than search for strategic opportunities for co-operation. He drew heavily on the history of US imperialism against Chile and Cuba, demonstrating how powerful the legacy of US actions has been in Latin America and how easily adopted by those who wish to use history as an avenging angel.

Even though an important 1974 study of Jamaican attitudes concluded that 'in Jamaica there is neither a will to achieve the socialist alternative nor the necessary political support to sustain it even if such a will existed',[3] Manley's massive electoral victory in the 1976 elections indicated that perhaps he was correct in believing that he could launch his 'democratic socialism' initiative on an anti-American note with full support of the masses. Under pressure from the 'radical' wing of his People's National Party (PNP), which showed increased strength, Manley began radicalizing his rhetoric and that of his party. The role of Cuba in that rhetoric was noticeable. As early as July 1975, during a visit to Cuba, his speeches had not only a strident pro-Cuban and anti-capitalist tone, but also an anti-US one. The US, Manley told the Cubans, now finds itself 'morally isolated.'[4] He appeared to take it for granted that the bourgeoisie would balk and migrate; he felt free, therefore, to tell them that three flights a day were scheduled to Miami. But, alas, Michael Manley should have known from his study of the Marcus Garvey period that the bourgeoisie would not be the only group to leave.

Migration to the US had always been polyclass and stemmed from a variety of motivations. The shifting social structure in Jamaica affected groups and individuals of different social status: some were affected economically, others politically, and others socially or occupationally. Since they had all become a part of the normative system of the metropolis, the socio-cultural area discussed in Chapter 9, they had all, in a way, engaged in a form of anticipatory socialization. This was all the more a reality since, as one US social scientist discovered, most of the political, economic, and professional (medical, judicial and religious) elites governing since independence had studied in the UK or the US.[5] These included Manley and his rival, Edward Seaga. These elites were, and so considered themselves, equipped to migrate if necessary. When Manley heated up his anti-American, pro-Cuban rhetoric, the technical class began to migrate in large numbers. Along with capital flight, this represented a serious blow to Jamaica's developmental capabilities.

Advocating socialism was one thing; quite another was cutting off historical avenues of 'escape' or opportunity. Not surprisingly, a Carl Stone poll of May 1977[6] indicated that only 14 per cent of the sample opposed seeking aid from Washington or receiving US or other foreign assistance and foreign investments. His poll also indicated that a major part of the radical Left campaign (the discrediting of those who were migrating to the US) had little public appeal. Fully 60 per cent of those in Stone's sample indicated they would go to the US if the opportunity presented itself. Moreover, the preference for the US cut across class and party lines. Interestingly, the urban working class appeared more eager to migrate to the US than the much criticized urban middle class – by 68 per cent to 45 per cent. In addition, the number willing to migrate had shown an increase across social class: those wanting to migrate to the US specifically, increased quickly from the early 1970s to 1977 – from 58 per cent to 68 per cent among the Kingston working class and from 20 per cent to 45 per cent among the Kingston middle class. The figure in peasant areas was 68 per cent in 1977. These figures should have come as no surprise. Jamaica's strong orientation toward the west in general, and the US in particular, had already been documented.[7]

Many of the new emigrants settled in a city, Miami, that radicals denigrated in terms similar to those used in Cuba: a city laden with southern racial prejudice and Cuban-exile reactionary politics. As reflected in a Stone survey in November 1977, Jamaicans viewed their opportunities abroad differently. In fact Stone found that 62 per cent of the Kingston working class and 78 per cent of the peasantry held a favourable opinion of those who had migrated to Miami. The reality was that Jamaicans were most assuredly not opposed to migration, much less migration to the US. This country was still their favourite and in the US, Miami was fast becoming a preferred destination. A previous flood of refugees, the middle-class Cubans, had transformed that once sleepy city into a metropolis with a distinct Caribbean appeal. 'It is very difficult', wrote the radical Barbadian novelist, George Lamming, 'to get the local population of the Caribbean to think critically of the US.'[8]

There can be no doubt that the radical initiative of Michael Manley demonstrated an autonomous choice. The questions are, first, was that radicalism essential or even mildly beneficial to Jamaica's interests, and secondly, did it represent the will and wishes of the Jamaican people? The answer is negative in both cases. If it could not mobilize any particular resources in Jamaica, if as Manley himself admitted, US investments were not an obstacle to expansion of state initiatives,[9] if there was no real evidence that the US was attempting to 'destabilize' the Manley program,[10] why 'pick a fight'? Was neutralizing the internal left worth such a high cost? Evidently not.

Even two scholars quite well disposed towards Manley and his call for democratic socialism, felt that the most damaging effect of his anti-Americanism was to alienate the local technical and monied bourgeoisie:

> More distance from Cuba and less rhetorical anti-Americanism
> would have had further favourable effects on the government's
> relationship to these classes, besides sparing Jamaica some of
> the effects of US suspicion and hostility.[11]

It is a testament to Manley's democratic instincts and the depth of Jamaica's democracy that a 'new', more moderate Manley should have been re-elected in 1988. Alas, he had wasted at least four years.

For four and a half years, and despite the aggressive rhetoric of the Reagan administration, the Grenadian revolution had been governed on their own terms. Periodic attempts by Washington to 'punish' the Grenadians were adamantly rejected by that island's partners in the Caribbean Common Market (CARICOM). This was the case when the Reagan administration tried to block Caribbean Development Bank loans to Grenada or limit its participation in the newly-formed Caribbean Group of the World Bank. These small states even rebuffed Washington when President Reagan disinvited Bishop from a 'private' meeting in Barbados.[12]

This history is the backdrop against which the Peoples Revolutionary Government's (PRG) attempts from 1979 to 1983 to challenge the parameters of Grenadian decision-making should be examined.

The PRG Prime Minister, Maurice Bishop, grew up on the island of Aruba where his father worked in the oil refinery. Eric Gairy, the man he overthrew, began his career as a labour leader at the same refinery. The man who succeeded Bishop as Prime Minister in 1984, the moderate Herbert Blaize, worked for eight years at the same refinery. Of the three, only Bishop had the family means to go to England to study law. Gairy came from the poor peasantry, and Blaize was one of nine children whose father had migrated to the US in 1919 to work as a labourer; like most Grenadian immigrants who went to the US, he settled in Brooklyn. Not surprisingly, four of Prime Minister Blaize's six children presently live there; one lives in London. To Blaize, therefore, migration seemed quite natural: 'The question', he once said, 'is not whether to migrate, but when. It is the normal pattern of behaviour; you don't have to teach it.'[13] Like Seaga of Jamaica, but unlike Michael Manley, he did not intend to make migration a political issue since he knew that no Grenadian leader had ever controlled it or indeed been a stranger to it himself.

The PRG's Deputy-Prime Minister, Bernard Coard, should have known that. After all, he had two brothers residing in the US and had himself gone to Brandeis University in Massachusetts on a US scholarship. His grandfather was Barbadian, his grandmother was from St Vincent, and his wife was Jamaican. The family had been a proper middle-class one, and his father, a civil servant, had done what many place-bound West Indians do – taken various correspondence courses from the UK or the US. Bernard Coard's father certainly felt fully capable of much more than he was 'allowed' by the colonial situation to achieve in his occupation. Eventually, he would travel to the US, and, like so many others, he would write his autobiography.[14] In this touching story, the father's blocked status aspirations are seen to lead to vivid, vicarious pleasures with the successes of his three sons who resided in the US.

By late 1981, two years into their revolution, Bishop and the PRG leadership demonstrated their freedom of action by embarking on the planning of a series of radical internal reforms, many based on the Cuban model. These included the proposed creation of a Cuban-style national service and a labour army. By mid-1982 Grenada's Leninists had decided to move from the 'national democratic' or 'socialist emulation' stage to the 'construction of socialism' stage. They set up a Commission No. 5 to explore the possibilities and consequences of such a radical step.[15]

That this issue was extremely sensitive and even volatile is evidenced by the top secret classification of that report. 'The Commission has concluded', the report began, 'that our society is largely *petit bourgeois* in mentality as well as socially', and as such Grenadians would most probably not readily accept the restrictions necessary to implement the [Cuban style] service [called option 2]. Despite this, the Commission wished to go even further in its sociological analysis, probing the outer boundaries of Grenada's capacity for change along Cuban lines. Commission No. 5's study of the issue quickly refers to the fact that when the Cubans implemented national service 'there was a form of restriction on people leaving the country.'[16] The Commission then asks if Grenada could do the same. The answer was not long in coming: 'Our people, as a tradition, believe in going overseas to work for more money and there is at present an unsatisfactory level of patriotism among the masses. *In other words, we have grown up with a visa mentality.* The question we now pose is, can we apply restrictions to people wanting to leave the country?'[17]

Again, the Commission's response to that all-important question, the one relevant to the entire Caribbean Basin, was unequivocal since it immediately concluded that: 'Our country is a very open country. Anyone can turn on to any Radio Station and listen to all the imperialist propaganda. They can turn on to look at imperialist television. They can read any magazine, books, etc . . . , and have access to all the ways and means in which the imperialist can influence the mind.' Prohibiting migration to the US was out of the question. A new tack was necessary.

Exactly when a decision was made to attempt to cultivate the US is unclear. It is evident that since they realized that they could not stop, or indeed even control, emigration to the US, the decision to take what they termed Option 1, dealing with the Grenadians in the US, was strategically wise. However, as events would prove, it probably was taken too late. In any case, by February 1983 the PRG again showed its autonomy of action by switching courses: it launched a full-scale drive to gain support within the US. Something called 'The New York report' became a feature at Political Bureau meetings. For instance, the 23 February, 1983, report was made by Commander Liam James after visiting Washington, DC, and New York:[18]

> re-Grenadians abroad, the Party must look/develop a perspective on Grenadians abroad; seek to organize them wherever they go, develop, maintain links with them, not to be hostile to them (even those who left after the Revolution).

Part of Option 1's strategy was a visit to the US by Bishop, from 31 May to 10 June, 1983. During that visit Bishop met not only with large numbers of Grenadians but also with top US government officials. The real danger to Bishop from the *rapprochement* with Washington which seemed to have been in the offing,[19] came from his internal opposition, a fact he seemed to be aware of.[20] In a system divided between those like Bishop who favoured Option 1 and the hardliners who still preferred the politics of antagonism, any political decision had to involve a trade-off. Unlike Jamaica, where a democratic system permitted public opinion to 'weigh in' on such changes in policy, in Grenada's closed system, all this was occurring behind the backs of the people. Thus far, history does not reveal the internal facts of the trade-off but it does record that the strategy of greater co-operation, if not directly with Washington at least with sectors in the US, never got off the ground. On 19 October, 1983 the clash between the radical wing, led by Bernard Coard, and the Bishop faction escalated to the point of murder – the murder of Bishop and his most loyal followers.

Maurice Bishop had listened to his people and their socio-cultural ideals too late. Had he reflected on the history of their links with America rather than falling for the siren call of an ideology he had no proof his people preferred, he would have been able to make the dramatic conversion his Sandinista friends would later make in Nicaragua. This, however, would have required a pragmatism, even utilitarianism, which in the early 1980s was still anathema to those influenced by a Cuban revolution which had had quite a different experience with the US. Such pragmatism was much more characteristic of the majority of the leaders in the democratic Caribbean. The very dynamics of Caribbean relations with the rest of the world, especially the US, compel them to be so. Whenever Caribbean leaders have stood inflexibly on ideology or dogma, their societies (to the extent that democratic means existed) have forced them to relinquish such inflexibilities. Sadly, the atmosphere in the 1970s and 1980s was one in which everything was perceived through the prism of the Cold War. While intellectuals eulogized the Cuban 'model', in everything from strategies of securing power to economics, the US responded by promoting the Puerto Rican 'model'. Such was the one-upmanship about models that even Trinidad's Eric Williams offered his own to the Caribbean. As distinct from Cuba which had chosen the 'totalitarian framework', and Puerto Rico which in exchange for economic development had 'lost its soul', the Trinidad model promised democracy, economic self-reliance and cultural autonomy.[21]

Lost in all this geopolitical jousting was the irrefutable fact that national experiences cannot be packaged or precisely replicated. If the Caribbean stood for anything it was for the enormous variety of existential realities and the various ways in which Caribbean peoples and their leaders have confronted them. It was in the governance process as they related to two fundamental Caribbean values, democracy and human rights, that one could profitably make comparisons. On that score, it was a fact that Trinidad had little in common with Cuba and Williams's governance style even less with that of Castro. On the other hand, while Trinidad had little in common with Puerto Rico, Williams's approach shared a great deal with that of the founder of modern Puerto Rico, Luis Muñoz Marín. Unfortunately, both Williams and Muñoz were ignored in the stampede to celebrate something called 'revolution'. That myopic intellectual unidimentionality has to be corrected.

Muñoz began his political career as a socialist, a neo-Malthusian (i.e. an advocate of birth control) and an 'eclectic' Christian (i.e. anti-clerical). By 1922, however, he admitted that while he had not stopped being a socialist he was in the process of 'dedogmatizing' his beliefs. He was making the transition to pragmatism.[22] His thinking would evolve into an unadorned but cogent developmental theory of democracy. 'Democracy', he said on 4 July, 1940, 'is not a static force, it is a vital force, continually creating greater democracy not only in the political arena but also in economics and all other areas of human endeavour . . . it is constituted of equal parts of history and of future potential'.[23] It is not at all surprising, therefore, that all his close friends were the leaders of Latin American democracy: the Venezuelans Rómulo Gallegos and Rómulo Betancourt, the Colombian Carlos Lleras Camargo, the Costa Rican José Figueres. The Puerto Rico of Luis Muñoz Marín was a safe haven for the persecuted and discriminated against: Spanish Republicans, Latin American exiles, Americans fleeing the ravishes of the McCarthyite witchhunts or racial bigotry. To the aspiring colonial politician in the Caribbean he had a special appeal.

To an Eric Williams in 1940, Muñoz and his party represented 'possibilities that seemed remote from the seemingly eternal darkness of Trinidad and Jamaica . . . .'[24] Norman Manley in Jamaica saw his organizational skills as a model for his embryonic social-democratic party (PNP). To the intellectual creator of the Puerto Rican Associated Commonwealth status, any system had to help Puerto Ricans confront three major problems in this American sphere of influence:

1   The coexistence of two distinct *socio-cultural* traditions in mutual respect and constructive *co-operation*, not conflict.
2   The creation of an *economic* relationship which was beneficial to the islanders.
3. Building a political system which allowed 1 and 2 to be fulfilled according to the perceived needs of succeeding generations.

Given the importance of the concept of generations to Spaniards and Latin Americans alike, Muñoz' emphasis on each generation having the right to decide their own affairs is in contrast to the Marxist idea that the revolutionary elite of the present generation decides for the rest of history. In other words, Muñoz was calling for a political system which guaranteed Puerto Ricans the right to sovereign consent: an ongoing and increasingly perfectable system of self-determination. This meant building a political system premised on notions of development, flexibility and changeability, not inflexible structures. To achieve this, however, an ideological change had to occur. Puerto Rico had to move towards a system which could, in his celebrated phrase, 'break through from nationalism', constantly creating new ways and relationships between diverse peoples. He called for '*nacionalismo pueblo*', a people-centric self-determination rather than a state-centric concept of sovereignty. It had to be something 'quite distinct from the known constitutional forms'[25] and capable of continual evolution and improvement. Muñoz' speeches were full of words such as 'flexibility', 'adaptability', 'audaciousness', 'the will to experiment, to adapt and revise'.[22]

There is a lesson for the rest of the Caribbean – but especially for the growing numbers of Puerto Ricans who favour statehood in the US federation – in the fact that Muñoz never had any illusions about the implications of the distinct socio-cultural and racial divisions which separated the US and Puerto Rico. He was, said an admiring Rexford Tugwell, like Franklin Delano Roosevelt and Fiorello La Guardia, concerned with broad strategies, not merely tactical skirmishes. And of the three, Muñoz was judged the most successful;[27] in part because he had to overcome the same American racial attitudes which other Caribbean peoples had faced, and never did he allow that to divert him from his nationalist goals. In fact, he turned that adversity to his people's advantage. He was aware of the limited nature of the citizenship granted Puerto Ricans by the Jones Act of 1917. As Puerto Rican legal scholar J.A. Cabranes notes, the argument in favour of granting US citizenship to the Puerto Ricans and not to the Filipinos was that the former were white and European, but the latter not.[28] Later, as the mood in the US changed because of the civil rights movement, Puerto Ricans took advantage of the fact that, as Cabranes notes 'Citizenship of the 'second class' in a colonial setting was destined to fall into disrepute in the era of decolonization and the reassertion of claims to equality by long-oppressed racial minorities in the US.'[29] It was Muñoz' particular genius to understand that while Puerto Rico could not control the swings in American moods, it certainly could take advantage of them.

Gordon K. Lewis, no friend of Muñoz's political creation, the Associated Commonwealth, nevertheless put him in the mould of José Martí:

> A worthwhile leader', one thoughtful Puerto Rican told an American inquirer in 1938, 'will not come in on a wave of hatred and violence. He will not secure his following through attacks on specialized groups. Instead, he'll regard the entire interest of the island, and he should go further than that and think in terms of a world society.' Muñoz could with good reason claim to be the fulfilment, in his person, of that prophecy.'[30]

And yet, it was a reflection of the times that Lewis prophesied a Caribbean governed not by the Muñoz types but by the likes of Fidel Castro. To Lewis ' . . . it is Cuba, not Puerto Rico', that excited the Latin American world and that 'promises to become, so to speak, the guiding star of the hitherto repressed Latin American renaissance'. 'Fidelismo', he predicted 'will become a hemispheric idea which – like the idea of equality in Europe after 1789 – will create an entirely new world in the area'. The new Cuba of Fidel Castro was now 'the heart and centre of the Caribbean.'[31] Lewis's predictions on the future of Fidel Castro need not be discussed much further. The literature on the decline of socialist Cuba is now overwhelming,[32] with some of the most poignant critiques of its economic model coming from inside Cuba.[33]

What still lingers among many intellectuals, however, is Lewis's conviction that political independence with socialism is the only route for Puerto Rico and the rest of the non-independent Caribbean. Only these two together could break the stranglehold of US imperialism and ensure true sovereignty. Alongside the ideological inflexibility reflected in such views there is also an excessively static concept of sovereignty.

Their definition of sovereignty is that of Grotius to whom sovereignty was: 'that power whose acts are not subject to the control of another so that they may be made void by the act of any other human will.' Whatever one's ideological preferences might be, the fact is that any argument which sees sovereignty, political independence and self-determination as not only coterminous but synonymous, does a disservice to the principle of self-determination. The Puerto Rican case is a good illustration of the fact that political independence and self-determination are distinct attributes. Neither are natural rights, they are remedial rights, engendered by specific needs and undergoing specific historical evolutions. Bernard Crick might argue that the concept of 'sovereignty of the people' which once held sway in the US and France is 'almost meaningless rhetoric' because in both cases it strengthened what both Alexis de Tocqueville and John Stuart Mill called 'the tyranny of public opinion'. One wonders, however, what those two luminaries would have thought of the single-party or *caudillo* tyrannies in an age when: (1) we do have accurate ways to measure public opinion, and (2) many other people use those ways to govern themselves not only democratically but to great material advantage. Alas, Muñoz was going against the grain of Third World opinion when he advocated sovereign consent, that sovereignty resides in the will of the people, democratically expressed. He had to face the intellectuals of the region and even world-wide opinion.

Initially, the mood in the UN was not askance to respecting the will of the Puerto Rican people regarding status. General Assembly Resolution 748 (VIII) of 27 November, 1953 removed Puerto Rico from the list of 'non-self governing territories' which the General Assembly had targeted for decolonization. By 1960, however, the UN atmosphere and composition had changed; with the active advocacy by Cuba and in the milieau created by the post-Bandung emphasis on political independence, a new era of state-centric thought had begun. The Puerto Rican arrangement (as indeed that of the Kingdom of the Netherlands of 1954) would never have been taken off the list of 'colonies' under the new UN climate. On 14 December, 1960 the UN passed General Assembly Resolution 1514, the 'Declaration on the Granting of Independence to Colonial Countries and Peoples'. It accepted three procedural avenues for the decolonization of any non-self governing territory:[34] (1) emergence as an independent sovereign state; (2) free association with an independent state; (3) integration into an independent state.

The Caribbean became the area where all three options would be exercised. Puerto Rico had (through a free vote) opted for free association with the US, the French Antilles (1946) and Netherlands Antilles (1954) had been integrated into the systems of their respective metropolis. In 1957 the independent Federation of the West Indies came about; upon its demise, virtually all remaining English-speaking territories moved towards independence.

After 1960 the UN established the Committee of 24 to oversee and supervise the decolonization process. It became the guardian of self-determination. It is evident that while they showed a clear bias towards outright independence – Option 1, that Option was never assumed to have exhausted the principle of self-determination. Be that as it may, it is clear that the UN's General Assembly did have distinct preferences. That was evident in the very different requisites and criteria they established for evaluating each of the three avenues to self-determination.

After 1960 the Committee of 24 was determined not to give the UN's blessing to any 'act of self-determination short of accession to full independence, without having been a party or a witness *in loco* to the exercise of this right.'[35] The requisites for movements towards independence were by far the easiest to meet. It was, and still is, the most unencumbered avenue to self-determination from the point of view of international law and the UN. The criteria for free association (the Puerto Rican option) was the most difficult. Resolution 1541 requires that any 'voluntary limitation of sovereignty', i.e. free association, be 'expressed through an informed and democratic process', through guaranteed 'freedom of choice'. The 'fine print', however, was crucial: the 'political level' of the population would be taken into account and the choice should in no way be detrimental to existing sentiments of 'ethnic and cultural' integrity and identity.

Independence, on the other hand, according to Resolution 1514, need not meet any such tests. 'Inadequacy of political, economic, social or education preparedness', said the GA, 'should never serve as a pretext for delaying independence.'[36] Why demand 'adequacy' in a range of human rights and socio-economic areas for any status short of independence, while holding 'inadequacy' in the same areas no obstacle to independence? The answer is all too evident in General Assembly Resolution 742 which notes that independent status under international law is recognized by a series of acts which measure state power, not freedom of popular choice.[37] An independent (i.e. sovereign) state is one which has: (1) unqualified juridical power; (2) the full international responsibility for acts inherent in the exercise of its external sovereignty; (3) full responsibility for acts inherent in the administration of its internal affairs. All state-centric criteria.

Again, the criteria of success of this status deals with state power not socio-political or cultural measures: (1) eligibility for membership in the UN; (2) sovereign power to enter into direct relations of all kinds with governments and international institutions; (3) power to negotiate, sign and ratify all sorts of international instruments; (4) the sovereign right to provide for its national defence as it deems appropriate (and consistent with international law).

The reality of the definition of sovereignty after 1960 is that once political independence is defined as a natural right, arguments about how it is brought about and then exercised are rendered redundant. Note the legal argument of Manuel Rodríguez-Orellana, who makes an articulate case that independence is 'the only' legitimate means of self-determination for Puerto Rico. Much of the cogency of Rodríguez-Orellana's case, however, rests on the acceptance of certain premises or doubts about the validity of public decision-making. The opinion of the population, 'its perception as to what it is free to decide and its voluntary limitation of sovereignty', he notes, 'are extremely susceptible to manipulation'.[38] This claim echoes the position of the Committee of 24 and reflects the generalized belief that a choice for independence is the only free one.

The point is, of course, that in the absence of any specific charges of manipulation or abuse, isn't this claim potentially true for any one of the three avenues leading to self-determination? Why should a presumption of elite malevolence and public gullibility be reserved for only one of the choices of self-determination? Not unrelated to this attitude is the following often-voiced charge, repeated by Rodríguez-Orellana:

> How voluntary can any limitation of sovereignty be when the Metropolitan Power exercising the colony's sovereignty is always silent regarding what a period of economic transition to independence would entail?

The answer is both logical and empirical. From a logical point of view, freedom of choice has to incorporate freedom to arrive at one's own assessment of results and consequences. It stands to reason that any metropolitan-directed assessment of consequences of this or that decision on status could be considered an imposition by one group or the other. This is especially the case where sustaining the non-independent status – still the case of 15 per cent of the Caribbean population – is quite costly to the metropolis. Nothing illustrates this better than the heavy transfer costs of social welfare in the French, Dutch and Puerto Rican cases. A situation such as the one in which The Netherlands advanced payments to Suriname in order to accelerate that prevaricating population's 'choice' of independence, hardly made the Surinamese choice a totally free one. The Dutch simply wished to stop: (1) more Surinamese migration, and (2) be rid of the 'guilt' which a colonial situation causes the metropolis. The Dutch response was not an isolated case. Max Beloff is brutally frank, but on the mark, when he attributes the western hesitation to criticize any Third World leader to their sense of guilt about their colonial pasts as well as fear that that would push them towards the Soviet camp.[39]

The difficulty of making choices about status in areas such as the Caribbean is illustrated by the case of Aruba.[40] The Aruban decision in 1983 to move to *status aparte* in 1986 was more geared to separating itself from the cluster of islands which form the Netherlands Antilles (perhaps especially from the hegemony of its largest member, Curaçao) than a move towards independence. Because they were not pleased with this split off, the Dutch decided to 'punish' the Arubanos by setting 1996 as the date for their full independence. Whatever their ultimate status goals, the Arubano's acceptance of that condition reflected a perception of self-sufficiency which was belied by economic realities. The point is that in 1983, the island's largest employer Isla, the Esso oil refinery, was still operative. When, soon afterwards, the refinery was completely closed, there was no mention any more of independence in 1996. The mood had changed, and Aruba rushed to join the Antillean chorus against independence. As two Dutch scholars note: 'Ironically, pushing the Netherlands Antilles into independence today might be considered a repulsive colonial act.'[41] In other words, a denial of sovereign consent. Would the group in Aruba who initially wished to have *status aparte* at any cost have thought differently if they had been well-informed about the economic situation which was just around the corner? The case of Puerto Rico, where issues of political viability are intimately linked to issues of both cultural and economic viability, indicates that it might well have been. None of these viabilities is grounded in natural law, but in socio-political perceptions shaped by interests and levels of information.

From a factual point of view I know of no Caribbean constitutional case which has been more studied and analyzed than Puerto Rico's. And this includes not only dispassionate political and juridical studies but socio-logical analyses of recognized scholarship and economic studies of admir-able objectivity and comprehensiveness.[42]

There exists in the Puerto Rican case the data, conceptual and empir-ical, to form the basis for an analysis and determination of probable costs and benefits of any particular decision on status. Puerto Rican scholars such as Rodríguez-Orellana himself, are often too close to the problem to realize that they have contributed to one of the great debates about political status, colonialism and the true nature of self-determination of the post-World War II period. The Puerto Rican intellectual debate is rich and universal in its content and implications for small nations everywhere, but especially in the Caribbean. Yet, such is the self-effacing nature of Puerto Rican scholarship that even a Gordon Lewis, who in his seminal early work on the issue called the Puerto Rican preoccupation with its status: 'a magnificent obsession that infects every other facet of the public debate'[43] – can later question the merits of that literature in comparison to that on the Cuban Revolution.[44]

Admittedly, the two literatures are different: the literature on and of Cuba deals with 'total' revolution, that of Puerto Rico with the pros and cons – legal, political, economic, cultural – of this or that status. With all due respect to the valuable literature on Cuba, it is doubtful that there is anything as thoughtful and analytical about Cuba-US relations as Lewis's *Puerto Rico* or José Luis González' *El pais de cuatro pisos* (1980) and *Nueva visita al cuarto piso* (1986.) The latter especially makes a plausible argument that Puerto Rico has an integral cultural viability, both Latin American and Caribbean. How that translates into political and economic viablity is another issue which will not be easily resolved.

Those who favour independence for cultural reasons have to face the economic issue. This is especially true given the probable dismantling of the privileged taxation system on which the island's advanced technological industries have been based.[45] On the other hand, the fastest growing sector, those who seek economic security in statehood, will have to confront the cultural opposition not just of Puerto Ricans but even of liberal US politicians who fear the ethnic 'balkanization of America'.[46] This growing congressional apprehension about Puerto Rican statehood might well explain Juan Manuel García-Passalacqua's thesis that since 1990 Congress has been giving the independence option 'an obvious preferential treatment'.[47] Since the 1950s, the independence vote has hovered between 3 and 6 per cent while the rest of the electorate alternates between the commonwealth and the statehood choices, with the latter appearing to be gaining. All this leads to the conclusion that it is the Puerto Rican case, in terms of democratic decision-making and in terms of the relations which this Hispanic people have with the US, which illustrates the best and the worst in situations where there exist enormous asymmetries of power.

The late Arturo Morales Carrion, close friend of Muñoz and a luminary among that extraordinary generation of 1930, had a singularly clear perspective on the challenges and probable synergies of US-Puerto Rican relations, which applies most assuredly also to the rest of the Caribbean. 'In Puerto Rico', said Morales Carrion, 'the US is subject to a difficult test. It is a test of both its altruism and its national egoism; its capacity to understand and its proclivity to misunderstand, its mature world view and its self-centered parochialism.'[48] The crux of self-determination is that leaders (whether independent or not) have to make autonomous decisions as to how to maximize the advantages and reduce the costs of dealing with the US. The way to begin is by recognizing the complexities of that relationship, invariably a mix of positive and negative elements.

The call to re-evaluate conceptions of sovereignty is not a defence of an associated status with the US or any other metropolitan state, it is an appeal for a new discussion of the nature and exercise of sovereign consent in both independent and non-independent societies.

The argument is not, of course, that there should be such stringent tests for a 'voluntary limitation of sovereignty' (free association) but that there were and are so few for independence. There was and is a clear double standard which – along with the ideological pressure of the Cuban Revolution and the 'non-aligned' block in the UN – presents the independence option as virtually the only form of self-determination. But, as one surveys the grip that brutal dictators have had on so many of these countries, one must agree with Rupert Emerson that the principle of self-determination has been interpreted in such a fashion as to serve the interests of those who manipulate it. 'What emerges beyond dispute', says Emerson, 'is that all people do *not* have the right of self-determination . . . .'[49]

The fact is that in the Caribbean at least, it has been the non-independent statuses which have been debated, studied, analyzed and surveyed through polls and repeatedly voted on. This has been true in Puerto Rico, in the Netherlands Antilles and Suriname and in the French West Indies and Guiana. Certainly, 'political status' was not the only issue in these elections; everyday concerns with economics, with issues of race and class and the appeals of particular charismatic figures, all played their part as they do in democracies everywhere.[50] Clearly freedom of choice ought to be emulated in all the independent countries, especially those like Cuba and Haiti where 'enlightened' elites have governed at will the destiny of their peoples.

The first step towards a new Caribbean discourse is to reconcile the definition, legal and socio-political, of self-determination with the institutional requirements for achieving it and judging its performance; that is, a discourse on democratic procedure. Such a discourse might begin by admitting that the plebiscites and referenda held in Puerto Rico reflect greater self-determination than the 'mobilization' systems of independent Cuba or Haiti.[51]

The emphasis, therefore, should be on the nature and benefits of self-determination in all the islands, independent and non-independent alike. In this regard, a sincere interest in the methods through which that self-determination is expressed and measured (i.e. democratic elections) might serve the people better than a discussion which focuses solely on sovereignty as a natural right.[52] And a major part of such a debate would be questions as to how not only the difficulties, but also the possible benefits embodied in the asymmetry of power between the US and the Caribbean, impact on the exercise of self-determination.

There can be little dispute with the general assertion that small democratic countries – at least those which attempt to sustain a good standard of living for their populace – will be more economically dependent than larger ones. As a rule, also, the smaller the political system, the more 'open' the society is, i.e. the more the actions of outside actors count. In this sense the autonomy of the smaller state is reduced. Similarly, the greater the dependence on multilateral or supranational organizations, the greater the reduction of outright autonomy. Yet none of this should be interpreted to mean total dependence or lack of autonomy in making decisions which affect self-determination.

In closing, two fundamental principles seem relevant. First, as Dahl and Tufte tell us, 'no democratic system has ever been completely autonomous' and that since the second half of the twentieth century, state sovereignty has been in steady decline.[53] But even if sovereignty is asserted, it does not negate existing dependencies. As Kenneth N. Waltz notes: 'It is no more contradictory to say that sovereign states are always constrained, and often tightly so, than it is to say that free individuals often make decisions under the heavy pressure of events.'[54] The constant, and mostly ideological discourse on the 'dependency' of Third World countries misses this point. It also misses another fact of contemporary US-Caribbean relations: the proven skills and manoeuvering capabilities of the region's democratic leaders.

These leaders have realized that despite its role as the keeper of the geopolitical status quo in the Caribbean, the US is itself an open system. They understand that the US is in fact a most complex democracy. So much so that Gunnar Myrdal believed that the US had developed 'the most explicitly expressed system of general ideals in reference to human interrelations' of any western society.[55] He called this the American Creed which, despite its dilemmas, was upheld by a whole gamut of legal and political avenues.

Caribbean leaders have to perfect their capacity to make use of these political and legal avenues. This will surely involve the strategic use – the strengthening and broadening – of a variety of 'diffused reciprocities' between the great power and the small state. This should include the highlighting of shared values as well as the skilful use or mobilization of the transnational networks created by immigration and racial and ethnic allies in the metropolis. This can result in their participation in the setting of the bilateral and multilateral agenda of the region's international relations, as well as influencing the nature of the language of the diplomacy of those agendas.

No claim to a 'special' relationship need be made. International relations need not be a question of homogenizing cultural identities. A 'strategic relationship' should have as its central goal an effect on US elite perceptions in two fundamental ways. First, that the fundamental geopolitical parameters of the region are not being challenged, i.e. that the behaviour of the small state is not only not intended to be threatening to the superpower's perceived geopolitical interests but that, indeed, these interests are shared in the broad outline. In the post-Cold War era, and given the range of problems the region shares, this does not represent a major problem to the exercise of full self-determination. Only by the conversion of a small state into a full-blown criminal enterprise, as discussed in Chapter 7, or into a major facilitator of tax evasion, as discussed in Chapter 8, would the US and the region be so threatened. All Caribbean states have an interest in avoiding such a calamity.

The real synergies of US-Caribbean relations, however, are to be found in the second set of US perceptions to be influenced: that the small state's behaviour is, in fact, in keeping with either the actual or the professed democratic beliefs of the great power's own interest to strengthen the position of the smaller state. A collective commitment to democracy and true self-determination is the best way to maximize the synergies of US-Caribbean relations.

The whole Caribbean should now hope that the age of insurgency and counter-insurgency, of covert and 'back channel' negotiations, of imperial and racial haughtiness followed by colonial guilt, is finally over. There are other serious problems to attend to, synergies to discover and push to their maximum. A truly self-determining new world to create.

Notes

1   Dudley Seers, *The Political Economy of Nationalism* (New York: Oxford University Press, 1983), p. 91. To his credit Seers did see a role for political leadership and noted that 'no government is completely without policy options'. p. 92.

2   While these are quite general principles of the large body of theory which emphasizes co-operation in international relations. I am particularly indebted to Duncan Snidal's clear and persuasive analyses in 'The Game Theory of International Politics'. *World Politics*, 38 (October 1985) pp. 25–7, and Robert O. Keohane, 'Reciprocity in International Relations', *International Organization*, 40 (Winter 1986) pp. 1–27.

3   Carl Stone, *Electoral Behaviour and Public Opinion in Jamaica* (Mona: Institute of Social and Economic Research, 1974), p. 96.

4   'Excerpts from Address to Cuban Workers, Alamar, 12 July 1975' in Hearne, (ed.), *The Search for Solutions*, pp. 205–6. For an example of party rhetoric, see the speech by the Minister of Foreign Affairs, Dudley Thompson, to the Second Socialist International Meeting, Caracas, 25 May, 1976.

5   Wendell Bell, *Jamaican Leaders* (Berkeley: University of California Press, 1964), p. 65.

6   Cf. Carl Stone, *The Political Opinions of the Jamaican People (1976–1981)* (Kingston: Blackett Publishers, 1982), p. 53. Further on Caribbean political conservatism see by Anthony P. Maingot, 'The Difficult Road to Socialism in the English-Speaking Caribbean', in Richard Fagen (ed.), *Capitalism and the State in US-Latin American Relations* (Stanford, Ca.:Stanford University Press, 1979), pp. 254–89; 'The Caribbean: The Structure of Modern-Conservative Societies', in Jan Knippers Black (ed.), *Latin America: Its Problems and its Promise* (Boulder: Westview Press, 1984), pp. 362–80.

7   See especially in Bell, *Jamaican Leaders*, an analysis of the preference among Jamaican elites across the political ideological spectrum, for the US over the Soviet Union.

8   Cited in Evelyne Huber Stephens and John D. Stephens, *Democratic Socialism in Jamaica* (Princeton, N.J.: Princeton University Press, 1986), p. 33.

9   Manley admitted on 19 September, 1976 that what was affecting Jamaica were global forces: rises in oil prices and the world recession. He celebrated the bauxite levy which the multinational companies had accepted as Jamaica's 'use of the sovereign power of a Third World nation. . . .' Michael Manley, *Not For Sale* (San Francisco: Editorial Consultants, n.d.), p. 17.

10   In Manley's *Jamaica: Struggle in the Periphery* (London: Third World Media, 1982) he discusses the 'destabilization' issue quite a bit but never in reference to Jamaica. There is, however, much about the fall of Allende in Chile and its role in Cuba. All true, of course, but of what use to Jamaica's development?

11   Stephens and Stephens, p. 319.

12   Cf. A.P. Maingot, 'Grenada and the Caribbean: Mutual Linkages and Influences', in Herbert Ellison and Jiri Valenta (eds), *Soviet/Cuban Strategy in the Third World* (Boulder: Westview Press, 1986), pp. 130–47.

13   *The Miami Herald*, 16 December, 1984, p. 24.

14   F. M. Coard, *Bitter Sweet and Spice* (Ilfracombe: Arthur H. Stockwell, Ltd., 1970).

15   Grenada Document (hereafter cited as GD), 'Top Secret Progress Report of Commission No. 5' (n.d. but apparently early 1982).

16   *Ibid.*

17   *Ibid.*

18   GD, Minutes, PB Meeting, 23 February, 1983.

19   G.D., Report, 21 April, 1983 by Ian Jacobs.

20   Quite accurately the authors of a history of the PRG analyze this visit under the subheading, 'The Risks and Benefits of Rapprochement'. (Cf. Anthony Payne, Paul Sutton and Tony Thorndike, *Grenada: Revolution and Invasion* (New York: St Martin's, 1984), pp. 114–17.

21   Eric Williams, *From Columbus to Castro* (London: André Deutsch, 1970), pp. 510–11.

22   The most comprehensive biography of Muñoz' early years is Carmelo Rosario Natal, *La Juventud de Luis Muñoz Marin* (Rio Piedras: Editorial Edil, 1989).

23   Luis Muñoz Marín, *Memorias, 1940–1952* (San German: Universidad Inter-Americana de Puerto Rico, 1992), p. 39.

24   Eric Williams, *Inward Hunger* (London: André Deutsch, 1969), p. 67.

25   Luis Muñoz Marín, *Breakthrough from Nationalism: A Small Island Looks at a Big Trouble*. The Godkin Lectures, Harvard University, April 1959. His first major statement of this position was the 'Discurso de Barranquitas' in 1954.

26   Cf. Muñoz speech to the American Assembly meeting in Puerto Rico, 1 March, 1960 (Estados Unidos y América Latina), 1960, pp. 7–10.

27   Rexford G. Tugwell, *The Art of Politics* (New York: Doubleday and Co. 1958), p. 17. Tugwell was the last appointed Governor of the island.

28   J.A. Cabranes, *Citizenship and the American Empire* (New Haven: Yale University Press, 1979).

29   *Ibid.*, p. 101.

30   Gordon K. Lewis, *Puerto Rico: Freedom and Power in the Caribbean* (New York: Monthly Review Press, 1963), p. 148.

31   *Ibid.*, pp. 17, 23, 503.

32   A good sense of this literature is contained in Damian Fernandez (ed.), *Cuban Studies Since the Revolution* (Gainesville: University Press of Florida, 1992).

33   See especially the studies emanating from the Centro de Estudios Sobre America and especially Julio Carranza Valdes' 'Cuba: los retos del futuro', *Cuadernos de Nuestra America*, 7, Vol. 19 (1993), pp. 131–59.

34   UN General Assembly Resolution 1541, Principle VI. *UN Document A/15*, Supp. 16 (1960).

35   Cited in Humberto García Muñiz, 'Puerto Rico and the US: United Nations Role 1953–1975', *Revista Jurídica de la Universidad de Puerto Rico*, LIII, no. 1 (1984), p. 177.

36   'Declaration on the Granting of Independence to Colonial Countries and Peoples', (G.A. Res. 1514, 15 UN GAOR Supp (No. 16), UNDOC A/15 Supp 16 (1960)).

37   G.A. Res. 742, 8 UN GAOR Supp. (No. 17) UN DOC. A/2630 (1953), p. A-1.

38   'In Contemplation of Micronesia: The Prospects for the Decolonization of Puerto Rico Under International Law', *The University of Miami Inter-American Law Review*, 18 (Spring, 1987), no. 68, pp. 471.

39 Max Beloff, 'The Third World and the Conflict of Ideologies', in W. Scott Thompson (ed.), *The Third World: Premises of US Policy* (San Francisco, Ca.: ICS Press, l983), p. 29.

40 Cf. Gert Oostindie, 'The Dutch Caribbean in the 1990s: Decolonization or Recolonization?', *Caribbean Affairs*, Vol. 5 (January–March, 1992), pp. 103–19.

41 Rosemary Hoffe and Gert Oostindie, 'Upside-Down Decolonization', *Hemisphere*, Vol. I (1989), p. 29.

42 For a good overview of the political issue, see Juan Manuel Garcia-Passalacqua, 'The Grand Dilemma: The Viability v. Sovereignty Debate in the Case of Puerto Rico', forthcoming in *The Annals of the American Academy of Political and Social Sciences* (May, 1994). On the economic front one has to note the US Department of Commerce's three volume *Economic Study of Puerto Rico* (December 1979). A report to President Jimmy Carter, it originated in a meeting between Carter and Puerto Rican Governor C. Romero-Barceló in 1977 who wished to understand the economic consequences of all three political options.

43 Gordon K. Lewis, *Puerto Rico: A Case Study in the Problems of Contemporary American Federalism* (Trinidad's Office of the Prime Minister, 1960), p. 5.

44 In his 1963 *Puerto Rico*, Lewis speaks of the 'mere handful of books' on Puerto Rico compared to 'the mere size' of the output on the Cuban Revolution as proof that 'Havana, not San Juan' was now 'in the forefront of international attention'. (p. 503).

45 As part of its deficit-cutting scheme, the Clinton administration is threatening to cut Section 936 of the US Internal Revenue Code which allows federal tax exemption to Puerto Rican subsidiaries of US companies as long as the profits are deposited in Puerto Rican banks. These deposits amounted to over US$15 billion in 1992; both Puerto Rico and other Caribbean nations are served by the loans made out of these funds.

46 Daniel Patrick Moynihan addresses the 'seemingly intractable problem of resolving the status of Puerto Rico' and the 'defensible' opposition of the US Congress of admitting a Spanish-speaking Puerto Rico to statehood. *Pandemonium. Ethnicity in International Politics* (New York: Oxford University Press, 1993), pp. 73–5.

47 Juan Manuel García-Passalacqua, 'La Crisis del Independentismo', *El Nuevo Herald*, 18 December, 1992, p. 12.

48 Arturo Morales Carrión, *Puerto Rico: A Political and Cultural History* (New York: WW Norton and Co. Ltd., l983), p. 316.

49 Rupert Emerson, *Self-Determination Revisited in the Era of Decolonization* (Harvard University: Centre for International Affairs, Occasional Paper No. 9, December 1964), pp. 63–4.

50 See the excellent set of essays on electoral politics in Colin Clarke (ed.), *Society and Politics in the Caribbean* (New York: St Martin's Press, 1991). Clarke quite correctly establishes a separate category ('independent authoritarian regimes') for Cuba and Haiti.

51 Cf. David Butler and Austin Ranney (eds), *Referendums: A Study in Practice and Theory* (Washington, D.C.: American Enterprise Institute, 1978).

52 See the discussions by Sutton and Maingot in Paul Sutton (ed.), *Dual Legacies in the Contemporary Caribbean* (London: Frank Cass, 1986), pp. 9–10, 120–40.

53 Robert A. Dahl and Edward R. Tufte, *Size and Democracy* (Stanford University Press, 1973), pp. 119–29.

54 Kenneth N. Waltz, 'Political Structures', in Robert O. Keohane (ed.), *Neorealism and Its Critics* (New York: Columbia University Press, 1986), p. 91.

55 Gunnar Myrdal, *The American Dilemma* (New York: Harper and Row, 1944), p. 3.

Bibliography

Apart from the references which accompany each of the chapters in this book – which shall not be repeated here – there is a considerable body of other relevant literature, published inside and outside the Caribbean. It reflects the growth of Caribbean Studies as a field.

An indispensable bibliographical source is the *Handbook of Latin American Studies* of the Library of Congress published by the University of Texas Press, Austin, Texas. The Department of Caribbean Studies of the Royal Institute of Linguistics and Anthropology, Laiden, The Netherlands, publishes the very valuable *Caribbean Abstracts* of books and articles. Also from Europe, the *European Review of Latin American and Caribbean Studies* (Amsterdam) is a useful bibliographic source. There are specific sections on the Caribbean in each subheading. A timely update on Caribbean books appears in each trimesterly issue of *Hemisphere*, published at Florida International University, Miami, Florida.

Of the general histories of the Caribbean which are comparative and interdisciplining in approach, the most outstanding is Franklin W. Knight's *The Caribbean: The Genesis of Fragmented Nationalism*, published in 1978 by Oxford University Press and now in a second edition. Somewhat dated, and limited to the English-speaking Caribbean but excellent on the periods they study, are David Lowenthal, *West Indian Societies* (Oxford: Oxford University Press, 1972) and Gordon K. Lewis, *The Growth of the Modern West Indies* (New York: Monthly Review Press, 1969). For a broader hemisphere-wide historical treatment, J.H. Parry, Philip Sherlock and Anthony P. Maingot, *A Short History of the West Indies* (New York: St Martin's Press, 1987) is still a significant resource.

Edited volumes are especially useful as introductory material, with several outstanding recent ones. Sidney W. Mintz and Sally Price (eds) *Caribbean Contours* (Baltimore, MD: The Johns Hopkins University Press, 1985) contains some basic writings on a range of topics by recognized Caribbeanists. Particularly important for politics and international relations are the following five readers: Anthony Payne and Paul Sutton (eds), *Caribbean Politics: A Comparative Analysis* (Baltimore, MD: The Johns Hopkins University Press, 1993); Jorge Dominguez, Robert Pastor and R. Delisle Worrell (eds) *Democracy in the Caribbean: Political, Economic and Social Perspectives* (Baltimore, MD: The Johns Hopkins University Press, 1993); Paul Sutton (ed.) *Europe and the Caribbean* (London: Macmillan/Warwick University Caribbean Studies, 1991); Colin Clarke (ed.) *Society and Politics in the Caribbean* (New York: St Martin's Press, 1991); and Franklin W. Knight and Colin A. Palmer (eds) *The Modern Caribbean* (Chapel Hill: The University of North Carolina Press, 1989). The most comprehensive coverage of Caribbean intellectual history is Alistair Hennessy (ed.) *Intellectuals in the Twentieth-Century Caribbean*, 2 vols. (London: Macmillan/Warwick University Caribbean Studies, 1992). Also useful is the Special Issue on 'Trends in US-Caribbean Relations' edited by this author for *The Annals of the American Academy of Political and Social Sciences* (Vol. 533, May 1994).

By far the greatest volume of writing on the Caribbean deals with Cuba, since the Revolution. The most complete bibliographical source for this period is Damian J. Fernandez (ed.) *Cuban Studies Since the Revolution* (Gainesville, Fl.: University Press of Florida, 1992). There is very little on the pre-revolutionary years, just as there is virtually nothing written in Cuba about the early revolutionary period. Only one study I know attempts to do a comparative analysis of socialist revolutions in the area, Brian Meeks' very competent, *Caribbean Revolutions and Revolutionary Theory: An Assessment of Cuba, Nicaragua and Grenada* (London: Macmillan/Warwick University Caribbean Studies, 1993). However, there is 40 years of interest in Fidel Castro (since Moncada in 1953). Generally there are four fundamental schools of thought about Cuban political culture:

1 Those who see a causal relationship between 1933 and 1959: a political culture composed of pent-up frustrations of many types: psychological, political and economic. In this school are Luis E. Aguilar, *Cuba 1933: Prologue to Revolution* (Ithaca, N.Y.: Cornell University Press, 1972); Irwin F. Gellman, *Roosevelt and Batista. Good Neighbour Diplomacy in Cuba, 1933–1945* (Albuquerque, NM: University of New Mexico Press, 1973); Jaime Suchlicki, *University Students and Revolution in Cuba, 1960–1968* (Coral Gables, Fl: University of Miami Press, 1969).

2 Those who believe that a new revolutionary culture crystallized by 1945–50, which was qualitatively different from the previous revolutionary tradition of Cuba. Fidel Castro belonged to the new political culture. Cf. Rolando E. Bonachea and Nelson Valdes (eds) *Revolutionary Struggle, 1947–1958* (Cambridge, MA: The MIT Press, 1972).

3 Those who pay lip service to context (i.e. political culture) but end up emphasizing the role of the 'hero'. From James Nelson Goodsell's *Fidel Castro: Personal Revolution in Cuba* (New York: Alfred A. Knopf, 1975) and Maurice Halperin's *The Rise and Decline of Fidel Castro* (Los Angeles, CA: University of California Press, 1972) to the recent, and ever-growing stock of works. Among the latter, only Andres Oppenheimer, *Castro's Final Hour* (New York: Simon and Schuster, 1992) presents any new information. Oppenheimer is especially valu-

able for his analysis of the sensational trial of revolutionary hero, General Arnaldo Ochoa.

4   The literature which began sympathetic to the revolutionary process but was very prescient about warning about the dangers of a militarized society. The most perceptive of this group are Hugh Thomas, *The Pursuit of Freedom* (New York: Harper and Row, 1971); René Dumont, *Cuba, est-il socialiste?* (Paris: Editions du Seuil, 1970); and K.S. Karol, *Guerrillas in Power* (New York: Hill and Wang, 1970).

One can accept the interpretations of all four schools as far as description is concerned. With a movement as complex as the Cuban Revolution, providing accurate causal explanations of why the revolution went this way or that still remains to be done. For example, the three most complete studies of Fidel Castro and his revolutionary context, Hugh Thomas, *Cuba*, Jorge Domínguez, *Cuba: Order and Revolution* (Cambridge, MA: Harvard University Press, 1978) and Taz Szulc, *Fidel a Critical Portrait*, arrive at totally different causal explanations on a key issue: did Castro plan to do what he did, i.e. turn left? Szulc says yes, this was his original plan but Domínguez and Thomas maintain that it was a mixture of Fidel Castro's competence, shrewdness and 'luck' which brought him to 1959, at which point he could have gone in one of various directions. The events described in Chapter 5 of this study inclines towards the Thomas and Domínguez thesis.

After Cuba, Haiti is the most studied country in the Caribbean. The most complete bibliography is Michel S. Laguerre (ed.) *The Complete Haitiana. A Bibliographical Guide to the Scholarly Literature, 1900–1980* (Millwood, N.Y.: Kraus International Publications, 1982). The best overall study of that island's political and intellectual history is David Nicholls, *From Dessalines to Duvalier*, first published 1979; 1988 paperback edition, Macmillan/Warwick University Caribbean Studies series. Richard M. Morse's *Haiti's Future* (Washington, D.C.: The Wilson Center Press, 1988), provides a good perspective on what twelve key Haitian intellectuals were thinking and hoping for soon after the fall of Jean-Claude Duvalier in 1986.

Good insights into the nature of traditional Haitian *revanchisme* after the fall of Jean Claude Duvalier are provided by Elizabeth Abbott, *Haiti. The Duvaliers and Their Legacy* (New York: McGraw Hill, 1988). Haitian efforts to make the transition to democracy, after 1986, is extensively analyzed in Claude Möise's *Constitutions et Luttes en Haiti, 1804–1987*, two vols. (Quebec: Editions CIDIHCA, 1990). Vol. II covers the new 1987 Constitution. The central role of Father Jean-Bertrand Aristide, before he was elected president in 1990, is outlined in Amy Wilentz, *The Rainy Season: Haiti Since Duvalier* (New York: Simon and Schuster, 1989). Aristide's own accounts are important to build a picture of this complex charismatic figure. His original defence of his political position as a priest, *La verite! En verite!* (Port-au-Prince: l'Imprimerie Le Natal, 1989) was followed by *In the Parish of the Poor*, translated and edited by Amy Wilentz. (New York: Orbis Books, 1990). Aristide gave two most revealing interviews: one with Gregorio Selser of Mexico before he came to office, in *El Caribe contemporáneo*, the other in Puerto Rico with Rosita Marrero after he had been overthrown: *Testigo de cargo* (San Juan: Coleccion Blanco y Negro, 1992). Aristide's premature autobiography, written with Christophe Wargny, *Aristide. An Autobiography* (New York: Maryknoll, 1993) is quite revealing about his 'anti-capitalist' sentiments.

The Dominican Republic is also well studied. The nature of Dominican political culture is competently analyzed by Rosario Espinal, *Auto-ritarismo y democracia en la polítical dominicana* (San José, Costa Rica: CAPEL, 1987). Richard S. Hillman and Thomas J. D'Agostino, *Distant Neighbours in the Caribbean* (Westport, Conn: Praeger, 1992) is enlightening about both the Dominican Republic and Jamaica. An important and rare Cuban contribution to the understanding of another political system is Haraldo Dilla and Felix Calvo, *Crisis y evolucion del sistema politico dominicano, 1982–1986* (Havana: Centro de Estudios sobre America, 1985).

There are big gaps in the comparative study of race and politics, especially as they affect social stratification. A rare study of a Caribbean oligarchy is Esteban Rosario's *La oligarquia dominicana* (Santo Domingo: Editorial Gente, 1987), contrasting with Lisa Douglass, *The Power of Sentiment: Love, Hierarchy and the Jamaican Family Elite* (Boulder, Co: Westview Press, 1992) and Micheline Labelle, *Ideologie de couleur et de classes sociales en Haiti* (Quebec: Les Editions du CIDHCA, 1987). Carlos Moore, *Castro, the Blacks and Africa* (Los Angeles, Ca: Centre for Afro-American Studies, 1988) looks at the race issue in Cuba. A good analysis of race, popular culture and political philosophy is Patrick Taylor, *The Narrative of Liberation* (Ithaca, N.Y.: Cornell University Press, 1989). One of the most perceptive studies of the role of race and ethnicity in Caribbean political culture is in Spanish: Andrés Serbín, *Ethnicidad, clase y nación en la cultura política del Caribe* (Caracas: Academia Nacional de Historia, 1987).

Failures of revolutionary attempts are well recorded. Jorge Heine, *A Revolution Aborted* (Pittsburgh, PA: University of Pittsburgh Press, 1990) is an excellent compilation of essays on the Grenadian revolution (1979–83) which committed suicide. Selwyn Ryan's *Revolution and Reaction* (St Augustine, Trinidad: ISER, 1989) contributes solid insights into the aftermath of the 1970 Black Power rebellion in Trinidad.

Essays in Paul Sutton's book, *Europe and the Caribbean* (cited above) contain reminders that many of the islands in the region still maintain intimate ties with their respective metropoli. The complexities of the US/Puerto Rican relationship is comprehensively dealt with by the various essays in Jorge Heine (ed.), *Time for Decision: The United States and Puerto Rico* (Lanham, MD: North-South Publishing Co., 1983) and in Juan Manuel Garcia-Passalacqua, *Puerto Rico: Equality and Freedom at Issue* (New York: Praeger, 1984). Richard Weiskoff, *Factories and Foodstamps; The Puerto Rican Model of Development* (Baltimore, MD: Johns Hopkins University Press, 1985) is still the best treatise on this vital issue.

Evidence of the vibrancy of democratic politics in the region is the growing literature on and by Caribbean democratic leaders, much of it published in the region, for example, Theodore Sealy, *Caribbean Leaders* (Kingston: Kingston Publishers, 1991). F.A. Hoyos, *Tom Adams: A Biography* (London: Macmillan Caribbean, 1988) is the only writing of this important Caribbean leader. The preference for 'revolutionaries' is all too evident. J.F. Mitchell's *Caribbean Crusade* (Waitsfield, Ut.: Concepts Publishing, 1989) contains the speeches of Eugenia Charles, St Vincent's premier politician, in Janet Higbie, *Eugenia Charles, The Caribbean's Iron Lady* (London: Macmillan Caribbean, 1993) does justice to this remarkable politician.

The distinguished Caribbean jurist, Sir Fred Phillips of Barbados, recounts his own involvements in the constitutional history of the islands in *Caribbean Life and Culture: A Citizen Reflects* (Kingston: Heinemann Publishers, 1991). The St Lucian democrat and Nobel Prize winner in economics, Arthur Lewis, is analyzed in Ralph Premdas and Eric St Cyr (eds) *Sir Arthur Lewis: An Economic and Political Portrait* (Mona, Jamaica: ISER, 1991). The role of an opposition leader in a democracy is explained in the collected speeches of Trinidad's Basdeo Panday, *An Enigma Answered* (Curepe, Trinidad: Chakka Publishing House, 1991).

Finally, two books reflect the dramatic changes sweeping the region. Darrell E. Levi's *Michael Manley: The Making of a Leader* (Athens, GA: The University of Georgia Press, 1990) indicates the speed with which Caribbean history moves: ending with Manley the radical politician of the 1970s. There is nothing on the 'new' Manley who, after his defeat in 1980 began to abandon radicalism. Regaining power in 1989, Manley had, in fact, returned to the earlier, more moderate, social democrat politics of his father and the Peoples National Party.

A welcome change from the determinism of prevalent theories of development is Mark Moberg, *Citrus, Strategy, and Class: The Politics of Development in Southern Belize* (Iowa City: University of Iowa Press, 1992). Through careful field research, Moberg demonstrates how a democratically mobilized peasantry squeezed real concessions out of metropolitan-based business giants. It is a model of the specific case study with comparative references which the new era in the region's international relations needs.

Index